CLASS 10

PHYSICS WALLAH

AF655212

CBSE 15 SAMPLE QUESTION PAPERS

NEW PATTERN

As per Latest CBSE SQP (Dated 30 July 2025)

SOCIAL SCIENCE

With CBSE SQP, 2024 & 2025 Solved Papers

2026 EXAMINATION

EDITION : Third

Published By: Physicswallah Limited

Physics Wallah Publication

ISBN: 978-93-7153-542-7

MRP: 349/-

Mobile App: Physics Wallah (Available on Play Store)

Printed by: PWP

Website: www.pw.live

Youtube Channel: Physics Wallah - Alakh Pandey
Alakh Pandey - Class 10
Physics Wallah Foundation
Competition Wallah
NCERT Wallah

Email: publication@pw.live

SKU Code: 3afd6444-3396-4a76-80c8-e3733b1c5b06

PREFACE

A step to make our book even better for our students:

Provide your valuable feedback or Report the Error

View Errata (Error Correction from our end)

In this era of cut throat competition among class 10th aspirants for great marks in Board Exams, only a few are prepared enough to achieve it. The key to success lies not just in hard work, but in smart work—knowing what to study, how to study, and how to evaluate oneself before the actual exams. While there is a plethora of study materials available, what often goes missing is a comprehensive, well-structured, and self-assessment tool that aligns with the CBSE curriculum.

To bridge this gap, we are pleased to introduce our latest offering: **15 Sample Question Papers for CBSE Class 10: Academic Year 2025-26**. This book aims to provide students with a robust platform to assess their preparation level, fine-tune their strategies, and ultimately excel in the CBSE Class 10th Board Exams.

The content is fully aligned with the CBSE curriculum and NCERT books, ensuring that you are studying the most relevant material. This makes your preparation more focused and effective. It has been curated by **Physics Wallah Editorial Team** under the careful observation of Physics Wallah Faculties.

This Book Consists of following Features:

The content is made in such a way that you can invest your time to make a strong fundamental that will get compounded and will pay you the interest in every upcoming year of your competitive exam's preparation and board exam preparation. Such that you will always stand ahead of your competitors.

Following are the different sections that we have provided to develop your skills:

- CBSE Latest Syllabus 2025-26
- Frequently Asked Questions
- Self-Assessment Sheet
- CBSE Past 5 Years' Paper Trend Analysis
- Question Typology, Evolving Trends in CBSE Exam Patterns, Preparation Guide.
- CBSE Solved Papers 2024 & 2025
- CBSE Sample Question Paper 2025-26 (with CBSE Marking Scheme)
- Cheat Sheets (Mind Maps)
- 111 Most Probable Questions
- 8 Sample Papers with detailed explanations (Step-wise Marking)
- 4 Sample Papers with handwritten explanations through QR code
- Level-wise (Easy, Medium, Hard) Sample Papers
- CBSE Board Exams 2026: Two-Exam Policy Decoded
- Exam Ready: Answering Templates that Score
- Topper's Explanations
- Mistake 101: What not to do! and Nailing the Right Answer

By using this book as a part of your study plan, you are arming yourself with a powerful tool that will help you secure excellent marks in your CBSE Class 10th Board Exams. We wish you all the best in your preparation and are confident that this book will serve as a valuable resource in your journey towards academic excellence.

**Please note 'Cheat Sheet' is just a terminology, we do not promote cheating.*

Chapter-wise Weightage & Trend analysis

CBSE PAST 5 YEARS' PAPERS

SOCIAL SCIENCE

CHAPTERS	2020		2022		2023		2024		2025	
	DL	ODL	DL	ODL	DL	ODL	DL	ODL	DL	ODL
HISTORY										
The Rise of Nationalism in Europe	11	4	-	-	4	4	8	4	4	5
Nationalism in India	9	10	10	13	8	12	6	8	8	8
The Making of a Global World (*Some portion is Rationalised*)	6	4	-	-	3	-	2	3	3	1
The Age of Industrialisation	1	4	-	-	1	-	-	-	-	-
Print Culture and the Modern World	4	5	-	-	4	3	4	5	5	6
GEOGRAPHY										
Resources and Development (*Some portion is Rationalised*)	7	1	-	-	1	1	1	2	3	2
Forest and Wildlife Resources (*Some portion is Rationalised*)	-	-	-	-	-	4	2	4	4	1
Water Resources	1	1	-	-	5	1	5	2	1	3
Agriculture (*Some portion is Rationalised*)	5	2	-	-	3	2	1	6	4	6
Minerals and Energy Resources	2	5	1	2	3	-	7	2	7	6
Manufacturing Industries (*Some portion is Rationalised*)	4	17	5	6	3	6	4	4	1	1
Lifelines of National Economy	4	6	5	3	5	2	1	1	1	2
POLITICAL SCIENCE										
Power-sharing	2	-	-	-	2	4	4	5	2	3
Federalism	8	4	-	-	5	1	5	4	6	6
Democracy and Diversity (*Rationalised*)	3	3	-	-	-	-	-	-	-	-
Gender, Religion and Caste (*Some portion is Rationalised*)	5	5	-	-	2	2	2	1	2	6
Popular Struggles and Movements (*Rationalised*)	8	8	4	5	-	-	-	-	-	-
Political Parties	5	12	5	12	4	4	4	4	4	2
Outcomes of Democracy	8	1	10	3	6	5	5	6	6	3
Challenges to Democracy (*Rationalised*)	-	-	-	-	-	-	-	-	-	-
ECONOMICS										
Development	5	6	-	-	5	5	6	5	5	2
Sectors of the Indian Economy	10	4	-	-	10	4	3	4	5	12
Money and Credit	5	9	5	5	5	4	5	5	5	3
Globalisation and the Indian Economy (*Some portion is Rationalised*)	5	1	5	5	3	6	6	6	5	3
Consumer Rights (*Rationalised*)	-	-	-	-	-	-	-	-	-	-

**The marks allotment mentioned above is chapter-wise and includes internal choice questions as well. Therefore, the total might not match the Maximum Marks of the respective Previous Year Paper. Here, DL is Delhi, ODL is Outside Delhi.*

**For the year 2021, the exam was not conducted.*

Preparation Guide!

❖ Chapter-wise Weightage & Trend Analysis

Revise smartly with a clear understanding of chapter-wise marks distribution based on the last 5 years of CBSE board exams. Identify high-weightage chapters and focus your efforts strategically.

❖ Answering Templates

Master the art of writing scoring answers using pre-designed templates. Learn how to structure your responses as per CBSE's expectations—write precisely, score efficiently.

❖ Board-based FAQs

Get clear, concise answers to all your common questions about the CBSE board exams and the latest 2026 exam pattern. Scan the QR provided for more FAQs.

❖ CBSE 2026: Two Board Exams Scheme

Understand the new Two-Exam System introduced by CBSE—its purpose, key features, and how it changes your preparation strategy. Gain clarity on what it means for phase 1 and phase 2.

❖ OMR Mastery

Follow step-by-step guidance on correctly filling the OMR sheet. Learn the dos and don'ts to ensure accuracy and avoid common mistakes.

❖ Practice Pack: 12 SQPs

Start with easy level SQPs to build confidence and move to medium difficulty level SQPs for skill-building. Challenge yourself with hard sample papers for full-syllabus preparation and deeper insight.

❖ Solutions with Step-wise Marking Scheme

Get detailed, stepwise solutions for every question. Understand answer logic, avoid frequent errors, and learn the marking scheme through 3 SQPs with marks breakdown table.

❖ Recent CBSE Board Papers & SQPs

Practice with the latest Sample Question Paper (2025–26), along with 2024 and 2025 Board Papers. Understand evolving patterns, new question types, and updated evaluation trends.

Question Typology

YEAR	Objective Questions		Subjective Questions				
	MCQs	A/R	VSA	SA	LA	Case/Source Based type	Map-Based type
2025	18	2	4	5	4	3	1
2024	19	1	4	5	4	3	1
2023	19	1	4	5	4	3	1
2022 (T-II)	-	-	5	3	2	2	1
2022 (T-I)	30	8	-	-	-	2	2
2021	Exam Not Conducted						
2020	6	-	10	8	5	1	1

Evolving Trends in CBSE Exam Patterns

Social Science

2020

- Source and Data Based Questions introduced.
- Some MCQs were included in VSA.
- Assertion and Reason type Questions added.
- Rationalised syllabus onwards in Economics and Pol. Science.

2021

- Exam Not Conducted

2022

- Term-I (objective) and Term-II (subjective).
- 2 Marks VSA instead of 1 Mark
- 1 Section of Case based questions added.
- Questions with "OR" option reduced.

2023

- Matching Based Questions introduced.

2024

- Image Based Question introduced.
- Rationalised syllabus in Economics.
- Chapter "Lifelines of National Economy" to be used for map based questions only.

2025

- Weightage of Competency Based Questions increased.

CONTENTS

Scan for Latest Syllabus & Upcoming CBSE SQPs

Frequently Asked Questions

Scan for More FAQs

1

Question: Has the paper pattern changed in CBSE SQP 2025-26 compared to 2025 Board Paper?

Answer: Yes. In 2025 Board Paper, questions from History, Geography, Political Science and Economics were intermixed throughout the paper, whereas in CBSE SQP 2025-26, the paper is divided into clear subject-wise sections:

Section A: History **Section B:** Geography
Section C: Political Science **Section D:** Economics

2

Question: Are the total number of questions, total marks and duration the same in CBSE SQP 2025-26 and 2025 Board Paper?

Answer: CBSE 2025 board paper had 37 questions, whereas CBSE SQP 2025-26 contains 38 questions. However, both papers carry a total of 80 marks and are scheduled for a duration of 3 hours.

3

Question: Is the subject-wise marks distribution in the CBSE SQP 2025–26 the same as that of the 2025 Board Paper?

Answer: Yes, the subject-wise marks distribution in the CBSE SQP 2025–26 is the same as that of the 2025 Board Paper. The distribution of marks across the four subjects is as follows:

History: 20 marks **Geography:** 20 marks
Political Science: 20 marks **Economics:** 20 marks

4

Question: Is there any change in the assessment scheme for the current academic session (2025–26)?

Answer: No. There is no change in the assessment scheme for 2025–26. It remains the same as that of the academic session 2024–25.

5

Question: If a choice is given to attempt any one of the questions in the Board exam, can we attempt both? If yes, which answer would be considered?

Answer: The instructions given in the question paper should be followed. Attempting both the options not only takes away much of the precious time but also confuses the examiner.

6

Question: Do examiners deduct marks for exceeding the word limit and spelling mistakes, especially in the language papers?

Answer: No marks are deducted for exceeding the word limit. Marks for spelling mistakes and other errors are deducted in the Language Papers.

7

Question: Will questions be asked from the Board's sample paper?

Answer: Sample question papers help you know the design, pattern and types of questions. Questions in the examination may be from any part of the syllabus. So, prepare thoroughly from the entire syllabus

8

Question: How can we obtain a copy of the Answers Book of Class 10th exam?

Answer: Applicant may apply for obtaining photocopy of answer books by paying prescribed processing charges as per time frame set by the Board. For details please see our website www.cbse.nic.in at the time of declaration of results.

CBSE Board Exam 2026: Two-Exam Scheme Decoded

1. What is the major change in Class X Board exams from 2026?

Ans: Starting in 2026, CBSE will conduct two Board exams per year for Class X, one main examination and one for improvement, if desired. This aims to offer students more flexibility and reduce pressure.

2. Why are two Board exams being introduced?

Ans: This is in line with the National Education Policy (NEP) 2020, which emphasizes holistic assessment, focus on core competencies, and reducing rote memorization.

Two Board exams aim to eliminate the high-stress/high-stakes nature of a single final exam and provide students more opportunities to improve.

3. Can I appear for both exams in the same year?

Ans. Yes, you can appear in both exams within the same school year:

First Board Examination (Main Exam)

You must appear in the first Board Examination, as it is mandatory for all students.

Eligible categories:

- Fresh students of Class X
- Students in Compartment (2nd Chance)
- Students repeating the year (Essential Repeat)
- Students appearing for improvement of previous performance

Second Board Examination

You can appear in the second examination in the following cases:

- Improvement: For up to 3 subjects to improve your score.
- Compartment: If you were placed in Compartment in the first phase exam.
- Improvement + Compartment: You can appear for both in May.
- Improvement for the students passed by the replacement of the subject.

Note: You are not allowed to take the second examination if you didn't appear in at least 3 subjects during the first examination. In such cases, you'll fall under the "Essential Repeat" category and have to wait until the next year.

4. When will the exams be held?

Ans. First Phase Examination: 17 February to 6 March 2026

Second Phase Examination: 5 May to 20 May 2026

5. Is it mandatory to attempt the First Phase exam for all students?

Ans. Yes, it is mandatory to attempt the First Phase Exam for all Class X students. It will be treated as the main board examination.

6. Is it mandatory to attempt the Second Phase exam? Who can appear for it?

Ans. No, the May exam is not mandatory. It is an optional attempt meant for:

- Students who want to improve their scores
- Students who were absent or could not perform well in the February exam
- Students who fail in one or more subjects in the first phase

7. Will the syllabus remain the same for both first and second examinations?

Ans. Yes, the syllabus will be the same for both the first and second examinations. Both examinations will be based on the full syllabus prescribed for the academic year.

8. Is it necessary to opt for the second examination at the time of filling the LOC for the first examination to be eligible for it?

Ans. Yes, you must opt for the second examination while filling the LOC (List of Candidates) for the first examination to be eligible for it.

As per CBSE policy:

- Filling the LOC for the first examination is mandatory.
- At that time, you must indicate whether you want to appear for the second examination.
- If you don't select this option, you cannot appear in the second examination later.
- No new name will be added to the LOC of the second examination.
- After the first exam result, you can opt out, but not opt in if you didn't choose the second examination earlier.

Tip: Always opt for the second examination—just in case.

9. Can I take admission in Class XI after the first examination result?

Ans. Yes, provisional admission to Class XI is allowed after the first examination result.

- Your performance of main/first examinations will be available in DigiLocker and can be used for admission to class XI if the student does not wish to appear in second examinations for improvement.
- Students not qualified in the main examination will be allowed provisional admission in Class XI and based on the result of the second examination, their admission will be confirmed.

10. Are the dates fixed for all subjects?

Ans. Major subjects like Maths, Science, Social Science, Hindi, and English will have fixed exam days.

Examination of Regional and Foreign Languages will be done in one go on a single day.

Examination of remaining subjects will be conducted 2 times to 3 times based on the choices of the students on 2 or 3 days.

11. Can I change my subjects after LOC Submission?

Ans. No. Once the List of Candidates (LOC) is submitted, no subject changes will be allowed except permitted as per policy.

12. Will special exams be conducted in case of emergencies?

Ans. No. Special exams will not be conducted under any circumstances.

13. When will the results be declared?

Ans. Results of the first examinations will be declared in the month of April.

Results of the second examinations will be declared in the month of June.

14. What details will be shown in the final Mark Sheet cum Passing Certificate?

Ans. The Mark Sheet cum Passing Certificate will include the following:

- Marks obtained in the first examination
- Marks obtained in the second examination (if attempted)
- Marks from the Practical/Internal Assessment
- Grades for each subject
- The better of the two marks (first or second examinations) will be clearly mentioned.

15. Will I get marksheets for both exams?

Ans. You'll receive your passing documents and merit certificates after the results of second examinations. Your first attempt's performance will be available in DigiLocker for Class XI admissions.

16. If I score well in the first examination, do I still need to appear in the second one?

Ans. No. If you're satisfied with your performance, you don't need to appear again. The second exam is optional for improvement.

17. Will Practical/Internal Assessment also be conducted twice?

Ans. No, Practical/Internal Assessment will be conducted only once.

INSTRUCTIONS FOR FILLING THE OMR SHEET

- Use a black or blue ballpoint pen to fill the OMR sheet. Pencils or gel pens are not allowed.
- Carefully read the instructions given on the OMR sheet before filling it out.
- While filling the name, leave a block between your first name, middle and last name.
- The student has to fill the following particulars in the answer sheet:

From Admit Card

1. Subject
2. Sub Code
3. Date of Examination
4. Candidate's Name
5. Father's Name
6. Roll No. (In digits)
7. Roll No. (In words)
8. Centre No.
9. School No.

From Question Paper

10. Set Number
11. Code Number

ADMIT CARD

CENTRAL BOARD OF SECONDARY EDUCATION, DELHI

ADMIT CARD FOR SECONDARY EXAMINATION 2026

LATEST ENTRY IN EXAMINATION CENTRE 30 MIN BEFORE THE EXAM START 10 AM (IST)

Digital CBSE

Roll No. (6) 22122532 **Date of Birth** 26/02/2008 **School No.** (9) 65345 **Centre No.** (8) 8407

Roll. No. (In words) (7) TWO CRORE TWENTY ONE LAKH TWENTY TWO THOUSAND FIVE HUNDRED THIRTY TWO ONLY

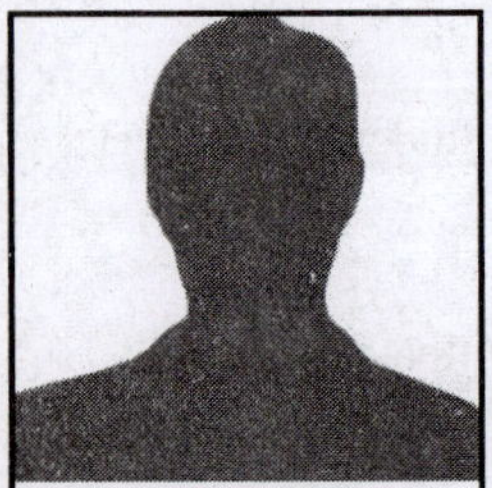

RAHUL KUMAR SINGH
11-04-2025

Examination	SECONDARY - CLASS: 10
Candidate's Name	(4) RAHUL KUMAR SINGH
Mother's Name	REKHA DEVI
Father/Guardian's Name	(5) OM PRAKASH SINGH
of School	***************************
Exam Centre	***************************
Category of PwD	Not Applicable
Admit Card ID	RR536521

SUB CODE (2)	SUBJECT NAME (1)	MEDIUM	DATE (3)
002	HINDI COURSE-A	...	21.02.2026
184	ENGLISH (LANGUAGE AND LITERATURE)	...	26.02.2026
086	SCIENCE	...	02.03.2026
087	SOCIAL SCIENCE	...	07.03.2026
041	MATHEMATICS STANDARD	...	11.03.2026

QUESTION PA-

Series WYXZ1/4

(10) **Set No. 2**

(11) Q.P. Code **2/4/2**

Roll No.

2	2	1	2	2	5	3	2

Candidates must write the Q.P. Code on the title page of the answer book.

Note: The details provided in the admit card are imaginary; if you found something resembling anyone's details, then it could be by chance.

केन्द्रीय माध्यमिक शिक्षा बोर्ड, दिल्ली
सीनियर स्कूल सर्टिफिकेट परीक्षा (कक्षा बारहवीं)
परीक्षार्थी प्रवेश-पत्र के अनुसार भरे

CENTRAL BOARD OF SECONDARY EDUCATION, DELHI
Secondary School Examination (Class-X)
To be filled in by the candidate as per as per Admit Card
लिखे तथा संगत गोले को पूरे गहरे निशान से भरें।
Write and darken the appropriate circle as applicable.

क्रम संख्या
Serial No.

SAMPLE

विषय Subject: SOCIAL SCIENCE

विषय कोड Subject Code: 087

परीक्षा का दिन एवं तिथि
Day & Date of the Examination: MONDAY 07/03/2024

उत्तर देने का माध्यम
Medium of answering the paper: ENGLISH

प्रश्न पत्र के ऊपर लिखे कोड को दर्शाएं:
Write code No. as written on the top of the question paper

Code Number	Set Number
2/4/2	1 ● 3 4

अतिरिक्त उत्तर-पुस्तिका (ओं) की संख्या
No. of supplementary answer-book(s) used

विकलांग व्यक्ति: हाँ / नहीं
Person with Disabilities: Yes / No — NO

किसी शारीरिक अक्षमता से प्रभावित हो तो संबंधित वर्ग में ✓ का निशान लगाएं।

If physically challenged, tick the category

B	D	H	S	C	A

B = दृष्टिहीन, D = मूक व बधिर, H = शारीरिक रूप से विकलांग,
S = स्पास्टिक, C = डिस्लेक्सिक, A = ऑटिस्टिक

B = Visually Impaired, D = Hearing Impaired, H = Physically Challanged
S = Spastic, C = Dyslexic, A = Autistic

क्या लेखन - लिपिक उपलब्ध करवाया गया: हाँ / नहीं
Whether writer provided: Yes / No — NO

यदि दृष्टिहीन है तो उपयोग में लाए गये सोफ्टवेयर का नाम:
If Visually challenged, name of software used:

एक खाने में एक अक्षर लिखें। नाम के प्रत्येक भाग के बीच एक खाना रिक्त छोड़ दें। यदि परीक्षार्थी का नाम 24 अक्षरों से अधिक है, तो केवल नाम के प्रथम 24 अक्षर ही लिखें।
Each letter be written in one box and one box be left blank between each part of the name. In case Candidate's Name exceeds 24 letters, write first 24 letters.

परीक्षार्थी का नाम बड़े अक्षरों में Candidate's Name in CAPITAL letters

R A H U L   K U M A R   S I N G H

(Bubble grid A–Z under each letter box; filled circles correspond to the letters above.)

अनुक्रमांक Roll No.

2	2	1	2	2	5	3	2

(Bubble grid 1–9, 0; filled circles correspond to the digits above.)

As per Admit Card

विषय कोड Sub. Code	केन्द्र संख्या Centre No.
0 8 7	8 4 0 7

विषय Subject: SOCIAL SCIENCE

School No. as per admit card:
विद्यालय संख्या जैसा प्रवेश पत्र में दिया गया है। 6 5 3 4 5

अनुक्रमांक (शब्दों में) Roll No. (in words) TWO Crore TWENTY ONE Lakhs TWENTY TWO Thousands FIVE HUNDRED THIRTY TWO ONLY

पिता/संरक्षक का नाम
Father's/Guardian's Name: OM PRAKASH SINGH

परीक्षार्थी के हस्ताक्षर Signature of Candidate: *(Candidate's signature in black/blue ballpoint pen)*

कार्यालय उपयोग के लिए
Space for office use

इस पृष्ठ पर परीक्षार्थी द्वारा भरे गए सम्पूर्ण विवरण की जांच कर ली गई है।
All the particulars filled in by the candidate on this page have been verified

सहायक अधीक्षक के हस्ताक्षर
Signature of Asstt. Supdt.

अधीक्षक की मोहर
Facsimile sstamp of the Centre supdt.

SELF ASSESSMENT SHEET

Self-assessment plays a crucial role in exam preparation and offers several advantages:

- **Enhanced Self-awareness:** Self-assessment sheets help students gain a deeper understanding of their strengths and weaknesses across various subjects. Specific feedback on their performance provides valuable insights into areas of excellence and those that require improvement.
- **Focused Study:** These sheets provide clear guidance to students on where to direct their efforts. Identifying which questions to review, reattempt, or practice allows for more efficient and purposeful study sessions.
- **Targeted Improvement:** By categorizing questions into different categories (e.g., Easy, Revise, Reattempt), students can concentrate on areas that require the most attention. This targeted approach can result in significant improvements in their comprehension and performance.
- **Motivation:** Self-assessment sheets serve as a source of motivation for students. Observing their progress and understanding the steps needed for improvement can boost their motivation to work harder and achieve better results.
- **Reduced Exam Anxiety:** Having a clear understanding of their preparation progress helps reduce exam-related anxiety. Students feel more confident when they know what aspects to focus on, leading to a calmer and more effective exam experience.
- **Time Management:** Self-assessment sheets aid students in managing their study time more effectively. They can allocate more time to areas requiring extensive revision or reattempt while spending less time on topics they have already mastered.

Self evaluation Instruction: After completing the test, evaluate it using the provided explanations. Use only a pencil to mark the evaluations (allowing for revisions and reattempts). Record the marks obtained in the Marks section and provide remarks in the Remarks column.

Remarks abbreviations:

- **Easy (E):** Use for questions that you should find straightforward, indicating a good understanding and correct answers.
- **Revise (R):** Assign to questions where your response contains minor errors or gaps in understanding, suggesting the need for topic review.
- **Reattempt (RA):** Use for questions with incorrect responses, significant misconceptions, or a lack of understanding. Students receiving this remark should revisit the topic thoroughly, seek additional help if necessary, and attempt similar questions to enhance their grasp of the concept.

	SQP 1		SQP 2		SQP 3		SQP 4		SQP 5		SQP 5		SQP 6	
S.No.	Marks	Remarks	Marks	Remarks	Marks	Remarks	Marks	Remarks	Marks	Remarks	Marks	Remarks	Marks	Remarks
Q.1														
Q.2														
Q.3														
Q.4														
Q.5														
Q.6														
Q.7														
Q.8														
Q.9														
Q.10														
Q.11														
Q.12														
Q.13														
Q.14														
Q.15														
Q.16														
Q.17														
Q.18														
Q.19														
Q.20														
Q.21														
Q.22														
Q.23														
Q.24														
Q.25														
Q.26														
Q.27														
Q.28														
Q.29														
Q.30														
Q.31														
Q.32														
Q.33														
Q.34														
Q.35														
Q.36														
Q.37														
Total														

	SQP 8		SQP 9		SQP 10		SQP 11		SQP 12		CBSE SQP	CBSE 2024 paper	CBSE 2025 paper
S.No.	Marks	Remarks	Marks	Remarks	Marks	Remarks	Marks	Remarks	Marks	Remarks	Remarks	Remarks	Remarks
Q.1													
Q.2													
Q.3													
Q.4													
Q.5													
Q.6													
Q.7													
Q.8													
Q.9													
Q.10													
Q.11													
Q.12													
Q.13													
Q.14													
Q.15													
Q.16													
Q.17													
Q.18													
Q.19													
Q.20													
Q.21													
Q.22													
Q.23													
Q.24													
Q.25													
Q.26													
Q.27													
Q.28													
Q.29													
Q.30													
Q.31													
Q.32													
Q.33													
Q.34													
Q.35													
Q.36													
Q.37													
Total													

EXAM READY: ANSWERING TEMPLATES THAT SCORE

Conceptual-Justification Type

Q. Why is the horizontal distribution of power-sharing important? Explain

Ans.

The Horizontal distribution of power-sharing is important for the following reasons:

(*i*) Reason 1 ____________________

(*ii*) Reason 2 ____________________

Begin with an introductory sentence. For example, you may start by defining Horizontal power distribution. In this case, the question directly asks for reasons so the introduction can be skipped.

Now, proceed with the reasons/measures/ functions/characteristics/examples, etc. as may be asked in the question.

Evaluating-Analyzing Type

Q. "The role of women is gradually enhancing in the politics of the country." Examine the statement.

Ans.

The statement "The role of women is gradually enhancing in the politics of the country is________. (True/Not true)

It stands true because ____________________

In the questions, which include examining, analyzing, and evaluating the statement, first verify its accuracy if the statement is true or false.

Provide reasons, or examples in support of your stance. Also, mention the positive and negative impact if this is worth more than 2 marks.

Comparison Type

Q. Differentiate between organized and unorganized sectors.

Ans.

Following are the differences between the __________ and __________:

Basis	Organized Sector	Unorganized Sector
(a) ________	________	________
(b) ________	________	________

In comparison / differentiate / distinguish / type questions, start with a general statement introducing the comparison between the two concept or topic given. This sets the context and keeps the examiner aware of the focus of your answer.

- **Avoid paragraphs:** Use a tabular format to compare.
- **Comparative Phrases:** Include terms such as in contrast, whereas, while, etc., to show the differences clearly.

Each point should address a different aspects such as **Definition, Term of Employment, Job Security, etc.**

Conceptual-Understanding Type

Q. "Democratic systems are based on political equality." Explain the statement.

Ans.

The statement "Democratic systems are based on political equality" highlights the ____

Practical examples: ____

Conclusion: ____

> Begin by explaining the meaning/fundamental principle of political equality in a democracy. For example, the concept of political equality in democratic systems emphasizes that all individuals have equal rights and influence in decision-making.

> Elaborate on how political equality operates practically by focusing on **Voting Rights, Equal opportunity of Participation, and Equal Value of Every Vote**.

> Conclude by emphasizing how political equality promotes inclusiveness and fairness within the political system.

Identification-Application

Q. "Mohan recently bought a farm and wants to grow crops such as sugarcane, cotton, and jowar. He is unfamiliar with the local soil types and climatic conditions." Help him identify the appropriate soil type and its properties for successful farming.

Ans.

For growing crops like sugarcane, cotton, and jowar, ________ soil is the most suitable due to its unique properties and availability in specific regions.

Soil's Characteristics: ____

It contains ________, carbonate, magnesium, ________, ________. Its nutrient richness and water-holding capacity support the growth of crops like cotton, sugarcane, and jowar effectively.

Climatic Adaptability: ____

Thus, ____________ is ideal for crops like sugarcane, cotton, and jowar due to its nutrient-rich composition, moisture retention, and adaptability to climatic conditions."

> Start with a brief introduction, explaining the relevance of **choosing the right soil** for specific crops.

> Explain Soil's Characteristics for example: formed from lava flows, covers Maharashtra, Saurashtra, Malwa, and extends along the Godavari and Krishna valleys. It is clay-rich, ensuring excellent moisture retention, and is ideal for crops.

> Mention the nutrients it carries and its benefits for agricultural productivity.

> Develops **deep cracks** during dry seasons, aiding **aeration**, becomes **sticky when wet**, making it difficult to manage in the rainy season but ideal for pre-monsoon plantation.

> Sum up the answer by linking soil's properties with crop suitability.

Map Based Question

Q. (*a*) Two places A and B have been marked on the given outline map of India. Identify them and write their correct names on the lines drawn near them.

A. The place where the Peasant Satyagraha took place.

B. Indian National Congress session was held at this place in Sept. 1920.

(*b*) On the same outline map of India locate and label any three of the following with suitable symbols

i. A Software Technology Park in Maharashtra.

ii. A coal mine in Jharkhand.

iii. The tallest dam in India.

iv. A seaport located in West Bengal.

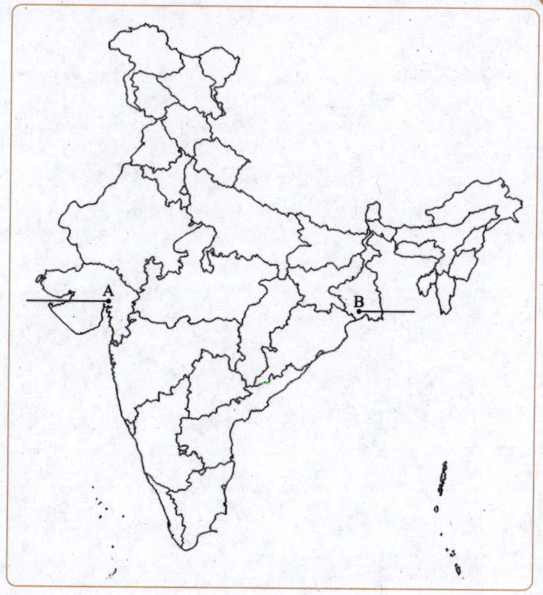

Ans.

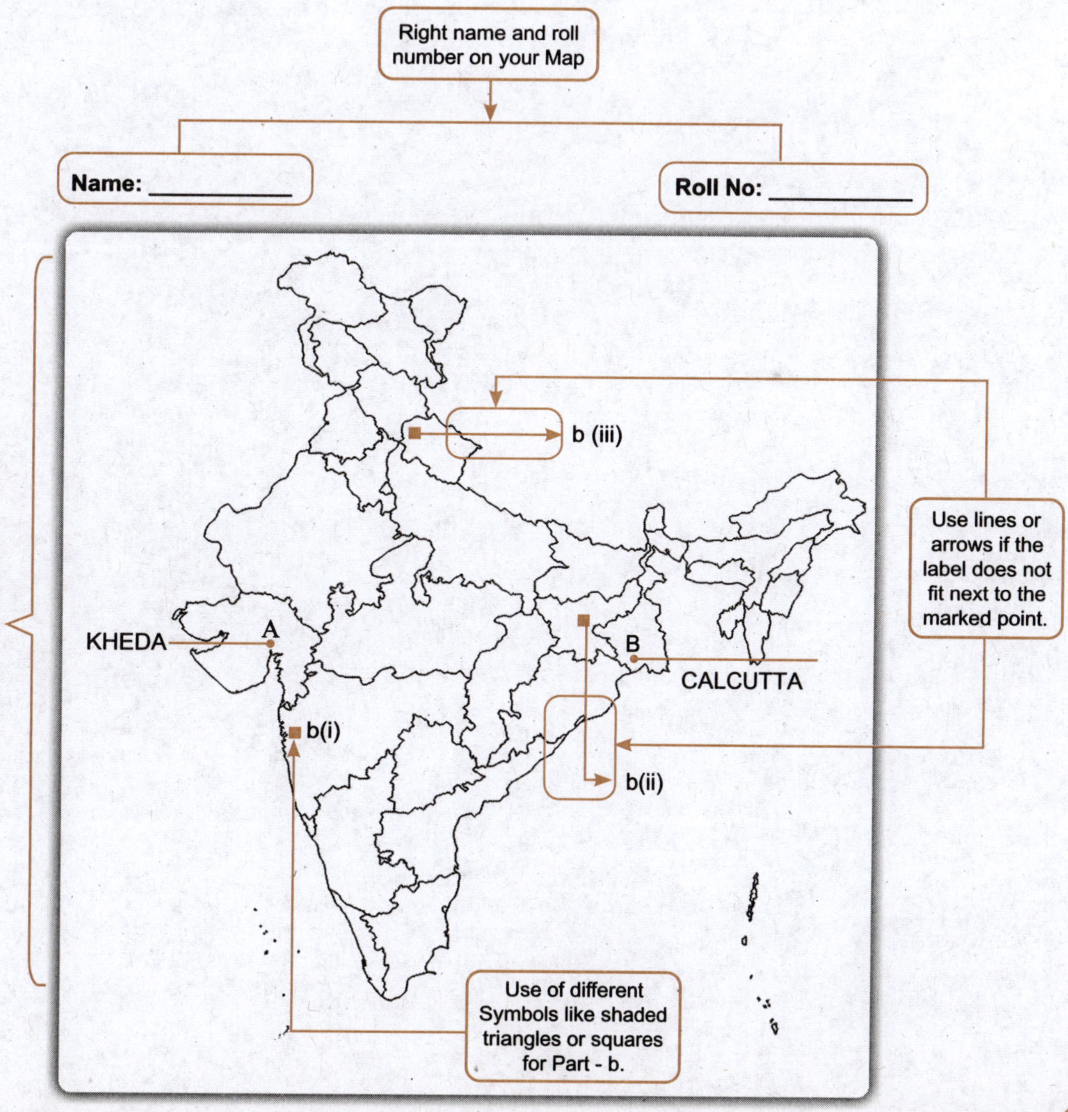

- In part b, locate and label only three of the four given, as marking all four won't give extra marks.
- Ensure all locations are labeled clearly without overcrowding the map to ensure the examiner can easily read your answer.
- Do not attach the map to the front and back of your answer booklet; instead, tie it in the middle to reduce the risk of tearing and misplacement.

CHAPTER-1
THE RISE OF NATIONALISM IN EUROPE

HISTORY

Cheat Sheet

To Access One Shot Revision Video Scan This QR Code

The Rise of Nationalism in Europe

The French Revolution and the idea of Nation (CBSE 2025)

French Revolution-1789 (CBSE 2020)
- La patrie (The father land)
- Le citoyen (The Citizen)
- Tricolour French flag
- Equal Rights

Administrative Changes
- Emergence of Constitution of France
- Estates General renamed as the National Assembly
- Centralised Administration
- Uniform system of weights measures and common currency
- French language made a common language

Napoleonic Code - (1804) (CBSE 2020)
- Introduction of civil code (1804)-(Napoleonic code)
- Equality before the law
- Secured right to property
- Privileges of high class abolished
- Feudal system ended
- Peasants freed from serfdom system
- Transport and communication improved

The age of Revolutions: 1830-1848 (CBSE 2022 Term-I)

Romantic Imagination & National Feeling

Romanticists criticised science and focussed instead on emotions, intuition and mystical feelings. Language and folklores were used to instil national spirit.

Hunger, Hardship & Popular Revolt

In 1830s, increased population, food shortages and widespread unemployment brought people out on the roads.

Liberal Revolts (CBSE 2022 Term-I)
- Upheaval in France in July 1830
- Uprising in Brussels
- Uprising in Greece 1821
- Treaty of Constantinople 1832

The Making of Nationalism in Europe (CBSE 2024)

Aristocracy and New Middle Class
- **Aristocrats:** Numerically small dominant social and political class united by common way of life. Emergence of commercial classes-existence band on production for market.
- **New middle class:** Working class, artisans, businessmen, professionals etc.

Liberal Nationalism (CBSE 2023, 2022 Term-I, 2020)
- **Political:** End of clerical privilege, autocracy, representative form of government through parliament, inviolability of private property, limited suffrage.
- **Economic:** Freedom of markets, abolition of state-imposed restrictions on movement of goods of capital.

Revolutionaries (CBSE 2023, 2022 Term-I)
- Secret societies sprang up in many parts of Europe to oppose monarchical forms and to fight for liberty and freedom.
- Giuseppe Mazzini, an Italian revolutionary founded 2 secret societies, **Young Italy** in Marseilles and **Young Europe** in Berne.

A New Conservatism after 1815 (CBSE 2022 Term-I)

Conservatists when they realised that modernisation could strengthen traditional institutions like the Monarchy introduced a modern army, an Efficient bureaucracy, a dynamic economy, abolition of serfdom and feudalism. Treaty of Vienna (1815)

The Rise of Nationalism in Europe

The Making of Germany and Italy

Unification of Germany

CBSE 2024, 2022 Term-I

- Attempt to set up a constitutional monarchy at Frankfurt in 1848 was suppressed by the monarchy, Military and Junkers.
- Prussian Chief Minister Otto Von Bismarck takes the lead in German unification.
- He planned the unification with the help of the Prussian Army and Bureaucracy.
- Ensured unification after 3 wars with France, Austria and Denmark over 7 years.
- Process completed with the crowning of Kaiser William I as King of Germany.

Strange Case of Britain

English, Welsh, Scot or Irish (ethnicity) was the primary identities of inhabitants of Britain Isles. United Kingdom of Great Britain was formed as a result of the Act of Union (1707).

Unification of Italy

CBSE 2024, 2023, 2022 Term-I

- Idea of unification was first given by Guiseppe Mazzini through his secret society called young Italy.
- The lead was taken by the king of Sardinia, Victor Emmanuel II.
- Count Cavour, Chief Minister of Sardinia, led the unification process by alliance with France to defeat Austria and unify its Northern territories.
- Guiseppe Garibaldi led a movement in Western part by involving local peasant support to attack Spanish rule.
- Process completed with the crowning of Victor Emmanuel II as king of Italy in 1861.

Visualising the Nation

CBSE 2025

Allegory of the Nation

Female figure (allegory) chosen to personify the nation, to give the abstract idea of nation a concrete form. 'Germania' in Germany and 'Christened Marianne' in Italy was chosen.

Nationalism and Imperialism

CBSE 2025

Nationalism in the Balkans State

- Tensions of Europe after 1971 was the area called the Balkans.
- First world war (1914-1918)
- In 1914, Europe was disastrous because of Nationalism, aligned with imperialism.
- Anti-imperial movements were developed but they all struggled to form independent nation-states.

CHAPTER-2

NATIONALISM IN INDIA

Cheat Sheet

To Access One Shot Revision Video Scan This QR Code

Nationalism in India

The First World war, Khilafat & Non-Cooperation
CBSE 2025, 2020

Rise of Nationalism after First World War

Reason — CBSE 2022 Term-II
- Increase in custom duties and introduction of income tax due to war loans.
- Extreme hardships due to increase in price of essential goods.
- Forced recruitment in the army.
- Shortage of food due to crop failure, famines and epidemics.

The way of Changes Nationalism
CBSE 2024

Satyagraha — CBSE 2022 Term-II
- Satyagraha is Mahatma Gandhi's concept of peaceful protest (fighting with peace).
  - Champaran Satyagraha 1917.
  - Mill worker's movement in Ahmedabad 1918.
  - Kheda Satyagraha 1918.

Rowlatt Act
- Rowlatt Act (1919) was passed in a hurry by the Imperial Legislative Assembly despite the opposition from the Indian members of the council.
- Local leaders were asserted in Amritsar and Gandhiji was barred from entering Delhi, martial law was imposed in Amritsar
- A number of people gathered in Jallianwala Bagh to celebrate Baisakhi unaware of the martial law.
- celebrate Baisakhi unaware of the martial law. General Dyer ordered open fire on them killing hundreds of people.
- People in India opposed the killings by attacking government offices, police stations etc.

Non-Cooperation Movement — CBSE 2022 Term-II, 2020
- Surrender of Govt. Titles.
- Boycott of civil services, army, police, courts and legislative councils. Schools and foreign goods.

Differing strands within Movement
CBSE 2020

The Movcment in the Towns
- Students left government schools, officers resigned, lawyers gave up their practices, and traders and merchants boycotted foreign goods.
- The movement experienced a slowdown due to the high price of Khadi cloth and the absence of adequate alternative Indian institutions to replace British-established systems.

Movement in the Countryside
- In Awadh Peasants were led by Ram Chandra - a Sanyasi, who had earlier been to Fiji as an indentured labourer.
- Peasants had to do begar and work at the landlord's farms without any payment. Peasants movement demanded abolition of begar and reduction of revenues.
- The movement in the countryside was against talukdars and landlords who demanded high rents and other cesses.

Swaraj in the Plantations — CBSE 2023, 2020
- Under the Inland Emigration Act of 1859, workers were not allowed to leave the plantations without permission, which was seldom granted.
- Workers defied the authorities, left the plantations.

Nationalism in India

Towards Civil Disobedience (CBSE 2025, 2024)

Aspects of the Movement

Re-launch of the Movement

- Mahatma Gandhi relaunched the Civil Disobedience Movement.
- For over a year, the movement continued, but by 1934 it lost its momentum.

Gandhi-Irwin Pact

- The pact was signed on March 5, 1931, wherein Mahatma Gandhi agreed to attend the Round Table Conference.
- The British government consented to release political prisoners as part of the pact's conditions.
- Held in London in 1931, this conference concluded without achieving any substantive results.

Salt March (CBSE 2025, 2022 Term-II)

- The Salt Satyagraha was a large-scale civil disobedience movement started by Mahatma Gandhi in response to the imposition of a salt tax in India by the British administration.
- Mahatma Gandhi initiated the Salt March from Sabarmati to Dandi with 78 followers, embarking on a profound act of civil disobedience.
- Arriving at Dandi on April 6, 1930, Gandhi defied British law by producing salt from sea water, symbolically challenging British authority.

Simon Commission

- The Simon Commission was established by Britain's Tory government
- Sir John Simon, to review nationalist demands and recommend changes to India's constitutional framework.
- The commission was met with widespread protest and the slogan "Go back Simon" in India due to its all-English membership.
- The Simon Commission proposed 'dominion status' as a topic for future discussions on India's Constitution.

Withdrawal of Non-Cooperation Movement

- Gandhiji ended the movement due to escalating violence.
- There was significant debate within the Congress about participating in council elections.

Formation of Swaraj Party

- C. R. Das and Motilal Nehru established the Swaraj Party within the Congress to advocate for council entry.
- Jawaharlal Nehru and Subhash Chandra Bose pressed for mass agitation and for full independence.

Effect of Civil Disobedience Movement (CBSE 2020)

- The movement spread to the entire nation.
- Colonial laws were violated, salt manufactured in numerous places.
- Foreign clothes were burnt and picketing liquor shops.
- Peasants refused to pay revenue and chaukidari tax.

Different Perspective of The Movement (CBSE 2024)

Business Class

- They wanted protection against imports of foreign goods.
- The Indian Industrial and Commercial Congress was established in 1920 and FICCI in 1927 by leading Indian industrialists.
- These groups opposed colonial economic policies and supported the initial launch of the Civil Disobedience Movement.

Poor Peasants (CBSE 2020)

- The poor peasants were interested in the reduction of the revenue demand.
- Congress was unwilling to support 'no rent' campaigns in most of the places.

Rich Peasants (CBSE 2023)

- The wealthy Patidars of Gujarat and the Jats of Uttar Pradesh were involved in the movement in the countryside.
- For them the fight for Swaraj was struggle against high revenues.

Industrial Worker

- The Industrial Working Classes did not participate in the Civil disobedience Movement in large numbers except in the Nagpur region.
- There were strikes by railway workers in 1930 and dock workers in 1932.

Participation of Women

- They participated in protest marches, manufactured salt and picketed foreign cloth and liquor shops.
- In Urban areas these women were from high-caste families; in rural areas they came from rich peasant households.

Nationalism in India

Towards Civil Disobedience

Feeling of Collective Belonging

CBSE 2020

- People began to see themselves as members of a unified nation, recognizing a common bond among diverse communities.
- To foster nationalism, communities developed folklore, and created national figures, symbols, and icons that encapsulated shared values and aspirations.

Positive and Negative aspects of Nationalism

- The Indian national struggle united various groups and classes in a collective effort for independence.
- Conflicts among different groups occasionally emerged, sometimes leading to the movement's failure.

Quit India Movement

- Launched in 1942 after the failure of the Cripps Mission.
- Led by Mahatma Gandhi with the slogan "Do or Die."
- Involved diverse sections of society including students, workers, and women.
- Marked by severe crackdowns, mass arrests, and violence.
- Weakened British control and paved the way for India's independence in 1947.

CHAPTER-3

THE MAKING OF A GLOBAL WORLD

Cheat Sheet

To Access One Shot Revision Video Scan This QR Code

The Making of a Global World → Important aspect (CBSE 2025, 2024)

Features of Pre-modern World (CBSE 2024, 2020)

- Human societies have become steady more interlinked.
- Travellers, Traders, Priest and Pilgrims travelled vast distance.
- Indus Valley civilisation was linked with west Asia.
- Cowries were used as a form of currency.

Conquest, Disease and Trade (CBSE 2025, 2023)

- In 16th century, Europe sailors found a sea route to Asia and America.
- The Portugese and Spanish conquest and colonisation of America was under way.
- The most powerful weapon of Spanish conquers, was small pox which they carried to America.

Silk Routes (CBSE 2025)

- Interconnected modern trade and cultural link between distant parts of the world.
- Most well known silk route connected China to Europe.

Food Travells

- Traders and Travellers introduced new crops of the land they travelled.
- Potatoes, Soya, Maize, Ground nuts, Tomatoes, Chillies introduced in Europe and Asia after America wad discovered.
- Noodles travelled west from China to become Spaghetti.

CHAPTER-4
PRINT CULTURE AND THE MODERN WORLD

Cheat Sheet

To Access One Shot Revision Video Scan This QR Code

Print Culture and the Modern World

The First Printed Books and Print Comes to Europe (CBSE 2020)

The First Printed Book

The First Printed Book
- China, Japan and Korea invented the very first type of print technology, which was a hand printing system.

Contribution

China
- Shanghai emerged as the center of the new print culture.
- Merchants utilized printed materials extensively.
- Affluent women started to read and publish their poetry and plays.

Japan
- Buddhist missionaries introduced print technology.
- The "Diamond Sutra" is considered the oldest known book in Japan.
- The printing of visual materials fostered unique publishing practices.

Print Culture in Europe

Origins
- Introduction of Chinese paper to Europe in the 11th century.
- Marco Polo's introduction of woodblock printing from his travels in Asia.
- Italians began producing books with woodblocks, and soon the technology spread to other parts of Europe.

Manuscript Culture
- The production of handwritten manuscripts could not satisfy the ever-increasing demand-for books because:
  - Copying was an expensive, laborious and time-consuming business.
  - Manuscripts were fragile, awkward to handle.

First Printing Press
- Johann Gutenberg developed the printing press for the first time in the 1430's Strasbourg.
- For the printing press, he used an olive press model and molds for the letters of the alphabet.
- The first book he printed with this technology was the Bible.

The Print Revolution & Its Impact and The Reading Mania

The Print Revolution and its Impact

A New Reading Public
- Printers began publishing popular ballads and folk tales and such books would be profusely illustrated.
- Printed material was orally transmitted.

Religious Debate
- In 1517, the religious reformer Martin Luther wrote Ninety-Five Theses criticizing many of the practices and rituals of the Roman Catholic Church.
- This led to a division within the Church and the Beginning of the Protestant Reformation.

Fear of Print
- People believed this can lead to the fear of the spread of rebellious and irreligious thoughts.

The Reading Mania

Increased Literacy Rates
- Literacy rates surged in Europe through the 17th and 18th centuries.
- Churches set up schools in villages, bringing education to a broader audience.

Emergence of New Readers
- The market was flooded with books catering to new demographics, including peasants, artisans, and women.
- Pedlars sold books, reaching audiences beyond the cities and towns.

Tremble, therefore, Tyrants of the World
- People believed books as a means of spreading progress and enlightenment.
- Printing Press believed to be a means of ending despotism.

Print Culture and the Modern World

The Nineteenth Century and India and the World of Print
CBSE 2025

Print in India

CBSE 2020

Manuscripts before the age of Print

- In India, manuscripts were copied on palm leaves or on handmade paper.

Print comes to India

- In the mid-sixteenth century, the printing press first came to Goa with Portuguese missionaries.
- By 1710, Dutch Protestant Missionaries had Printed 32 Tamil texts.
- James Augustus Hicky began to edit ***'Bengal Gazette'*** in 1780.

Important Aspect

Children, Women and Workers

- Children's Press was set up in France in 1857.
- Women became important as readers as well as writers.
- Penny Magazines were especially meant for women, manuals teaching proper behaviors and housekeeping.

Further Innovations

- By mid 19th Century, ***Richard M. Hoe*** perfected the power driven cylindrical press.
- In the late 19th century, an offset press was developed that can print up to six colours at a time.
- By the 20th century, electrically operated presses accelerated printing operations.

Religious Reform and Public Debates, New Forms of Publication and Print and Censorship
CBSE 2025

New Forms of Publication

CBSE 2023

Rise of the Novel

- The novel as a literary form found its unique place in India, reflecting the diverse experiences and emotions of its people.
- New Literary Forms- lyrics, short stories, essays.

Women & Print

- The prevalence of reading among women rose in middle-class households.
- Rashsundari Devi authored 'Amar Jiban,' recognized as the first extensive autobiography by a woman.
- Tarabai Shinde and Pandita Ramabai penned works that examined women's lives.
- In the early 20th century, journals composed by women began to gain popularity

Print & the Poor People

- In the 19th century, very cheap and small books were brought to markets.
- From the late nineteenth century, issues of caste discrimination began to be written about in many printed tracts and essays.
- A Kanpur mill worker published 'Sacchi Kavitayen' under the name of 'Sudarshan Chakra'.

Religious Reforms and Public Debates

CBSE 2025, 2024, 2020

- Raja Ram Mohan Roy released a publication called ***"Sambad Kaumudi"*** in the year 1821.
- In response, Hindu traditionalists started publishing a paper titled ***"Samachar Chandrika"*** also beginning in 1821.
- Muslim communities produced translations of sacred texts in Persian and Urdu.
- A variety of religious texts began to be widely printed in local languages starting in the 1880s.

Print and Censorship

CBSE 2020

Facts

- By the **1820s,** the Calcutta Supreme Court passed certain regulations to control press freedom.
- In **1835,** Thomas Macaulay formulated new rules that restored the earlier freedoms.
- In **1878,** the Vernacular Press Act was passed, modelled on the Irish Press Laws.

CHAPTER-1

POWER SHARING

POLITICAL SCIENCE

Cheat Sheet

To Access One Shot Revision Video Scan This QR Code

Power Sharing

Case Study: Sri Lanka (CBSE 2020)

Location & Population (CBSE 2025, 2020)

- An island nation, few kilometres off the southern coast of Tamil Nadu.
- The population of about two crore, the same as in Haryana
- **Majority-**
  - 74% Sinhalese speakers
- **Minority-**
  - 18% Tamil speakers (Hindus or Muslims)
    - → 13% Sri-Lankan Tamils
    - → 5% Indian Tamils
  - 7% Christians(Tamils and Sinhala speaker)

Reason of Conflict

Sinhala leaders adopted majoritarian measures to establish Sinhala supremacy after independence in 1948.

Response to Conflict → MAJORITARIANISM

- Paid no attention to minorities need and wishes.
- Sinhala was recognised as the only official language by an act in 1956.
- Preference to Sinhalese in government jobs and universities.
- Protected and fostered Buddhism.

Outcomes

- Feeling of alienation among Sri-Lankan Tamils
- **Tamils Started demanding-**
  - Recognition of Tamil as an official language
  - Regional autonomy
  - Equality of opportunity in jobs and education
  - Independent Tamil Ealam (State) in northern and eastern part of Sri Lanka
  - **Civil War-**
    - → Thousands of people were killed from both communities.
    - → Families were forced to leave the country as refugees.
    - → Many people lost their livelihood.

Case Study: Belgium

Location & Population (CBSE 2025)

- A small country in Europe(Smaller than Haryana).
- Share border with the Netherlands, France, Luxembourg, and Germany.
- Population- little over one crore(about the half of the Haryana's population)
- **Majority-**
  - Country- Dutch(59%, Flemish)
  - Capital city(Brussels)- French(80%)
- **Minority-**
  - Country- French(40%, Wallonia)
  - Capital city(Brussels)- Dutch(20%)

Reason of Conflict (CBSE 2025)

- The french speaking community was relatively rich and powerful.
- Dutch-speaking (majority) community got the benefit of economic development and education much later then the minority French-speaking community

Outcomes

- No civic strife between the two major communities
- Prevented the possible division of the country on linguistic lines.

Response to Conflict → ACCOMMODATION (CBSE 2024, 2020)

- Recognised the existence of regional differences and cultural diversities
- Amended constitution four times between 1970-1993 to ensure peaceful co-existence
- **Elements of Belgium model-**
  - Equal no. of Dutch and French speaking ministers in central government.
  - Support of majority of members from each linguistic group to prevent dominance of any one group.
  - Devolution of power to state government.
  - State government not subordinate to central government.
  - Separate government for brussel in which both communities have equal representation.
  - Community government- Elected by people belonging to one language community.

Power Sharing

Why power sharing is desirable?

Prudential Reasons

It can lead to better outcomes like less conflict, and more stability and keep the country running smoothly.

Moral Reasons

It is the right thing to do in a democracy because it respects everyone's rights and opinions.

Forms of Power Sharing (CBSE 2023)

(i) Horizontal Division of Power (CBSE 2025, 2024, 2020)

- Between the different organs of the government - Legislature, Executive and Judiciary.

(ii) Vertical Division of Power

- Between the different levels of government - Central, State & Local self government.

(iii) Power Sharing among different social groups (CBSE 2025)

- Between various social groups such as linguistic and religious groups.
- E.g.: Belgium's Community Government

(iv) Power Sharing among Influential groups

- Political Parties, Business men, Industrialists, Farmers Industrial workers.
- E.g.: Coalition Government.

Advantages of Power sharing (CBSE 2023)

- Bring peace, harmony and unity.
- Prevent discrimination, disintegration, conflicts and abuse of power.
- Ensure fair representation and political stability.

CHAPTER-2
FEDERALISM

To Access One Shot Revision Video Scan This QR Code

Cheat Sheet

Federalism

Meaning

A system of government in which the power is divided between central authority and various constituent units.

Features (CBSE 2020)

- Multiple levels (tiers) of Government.
- Each tier is accountable to the people.
- Each level has its own jurisdiction, specified in the constitution, guaranteeing their authority.
- Changes to fundamental provisions require the consent of both levels of Government.
- Courts interpret the Constitution & resolve disputes between levels of Government.
- Revenue sources for each level are specified to ensure financial autonomy

Type of federations

- **Coming Together Federation:** Independent states voluntarily coming together (example -USA, Switzerland, Australia)
- **Holding Together Federation:** Large country divides power between constituent states and the national government (example - India Spain, Belgium).

What Makes India A Federal Country? (CBSE 2025)

Constitution

Establishes a two-tier system of government namely union government (represent the country) and state government (represent a particular state). In 1992, the third tier was added with panchayats and municipalities.

Independent Judiciary

Judiciary interpret and oversee the implementation of constitutional provisions & in case of a dispute regarding the division of powers, the court makes the decision.

Amendment Process

Requires two-third majority in both the houses of the parliament and ratification by the legislature of at least half of the total states.

Power sharing arrangements (CBSE 2025, 2023)

Power sharing arrangements between union and state government.

State Government Legislate over

State list - Contains subject of state and local importance. Such as police, trade, agriculture etc.

Concurrent list - Both union and state government can make laws but in case of Conflict, the union government's law prevail

Special power (under article 371) - Granted to states like Assam, Nagaland, Arunachal Pradesh and Mizoram. Aim is to protect Culture, land rights and ensure preferential employment for indigenous people.

Union Government Legislate over (CBSE 2024, 2023)

Union list - Subjects of national importance such as defence, banking, foreign affair etc.

Concurrent list - Includes subjects of common interests to both union and state government such as education forest, trade union. In case of conflicts, union government's law prevail.

Union territories - Small areas that neither become independent state nor merge with existing States. E.g.- Chandigarh, Delhi etc.

Residuary power - Subjects that do not fall in any of the three lists or all subjects that came up after the constitution was made.

Federalism

Key Factors Behind The Success of Federalism in India (CBSE 2024)

Linguistic states

- State were created based on language.
- Some states were created on the basis of culture, ethnicity or geography also.
- **Initial concerns:** Linguistic states would lead to disintegration.
- **Outcomes:** United the country and facilitated better and efficient administration.

India's Language Policy (CBSE 2023, 2020)

- Indian constitution did not designate any language as the national language.
- Use of English along with Hindi for official purpose.
- 22 languages were recognised as scheduled language. (CBSE 2025)
- Candidates in central government examinations could opt for any of scheduled language.
- Each state has its own official language. Government work predominantly takes place in the respective states language

Decentralisation (CBSE 2025, 2023, 2020)

Meaning

Transferring power from central and state governments to local government bodies.

Promotes

- Local Self government Bodies - Municipalities & Municipal Corporation, Zilla Parishad, Gram Panchayat.
- Effective governance at the Grassroot level
- Democratic Participation
- Direct Participation of citizens in decision-making

Outcomes of Constitutional Amendment Act, 1992 (CBSE 2025)

- Regular Elections for local government bodies in every 5 year.
- Seats are reserved in elected bodies and the executive heads of these institutions for the SCs, STs and OBCs.
- At least 1/3rd of all positions are reserved for women.
- Independent state election commissions conduct panchayats & municipal elections.
- State government required to share powers & revenue with local government bodies.

CHAPTER-3

GENDER, RELIGION AND CASTE

Cheat Sheet

To Access One Shot Revision Video Scan This QR Code

Gender, Religion and Caste

→ Basis of Social Differences → Gender / Caste / Religion

Gender (CBSE 2025, 2023, 2020)

Meaning

Biological difference between males and females.

Gender division of labour

- **Meaning:** Social division under which unequal roles are assigned.
  - ▲ **Males:**

    Roles Assigned: Earning and all the work outside home.

    Result: Men becoming more powerful enjoying greater freedom and social respect.
  - ▲ **Females:**

    Roles Assigned: Household work, cooking, taking care of kids etc.

    Result:

    Minimum role in public life, women confined to home, no freedom

    Womens started demanding for voting rights, enhancement in political and legal status,improvement in educational and career opportunities, equality in personal and family life. It led to Improvement in women's role in public life.

Women in India

- **Status in Society** Indian women have low respect in society due to patriarchal society.
- **Literacy Rate:** only 54% compared with 76% among men
- **Unpaid Work:** Women works one hour more than men but do not get paid for household work.
- **Wage Difference:** Despite of Equal Renumeration Act 1976, women workers get less pay than men for equal work.
- **Child Sex Ratio:** Girl child is aborted due to preference of male which led to a decline in child sex ratio (919 girls per 1000 boys).
- **Violence against Women:** Exploitation, harassment and violence against women have increased in urban areas.
- **Political Representation:** Proportion of women in legislature is low.
- **Reservation of Seats:** In 1992, 1/3rd seats in local government bodies is reserved for women. Now, there are more than 10 lakh elected women representatives in rural and urban local bodies.
- In 2023, Nari Shakti Vandan Adhiniyam (Women's Reservation Act, 2023) was passed, which will give a 33 percent reservation of seats for women in the Lok Sabha, State Legislative Assemblies, and also the Delhi Assembly.

Caste

Religion

Religious Division

Meaning:

- Division of society on the basis of religion
- Leads to discrimination and opperession of minorities
- Also leads to Communalism.

Communalism (CBSE 2020)

Meaning

- When one community tries to promote itself on the cost of the other.
- **Communal Politics:** Using religion in politics to gain dominance
- **Forms of communalism:**
  - ▲ Religious beliefs in the superiority of one's religion
  - ▲ Use of sacred symbols, religious leaders, emotional appeal in politics
  - ▲ Communal violence, riots, massacre between different communities

Gender, Religion and Caste

Basis of Social Differences

- Gender
- Religion
- Caste

Caste

Brief

- Caste inequalities create social division
- In India, untouchability is an extreme form of casteism
- Government prohibited untouchability.
- Urbanisation and occupational mobility reduced caste hierarchy.

Caste in Politics CBSE 2020

Meaning:

- Using caste in politics to gain dominance

Negative Aspect

- Parties choose candidate according to caste composition of the electorate and not on qualification basis.
- Parties favour a particular caste to gain support

Positive Aspect

- Lower caste got the better representation in the government.
- Everyone gets a fair chance to contest in the elections

India as a Secular State CBSE 2025, 2020

- No official religion, of the country
- People have freedom to practice, follow and propagate their religion
- No discrimination on the basis of religion.

Politics is Caste

Influence of politics in caste:

- Each caste tries to gather more subcaste to increase its number
- One caste may make alliance with other castes to gain political support
- New kind of caste group such as 'backward' and 'forward' caste has emerged.

CHAPTER-4

POLITICAL PARTIES

Cheat Sheet

To Access One Shot Revision Video Scan This QR Code

Political Parties

Why do we need political parties?

Necessity (CBSE 2023, 2020)
- Bring together diverse views and interests
- Support or restrain govt. and make policies
- Ensure the functioning of a democratic system
- Form responsible governments
- Gather different opinions

Functions of political parties (CBSE 2024, 2022)
- Contesting Elections
- Formulating policies
- Law making
- Government formation
- Opposition role
- Shaping public opinion
- Access to Government machinery and welfare schemes.

Steps taken to reform Political Parties (CBSE 2022, 2020, 2017)

1. Every candidate must file an affidavit, sharing details of his **property** and **criminal cases** pending against him.
2. Parties must:
   (a) Hold regular elections within the party.
   (b) File income tax returns
3. Anti-Defection Law:
   (a) Now, the law says if any MLA or MP changes parties, he or she will lose the seat in the legislature.
   (b) This stops defection.

Challenges to political parties (CBSE 2020)
- Dynastic succession
- Influence of money and muscle power
- Lack of meaningful choice
- Lack of Internal democracy

Party System

Type (CBSE 2022)
- One-party system
- Two-party system (CBSE 2024)
- Multiparty system (CBSE 2025)

Depends on
- Nature of Society
- Social and regional divisions
- History of Politics
- Electoral system in each country

National parties and State parties (CBSE 2025, 2023)

National parties
- These parties have units across various states and follow same policies and strategies
- Must register with Election Commission and Enjoy special facilities and privileges
- There are six recognized national parties in the country as per notification of the Election Commission of India issued in 2023.

Aam Aadmi Party (AAP): Formed on 26 November 2012, following the 2011 anti-corruption movement. The party is based on the principles of accountability, clean administration, transparency, and good governance.

(CBSE 2020) **Bahujan Samaj Party (BSP):** Formed in 1984 under the leadership of Kanshi Ram, represents the interests of Bahujan samaj which includes Dalits, Adivasis, OBC and Religious minorities.

Bharatiya Janata Party (BJP): BJP was founded in 1980 by reviving Bharatiya Jana Sangh (1951) founded by Syama Prasad Mukherjee in 1951. It draws inspiration from India's ancient culture, Deendayal Upadhyaya's ideas of integral humanism, and Antyodaya. Emerged as the largest party with 303 members in the 2019 Lok Sabha elections.

Indian National Congress (INC): Founded in 1885, INC is one of the world's oldest political parties. INC is a centrist party promoting secularism, minority welfare, and economic reforms with a human face. Secured 19.5% votes and 52 seats in the 2019 Lok Sabha elections.

National People's Party (NPP): The National People's Party (NPP) was formed in July 2013 under the leadership of P.A. Sangma and is the first political party from Northeast India to attain the status of a national party. Its core philosophy revolves around providing education and employment to all while empowering all sections of society.

Communist Party of India - Marxist (CPI-M): Formed in 1964, adhere to Marxism-Leninism and supports socialism, secularism and democracy and opposes imperialism and communalism.

State Parties (CBSE 2025)
- ❒ Operate mainly in one or a few states.
- ❒ Recognized by the Election Commission if secure 6% of votes in a state and win atleast two seats in state elections.
- ❒ Have a limited presence in one or a few states.
- ❒ **Example:** Samajwadi Party (SP), All India Trinamool Congress (AITC), Rashtriys Janta Dal (RJD)

CHAPTER-5

OUTCOMES OF DEMOCRACY

Cheat Sheet

To Access One Shot Revision Video Scan This QR Code

Democracy

Meaning: A form of government where citizen have the power to choose their leader and have a say in decisions affecting them.

Democracy Or Dictatorship (CBSE 2023, 2020)

Democracy is better because dictatorships is often lack in:

- Promoting equality
- Facilitating better decision-making
- Providing peaceful way to resolve conflicts
- Provision of correcting mistakes
- Improving dignity and freedom of people.

Outcomes of Democracy (CBSE 2024)

Political Outcomes (CBSE 2025, 2024)

Expectations (CBSE 2023)

- **Accountable government:** Answerable to the citizen for the actions taken.
- **Responsive government:** Consider the needs and expectations of the people in decision-making.
- **Transparency:** Citizens can examine all the actions/decisions taken by the government.
- **Elections:** Regular, free and fair elections.
- **Public Debates:** Open public debates on major policies and legislation
- **Political Equality:** All individual have equal weight in electing representatives
- **Corruption Free:** Democracy is supposed to be free from corruption.

Outcomes

- Successful in setting up regular and free elections, but falls short in providing fair chance to everyone in elections.
- Successful in setting up condition for open public debates, but falls short in subjective every decision to public debates.
- Do not show good record when it comes to sharing information with citizens.
- Democracy is not free from corruption.
- Successful in providing political equality

Economic Outcomes (CBSE 2022, 2017)

Expectations

- Democracy is expected to bring economic growth and development.
- Government keenly take up the problem of poverty.
- Democracy is expected to decrease the income disparity between the people.

Outcomes (CBSE 2025)

- Democracy did not appear to be very successful in ensuring economic growth and development.
- Democratically elected governments do not appear to be as keen to address the question of poverty as one may expect.
- Many democracies have failed in reducing economic disparities.

Social Outcomes (CBSE 2023, 2017)

Expectations (CBSE 2022)

- **Accommodation of Social Diversity-** Proper handling of social difference, divisions and conflicts
- **Dignity and Freedom of People-** Respect and freedom of every individual living in the country.
- **Equal treatment of women-** Equal treatment of women in society and treating them with respect.
- **Equal status of all castes-** Respect and equal position in society to the backward classes.

Outcomes (CBSE 2025)

- Democracy stands much superior to any to any other form of government in promoting dignity and freedom of the individual.
- Democracy accommodates social diversity.
- Democracy provide dignity and freedom to every iindividual.
- Democracy prohibits discrimination based on caste, gender, etc., and treats every individual as equal.

CHAPTER-1
RESOURCES AND DEVELOPMENT

GEOGRAPHY

Cheat Sheet

To Access One Shot Revision Video Scan This QR Code

Resources and Development

Resources

CBSE 2020

A **resource** is anything in our environment that can be used to fulfill human needs — but only if it is: **Technologically accessible, Economically feasible and Culturally acceptable.**

Importance of Resources

Resources are important because they:
- Help in satisfying **human needs.**
- Support **economic development.**
- Improve the **quality of life.**
- Are essential for **survival and progress** of all life forms.
- Enable **technological advancement** and **social development.**

Classification of Resources

- **On the basis of origin:** biotic and abiotic
- **On the basis of exhaustibility:** renewable and non-renewable
- **On the basis of ownership:** individual, community, national and international
- **On the basis of status of development:** potential, developed stock and reserves.

Resource Planning in India

CBSE 2025, 2020

- **Resource planning** is the process of **judicious use of available resources** by assessing, mapping, and managing them efficiently for balanced development.
- **Resource planning in India** is a **multi-step; complex process** aimed at the **sustainable and equitable use** of natural resources across regions. It involves:

Three key stages of the resource planning process:

(*i*) Identification & Inventory

(*ii*) Planning Structure

(*iii*) Integration with National Goals

Land Use Pattern in India

- Land use is shaped by Topography, Climate, Soil, Population, Technology, and Culture. **Example:** Hilly areas → forest/tourism use Plains → agriculture/settlements
- The total geographical area of India is 3.28 million sq km.
- Net sown area ranges widely across states, exceeding 80% in **Punjab** and **Haryana**, but falls below 10% in **Arunachal Pradesh**, **Mizoram**, **Manipur**, and the Andaman Nicobar Islands.
- Forest area in the country is far lower than the desired 33% of geographical area, under the **National Forest Policy, 1952**
- Land degradation and conservation measures are about 130 Million of hectares of degraded in India.

Land use in India

CBSE 2024

- **Forests:** Land under forest, i.e. 22.78%
- **Land not available for cultivation:** Barren and wasteland, Land put to non-agricultural uses, e.g. buildings, roads, factories, etc.
- **Other uncultivated land (excluding fallow land):** Permanent pastures and grazing land, Land under miscellaneous tree crops groves, Culturable wasteland (left uncultivated for more than 5 agricultural years).
- **Fallow lands:** (a) **Current fallow** – Uncultivated for less than 1 year
  (b) **Other fallow** – Uncultivated for 1 to 5 years
- **Net Sown Area (NSA):** Area sown more than once in an agricultural year plus net sown area is known as gross cropped area.

Land Under Important Relief Features

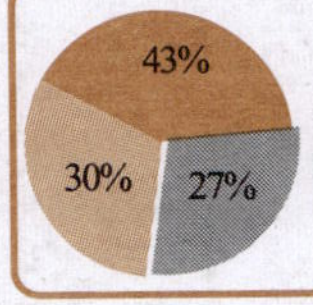

Classification of Soils in India

CBSE 2025, 2023

Soils in India are classified based on several factors such as: Soil formation, factors, Colour,Texture, Thickness, Age and Chemical and physical properties

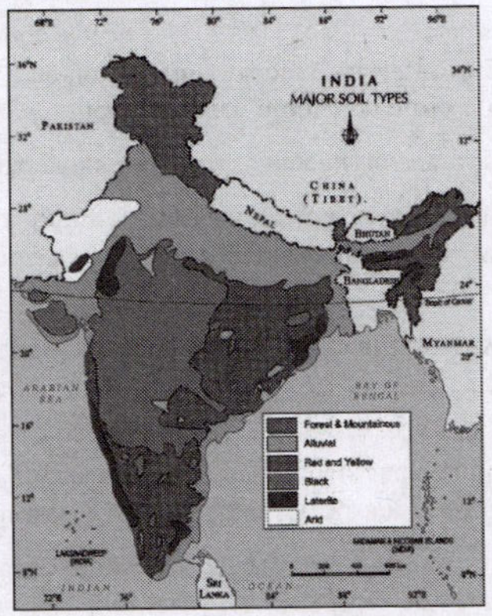

Soils	Major Regions
Alluvial Soil	Indo-Gangetic plain – Punjab, UP, Bihar, West Bengal
Black Soil	Deccan Plateau – Maharashtra, Gujarat, MP
Forest Soil	Odisha, Chhattisgarh, parts of Karnataka & Tamil Nadu
Red and Yellow Soils	Odisha, Chhattisgarh southern Deccan plateau
Arid Soil	Rajasthan parts. of Gujarat
Laterite Soil	Western Ghats – Kerala, Karnataka, parts of WB & Odisha

Soil Erosion and Soil Conservation

Soil Erosion: Soil erosion is the **removal of the top layer** of soil (soil cover) due to natural forces like **wind**, **water**, and **glaciers**, or by **human activities** like deforestation, overgrazing, and faulty farming.

The different types of soil erosion are: **Gully erosion, Sheet erosion and Wind erosion.**

Soil Conservation: Methods to protect soil from erosion and maintain its fertility, including planting trees, **contour ploughing**, and **terrace farming.**

CHAPTER-2
FOREST AND WILDLIFE RESOURCES

To Access One Shot Revision Video Scan This QR Code

Cheat Sheet

Forest and Wildlife Resources

Flora and Fauna

- Flora represents all the **plant life** in a certain area, including various types of plants like trees and flowers.
- Fauna means all the **animal life** in a specific area, including different animals like tigers, birds, and insects.

Biodiversity or Biological Diversity

- Biodiversity is the **variety of all living forms** and their ecosystems on Earth.

Project Tiger

- **Project Tiger** is one of the most famous wildlife conservation campaigns, launched in **1973**. It was introduced because:
  - Tiger population declined to **1,827** from over **55,000** a century ago
  - Reasons included **poaching, shrinking habitats, loss of prey,** and **illegal trade**

Community and Conservation

CBSE 2025

Community Involvement
- Support government conservation efforts
- Seek livelihood security through forests
- In some areas, independently manage forests.

Chipko Movement	**Origin:** Himalayas **Action:** Tree-hugging protest **Impact:** Stopped deforestation, encouraged local afforestation with native species
Joint Forest Management (JFM)	**Started:** 1988 in Odisha **Partnership:** Village + Forest Department **Benefits:** Non-timber produce, timber share, degraded forest restoration
Sacred Groves	**Forest patches protected due to religious/cultural beliefs** Remain untouched; promote biodiversity Sacred Plants & Animals (Region-wise) **Mundas & Santhals:** Mahua, Kadamba trees **Odisha & Bihar tribes:** Tamarind, Mango **Common Belief:** Peepal, Banyan – sacred

Depletion of the Flora and Fauna

- **Major Causes**
  - Development Projects – e.g., dams, highways
  - Shifting Cultivation – slash & burn method
  - Mining – destruction of vegetation
  - Grazing & Fuel Collection – overuse of plant resources
  - Overpopulation – rising demand for land and wood
- **Decline in Biodiversity**
  - Habitat Destruction – clearing of forests
  - Hunting & Poaching – for trade, sport
  - Over-exploitation – unsustainable use
  - Over-exploitation
  - Pollution – industrial, plastic, air, and water
  - Poisoning – chemicals & waste harming life
- **Human Role**

  Nature to Resource – forests used for:
  - Wood, bark, leaves
  - Rubber, dyes, medicines
  - Food, fuel, manure

Types and Distribution of Forest

- In India, much of its forest and wildlife resources are either owned or managed by the government through the Forest Department or other government departments.
- **Classification of forests:**
  - **Reserved Forests:** Most valuable forests, cover half of the total forest land.
  - **Protected Forests:** Protected from any further depletion, one third of total forest area.
  - **Unclassed Forests:** Other forests and wastelands belong to both govt. and private individuals and communities.

Conservation of Forest and Wildlife in India

CBSE 2024

Conservation: Preserves the ecological diversity and our life support systems – water, air and soil.
- The Indian Wildlife (Protection) Act of 1972 was enacted to safeguard endangered species by prohibiting hunting, protecting habitats, and limiting wildlife trade.
- National parks and wildlife sanctuaries were established by central and state governments.
- The government launched protection projects for critically threatened animals, including tigers, one-horned rhinoceroses, Kashmir stags, three types of crocodiles, Asiatic lions, and more.
- By 1986, protections were extended to include hundreds of butterflies, moths, beetles, and a dragonfly.
- In 1991, plants were added to the protection list for the first time, starting with six species.

CHAPTER-3

WATER RESOURCES

To Access One Shot Revision Video Scan This QR Code

Cheat Sheet

Water Resources

Water Resources

Water resources are sources like rivers, lakes, groundwater, and rainwater useful to humans.

Water Scarcity

Water scarcity is when there **isn't enough** readily **available freshwater** to meet the demands of a region.

Cause of Water Scarcity

- **Over-exploitation:** Excessive use of water resources (agriculture, industry)
- **Unequal access:** Disparity in water access between different regions. Eg.: Urban vs. rural water access
- **Population growth:** Increased demand for water due to rising population
- **Pollution:** Contamination of water sources. (industrial, agricultural waste) Eg.: Yamuna River pollution

Water Conservation and Management

CBSE 2025

Water conservation and management involve strategies to protect and efficiently use water to prevent scarcity and ensure future availability.

Multi-purpose River Projects

CBSE 2025, 2024, 2023

Large-scale initiatives using dams for multiple benefits like irrigation, power, and water supply, aiming for integrated resource management.

Examples:

- **Narmada Bachao Andolan:**

  Narmada Bachao Andolan is a movement for the rights of those impacted by the Sardar Sarovar Dam, focusing on conservation and fair resource share; Bhakra-Nangal is in the Satluj-Beas basin.

- **The Sardar Sarovar project:**

  The Sardar Sarovar Dam on the Narmada River in Gujarat is a major water project affecting four states: Maharashtra, Madhya Pradesh, Gujarat, and Rajasthan.

River Water Disputes

River water disputes arise from disagreements over sharing water from common rivers, like the Krishna-Godavari dispute among Indian states.

Classification of Dams

Dams are classified by structure (timber, embankment, masonry), purpose (multi, single), and height (large, medium, low) for various water management needs.

Mange and Conserve our Water Resources

- Water-resource management is the planning and managing of water resources focusing on quantity, quality, infrastructure, and sustainable use policies.
- To protect ourselves from risks to our health.
- To maintain our ability to eat, our way of life and constructive endeavours.
- In order to stop the destruction of our natural habitats.

Rain Water Harvesting

CBSE 2024, 2023

- Rainwater harvesting involves collecting and storing rainwater for reuse, enhancing water security, like rooftop collection in Rajasthan.
- Rainwater harvesting is seen as a **socio-economically** and **environmentally viable alternative** to large dams because it Involves **local, low-cost techniques**, Requires **less infrastructure** and **adapted to local ecological conditions**.

Rooftop Rainwater Harvesting

CBSE 2024, 2023

- It is a simple way of collecting rainwater for future use. rainwater can be stored, used in various ways, or immediately used for recharge.
- Rooftop rainwater collection is a prevalent practice in Rajasthan for storing drinking water.
- People in flood plains of Bengal created inundation canals to irrigate their land.
- People in hilly areas created diversion channels for agriculture similar to "guls" or "kuls" of the Western Himalayas.

Bamboo Drip Irrigation

A traditional system in Meghalaya using bamboo pipes to transport and distribute water directly to crops.

CHAPTER-4
AGRICULTURE

To Access One Shot Revision Video Scan This QR Code

Cheat Sheet

Agriculture

Subsistence Farming

Subsistence farming is a traditional method where families grow food for their own use with simple tools and local labour.

Types of Farming

CBSE 2024, 2023, 2020

(a) Primitive Subsistence Farming Key Features:

- Small land patches, Traditional tools **(Hoe, Dao and Digging sticks)** and family labour
- No HYV seeds or chemical fertilisers
- Depends on monsoon & natural soil fertility
- Also Known As **Slash and Burn agriculture** and in North-East India → Called **Jhumming**.

(b) Intensive Subsistence Farming Key Features:

- High Population – Pressure on land
- Small Landholdings – Maximum output focuss.
- **Regions practiced:** Uttar Pradesh, Bihar,West Bengal, Kerala,Tamil Nadu and Eastern and Northern parts of India where population density is high.

(c) Commercial Farming Key Features:

- **Market-Oriented** – Grown for sale, not consumption and **Modern Inputs** – HYV seeds, fertilisers, irrigation
- Large-Scale Production
- **Regional Variations:** Rice is Commercial Crop → Punjab, Haryana and Rice is Subsistence Crop → Odisha

Plantation Farming Key Features:

- Mono-crop Farming – Single crop over large area
- Capital & Labour Intensive – Requires investment & workforce

Examples: Tea, Coffee, Rubber, Sugarcane, Banana Transport and processing needs

Jhumming Agriculture

Trees are cut and burned to clear land for crops, then after a few years, farmers move to new areas. This practice is common in Northeast India.

Jhumming farming is mostly done in some northeast parts of India.

Slash and Burn

CBSE 2025

- Jhumming-Assam, Meghalaya, Mizoram and Nagaland, Pamlou- Manipur, Dipa-Chhattishgarh
- 'Milpa' in Mexico and Central America, 'Conuco' in Venzuela, 'Roca' in Brazil, 'Masole' in Central Africa, 'Ray' in Vietnam

Cropping Pattern

CBSE 2025, 2024

Cropping Seasons:

Rabi: Oct–Dec (sowing), Apr–Jun (harvest) e.g. wheat, barley, peas, gram, mustard

Kharif: With monsoon, harvested Sep–Oct e.g. paddy, maize, jowar, bajra, cotton, jute

Zaid: Summer season crops e.g. watermelon, cucumber, sugarcane (year-round)

Rabi Crops

CBSE 2024

Winter-grown crops like wheat and mustard, harvested in the summer.

Key Regions

Punjab, Haryana, Himachal Pradesh, Jammu and Kashmir, Uttarakhand, Uttar Pradesh.

Harvesting Period: April to June

Kharif Crops

CBSE 2024

Crops planted at the start of the rainy season, such as rice and maize, harvested in the fall.

Key Regions

Assam, West Bengal, Coastal Odisha, Andhra Pradesh, Telangana, Tamil Nadu, Kerala, Maharashtra, Uttar Pradesh, Bihar

Harvesting Period: September to October

Zaid Season

CBSE 2024

A brief farming period between Rabi and Kharif seasons for crops like watermelon and cucumber.

Key Regions

Various parts of India, mainly in northern and central regions.

Harvesting Period: Before Kharif season

Non-Food Crops

CBSE 2024

These are crops grown **not for consumption** but for other purposes such as manufacturing and industry.

Examples include **cotton**, **jute**, and **oil seeds**.

Harvesting Period: April to June

Food Grains

CBSE 2025, 2024

Staple crops such as rice, wheat, millets, and pulses, consumed as primary food sources.

CHAPTER-5

MINERALS AND ENERGY RESOURCES

To Access One Shot Revision Video Scan This QR Code

Cheat Sheet

Minerals and Energy Resources

Minerals (CBSE 2025,2024)

- Meaning: Homogeneous naturally occurring substance with a definable internal structure.
- **Metallic**
  - **Ferrous** (CBSE 2024)
    - **Major Iron ores Belts:**
      - Odisha-Jharkhand belt,
      - Durg-Bastar-Chandrapur belt lies in Chhattisgarh and Maharashtra
      - Ballari-Chitradurga-Chikkamagaluru-Tumakuru belt in Karnataka
      - Maharashtra-Goa belt includes the state of Goa & Maharashtra.
    - **Manganese:** (CBSE 2025)
      - Madhya Pradesh - 33%
      - Odisha - 16%
      - Andhra Pradesh - 10%
      - Maharashtra - 27%
      - Karnataka - 12%
      - Other states - 2%
  - **Non-Ferrous** (CBSE 2025, 2024)
    - **Copper:** Used in electrical cables, electronics and chemical industries, The Balaghat mines in Madhya Pradesh, Khetri mines in Rajasthan and Singhbhum district of Jharkhand are leading producers of copper.
    - **Bauxite:** Deposits are found in the Amarkantak plateau, Maikal hills and the plateau region of Bilaspur-Katni
  - **Precious**
    - Gold, Silver & Platinum
- **Non-metallic** (CBSE 2025)
  - **Mica:** Most indispensable minerals used in electronic industries, Mica deposits are found in the Chota Nagpur plateau, Koderma Gaya Hazaribagh belt of Jharkhand, Ajmer in Rajasthan and Nellore Mica belt in Andhra Pradesh.
  - **Limestone:** Found in sedimentary rocks. used raw material for the cement industry and essential for smelting iron ore in the blast furnace.

Energy Resources (CBSE 2025, 2024, 2023, 2022, 2020)

- **Conventional**
  - **Coal:** Decaying plants in swamps produce peat, Lignite is a low grade brown coal, which is soft with high moisture content. Bituminous is the most popular coal in commercial use. Anthracite is the highest quality hard coal.
  - **Petroleum:** Major petroleum production states are Mumbai High, Gujarat and Assam.
  - **Natural Gas:** Discovered in the Krishna-Godavari basin, the Gulf of Cambay Andaman and Nicobar islands. Hazira-Vijaipur-Jagdishpur cross country gas pipeline Links Mumbai High and Basin with the fertilizer, power & industrial complexes in western and northern India.
  - **Electricity**
    - **Thermal Electricity:** Generated by using coal, petroleum and natural gas in thermal power plants.
    - **Hydro Electricity:** Generated by fast flowing water, and by multi-purpose projects like the Damodar Valley Corporation, the Kopili Hydel Project, etc. producing hydroelectric power.
- **Non-Conventional**
  - **Tidal Energy:** Oceanic tides can be used to generate electricity. The Gulf of Khambat, the Gulf of Kuchchh in Gujarat on the western coast and Gangetic delta in Sunderban regions of West Bengal provide ideal conditions for utilising tidal energy.
  - **Biogas:** Shrubs, Farm waste, Animal and Human waste are used to produce biogas.
  - **Wind Power:** Located in Tamil Nadu, Andhra Pradesh, Karnataka, Rajasthan, Gujarat, Kerala, Maharashtra & Lakshdweep
  - **Solar Energy:** India has enormous possibilities of tapping solar energy. Photovoltaic technology converts sunlight directly into electricity
  - **Nuclear or Atomic Energy:** (CBSE 2025) Uranium and thorium available in Jharkhand and in Rajasthan are used for generating atomic or nuclear power. The Monazite sands of Kerala is also rich in Thorium
  - **Geo Thermal Energy:** Refers to the heat and electricity produced by using the heat from the heat from the interior of the Earth. Parvati Valley in Himachal and Puga Valley in Ladakh are 2 experimental projects.

CHAPTER-6

MANUFACTURING INDUSTRIES

To Access One Shot Revision Video Scan This QR Code

Cheat Sheet

Manufacturing Industries

- **On the basis of ownership**
  - **Public Sector:** like BHEL, SAIL etc.
  - **Private Sector:** like TISCO, Bajaj Auto Ltd. etc.
  - **Joint sector industries:** like Maruti Udyog Ltd., Oil India Ltd. etc.
  - **Cooperative sector industries:** like AMUL, Indian Coffee House etc.
- **Based on the bulk and weight raw material and finished good**
  - **Heavy Industries:** like Iron and Steel Industries
  - **Light Industries:** like Automobile and Kitchen items etc.
- **On the basis of capital investment**
  - **Small Scale Industries:** Max. investment upto ₹ 1 crore
  - **Large Scale Industries:** Investment more than ₹ 1 crore.
- **On the basis of source of raw materials used** (CBSE 2024, 2023, 2022, 2020)
  - **Mineral based:** like Iron and Steel, Cement, Aluminium etc.
  - **Agro based:** like Cotton, Woolen, jute, silk etc. (CBSE 2025)
- **According to their main role** (CBSE 2024)
  - **Consumer industries:** like Sugar, toothpaste, paper etc.
  - **Basic or key industries:** like Copper smelting, Aluminium smelting etc.
- **Environmental Degradation** (CBSE 2023)
  - Minimising the use of water for processing by reusing and recycling, harvesting of rainwater, treating hot water and effluents before releasing, etc.
- **Industrial Pollution** (CBSE 2023)
  - **Air Pollution:** Caused by undesirable gases like SO_2 and CO_2.
  - **Noise Pollution:** Caused due to industrial and construction activities.
  - **Water Pollution:** Caused by organic and inorganic industrial wastes discharged into rivers.
  - **Thermal Pollution:** Occurs when hot water from factories and thermal plants drained into rivers and ponds.

CHAPTER-7
LIFELINES OF NATIONAL ECONOMY

To Access One Shot Revision Video Scan This QR Code

Cheat Sheet

Lifelines of National Economy

Major Sea Ports

CBSE 2025, 2024, 2023, 2020

- Kandla (Gujarat)
- Mumbai (Maharashtra)
- Marmagao (Goa)
- New Mangalore (Karnataka)
- Kochi (Kerala)
- Tuticorin (Tamil Nadu)
- Chennai (Tamil Nadu)
- Vishakhapatnam (Andhra Pradesh)
- Paradip (Odisha)
- Haldia (West Bengal)

International Airports

CBSE 2025, 2023, 2022, 2020

- Amritsar (Raja Sansi - Sri Guru Ram Dass jee),
- New Delhi (Indira Gandhi International),
- Mumbai (Chhatrapati Shivaji),
- Chennai (Meenam Bakkam),
- Kolkata (Netaji Subhash Chandra Bose),
- Hyderabad (Rajiv Gandhi)

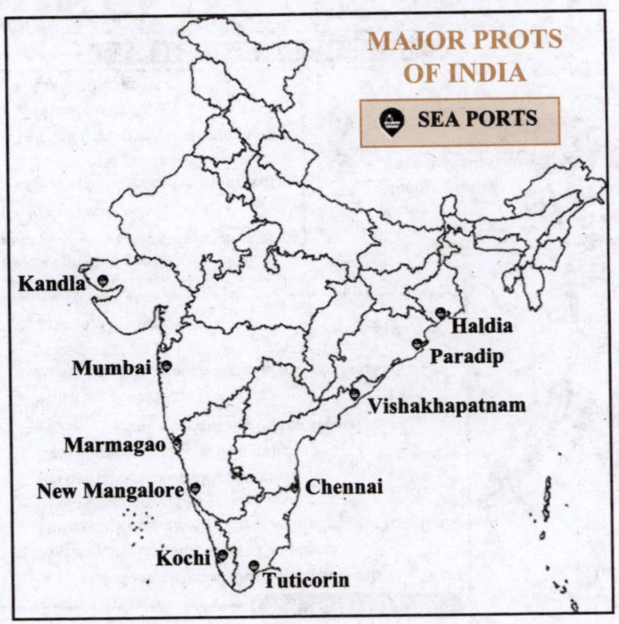

CHAPTER-1
DEVELOPMENT

ECONOMICS

Cheat Sheet

To Access One Shot Revision Video Scan This QR Code

Development

Income and Other Goals

CBSE 2023

Income Goals, What people desire is regular work, Better wages and decent prices for their crops or other products that people produce.

National Development

CBSE 2025, 2024, 2023, 2022 Term-II, 2020

It means thinking about a fair and just path for all, like Social Economic & Political welfare of the people.

How to compare different Countries:
On the basis of Development & Per Capita Income.

How to compare different States:
On the basis of Income, Infant mortality rate, Literacy rate & Net attendance ratio.

Average Income: Average earnings per person in a specific area within a specific time frame. The average income is also called **Per Capita Income.**
Average Income or Per Capita Income is calculated:

$$\text{Per Capita Income} = \frac{\text{Total Income}}{\text{Total Population}}$$

Used by the world bank to classify countries

- **High income:** ≥ $63,400 **(2023)**
- **Low income:** < US $24,00 **(2023)**
- **India:** Low middle income US $10,030 p.a. **(2023)**

Income and Other Criteria

Comparing states on the basis of (Haryana, Kerala, & Bihar)

Per Capita Income - Highest Harayana (₹264729) & Lowest Bihar (₹47,498)

Infant mortality rate - Highest Bihar (27) & Lowest Kerala (6)

Literacy Rate % - Highest Kerala (94%) & Lowest Bihar (62%)

Net Attendance Ratio - Highest Kerala (94) & Lowest Bihar (69)

Development Goals and Mixed Goals

CBSE 2025, 2024, 2023

Characteristics of Development Goals

- More equitable distribution of resources.
- Different people have different aspirations for & nations of development.
- Each person seeks a different goals.
- Development goals can be conflicting.

Characteristics of Mixed Goals

- Thinking about Equality.
- Better lifestyle through better administration and principles.
- Freedom, Money, etc.

Meaning and Characteristics

Refers to the process by which an individual grows and changes throughout the life cycle.

Characteristics of Development

- Continuous process
- Income as an essential component
- Mixed goals
- Conflicting goals etc.

Sustainable Development

CBSE 2024, 2023, 2022 Term-II, 2020

Sustainable: Maintain for long term of time (for future generation) + **Development**: Economic Development (for current generation) = Sustainable development which meet needs of current generation without compromising ability of future generation to meet their needs.

Balance use of Natural Resources

Conservation & finding alternatives of non-renewable resources. Eg. Petrol.

Using renewable resources carefully. E.g. Ground water.

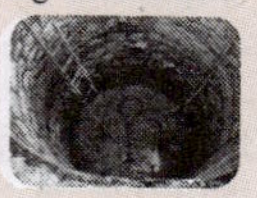

Features of Sustainable Development

- Efficient use of natural resources.
- No ↑ in the pollution.
- Improve Quality of human life.
- To fulfill the requirements of future generations.

Pillars of Sustainable Development

- Social Sustainability
- Economics Sustainability
- Environmental Sustainability

Human Development Report

CBSE 2025, 2020

Prepared by UNDP [United Nations Development Programme] in 1990.

Components of Human Development Index

- Living Standard (Per Capita Income)
- Health Indicator (Life Expectancy at Birth)(BMI)
- Body Mass Index (BMI) = $\frac{\text{Weight in kilogram}}{(\text{Height in meter})^2}$
- Education Indicator (Literacy rate, Enrollment ratio)

India Vs. Neighbours (2023-24)

- **Sri Lanka:** Best HDI (Rank 78)
- **India:** Rank 134.
- Bangladesh ahead of India in life expectancy.

Other Elements

- Consumption
- Freedom
- Health
- Security, etc.
- Environment

Public Facilities

CBSE 2023, 2020

Provided facilities by the government. E.g. Schools, Hospital, Community Halls, Transport, Electricity etc. These facilities are important as we cannot purchase every major facility.

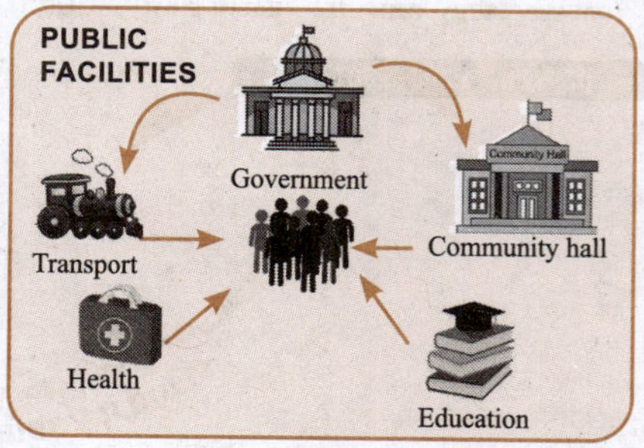

CHAPTER-2

SECTORS OF THE INDIAN ECONOMY

Cheat Sheet

To Access One Shot Revision Video Scan This QR Code

Sectors of the Indian Economy

Economic Activities (CBSE 2025, 2023, 2020)

- **Primary Sector (Agriculture)**: Agriculture, Fishing, Forestry, Poultry Farming, Animal Husbandry etc.
- **Secondary Sector (Industry)**: Manufacturing take place in factories, workshops or homes. E.g., Sugar from Sugar cane, cloth from cotton
- **Tertiary Sector (Service)**: Transportation, Banking, Warehousing, Communication, Education, Tourism, IT services etc.

Comparison and Dependence among Sectors (CBSE 2023, 2022 Term-II, 2020)

- ❑ All sectors are **interdependent**
- ❑ **Example:** Farmer → Sugarcane → Sugar Mill → Transport → Retailer
- ❑ Final goods are used to avoid double counting

Final Goods vs. Intermediate Goods:

- ❑ **Final goods:** Used by consumers
- ❑ **Intermediate goods:** Used in production (e.g., flour used for biscuits)

GDP (Gross Domestic Product)

- ❑ Total value of final goods and services produced in a country in a year
- ❑ Calculated by a central government ministry
- ❑ Now replaced globally by Gross Value Added (GVA)

Historical Changes in Sectors (CBSE 2023, 2022 Term-I, 2020)

In Developed Countries

Primary → Secondary → Tertiary

- ❑ Primary was initially dominant
- ❑ With industrialisation, secondary became dominant
- ❑ Now tertiary is most important

In India

- ❑ Tertiary sector became largest in production by 2017–18
- ❑ Still, primary sector remains the largest employer

Rising Importance of Tertiary Sector

Reasons

- ❑ Need for basic services (education, health, administration)
- ❑ Growth of agriculture and industry
- ❑ Rising income levels → demand for tourism, shopping, private services
- ❑ Rise of IT and communication-based services

Note: Not all service sector jobs are well-paid or regular Many work as shopkeepers, repair persons etc.

Public & Private Sector (CBSE 2025 2020)

- Public Sector is the sector in which government owns most of the assets and provides all the services. e.g., Railways, post office etc. — Motive is Social Welfare
- Private Sector is the sector in which ownership of assets and delivery of services is in the hands of private individuals/companies. e.g., TISCO, RIL etc. — Motive is profit earning

Organised & Unorganised Sector (CBSE 2025, 2024, 2023 2020)

Advantages of Organised Sector

- Job Security
- Fixed number of working hours
- Overtime payment for more work
- Other benefits like paid leave, payment during holidays, PF, Gratuity etc.
- Pension on retirement

Disadvantages of Unorganised Sector

- Job Insecurity
- Rules and Regulations are not followed
- No Provision for overtime, paid leaves, holidays etc.
- Low paid and irregular job
- High degree of exploitation of workers

Employment & Unemployment (CBSE 2025 2022 Term-I)

Unemployment

- A situation when a person who is actively seeking a job, is unable to find work.
- **Underemployment/ Disguised Unemployment:** A situation where people are working but all of them are made to work less than their potential

Methods to create more employment

- **Short-term**
  - **MGNREGA:** It provides 100 days of guaranteed employment every year, Unemployment allowance in case of not having employment, application of Right to work ethics, targeted on SC/ST and Poor women folk etc.
- **Long-term**
  - Providing Cheap Credit
  - **Promotion of local industries:** SSI and Cottage
  - Improving agriculture sector
  - Provision of basic facilities like transportation and storage etc.
  - Other new services like Tourism, IT etc.
  - Improving Education and Health sector

CHAPTER-3
MONEY AND CREDIT

To Access One Shot Revision Video Scan This QR Code

Cheat Sheet

Money and Credit

- **Money**
  - **Various forms of money** (CBSE 2022 Term-II, 2020)
    - **Early Ages**
      - Barter System
        - **Limitation:** Double coincidence of wants
    - **Middle Ages**
      - Cattle, Grains, Gold, Silver and Copper Coins
    - **Modern Ages**
      - Currency Notes and Coins (authorised by RBI)
      - Demand Deposits with bank like cheque
  - **Why transactions are made in Money?**
    - Many transactions involve buying and selling of goods using money.
    - A person with money can easily exchange it for any commodity or service, he/she desires.
- **Bank** (CBSE 2025, 2024)
  - **Depositors**
    - Make deposits and withdrawals and get interest.
  - **Borrowers**
    - Take loan and repay loan with higher interest.
- **Credit** (CBSE 2024, 2022 Term-II, 2020)
  - **Terms of Credit**
    - Interest rate
    - Collateral and documentation
    - Mode of repayment
  - **Positive role of Credit**
    - Credit helps to meet expenses, production on time, and thereby increases earnings.
  - **Negative role of Credit**
    - Credit pushes the borrower into debt-trap from which recovery is very painful.

Money and Credit

Self Help Group
CBSE 2025, 2023, 2022 Term-II

Advantages
- Gender Equity
- Social Integrity
- Impact on housing & health
- Improvement in standard of living
- Women empowerment etc.

Disadvantages
- Dependence on group participation
- Lack of upgrading skills & professional guidance
- Lack of qualified facilitators
- Limited availability, Inadequate financial assistance
- Too much depend on Govt.
- NGOs etc.

Functions
- Offer collateral-free loans
- Build the functional capacity
- Initiate and maintain savings
- Resolves conflicts, common problems, etc.

Purpose
- **SHG:** 15–20 women from same neighborhood pool savings.
- Rural areas depend on informal sectors
- Poverty relief
- Improve social status etc.
- Providing small loans at lower interest
- Can get back loans in group's name

Credit sources of India
CBSE 2025, 2024, 2023, 2022 Term-II

Formal Sector
Refer to those sources that are regulated by the government and are subject to legal requirements & formalities.

- Lower Interest Rates
- E.g., Cooperative societies, Commercial Banks, etc.
- Requires documentation and collateral.

Informal Sector
Refer to those sources that are not regulated by the government are based on personal relationships & trust.

- Higher Interest Rates
- E.g., Money lenders, landlords, relatives etc.
- Not requires documentation and collateral.

CHAPTER-4

GLOBALISATION AND THE INDIAN ECONOMY

To Access One Shot Revision Video Scan This QR Code

Cheat Sheet

Globalisation and the Indian Economy

Meaning (CBSE 2024)

It is the process of rapid integration and interaction among people, companies, and governments worldwide.

Factors Enabling Globalisation

Factors (CBSE 2025, 2024, 2023, 2020)

- Liberalisation of Foreign Trade & Foreign Investment
- Technology

Early Phase

Colonial Countries (e.g. India) → Industrial Developed Countries (e.g. European Countries and USA)

- **Raw material** — Export → **Finished products**
- **Finished products** — Import → **Raw material**

Modern Phase

MNC: A multinational corporation (MNC) is a corporation that owns or controls production in more than one country.

Offices and Factories → Located where cheap labour and other Resources available i.e., Minimum Cost of Production and Maximum profit.

Role of MNCs (CBSE 2025, 2022 Term-II)

- Spread production
- Influence local markets
- Global production chains

111 MOST PROBABLE QUESTIONS (ANALYZED & SELECTED FROM PYQs)

To Access Detailed Explanations
Scan This QR Code

Note: *Questions in this section are selected based on repetitive themes and concepts from past examinations, though patterns and typologies may vary.*

HISTORY

The Rise of Nationalism in Europe

1. Who among the following remarked "When France sneezes, the rest of Europe catches cold"?

***(1 M)* (2022 Term-I, 2020, 2016 Term-II)**

(*a*) Lord Byron (*b*) Metternich

(*c*) Johann Herder (*d*) Napoleon

2. How did the 'Treaty of Constantinople' of 1832 recognise Greece as an independent nation? Explain.

***(2 M)* (2023, 2016 Term-II)**

3. Describe the great economic hardship that prevailed in Europe during the 1830s. ***(3 M)* (2019, 2016 Term-II)**

4. How had Napoleonic code exported to the regions under French control? Explain with examples.

***(3 M)* (2025, 2019, 2017)**

5. Analyse the process of German Unification.

***(3 M)* (2024, 2015 Term-II)**

6. Analyse the measures and practices introduced by the French revolutionaries to create a sense of collective identity amongst the French people.

***(5 M)* (2025, 2017, 2016 Term-II, 2015 Term-II)**

7. How did the ideology of 'liberalism' affect the Europe in early nineteenth century? Explain.

***(5 M)* (2025, 2024, 2023, 2020)**

Nationalism in India

8. Mention any two causes that led to the Civil Disobedience Movement. ***(2 M)* (2024, 2023, 2022 Term-II)**

9. "There were variety of cultural processes through which Indian Nationalism captured people's imagination." Explain the statement with examples.

***(3 M & 5 M)* (2024, 2019)**

10. Why did Mahatma Gandhi decide to withdraw the Non-Cooperation Movement in February 1922? Explain.

***(3 M)* (2025, 2022 Term-II, 2017)**

11. How did the First World War create a new economic situation in India? Explain.

***(3 M)* (2025, 2022 Term-II, 2020, 2019)**

12. Why did Mahatma Gandhi decide to launch a nationwide Satyagraha against the proposed Rowlatt Act 1919? Explain any three reasons.

***(3 M)* (2017, 2016 Term-II, 2015 Term-II)**

13. 'The Treaty of Vienna was drawn up in 1815 with the object of undoing most of the changes that had come about in Europe during the Napoleonic wars.' Highlight the significant provisions of this treaty.

***(5 M)* (2025, 2024, 2023)**

14. How were the various social groups involved in the Civil Disobedience Movement? Explain with examples.

***(5 M)* (2024, 2023, 2016 Term-II)**

15. "Plantation workers had their own understanding of Mahatma Gandhi's ideas and the notion of 'Swaraj'." Support the statement. ***(5 M)* (2017, 2016 Term-II)**

16. Why was the Salt March considered an effective symbol of resistance against colonialism? Explain.

***(5 M)* (2018, 2015 Term-II)**

17. Two places **(A)** and **(B)** have been marked on the given political outline map of India. Identify them with the help of given information and write their correct names on the lines drawn near them.

(A) The place where Indian National Congress Session was held in 1927.

***(1 M)* (2025, 2024, 2023, 2015 Term-I, 2015 Term-II)**

(B) The place where Mahatma Gandhi broke Salt law.

***(1 M)* (2025, 2024, 2023, 2019, 2017)**

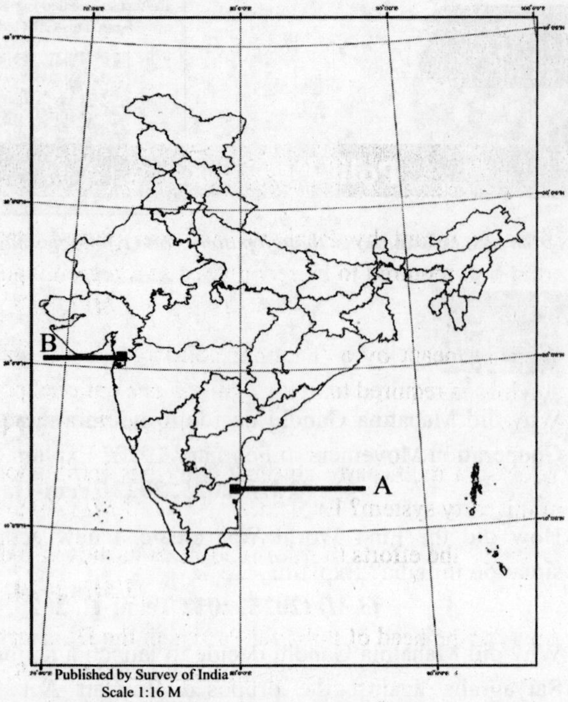

The Making of a Global World

18. "Trade and cultural exchange always went hand in hand". Explain the statement in the context of pre-modern world. ***(2 M)* (2025, 2024)**

19. 'Sometimes the new crops could make the difference between life and death.'. Explain the statement. ***(2 M)* (2025, 2024)**

20. "The Silk route was a good example of vibrant pre-modern trade and cultural links between distant parts of the world." Explain the statement with any two examples. ***(2 M)* (2024, 2016 Term-I)**

21. How had Indian trade been beneficial for the British during seventeenth century? Explain. ***(3 M)* (2020, 2019)**

Print Culture and the Modern World

22. How had the printing press created a new culture of reading in Europe? Explain with examples. ***(3 M)* (2024, 2019)**

23. How had the Imperial State in China been the major producer of printed material for a long time? Explain with examples. ***(3 M)* (2019)**

24. How did a new reading public emerge with the printing press? Express in your opinion. ***(3 M)* (2016, 2015)**

25. What led to the colonial government to pass the Vernacular Press Act in 1879? How did it affect the vernacular newspaper? ***(5 M)* (2020, 2015)**

26. 'The shift from hand printing to mechanical printing led to the print revolution in Europe.' Explain the statement with examples. ***(5 M)* (2018, 2015 Term-I)**

27. Read the following source and answer the questions that follow:

Why Newspapers?

'Krishnaji Trimbuck Ranade inhabitant of Poona intends to publish a Newspaper in the Marathi Language with a view of affording useful information on every topic of local interest. It will be open for free discussion on subjects of general utility, scientific investigation and the speculations connected with the antiquities, statistics, curiosities, history and geography of the country and of the Deccan especially… the patronage and support of all interested in the diffusion of knowledge and Welfare of the People is earnestly solicited.'

Bombay Telegraph and Courier, 6 *January* 1849.

'The task of the native newspapers and political associations is identical to the role of the Opposition in the House of Commons in Parliament in England. That is of critically examining government policy to suggest improvements, by removing those parts that will not be to the benefit of the people, and also by ensuring speedy implementation. These associations ought to carefully study the particular issues, gather diverse relevant information on the nation as well as on what are the possible and desirable improvements, and this will surely earn it considerable influence.'.

Native Opinion, 3 April 1870. ***(1 + 1 + 2 M)***
(2025, 2024, 2023)

1. Analyse the primary objective proposed by Ranade for publishing Marathi Language newspaper. ***(1 M)***
2. Why did the Bombay Telegraph emphasize the role of newspaper in promoting welfare of Deccan region? ***(1 M)***
3. What were the key responsibilities attributed to native newspapers? Mention any two. ***(2 M)***

POLITICAL SCIENCE

Power-Sharing

28. Describe the elements of the Belgian model for accommodating diversities. ***(3 M)* (2020)**

29. Evaluate the Power-sharing in India. ***(3 M)* (2019)**

30. How did the idea of power-sharing emerge? Explain different forms that have common arrangements of power sharing. ***(5 M)* (2024, 2023, 2019)**

31. How did the feeling of alienation develop among the Sri Lankan Tamils? What were the demands of the Sri Lankan Tamils? ***(5 M)* (2019)**

Federalism

32. Differentiate between federal and unitary form of government with examples. ***(3 M)* (2025)**

33. "India has a large cultural, regional, and religious diversity but there is a unity among people". What factors are responsible for this? Elaborate. ***(3 M)* (2017, 2016)**

34. Describe any three steps taken to strengthen local self-government, by the Constitutional Amendment, 1992. ***(3 M)* (2019, 2018)**

35. Describe any three features of the federal government. ***(3 M)* (2020, 2019, 2018)**

36. Describe the importance of a third tier of government in a vast country like India. ***(5 M)* (2019)**

Gender, Religion and Caste

37. Suggest any two measures to increase the representation of women in the legislatures of India. ***(2 M)* (2025)**

38. Mention different aspects of life in which women are discriminated or disadvantaged in India. ***(3 M)* (2023, 2020, 2019)**

39. "Caste inequalities are still prevalent in India." Examine the statement. ***(3 M)* (2019)**

40. Explain the role of castes in Indian politics. ***(5 M)* (2020, 2019, 2015)**

41. Define the term secularism. Explain any four features of secularism in india. ***(5 M)* (2025, 2020, 2019)**

Political Parties

42. What is meant by Regional political party? State the condition required to be recognized as a regional political party. ***(1 + 2 = 3 M)* (2019, 2016)**

43. What is meant by a 'national political party'? State the conditions required to be recognized as a national political party. ***(1 + 2 = 3 M)* (2016)**

44. What is a multi-party system? Why has India adopted a multi-party system? Explain. ***(3 M)* (2025, 2016)**

45. Describe the efforts to reform political parties in India ***(3 M)* (2020, 2017)**

46. Analyze the need of Political Parties in the Democracy. ***(3 M)* (2023, 2020, 2016)**

47. Describe any five functions of political party in a democracy. ***(5 M)* (2025, 2024, 2020, 2018)**

48. Examine any five major challenges faced by the political parties in India. ***(5 M)* (2025, 2024, 2022, 2016)**

49. What is meant by a Political party? Describe the three components of a political party. ***(5 M)* (2016, 2015)**

Outcomes of Democracy

50. Analyze the role of democracy in reducing inequality and poverty. ***(5 M)* (2019, 2025)**

51. Evaluate the outcomes of democracy in the social sector of the country. ***(5 M)* (2025, 2022, 2017)**

52. "Democratic systems are based on political equality." Examine the statement. ***(5 M)* (2024, 2015)**

53. "Democracy stands much superior to any other forms of government in promoting dignity and freedom of the individual." Support the statement with arguments. ***(5 M)* (2023, 2018, 2017)**

54. "Democracy produces an accountable, responsive and legitimate government." Support the statement with arguments. **(2023, 2019, 2016, 2015)**

55. How is democracy a better from of government in comparison to dictatorship? Explain ***(5 M)* (2025, 2023, 2020, 2019, 2016)**

56. "There is overwhelming support for the idea of democracy all over the world." Support the statement. ***(5 M)* (2017, 2015)**

GEOGRAPHY

Resources and Development

57. Why is planning necessary for judicious use of resources? Explain. ***(2 M)*** **(2025, 2020)**

58. How is the issue of sustainability important for development? Explain. ***(3 M)*** **(2024, 2018)**

59. Describe any three main features of 'Alluvial soil' found in India. ***(3 M)*** **(2019, 2013)**

60. Describe any three main features of 'Black soil' found in India. ***(3 M)*** **(2019, 2013)**

Water scarcity

61. Explain any three causes of water scarcity. ***(3 M)*** **(2015 Term-I)**

62. "Water scarcity may be an outcome of large and growing population in India." Analyse the statement. ***(3 M)*** **(2019)**

63. Discuss how rainwater harvesting in semi-arid regions of Rajasthan are carried out. ***(5 M)***

Agriculture

64. Give one example of the commercial crops cultivable in laterite soil. ***(2 M)*** **(2020, 2015)**

65. "Agriculture and industry move hand in hand." Support the statement with examples. ***(2 M)*** **(2025, 2023, 2013, 2012)**

66. Write the amount of annual rainfall required for the cultivation of Wheat. ***(2 M)*** **(2020, 2011)**

67. Name one important beverage crop and specify the geographical conditions required for its growth. ***(2 M)***

68. Explain any three factors responsible for soil formation. ***(3 M)*** **(2012, 2011)**

69. Describe any three main features of "Rabi crop season". ***(3 M)*** **(2019)**

70. Describe any three main features of "Kharif crop season". ***(3 M)*** **(2019)**

71. Explain the features of Commercial Farming. ***(5 M)*** **(2024, 2019, 2015, 2011)**

72. Explain the features of Primitive Subsistence Farming. ***(5 M)*** **(2024, 2019, 2015, 2011)**

73. Compare 'intensive subsistence farming' with that of 'commercial farming' practiced in India. ***(5 M)*** **(2019, 2018)**

74. Name the two major beverage crops grown in India. Describe their growing areas. ***(5 M)*** **(2019, 2015)**

Minerals and Energy Resources

75. Suggest any two ways to conserve energy resources in India. ***(2 M)*** **(2025, 2024)**

Manufacturing Industries

76. How is cement industry responsible for land degradation? ***(1 M or 2 M)*** **(2019)**

77. Classify industries on the basis of raw materials. ***(2 M)*** **(2022 Term-II, 2022 Term-II, 2016 Term-II)**

78. "Efficient means of transport are pre-requisites for fast development of the country." Support the statement with examples. ***(3 M)*** **(2020, 2016 Term-II)**

79. "The textile industry is the only industry in the country which is self-reliant and complete in the value chain." Justify the statement. ***(3 M)*** **(2016 Tern-II)**

80. "Manufacturing industries are considered the backbone of the economic development of a country." Justify the statement. ***(5 M)*** **(2020, 2018, 2015)**

81. How can the industrial pollution of fresh water be reduced? Explain with examples. ***(5 M)*** **(2013, 2020, 2019)**

82. Explain the factors which are responsible for location of industries. ***(5 M)*** **(2020, 2015, 2012, 2011)**

83. How can the industrial pollution of fresh water be reduced? Explain with examples. ***(5 M)*** **(2023, 2020, 2019)**

ECONOMICS

Development

84. Define the term 'literacy rate'. *(1 M)* **(2020, 2015)**

85. How does the United Nations Development Program's (UNDP's) developmental criterion differ from the World Bank? Explain. *(2 M)* **(2024)**

86. "Different persons can have different developmental goals." Support the statement with an example. *(2 M)* **(2025, 2023, 2019, 2018)**

87. Why is the issue of sustainability important for development? Explain with examples. *(3 M or 5 M)* **(2025, 2024, 2023, 2020)**

88. What is human development? Explain its indicators. *(5 M)* **(2020, 2015)**

89. How has the World Bank classified countries? What are the limitations of this report? *(5 M)* **(2025, 2017, 2016)**

Sectors of Indian Economy

90. Explain the difference between public and private sector of Indian economy with example. *(3 M)* **(2025)**

91. Analyse the problem of underemployment in agriculture sector in India. *(3 M)* **(2025)**

92. Examine the role of Tertiary sector in the development of the country. *(3 M)* **(2024, 2016)**

93. Why is there a need to protect workers in the Unorganized Sector? *(3 M)* **(2023, 2020)**

94. "Tertiary sector activities help in the development of the primary and secondary sectors." Evaluate the statement. *(1 M or 3 M)* **(2024, 2020, 2016)**

OR

Which sector helps in the development of the primary and secondary sectors?

95. Distinguish the service conditions of organized sector with that of unorganized sector. *(2 M, 3 M or 5 M)* **(2024, 2020, 2019, 2018)**

96. Why is 'Tertiary Sector' becoming important in India? Explain. *(3 M or 5 M)* **(2023, 2020, 2019)**

Money and Credit

97. Highlight the inherent problem in double coincidence of wants. *(1 M)* **(2017, 2015)**

98. 'Formal sector of credit better than informal sector.' Give arguments in support of your answer. *(3 M)* **(2024, 2019)**

99. Distinguish between formal and informal sources of credit. *(3 M)* **(2025, 2023, 2022 Term-II)**

100. In what ways does the Reserve Bank of India supervise the functioning of banks? Why is this necessary? *(2 M or 3 M)* **(2019, 2012)**

101. Why is it necessary to for the banks and cooperative societies to increase their lending facilities in rural areas? Explain. *(3 M)* **(2019, 2017, 2015)**

102. "Cheap and affordable credit is crucial for the country's development." Justify the statement. *(3 M or 5 M)* **(2024, 2023, 2018)**

103. Justify the role of 'Self Help Groups' in the rural economy. *(3 M or 5 M)* **(2025, 2023, 2022 Term-II)**

104. "Bank plays an important role in the economic development of the country." Support the statement with examples. *(5 M)* **(2020, 2019, 2015)**

105. "Credit sometimes pushes the borrower into a situation from which recovery is very painful." Support the statement with examples. *(5 M)* **(2024, 2020)**

Globalisation

106. Why had the Indian government put barriers to foreign trade and foreign investments after independence? Analyse the reasons. *(1 M or 3 M)* **(2016, 2015)**

107. How did the process of liberalisation initiated in India in the 1990s, promote globalisation? Explain *(2 M)* **(2025, 2024, 2023, 2017)**

108. 'Improvement in technology has stimulated the globalisation process.' Explain the statement with examples. *(5 M)* **(2025, 2024, 2022 Term-II)**

109. "Globalisation is the process of rapid integration and interconnection between countries". Explain the statement with examples. *(2 M, 5 M)* **(2025, 2024)**

110. 'Among producers and workers, the impact of globalisation has not been uniform.' Support the statement with suitable arguments. *(5 M)* **(2023, 2022 Term-II, 2016)**

111. Why do multinational corporations (MNCs) set up their offices and factories in certain areas only? Explain any five reasons. *(5 M)* **(2019, 2016)**

Roll No. | | | | | | | | Q.P. Code **01**

Candidates must write the Q.P. Code on the title page of the answer book.

SAMPLE QUESTION PAPER- I
SOCIAL SCIENCE

Time allowed : 3 hours | Maximum Marks : 80

General Instructions:

Read the following instructions carefully and follow them:

(i) There are 38 questions in the Question paper. All questions are compulsory.

(ii) The question paper has Four Sections – A-History, B-Geography C- Political Science, and D- Economics.

(iii) Each Section is of 20 Marks and has MCQs, VSA, SA, LAs and CBQ.

(iv) Very Short Answer Type Questions (VSA), carry 2 Marks each. Answers to each question should not exceed 40 words.

(v) Short Answer Type Questions (SA), carry 3 Marks each. Answers to each question should not exceed 60 words.

(vi) Long answer type questions (LA), carry 5 Marks each. Answers to each question should not exceed 120 words.

(vii) There are case based questions (CBQ) with three sub questions and are of 4 Marks each. Answers to each question should not exceed 100 words.

(viii) The map-based questions, carry 5 Marks with two parts- Q10. In Section A-History (2 Marks) and Q18. In Section B -Geography (3 Marks)

(ix) There is no overall choice in the question paper. However, an internal choice has been provided in few questions. Only one of the choices in such questions must be attempted.

SECTION - A
HISTORY (20 Marks)

1. What was the primary aim of the Non-Cooperation Movement in India? **1**

(*a*) Complete independence from British rule

(*b*) Economic reforms and land redistribution

(*c*) Social equality and religious harmony

(*d*) Restoration of the Khalifa's temporal powers

2. Identify the painting from the options given below. **1**

(*a*) Frankfurt Parliament
(*b*) Reichstag
(*c*) Duma
(*d*) The House of Parliament

3. Arrange the following historical events in the correct chronological order: **1**

A. Khilafat movement
B. Second round table conference
C. Chauri Chaura
D. Ambedkar establishes depressed classes associations

Choose the correct option:

(*a*) A-C-D-B (*b*) C-B-D-A
(*c*) B-A-D-C (*d*) D-A-C-B

4. Which one of the following pairs regarding indian nationalism is correctly matched? **1**

	Leaders	Contribution
(*a*)	Sardar Patel	: Hindustan Socialist Republican Army
(*b*)	Bhagat Singh	: Swaraj Party
(*c*)	C R Das	: Bardoli Satyagraha
(*d*)	J L Nehru	: Oudh Kisan Sabha

5. Which one of the following Italian states was ruled by an Italian princely house? **1**

(*a*) Papal State
(*b*) Lombardy
(*c*) Venetia
(*d*) Sardinia-Piedmont

6. "Trade and Cultural exchange always went hand in hand."Explain the statement in the context of the pre-modern world. **2**

7A. Explain any two beliefs of conservatism that emerged after 1815. **2**

OR

7B. Who led the liberal-nationalist revolutions during 1830-1848 period? **2**

8A. Mahatma Gandhi's concept of satyagraha was central to the Indian independence movement. Imagine you are a journalist in the early 20th century who has the opportunity to interview Mahatma Gandhi. During the interview, Gandhi explains that satyagraha is not merely passive resistance but involves active, non-violent resistance to injustice. Based on this explanation, how would you, as the journalist, describe the principles of satyagraha to your readers? **5**

OR

8B. "The most striking evidence of continued popular militancy came from the ever- restive semi-tribal Rampa region in the north of the Godavari, scene of a veritable guerrilla war between August 1922 and May 1924. [The leader of the revolt] won the grudging admiration of the British As a formidable guerrilla tactician. That the Government had to spend over Rs 40 lakhs in those days to defeat the rebellion speaks volumes about the success of the Rampa rebellion."

Source: The Hindu

State the causes of the rebellion that the passage talks about. **5**

9. Read the text carefully and answer the following questions: (1 + 1 + 2 = 4) 4

The Non-Cooperation-Khilafat Movement began in January 1921. The movement started with middle-class participation in the cities. Thousands of students left government-controlled schools and colleges, headmasters and teachers resigned, and lawyers gave up their legal practices. The council elections were boycotted in most provinces except Madras, where the Justice Party, the party of the non-Brahmans, felt that entering the council was one way of gaining some power- something that usually only Brahmans had access to. The effects of non-cooperation on the economic front were more dramatic. Foreign zgoods were boycotted, liquor shops picketed, and foreign cloth burnt in huge bonfires. The import of foreign cloth halved between 1921 and 1922, its value dropping from ₹ 102 crores to ₹ 57 crores. In many places, merchants and traders refused to trade in foreign goods or finance foreign trade. As the boycott movement spread, and people began discarding imported clothes and wearing only Indian ones, the production of Indian textile mills and hand looms went up.

9.1 Explain the meaning of picketing liquor shops.

9.2 When did the Non-Cooperation-Khilafat Movement begin?

9.3 Why did the movement in the cities gradually slow down?

MAP SKILL-BASED QUESTION (2 Marks)

10. Two places **A** and **B** have been marked on the given outline map of India. Identify them and write their correct names on the lines drawn near them. **(1 + 1 = 2)**

A. The place where Indian National Congress session was held in 1927

B. The place where Gandhi ji started first Satyagraha.

SECTION - B

GEOGRAPHY (20 Marks)

11. Which of the following is an example of a multipurpose project in India? **1**

(*a*) Bhakra Nangal Dam
(*b*) Golden Quadrilateral highway project
(*c*) Mumbai Metro rail project
(*d*) Bhopal gas tragedy

12. Identify the National Park dedicated to the preservation of one-horned rhinoceros from the image below: **1**

(*a*) Bandhavgarh National Park
(*b*) Buxa Wildlife Reserve
(*c*) Kaziranga National Park
(*d*) All of the above

13. Study the pie charts given below showing land use categories in India for the years 1960–61 and 2014–15. Using the data, identify which land-use category has shown an increase in percentage from 1960 to 2014.

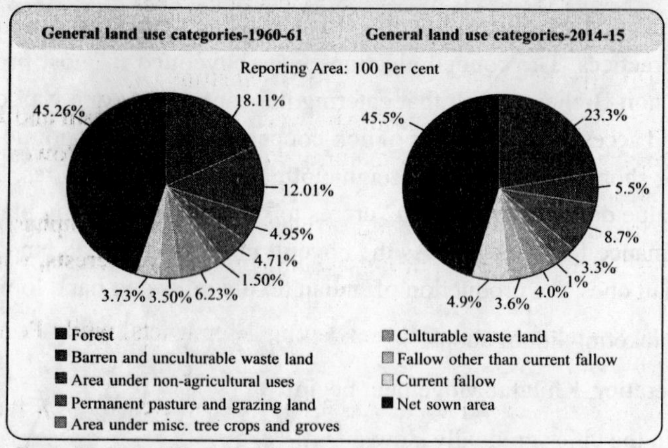

Source: *Directorate of Economics and Statistics, Ministry of Agriculture, 2017*

(*a*) Barren and unculturable waste land
(*b*) Unculturable waste land
(*c*) Forest
(*d*) Area under miscellaneous tree crops and groves.

14. "Agriculture and industry move hand in hand." Support the statement with examples. **2**

15. Examine the significance of agriculture contributes in the Indian economy. **3**

16A. Differentiate between metallic and non-metallic minerals with examples. **5**

OR

16B. "Minerals are indispensable part of our lives". Support the statement with examples. **5**

17. Read the given text and answer the following questions: (1 + 1 + 2 = 4) **4**

Conservation in the face of rapid declines in wildlife populations and forests has become essential. Conservation preserves ecological diversity and our life support systems – water, air, and soil. It also maintains the genetic diversity of plants and animals for better growth and breeding. For instance, agriculture depends on traditional crop varieties, and fisheries rely on aquatic biodiversity. In the 1960s and 1970s, conservationists demanded a national wildlife protection program. The Indian Wildlife (Protection) Act of 1972 was implemented to protect habitats and publish a list of protected species. The Act aimed to protect endangered species by banning hunting, securing habitats, and restricting wildlife trade. Subsequently, central and state governments established national parks and wildlife sanctuaries. Projects were launched to protect specific threatened animals like the tiger, one-horned rhinoceros, and Asiatic lion. Recently, animals like the Indian elephant, blackbuck, great Indian bustard, and snow leopard received legal protection against hunting and trade.

17.1 Give the importance of conserving forests and wildlife.
17.2 Describe the role of the Indian Wildlife (Protection) Act of 1972 in wildlife conservation.
17.3 Distinguish between the conservation measures taken in the 1960s and 1970s and those taken more recently.

MAP SKILL-BASED QUESTION (3 Marks)

18. On the same outline map of India locate and label the following with suitable symbols: **1**

I. (*p*) The high dam built at the confluence of Bhagirathi and Bhilangana rivers in Uttarakhand for power generation and water supply.

OR

(*q*) The dam constructed on the Chambal River in Rajasthan, named after a famous king, known for power and irrigation.

II. Any two of the following **(1 × 2 = 2)**
(*i*) Narora Nuclear Power Plant
(*ii*) An International Airport in Chennai
(*iii*) An International Airport in Mumbai

SECTION - C

POLITICAL SCIENCE (20 Marks)

19. Most of the Sinhala-speaking people are________ **1**

(*a*) Buddhists (*b*) Hindus (*c*) Muslims (*d*) Christians

20. Which of the following statements accurately distinguishes between Majoritarianism and Power sharing? **1**

(*a*) Majoritarianism emphasizes the dominance of the majority community, while Power sharing emphasizes the sharing of power among different groups.

(*b*) Majoritarianism emphasizes the need for consensus building, while Power sharing emphasizes the exclusion of minority groups.

(*c*) Majoritarianism emphasizes the importance of accommodating minority interests, while Power sharing emphasizes the need for majority rule.

(*d*) Majoritarianism emphasizes the need for peaceful resolution of conflicts, while Power sharing emphasizes the use of force to impose the majority's will

21. In the following questions, two statement are given as Assertion (A) and Reason (R). Read the statements and choose the correct option. **1**

Assertion (A): In poor countries, the rate of economic growth under dictatorships and democracies is drastic.

Reason (R): The form of governance does not directly determine a country's economic growth rate.

(*a*) Both Assertion (A) and Reason (R) are true and Reason (R) is the correct explanation of Assertion (A).

(*b*) Both Assertion (A) and Reason (R) are true and Reason (R) is not the correct explanation of Assertion (A).

(*c*) Assertion (A) is true but Reason (R) is false.

(*d*) Assertion (A) is false but Reason (R) is true.

22. What was the purpose of the amendments to the Belgian constitution between 1970 and 1993? **1**

(*a*) To establish separate state governments

(*b*) To promote regional differences

(*c*) To divide the country on linguistic lines

(*d*) To enable everyone to live together within the same country.

23. Which of the following statements is not true about Democracy? **1**

(*a*) People wish to be ruled by representatives elected by them.

(*b*) It is free of corruption.

(*c*) It is expected to produce good governments.

(*d*) Guarantees rights of citizens.

24. Communal politics is based on the belief that: **1**

Statement-I: One religion is superior to that of others.

Statement-II: Followers of a particular religion constitute one community.

Read the following statements and select the correct options.

(*a*) Both Statement-I and Statement-II are correct.

(*b*) Both Statement-I and Statement-II are incorrect.

(*c*) Statement-I is correct & Statement-II is incorrect.

(*d*) Statement-I is incorrect & Statement-II is correct.

25. Read the statements given below regarding Federalism in India. **2**

Statement 1 (S1): India's constitution originally provided for a two-tier system of government.

Statement 2 (S2): Later, a third tier of federalism was added.

Explain what trend these statements - S1 and S2- reflect in the governance system of India.

26. "Caste inequalities are still prevalent in India." Examine the statement. **3**

27A. "Democratic systems are based on political equality." Examine the statement. **5**

OR

27B. How has democracy strengthened the claims of disadvantaged and discriminated castes in India? **5**

28. Read the given text and answer the following questions: (1 + 1 + 2 = 4) **4**

A political party is a group of people who come together to contest elections and hold power in the government. They agree on some policies and programs for society with a view to promoting the collective good. Since there can be different views on what is good for all, parties try to persuade people why their policies are better than others. They seek to implement these policies by winning popular support through elections.

28.1 What are the main functions of a political parties?

28.2 Why do political parties try to persuade people about their policies?

28.3 How do political parties seek to implement their policies?

SECTION - D

ECONOMICS (20 Marks)

29. Assume there are four families in a country. The average per capita income of these families is ₹ 5000. If the income of three families is ₹ 4000, ₹ 7000 and ₹ 3000 respectively, what is the income of the fourth family? **1**

(*a*) ₹ 7500 (*b*) ₹ 3000 (*c*) ₹ 2000 (*d*) ₹ 6000

30. What do the banks do with the major deposits that they accept from the customers? **1**

(*a*) Banks use these deposits for their infrastructure.

(*b*) Banks use a major portion of deposits to extend loans.

(*c*) Banks use deposits to buy shares in the share market.

(*d*) Banks use deposits to set up more branches in the country.

31. Match the Column-I with Column-II and choose the correct option from the following: **1**

	Column-I		Column-II
A.	Liberalisation	(*i*)	The purchase of assets in another country by an individual or a company
B.	Investment	(*ii*)	Removing barriers or restrictions set by the government
C.	Foreign Investment	(*iii*)	Electronic mail (e-mail) and talk (voice-mail)
D.	Internet Facilities	(*iv*)	The money spent to buy assets such as land

(*a*) A-(*iv*), B-(*iii*), C-(*ii*), D-(*i*)

(*b*) A-(*iv*), B-(*ii*), C-(*i*), D-(*iii*)

(*c*) A-(*ii*), B-(*iv*), C-(*i*), D-(*iii*)

(*d*) A-(*iii*), B-(*iv*), C-(*ii*), D-(*i*)

32. Meena owns a fishing boat and catches fish from the nearby river. She sells the fish directly to the local market, where they are purchased by consumers for their consumption. **1**

In which sector does Meena's fishing activities fall?

(*a*) Primary Sector

(*b*) Secondary Sector

(*c*) Tertiary Sector

(*d*) Quaternary Sector

33. Identify the reason as to why MNCs would like to collaborate with India in producing goods. Choose from the appropriate statements among the following options: **1**

(*i*) India has highly skilled engineers who can understand the technical aspects of production.

(*ii*) It also has educated English-speaking youth who can provide customer care services. This means 50-60 percent cost savings for the MNC.

(*iii*) It's the cheapest manufacturing location.

(*iv*) It's close to the markets in the US and Europe.

(*a*) Statements i and ii are appropriate.

(*b*) Statements i, ii, and iii are appropriate.

(*c*) All the statements are appropriate.

(*d*) Only statement iv is appropriate.

34. Rajesh is a farmer who needs to borrow money to buy seeds and fertilizers for the upcoming planting season. He is considering both formal and informal sources of credit. **1**

Which of the following is an example of a formal source of credit for Rajesh?

(*a*) Borrowing money from a moneylender in his village

(*b*) Taking a loan from a Self-Help Group (SHG)

(*c*) Receiving money as a gift from a relative

(*d*) Borrowing from a friend without any written agreement

35A. Distinguish between open unemployment and disguised unemployment. **3**

OR

35B. Explain reasons for the rising importance of the tertiary sector in India. **3**

36. In Araville, liberalization has allowed multinational corporations to enter the market, increasing product choices and sparking local economic growth. This policy shift introduces both competition for local businesses and a wealth of opportunities for consumers, enhancing overall market dynamism and community prosperity. Evaluate the effectiveness of foreign investment in improving the standard of living for Araville's residents. What measures can be taken to ensure that these benefits are distributed equitably? **3**

37. The following table gives the GDP in Rupees (crores) by the three sectors: **3**

Year	Primary	Secondary	Tertiary
2000	52,000	48,500	1,33,500
2013	8,00,500	10,74,000	38,68,000

(*i*) Calculate the share of all the three sectors in GDP for 2000 and 2013.

(*ii*) Show the data as a bar diagram for the year 2000 and 2013.

(*iii*) What conclusions can we draw from the bar graph?

38A. In what ways does the Reserve Bank of India supervise the functioning of banks? Why is this necessary? **5**

OR

38B. "Money cannot buy all the goods and services that you may need to live well." Explain the statement. **5**

Map for Q. no. 10 (Section A) & Q. no. 18 (Section B)

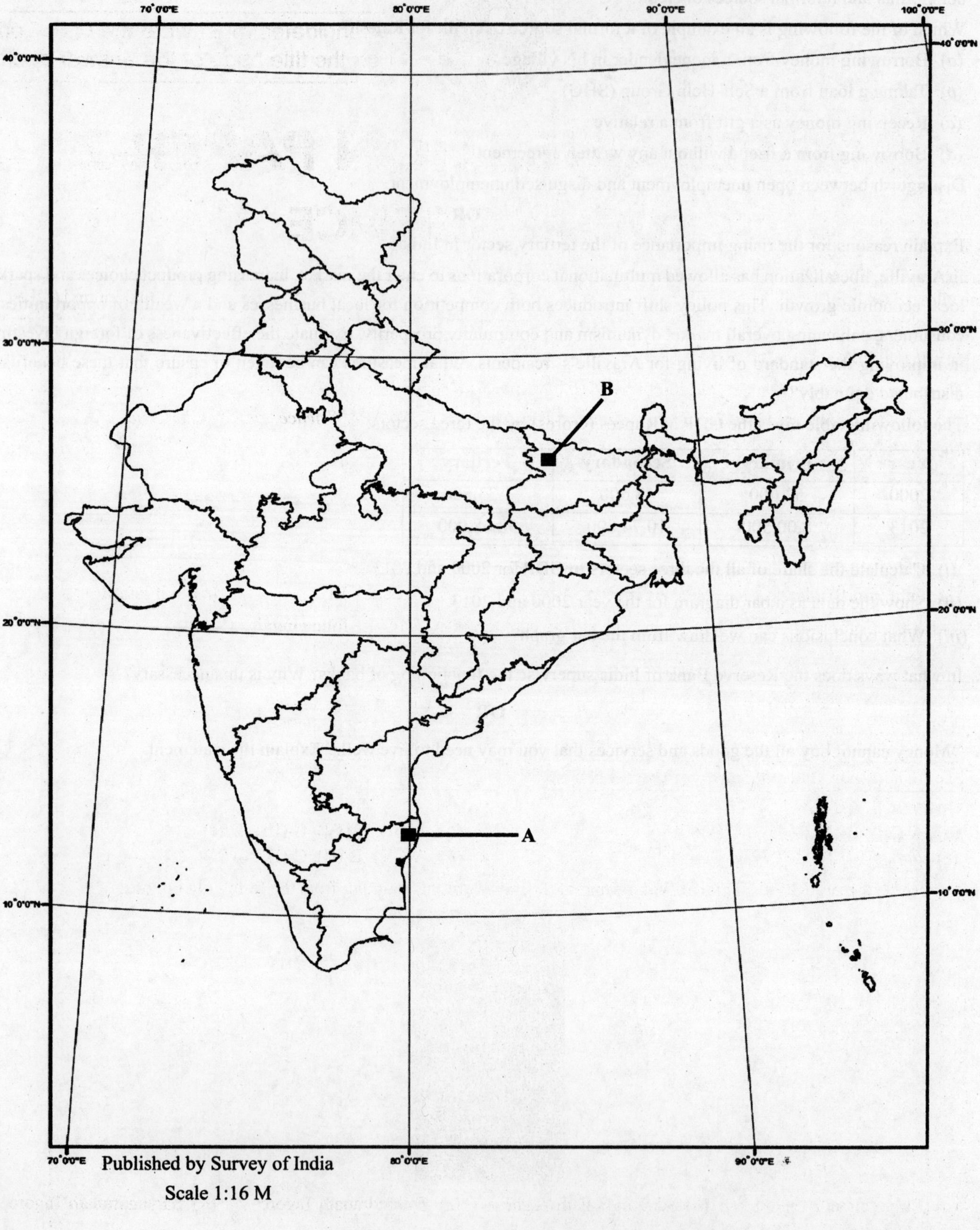

Published by Survey of India

Scale 1:16 M

Roll No. | | | | | | | |

Q.P. Code 02

Candidates must write the Q.P. Code on the title page of the answer book.

SAMPLE QUESTION PAPER-2

SOCIAL SCIENCE

Time allowed : 3 hours | Maximum Marks : 80

GENERAL INSTRUCTIONS:

(i) There are 38 questions in the Question paper. All questions are compulsory.

(ii) The question paper has Four Sections – A-History, B-Geography C- Political Science, and D- Economics.

(iii) Each Section is of 20 Marks and has MCQs, VSA, SA, LAs and CBQ.

SECTION - A

HISTORY (20 Marks)

1. Who among the following was the architect for the unification of Germany? **1**

(*a*) Otto Von Bismarck (*b*) William I (*c*) Frederick III (*d*) William II

2. Match the Column-I with Column-II and choose the correct option from the following: **1**

	Column-I		Column-II
A.	Gita Govind	(I)	B G Tilak
B.	Kesari	(II)	Rammohan Roy
C.	Sambad Kaumudi	(III)	Jaydev
D.	Chhote aur Bade ka Sawal	(IV)	Kashibaba

Options:

(*a*) A-(III), B-(I), C-(II), D-(IV) (*b*) A-(II), B-(IV), C-(III), D-(I)

(*c*) A-(I), B-(III), C-(IV), D-(II) (*d*) A-(IV), B-(II), C-(I), D-(III)

3. Look at the given picture and identify the name of the painter of this painting from the following options: **1**

(*a*) Rabindranath Tagore (*b*) Abanindranath Tagore (*c*) Debindranath Tagore (*d*) Satyendranath Tagore

4. Reason for decline of cotton textile export from India to Britain in the early 19th century: **1**

(*a*) Imposition of tariff on cotton import into Britain. (*b*) Quality of cotton textile was poor.

(*c*) Shortage of raw cotton in India. (*d*) Cotton producers had found other buyers.

5A. Why was the Indian subcontinent significant to trade networks before European intervention? Explain. **2**

OR

5B. Food offers many examples of long-distance cultural exchange. Justify this statement. **2**

6A. "The merchants and industrialists made a significant contribution to the Civil Disobedience Movement". In the light of the above statement, explain their role in the movement. **3**

OR

6B. 'A variety of political agreements played an important role in shaping the Indian freedom struggle.' Support the statement with reference to the Gandhi-Irwin Pact, giving suitable examples. **3**

7A. "Equality before law did not stand for universal suffrage in France after the revolution". Explain with suitable examples. **5**

OR

7B. Explain the conditions that were viewed as obstacles to economic exchange and growth by the new commercial classes. How did it end in 1834? **5**

8. Read the given text and answer the following questions: (1 + 1 + 2 = 4) **4**

Why Newspapers?

'Krishnaji Trimbuck Ranade inhabitant of Poona intends to publish a Newspaper in the Marathi Language with a view of affording useful information on every topic of local interest. It will be open for free discussion on subjects of general utility, scientific investigation and the speculations connected with the antiquities, statistics, curiosities, history and geography of the country and of the Deccan especially… the patronage and support of all interested in the diffusion of knowledge and Welfare of the People is earnestly solicited.' Bombay Telegraph and Courier, 6 January 1849 'The task of the native newspapers and political associations is identical to the role of the Opposition in the House of Commons in Parliament in England. That is of critically examining government policy to suggest improvements, by removing those parts that will not be to the benefit of the people, and also by ensuring speedy implementation. These associations ought to carefully study the particular issues, gather diverse relevant information on the nation as well as on what are the possible and desirable improvements, and this will surely earn it considerable influence.'

Native Opinion, 3 April 1870.

8.1 Analyse the primary objective proposed by Ranade for publishing Marathi Language newspaper.

8.2 Why did the Bombay Telegraph emphasize the role of newspaper in promoting welfare of Deccan region?

8.3 What were the key responsibilities attributed to native newspapers? Mention any two.

MAP SKILL-BASED QUESTION (2 Marks)

9. Two places **A** and **B** have been marked on the given outline map of India. Identify them and write their correct names on the lines drawn near them. **(1 + 1 = 2)**

(A) The place where Indian National Congress session was held in September, 1920.

(B) The place where Mahatma Gandhi started first Satyagraha.

SECTION - B

GEOGRAPHY (20 Marks)

10. Two statements are given below. They are Assertion (A) and Reason (R). Read both the statements and choose the correct option. **1**

Assertion (A): Conservation of forests and wildlife is not essential for maintaining ecological balance.
Reason (R): Forests and wildlife provide essential ecosystem services such as carbon sequestration, soil conservation, water regulation, and climate regulation.

(*a*) Both (A) and (R) are true and (R) is the correct explanation of (A)

(*b*) Both (A) and (R) are true but (R) is not the correct explanation of (A)

(*c*) (A) is true but (R) is false.

(*d*) (A) is false but (R) is true.

11. Identify the crop with the help of the following information. **1**

(*i*) It is a crop which is used both as food and fodder

(*ii*) It is a Kharif crop which requires a temperature between 21°C to 27°C.

(*iii*) It grows well in old alluvial soil.

(*iv*) Use of modern inputs have contributed to the increasing production of this crop.

(*a*) Wheat (*b*) Maize (*c*) Rice (*d*) Sugarcane

12. The given feature is representing which one of the following type of soil- According to their age this soil can be classified as old soil (Bangar) and new soil (Khadar). **1**

(*a*) Alluvial soil (*b*) Laterite soil (*c*) Black soil (*d*) Arid soil

13. Identify the appropriate option to fill in the empty boxes:

Factors Affecting Arabica Coffee Cultivation in India **1**

	Geographical Factor		Explanation
A.	High Altitude	(*i*)	?
B.	Ideal Climate	(*ii*)	Temperature between 15–24°C and rainfall of 150–250 cm
C.	Soil Type	(*iii*)	?

(*a*) Grown in desert plains; Rich red soil

(*b*) Grown in Nilgiri Hills; Loamy, well-drained, slightly acidic soil

(*c*) Cultivated in Indo-Gangetic plains; Sandy soil

(*d*) Found in coastal plains; Clayey soil

14. Conservation of forest is a key to the survival of human mankind. Some of the practices undertaken in India in this direction is Joint Forest Management. Identify the correct information related to Joint Forest Management. **1**

(*i*) It involves local communities in the management and restoration of degraded forests.

(*ii*) The programme has been in formal existence since 1980.

(*iii*) Jharkhand passed the first resolution for Joint Forest Management.

(*iv*) The members of local village communities are entitled to intermediary benefits like non timber forest producers.

(*a*) (*i*) and (*ii*) only

(*b*) (*ii*) and (*iii*) only

(*c*) (*i*) and (*iv*) only

(*d*) (*iii*) and (*iv*) onlyfrom protected areas.

15. Deforestation due to mining has caused severe land degradation in which one of the following states? **1**

(*a*) Odisha (*b*) Tamil Nadu (*c*) Kerala (*d*) Gujarat

16. Sameer is an energy consultant at the Global Energy Research Institute (GERI). The government of India has tasked you with assessing the current state of atomic or nuclear power resources in the country. Identify the main resources for generating atomic or nuclear power in India. **2**

17A. Mr. Gautam, a city planner was tasked with addressing the water scarcity challenges in a rapidly urbanizing area that is also undergoing significant industrialization. The local government is considering expanding hydroelectric power facilities as part of the solution. Analyze the impact of industrialization and urbanization on water scarcity. Discuss the role of hydroelectric power in this context. **5**

OR

17B. Kushagra belongs to a rural family in arid Rajasthan. His community faces significant challenges in accessing clean water, primarily due to the region's dry climate and infrequent rainfall. The local government has introduced a rainwater harvesting project to help alleviate water scarcity. He and his family decided to implement this system in their home.

Explain how rainwater harvesting in Rajasthan adapts to its arid and semi-arid conditions and its impact on local households. **5**

18. Read the given text and answer the following questions: (1 + 1 + 2 = 4) 4

Narmada Bachao Andolan or Save Narmada Movement is a Non-Governmental Organisation (NGO) that mobilized tribal people, farmers, environmentalists and human rights activists against the Sardar Sarovar Dam being built across the Narmada river in Gujarat. It originally focused on the environmental issues related to trees that would be submerged under the dam water. Recently it has re-focused the aim to enable poor citizens, especially the oustees (displaced people) to get full rehabilitation facilities from the government. People felt that their suffering would not be in vain and accepted the trauma of displacement believing in the promise of irrigated fields and plentiful harvests. So, often the survivors of Rihand told us that they accepted their sufferings as sacrifices for the sake of their nation. But now, after thirty bitter years of being adrift, their livelihood having even being more precarious, they keep asking: "Are we the only one chosen to make sacrifices for the nation?"

18.1 Why was the Sardar Sarovar Dam constructed?

18.2 Examine the tribal people's reasons for protesting.

18.3 Describe the issues that the "Save Narmada Movement" worked to resolve.

MAP SKILL-BASED QUESTION (3 Marks)

19. On the same outline map of India locate and label the following with suitable symbols: 1

I. (*p*) The dam built on the Chenab River in Jammu and Kashmir for hydroelectric power generation.

OR

(*q*) The dam constructed at the confluence of the Bhagirathi rivers, providing hydel power and water supply in Uttarakhand.

II. Any two of the following: **(1 × 2 = 2)**

(*i*) Ramagundam Thermal Power Station

(*ii*) An international airport in Hyderabad

(*iii*) An international airport in Amritsar

SECTION - C

POLITICAL SCIENCE (20 Marks)

20. Which one among the following pairs is correctly matched? 1

	Column-I		Column-II
A.	Bharatiya Janata Party	(I)	National Democratic Alliance
B.	Congress Party	(II)	Left Front
C.	Communist Party of India (Marxist)	(III)	Regional Party
D.	Mizo National Front	(IV)	United Progressive Alliance

Options:

(*a*) A-(II), B-(I), C-(III), D-(IV)
(*b*) A-(III), B-(II), C-(IV), D-(I)
(*c*) A-(I), B-(IV), C-(II), D-(III)
(*d*) A-(I), B-(IV), C-(III), D-(II)

21. There are two statements marked as Assertion (A) and Reason (R). Mark your answer as per the codes provided below: 1

Assertion (A): Women's political participation is crucial for achieving gender equality in society.

Reason (R): Women's perspectives and experiences are often different from men's, and their inclusion in decision-making processes can lead to more equitable policies

(*a*) Both (A) and (R) are true, and (R) is the correct explanation of (A).
(*b*) Both (A) and (R) are true, but (R) is not the correct explanation of (A).
(*c*) (A) is true, but (R) is false
(*d*) (A) is false, but (R) is true

22. Consider the following statements on power sharing and choose the correct option. 1

(*i*) Imposing the will of the majority community over others.
(*ii*) It helps in reducing the possibility of conflict between social groups.
(*iii*) Power sharing is a good way to ensure the stability of political order.
(*iv*) It brings socio-political opposition among parties.

(*a*) (*i*) and (*iii*) (*b*) (*ii*) and (*iii*) (*c*) (*i*) and (*iv*) (*d*) (*i*) and (*ii*)

23. The Constitution of India provides for a division of power between the Union and the States enumerated in three lists. Based on the division of subjects in the lists, Identify the ones that are correctly matched. **1**

(*i*) Defence and Banking - Union List

(*ii*) Police and Commerce - State list

(*iii*) Forest and Trade Unions - Concurrent list

(*iv*) Artificial intelligence - State list

Choose the correct option:

(*a*) (*i*) and (*ii*)

(*b*) (*i*), (*ii*) and (*iii*)

(*c*) (*i*), (*iii*) and (*iv*)

(*d*) (*i*), (*ii*), (*iii*) and (*iv*)

24. What is a political party? Name two components of a political party. **2**

25. What are the residuary subjects? Who has the power to legislate on "residuary" subjects in India? **2**

26. What changes occurred in Centre-State relations after 1990? What role did the Supreme Court play in this? **3**

27A. "Democracy promotes the dignity and freedom of the people." Examine the statement. **5**

OR

27B. "Democracy has failed to reduce economic inequality and poverty." Do you agree? Give arguments in support of your answer. **5**

28. Read the given text and answer the following questions: (1 + 1 + 2 = 4) **4**

Power sharing arrangements can also be seen in the way political parties, pressure groups and movements control or influence those in power. In a democracy, the citizens must have freedom to choose among various contenders for power. In contemporary democracies, this takes the form of competition among different parties. Such competition ensures that power does not remain in one hand. In the long run, power is shared among different political parties that represent different ideologies and social groups. Sometimes this kind of sharing can be direct, when two or more parties form an alliance to contest elections. If their alliance is elected, they form a coalition government and thus share power. In a democracy, we find interest groups such as those of traders, businessmen, industrialists, farmers and industrial workers. They also will have share in governmental power, either through participation in governmental committees or bringing influence on the decision-making process.

28.1 "Power sharing is an essential component of democracy". Support the statement with an example.

28.2 How does forming alliances show power-sharing?

28.3 How do political parties, pressure groups, and movements help restrict or influence those in positions of authority?

SECTION - D

ECONOMICS (20 Marks)

29. Rohan has taken a loan of ₹ 5 lakh from the bank to purchase a house at a 12% rate of interest. He has to submit papers for the new house and his salary record to the bank. What is this process called? **1**

(*a*) Interest Rate

(*b*) Collateral

(*c*) Principal Amount

(*d*) Installments

30. Globalisation is the increasing interconnectedness of the world through the flow of goods, services, capital, ideas, and people. Which of the following examples represents globalisation? **1**

(*a*) an online advertising portal for goods sold by local vendors run by the Indian government

(*b*) an IKEA store in Bengaluru selling products manufactured in China

(*c*) a traditional Vietnamese market selling handicrafts in Hanoi

(*d*) a Sunday market selling groceries produced locally

31. In the village of Econville, a local farmer, Mr.Arjun, grows wheat and sells it to a bakery, Mr.Sweet's Bakery, at ₹ 20 per kg. The bakery uses this wheat to make delicious biscuits, which are then sold in the local market at ₹ 80 per packet. Assume that there are no other production costs involved. Select among the following how should this transaction be reflected in the GDP? **1**

(*a*) Include the value of both the wheat and biscuits separately to highlight all economic activities.

(*b*) Include only the value of the wheat, as it is the raw product and the basis of further production.

(*c*) Include only the value of biscuits, as it represents the final consumption goods.

(*d*) Exclude both values, as they do not contribute directly to the village's retail market.

32. Identify the correct statements about globalization. **1**

(*i*) Removal of barriers by the government
(*ii*) Foreign companies are allowed to set up factories
(*iii*) has enabled all companies to increase their investments
(*iv*) has lessened foreign investment and foreign trade

(*a*) (*i*), (*ii*) and (*iii*)
(*b*) (*ii*) and (*iii*)
(*c*) (*i*) and (*iii*)
(*d*) (*ii*) and (*iv*)

33. Read the following data and select the appropriate option from the following. **1**

Educational Achievement of Rural Population of Uttar Pradesh		
Category	**Male**	**Female**
Literacy rate for the rural population	76%	54%
Literacy rate for rural children in the age group 10-14 years	90%	87%
Percentage of rural children aged 10-14 attending school	85%	82%

How much percentage of girls are not attending school?

(*a*) 82% (*b*) 15% (*c*) 13% (*d*) 18%

34. At the initial stages of development, which one of the following sectors was the most important for economic activity? **1**

(*a*) Tertiary (*b*) Secondary (*c*) Primary (*d*) Quaternary

35. "All the services of the 'service sector' are not growing equally well." Evaluate the statement. **3**

36. Two families in a village – one wealthy and the other of modest means—both need to borrow money for agricultural activities. The wealthier family easily secures a loan from a formal banking institution, while the poorer family struggles to find a reliable lender and ends up borrowing from an informal source with higher interest rates. Analyze the reasons behind the disparity in access to formal sector credit between these two families. **3**

37. Assess any three advantages of globalisation. **3**

38A. What should India do or achieve to become a developed country? Explain. **5**

OR

38B. Kerala, with lower per capita income has a better human development ranking than Haryana. Hence, per capita income is not a useful criterion at all and should not be used to compare states. Do you agree? Give reasons in support of your answer. **5**

Map for Q. no. 9 (Section A) & Q. no. 19 (Section B)

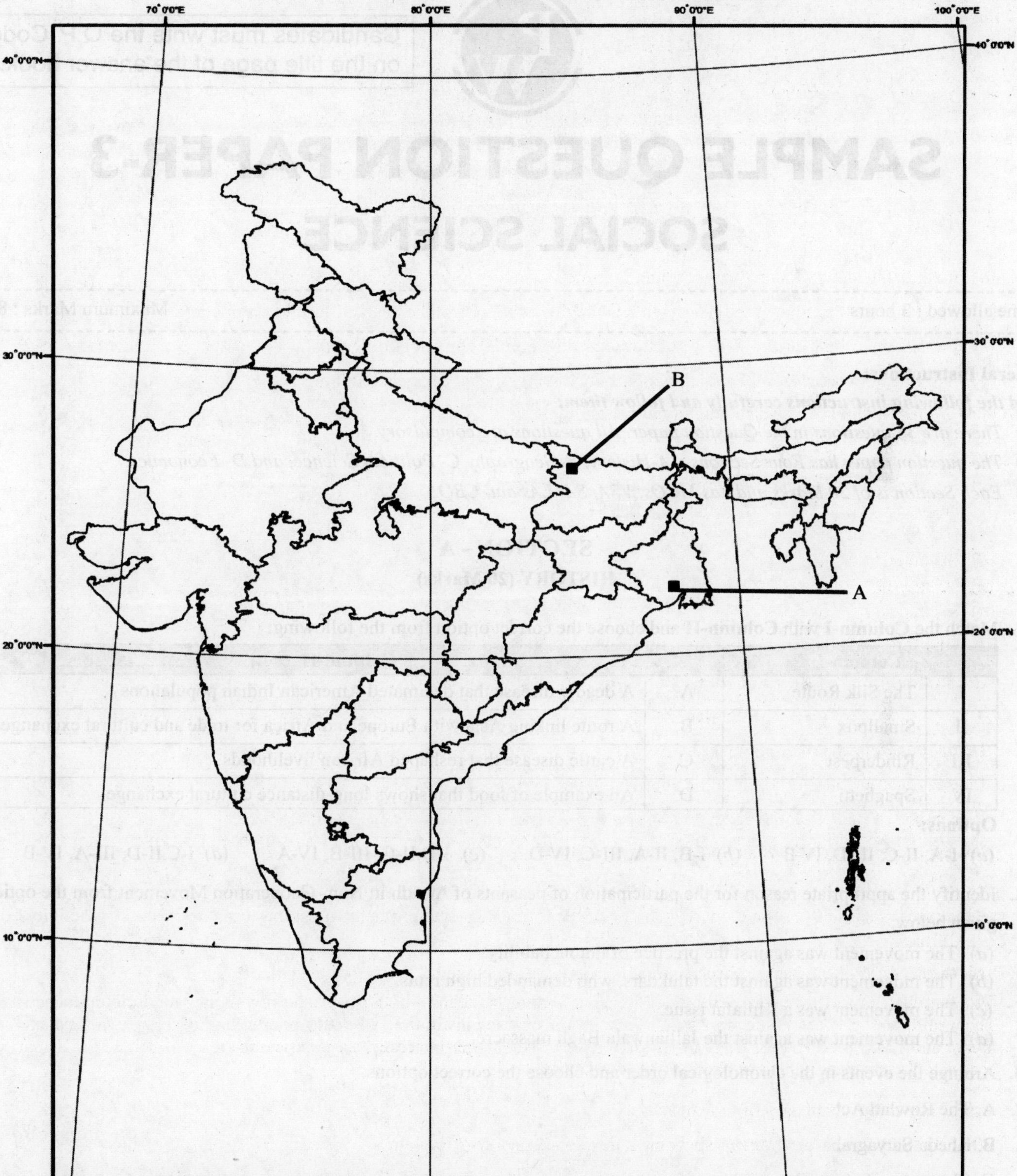

Published by Survey of India
Scale 1:16M

Roll No. | | | | | | | | |

Q.P. Code 03

Candidates must write the Q.P. Code on the title page of the answer book.

SAMPLE QUESTION PAPER-3

SOCIAL SCIENCE

Time allowed : 3 hours — Maximum Marks : 80

General Instructions:

Read the following instructions carefully and follow them:

(i) There are 38 questions in the Question paper. All questions are compulsory.

(ii) The question paper has Four Sections – A-History, B-Geography C- Political Science, and D- Economics.

(iii) Each Section is of 20 Marks and has MCQs, VSA, SA, LAs and CBQ.

SECTION - A

HISTORY (20 Marks)

1. Match the **Column-I** with **Column-II** and choose the correct option from the following: 1

	Column-I		Column-II
I	The Silk Route	A.	A deadly disease that decimated American Indian populations
II	Smallpox	B.	A route linking Asia with Europe and Africa for trade and cultural exchange
III	Rinderpest	C.	A cattle disease that reshaped African livelihoods
IV	Spaghetti	D.	An example of food that shows long-distance cultural exchange

Options:

(*a*) I-A, II-C, III-D, IV-B (*b*) I-B, II-A, III-C, IV-D (*c*) I-D,II-C, III-B, IV-A (*d*) I-C,II-D, III-A, IV-B

2. Identify the appropriate reason for the participation of peasants of Awadh in Non- Cooperation Movement from the options given below: 1

(*a*) The movement was against the practice of untouchability.

(*b*) The movement was against the talukdars, who demanded high rents.

(*c*) The movement was a Khilafat issue.

(*d*) The movement was against the Jallianwala Bagh massacre.

3. Arrange the events in the chronological order and choose the correct options. 1

A. The Rowlatt Act

B. Kheda Satyagraha

C. Champaran Satyagraha

D. Beginning of Non-Cooperation

(*a*) A-C-B-D (*b*) C-B-A-D (*c*) B-D-C-A (*d*) B-C-D-A

4. Identify the correct option that describes the book given below. 1

A. The oldest Japanese book

B. Pictures were printed on textiles, playing cards and paper money

C. Containing six sheets of text and woodcut illustrations

Options:

(*a*) Diamond sutra (*b*) The Jikji (*c*) Chapbooks (*d*) Bible

5. Why were the Spanish successful in establishing colonies in America? 2

6. "The effects of the Non-Cooperation Movement on the economic front were more dramatic." Support the statement with examples. 3

7A. Discuss the role of liberal ideas and ideologies during the revolution of the liberals in the context of the rise of nationalism in Europe. 5

OR

7B. How did the French Revolution contribute to the development of the idea of the nation? 5

8. **Read the given text and answer the following questions: (1 + 1 + 2 = 4)** 4

Lives and feelings of women began to be written in particularly vivid and intense ways. Women's reading, therefore, increased enormously in middle-class homes. Liberal husbands and fathers began educating their womenfolk at home, and sent them to schools when woman' schools were set up in cities and towns after the mid-nineteenth century. Many journals began carrying writings by women, and explained why women should be educated. They also carried a syllabus and attached suitable reading matter which could be used for home-based schooling. But not all families were liberal. Conservative Hindus believed that a literate girl would be widowed and Muslims feared that educated women would be corrupted by reading Urdu romances. Sometimes, rebel women defied such prohibition.

Since social reforms and novels had already created a great interest in women's lives and emotions, there was also an interest in what women would have to say about their own lives. From the 1860s, a few Bengali women like Kailashbashini Debi wrote books highlighting the experiences of women – about how women were imprisoned at home, kept in ignorance, forced to do hard domestic labour and treated unjustly by the very people they served. In the 1880s, in present-day Maharashtra, Tarabai Shinde and Pandita Ramabai wrote with passionate anger about the miserable lives of upper-caste Hindu women, especially widows.

8.1 Why did some families oppose the education of women?

8.2 How did the lives and feelings of women change during this time period?

8.3 What did Kailashbashini Debi and other Bengali women write about in their books?

MAP SKILL-BASED QUESTION (2 Marks)

9. Two places **A** and **B** have been marked on the given political outline map of India. Identify them and write their correct names on the lines drawn near them: (1 + 1 = 2)

A. The place where Indian National Congress session was held in 1927.

B. The place where Non-Cooperation Movement was called off.

SECTION - B

GEOGRAPHY (20 Marks)

10. Identify the industry with the help of following information: 1

(*i*) India is the largest producer and stands at second place as an exporter after Bangladesh

(*ii*) Most of the mills are located in West Bengal

(*a*) Jute Textiles (*b*) Fertilizer Industry (*c*) Chemical Industry (*d*) Iron & Steel Industry

11. Which one of the following industries uses bauxite as a raw material? **1**

(*a*) Aluminium Smelting (*b*) Cement (*c*) Paper (*d*) Steel

12. Which of the following statements about conservation reserves is/are correct? **1**

(*i*) Conservation reserves are established to protect specific species or habitats.

(*ii*) They are areas where controlled hunting and fishing are allowed.

(*iii*) Conservation reserves focus on the restoration of degraded ecosystems.

(*iv*) Human activities, such as industrial development, are permitted within conservation reserves.

(*a*) Statement (*i*) and (*iii*) are correct. (*b*) Statement (*i*), (*ii*) & (*iii*) are correct

(*c*) Statement (*ii*) is correct. (*d*) Statement (*i*), (*iii*) & (*iv*) are correct.

13A. What are the reasons for the availability of bad quality of water? **2**

OR

13B. What are the advantages of multi purpose projects? **2**

14. Explain the ways through which the industrial pollution of fresh water can be reduced. **3**

15A. What is the importance of soil? Explain factors responsible for soil formation. **5**

OR

15B. What is land degradation? Explain its causes. **5**

16. Read the given text and answer the following questions: (1 + 1 + 2 = 4) **4**

Minerals are valuable natural resources that are found in the earth's crust. They are essential for various industries and play a crucial role in the development of a country. India is rich in mineral resources, with a wide variety of minerals found in different parts of the country. These minerals can be broadly classified into metallic minerals and non-metallic minerals. Metallic minerals include iron ore, manganese, copper, lead, zinc, gold, and silver. These minerals are used in the production of metals and alloys, which are then used in industries such as construction, manufacturing, and transportation. India is one of the largest producers of iron ore and manganese in the world. Non-metallic minerals include limestone, gypsum, mica, and salt. These minerals are used in various industries such as cement, fertilizers, ceramics, and chemicals. India has abundant reserves of limestone, which is used in the production of cement. Apart from minerals, energy resources are also crucial for the development of a country. India relies heavily on coal for its energy needs. Coal is used in thermal power plants to generate electricity. India is the third-largest producer of coal in the world. In recent years, there has been a growing focus on renewable sources of energy such as solar and wind power. These sources of energy are clean and sustainable and can help reduce the dependence on fossil fuels. India has vast potential for solar and wind energy, and efforts are being made to harness these resources.

16.1 What are metallic minerals and non-metallic minerals?

16.2 How can renewable sources of energy help reduce the dependence on fossil fuels?

16.3 Why are minerals and energy resources important for the development of a country?

MAP SKILL-BASED QUESTION (3 Marks)

17. On the same outline map of India locate and label the following with suitable symbols. **1**

I. (*p*) The northeastern state famous for tea gardens in Brahmaputra Valley.

OR

(*q*) The hill state of South India known for Nilgiri tea production.

II. Any two of the following: **(1 × 2 = 2)**

(*i*) The southern state that leads in Arabica coffee production.

(*ii*) A neighboring state of Karnataka also contributing to coffee cultivation in the Western Ghats.

(*iii*) The leading cotton-growing state in the Deccan Plateau, known for black soil.

SECTION - C

POLITICAL SCIENCE (20 Marks)

18. Considering the expectations and actual outcomes in democracies, which of the following is true about the reduction of inequality and poverty? **1**

A. Democratically elected governments do not appear to be as keen to address the question of poverty as you would expect them to.

B. Economic growth in democracies is always accompanied by just distribution of goods and opportunities.

C. Democratically elected governments are highly attentive to addressing the question of poverty.

D. Despite high expectations, democracies do not appear to be very successful in reducing economic inequalities.

(*a*) Only A (*b*) Only D (*c*) B and C (*d*) A and D

19. Changing party allegiance from the party on which a person got elected (to a legislative body) to a different party is called __________. **1**

(*a*) Separation (*b*) Diversion (*c*) Defection (*d*) Cancellation

20. Identify the appropriate reason for introduction of Community Government in Belgium: **1**

(*a*) To enable power sharing among various political parties.

(*b*) To ensure power sharing among various organs of government.

(*c*) To give more power to the Dutch-speaking community.

(*d*) To share power among different religious and linguistic social groups.

21. Which one of the following is a 'National Political Party'? **1**

(*a*) Rashtriya Lok Dal

(*b*) All India United Democratic Front

(*c*) Samajwadi Party

(*d*) Bahujan Samaj Party

22. Which among the following is correctly paired? **1**

	Column-I		Column-II
A.	Coalition	I.	Two-party system
B.	Union Territory	II.	Controlled by the state
C.	Federalism	III.	Power sharing
D.	Unitary	IV.	Concentration of power

(*a*) Only (A) (*b*) Only (C) (*c*) (C) and (D) (*d*) (A), (C) and (D)

23. Two statements are given as Assertion (A) and Reason (R). Read the statements and choose the correct option. **1**

Assertion (A): In poor countries, the rate of economic growth under dictatorships and democracies is negligible.

Reason (R): The form of governance directly determine a country's economic growth rate.

(*a*) Both A and R are true and R is the correct explanation of A.

(*b*) Both A and R are true but R is not the correct explanation of A.

(*c*) A is true but R is false.

(*d*) A is false but R is true.

24. How was federalism fostered in India after 1990? **2**

25. How is democracy considered a better form of government than dictatorship or any other form of government? **3**

26A. Explain with examples the accommodative experience of Belgium for peace and harmony. **5**

OR

26B. Compare the situation of Belgium and Sri Lanka considering their location, size and cultural aspects. **5**

27. Read the given text and answer the following questions: (1 + 1 + 2 = 4) **4**

The gender division tends to be understood as natural and unchangeable. It is not based on biology but on social expectations and stereotypes. The result of this division is that though women constitute half of humanity, their role in public life, especially politics, is minimal in most societies. Issues related to women are not given adequate attention. This has led many feminists and women's movements to the conclusion that unless women control power, their problems will not get adequate attention. In India, the percentage of elected women members in Lok Sabha touched 12 percent of its total strength for the first time in 2014. Their share in the state assemblies is less than 5 per cent. One way to solve women's problems is to have a fair proportion of women in the elected bodies. In Panchayats and Municipalities, one-third of seats in local government bodies are reserved for women. Now there are more than 10 lakh elected women representatives in rural and urban local bodies. Gender division is an example that some form of social division needs to be expressed in politics. This also shows that disadvantaged groups do benefit when social divisions become a political issue.

27.1 What is the main reason for the minimal representation of women in politics according to the passage?

27.2 Why do feminists and women's movements believe that women need to control power in order to address their problems adequately?

27.3 How has India attempted to address the underrepresentation of women in politics?

SECTION - D

ECONOMICS (20 Marks)

28. What can be inferred about the reliance on moneylenders for credit in rural India based on the graph? **1**

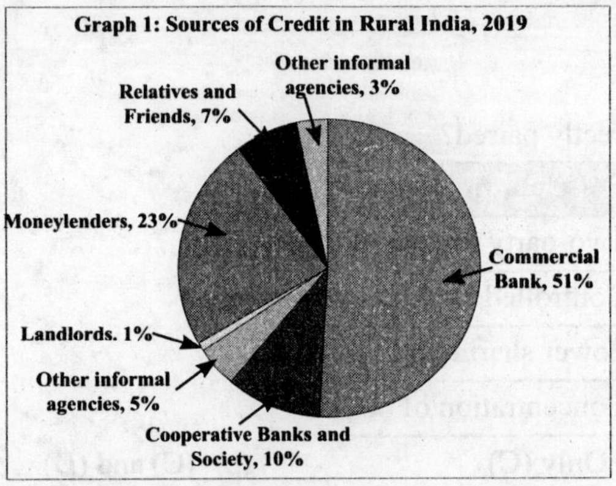

(*a*) Moneylenders are the least trusted source of credit.

(*b*) Moneylenders are still a significant source due to lack of access to formal banking.

(*c*) Moneylenders charge the lowest interest rates.

(*d*) Most people in rural areas prefer moneylenders over banks.

29. Shyama is working in a nearby grocery shop. She works from 7.30 in the morning to 8.00 p.m. in the evening. She does not get any allowance, leave or paid holiday. She has not been confirmed though she has been working for the past three years. Name the sector which she is employed in. **1**

(*a*) Organised sector (*b*) Primary sector

(*c*) Unorganised sector (*d*) Public sector

30. Meeta, owning about two hectares of unirrigated land-dependent only on rain and growing crops like jowar and arhar. All five members of her family work in the plot throughout the year. Everyone is working, none remains idle, but in actual fact their labour effort gets divided. Each one is doing some work but no one is fully employed. **1**

The situation given in the above lines can be termed as

(*a*) Unemployment

(*b*) Disguised unemployment

(*c*) Seasonal unemployment

(*d*) Open unemployment

31. Who among the following takes the decision regarding saving and loan activities in the Self-Help Groups (SHGs)? **1**

(*a*) Manager of a Bank

(*b*) Members of Non-Governmental Organisation (NGO)

(*c*) Local Money Lenders

(*d*) Members of Self-Help Group (SHG)

32. An industrialist has to make a payment to the supplier and writes a cheque for a specific amount. The supplier takes this cheque, and deposits it in his own account in the bank. Why has the supplier deposited the cheque in his account? **1**

(*a*) Money will automatically get transferred to his account.

(*b*) He will get the cash payment immediately.

(*c*) The cash will remain safe in the account.

(*d*) None of the above

33. Why do MNCs get their production process completed in different countries? **1**

(*a*) To minimize the cost of production

(*b*) To get the varieties in production

(*c*) To maximize the cost of production

(*d*) None of these

34. Identify the correct statements from the following: **1**

(*i*) Different people have different developmental goals and the goals cannot be conflicting.

(*ii*) People want more income to get material goods.

(*iii*) Quality of life depends only on material things.

(*iv*) Different people can have different and conflicting notions of development for the country.

Options:

(*a*) (*i*) and (*ii*) (*b*) (*ii*) and (*iii*)

(*c*) (*ii*) and (*iv*) (*d*) (*i*) and (*iii*)

35. Why is Per Capita Income always considered as an important parameter of measuring development? **2**

36. "The Impact of Globalization has not been uniform". Explain with examples. **3**

37. Why do banks and cooperative societies need to lend more? Explain. **3**

38A. "Public sector plays a crucial role in the economic development of a nation." Explain the statement. **5**

OR

38B. Distinguish between public sector and private sector. **5**

Map for Q. no. 9 (Section A) & Q. no. 17 (Section B)

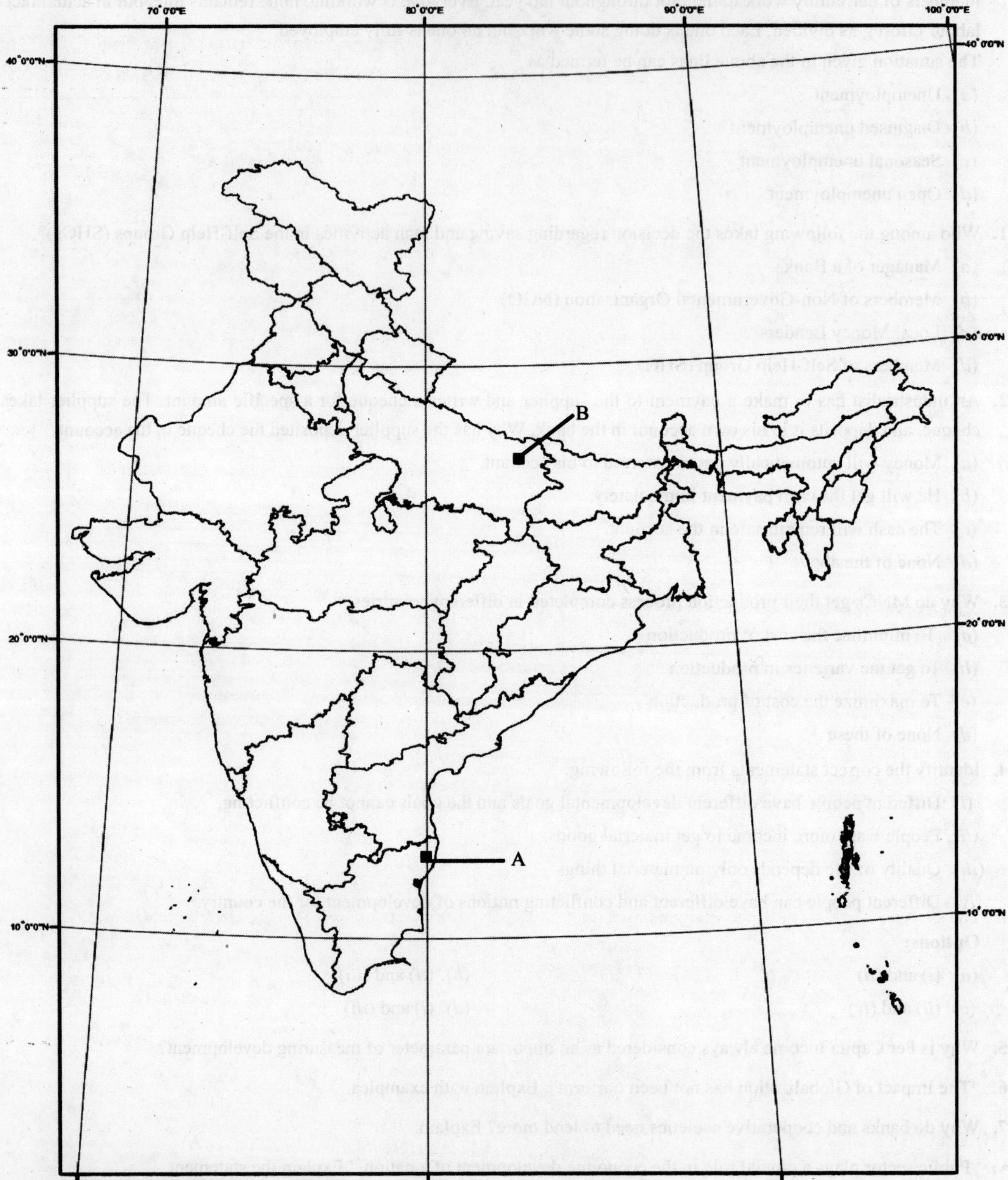

Published by Survey of India

Scale 1:16 M

Roll No. | | | | | | | |

Q.P. Code 04

Candidates must write the Q.P. Code on the title page of the answer book.

SAMPLE QUESTION PAPER-4
SOCIAL SCIENCE

Time allowed : 3 hours | Maximum Marks : 80

General Instructions:

Read the following instructions carefully and follow them:

(i) There are 38 questions in the Question paper. All questions are compulsory.

(ii) The question paper has Four Sections – A-History, B-Geography C- Political Science, and D- Economics.

(iii) Each Section is of 20 Marks and has MCQs, VSA, SA, LAs and CBQ.

SECTION - A
HISTORY (20 Marks)

1. Which of the following newspaper was started by Bal Gangadhar Tilak? **1**

(*a*) Hindu (*b*) Kesari (*c*) Gulamgiri (*d*) Pratap

2. What led to the diversification of print use in China in the seventeenth century? **1**

(*a*) Urban culture blooming (*b*) Western printing techniques

(*c*) Increase in trade information (*d*) Introduction of civil service examinations

3. Certain events are given below. Choose the appropriate chronological order: **1**

A. Coming of Simon Commission to India.

B. Demand of Purna Swaraj in Lahore Session of INC.

C. Government of India Act, 1919.

D. Champaran Satyagraha.

(*a*) C-B-D-A (*b*) A-B-D-C (*c*) B-C-A-D (*d*) D-C-A-B

4. The Cover of German almanac designed by the journalist Andreas Rebmann in 1798 Describes which event? **1**

(*a*) Storming of Bastille fort (*b*) The city of Mainz

(*c*) Two buildings of France (*d*) None of the above

5. How did the print revolution change the accessibility of books? **2**

6. Explain in what circumstances Gandhiji decided to call off the non-cooperation movements? **3**

7A. Describe the unification of Germany. **5**

OR

7B. Describe the unification of Italy. **5**

8. **Read the given text and answer the following questions: (1 + 1 + 2 = 4)** **4**

Printed Words

This is how Mercier describes the impact of the printed word, and the power of reading in one of his books: "Anyone who had seen me reading would have compared me to a man dying of thirst who was gulping down some frest" pure water... Lighting my lamp with extraordinary caution, I threw myself hungrily into the reading. An easy eloquence, effortless and animated, carried me from one page to the next without my noticing it. A clock struck off the hours in the silence of the shadows, and I heard nothing. My lamp began to run out of oil and produced only a pale light, but still I read on. I could not even take out time to raise the wick for fear of interrupting my pleasure. How those new ideas rushed into my brain! How my intelligence adopted them!

8.1 How does the passage reflect the immersive nature of reading Mercier?

8.2 Why did Mercier describe himself as a virtual writer?

8.3 How did reading influence Mercier's intellectual capacity and his engagement with new concepts? Explain any two points.

MAP SKILL-BASED QUESTION (2 Marks)

9. Two places A and B have been marked on the given outline map of India. Identify them and write their correct names on the lines drawn near them. **(1 + 1 = 2)**

(A) The place where the Indian National Congress session was held in Dec 1920.

(B) The place where Mahatma Gandhi broke Salt law.

SECTION - B

GEOGRAPHY (20 Marks)

10. Which of the following description of forest is **NOT** correct? **1**

(*a*) Reserved Forest -Reservation of more than half of forests

(*b*) Protected Forest- Reservation of 1/3 of the forests

(*c*) Unclassed Forest- other forest and wasteland belonging to both government and private individuals and communities.

(*d*) Permanent Forest-Reserved and unclassed forest for the production of Timber

11. Match the Column-I with Column-II and choose the correct option: **1**

	Column-I		Column-II
A.	Arid soil	I.	Red to brown in colour
B.	Alluvial soil	II.	Sand, silt and clay
C.	Red soil	III.	Crystalline igneous rocks
D.	Arid soil	IV.	Support deciduous & amp; evergreen forests

(*a*) A-I, B-II, C-III, D-IV. (*b*) A-II, B-I, C-IV., D-III

(*c*) A-IV., B-II, C-III, D-I (*d*) A-I, B-IV., C-II, D-III

12. Which state passed the first resolution for the Joint Forest Management Program? **1**

(*a*) Bihar (*b*) Jharkhand (*c*) Uttar Pradesh (*d*) Odisha

13. Suggest any two ways to conserve energy resources in India. **2**

14A. "A concerted effort has to be made in order to use mineral resources in a planned and sustainable manner." Suggest and explain any three measures. **3**

OR

14B. What are the uses of copper? Name the two leading copper producing states of India. **3**

15A. Manufacturing sector is considered as the backbone of general and economic development.' Examine the statement in the context of India. **5**

OR

15B. Explain the role of agro-based industries in the Indian economy. **5**

16. Read the given text and answer the following questions: (1 + 1 + 2 = 4) **4**

Dams were traditionally built to impound rivers and rainwater that could be used later to irrigate agricultural fields. Today, dams are built not just for irrigation but for electricity generation, water supply for domestic and industrial uses, flood control, recreation, inland navigation and fish breeding. Hence, dams are now referred to as multi-purpose projects where the many uses of the impounded water are integrated with one another. For example, in the Sutlej-Beas river basin, the Bhakra – Nangal project water is being used both for hydel power production and irrigation. Similarly, the Hirakud project in the Mahanadi basin integrates conservation of water with flood control. Multi-purpose projects, launched after Independence with their integrated water resources management approach, were thought of as the vehicle that would lead the nation to development and progress, overcoming the handicap of its colonial past. Jawaharlal Nehru proudly proclaimed the dams as the 'temples of modern India'; the reason being that it would integrate development of agriculture and the village economy with rapid industrialisation and growth of the urban economy.

16.1 What are some of the uses of dams mentioned in the passage?

16.2 Explain how the Bhakra-Nangal project in the Sutluj-Beas river basin is an example of a multi-purpose project.

16.3 Why are dams referred to as multi-purpose projects?

MAP SKILL-BASED QUESTION (3 Marks)

17. On the same outline map of India locate and label the following with suitable symbols: **1**

I. (*p*) The longest dam in India, built across the Mahanadi River in Odisha for flood control and irrigation.

OR

(*q*) The dam built across the Tungabhadra River, a tributary of Krishna, providing irrigation to Karnataka and Andhra Pradesh.

II. Any two of the following: **(1 × 2 = 2)**

(*i*) Bhilai Steel Plant

(*ii*) Noida Software Technology Park

(*iii*) Bengaluru Software Technology Park

SECTION - C

POLITICAL SCIENCE (20 Marks)

18. Consider the following statements regarding power-sharing arrangements in Belgium and identify the incorrect one from the following: **1**

(*i*) Equal number of members from dutch and french communities in the central government.

(*ii*) Separate government for brussels with equal representation of communities.

(*iii*) The State government is subordinate to the central government.

(*iv*) Community government elected by people belonging to one language community.

(*a*) (*i*) and (*ii*) (*b*) Only (*iv*) (*c*) Only (*iii*) (*d*) (*i*), (*ii*) and (*iv*)

19. Which one of the following subjects comes under the legislation of the Centre and State in India? **1**

(*a*) Education (*b*) Police (*c*) Banking (*d*) Trade

20. Which of the following statement is true regarding Feminist Movements? **1**

(*a*) A group which favors giving more power to working women at the rural and urban levels.

(*b*) A movement that believes in giving exclusive rights to females in urban areas.

(*c*) Radical women's movements aimed at equality in personal and family life as well.

(*d*) It is the practice of placing a feminine and masculine point of view in decision-making.

21. Match the **Column-I** with **Column-II** and choose the correct option: 1

Column-I (List)		Column-II (Jurisdiction Sphere)	
I.	Union list subjects	A.	State Government alone make laws on it
II.	State list subjects	B.	For uniformity Central Government Legislates on it
III.	Concurrent subjects	C.	Subjects under Jurisdiction of Centre and State Government
IV.	Residuary subjects	D.	Central Government legislates on new subjects

(*a*) I-A, II-B, III-C, IV-D (*b*) I-C, II-D, III-A, IV-B

(*c*) I-D, II-C, III-B, IV-A (*d*) I-B, II-A, III-C, IV-D

22. There are two statements marked as Assertion (A) and Reason (R). Mark your answer as per the codes provided below: **1**

Assertion (A): Democracy is an accountable, responsive, and legitimate government

Reason (R): Democracies have regular, free and fair elections and decision-making is based on norms and procedures

(*a*) Both A and R are true and R is the correct explanation of A.

(*b*) Both A and R are true but R is not the correct explanation of A.

(*c*) A is true, but R is false.

(*d*) A is false, but R is true.

23. Analyse the map and answer the question by choosing the correct option: **1**

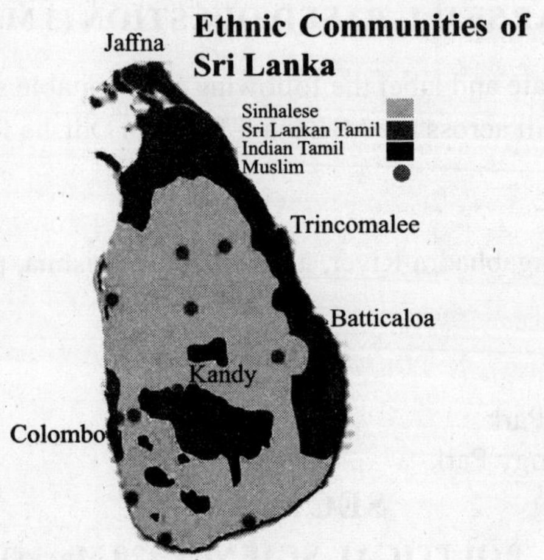

Which religion is followed by the majority in the Sri-Lanka?

(*a*) Hinduism (*b*) Islam (*c*) Buddhism (*d*) Christian

24A. Define majoritarianism. **2**

OR

24B. Why did the feeling of alienation develop among the Sri-Lankan Tamils? **2**

25. Suggest any three measures to enhance the participation of women in politics. **3**

26A. What functions do political parties perform in India? **5**

OR

26B. Identify the national political party that draws its inspiration from India's ancient culture and values. List four characteristics of that party. **5**

27. Read the given text and answer the following questions: (1 + 1 + 2 = 4) **4**

The Belgian leaders recognised the existence of regional differences and cultural diversities. Between 1970 and 1993, they amended their constitution four times so as to work out an arrangement that would enable everyone to live together within the same country. The arrangement they worked out is different from any other country and is very innovative. Here are some of the elements of the Belgian model:

The Constitution prescribes that the number of Dutch and French-speaking ministers shall be equal in the central government. Some special laws require the support of the majority of members from each linguistic group.

Many powers of the central government have been given to state governments of the two regions of the country. The state governments are not subordinate to the Central Government.

Brussels has a separate government in which both the communities have equal representation. The French-speaking people accepted equal representation in Brussels because the Dutch-speaking community has accepted equal representation in the Central Government.

Apart from the Central and the State Government, there is a third kind of government. This 'community government' is elected by people belonging to one language community – Dutch, French and German-speaking – no matter where they live. This government has the power regarding cultural, educational and language-related issues.

27.1 Why did the French-speaking people accept equal representation in Brussels?
27.2 Why do you think Belgian leaders felt the need to amend their constitution multiple times between 1970 and 1993?
27.3 What are some elements of the Belgian model mentioned in the passage?

SECTION - D

ECONOMICS (20 Marks)

28. The full form of IMR is **1**

(*a*) Indian Mortality Rate
(*b*) Infant Mortality Rate
(*c*) International Mortality Rate
(*d*) Infant Morbidity Rate

29. Inexpensive Chinese locks are flooding the Indian markets, thus destroying the traditional lock industry of India. Which of the following methods can the Government of India take up to protect the Indian lock industry? **1**

(i) Revalue Indian currency.
(ii) Give subsidies on the import of Chinese locks.
(iii) Impose an import tax on the import of Chinese locks.
(iv) Place a limit on the number of goods that can be imported.

(*a*) (i) and (iii)
(*b*) (i) and (iv)
(*c*) (ii) and (iv)
(*d*) (iii) and (iv)

30. Read the given data and answer the question that follows: **1**

States	Per Capita Income For 2018– 19 (in Rs)	Infant Mortality Rate per 1,000 live births (2018)	Literacy Rate % 2017–18	Net Attendance Ratio (per 100 persons) secondary stage (age 14 and 15 years) 2017–18
Haryana	2,36,147	30	82	61
Kerala	2,04,105	7	94	83
Bihar	40,982	32	62	43

Sources: Economic Survey 2020–21, P.A 157, National Sample Survey Organisation (Report No. 585), National statistical office, Government of India.

Based on the table provided above, which of the following statements are correct?

Statement-I: Bihar has the lowest per capita income among the three states.

Statement-II: Kerala has the highest literacy rate among the three states.

Statement-III: Haryana has the lowest infant mortality rate among the three states.

Statement-IV: Bihar has the highest net attendance ratio at the secondary stage among the three states.

Which of the following options is correct:

(*a*) Statment-I, II and III only
(*b*) Statement-I and II only
(*c*) Statement-II and IV only
(*d*) Statement-I, III and IV only

31. What might be a developmental goal for a girl from a rich urban family? **1**

(*a*) Equal political rights
(*b*) Access to urban amenities
(*c*) As much freedom as her brother
(*d*) Higher per capita income

32. Fill in the blank: **1**

SECTOR	CRITERIA USED
Primary, Secondary & Tertiary	Nature of Economic activity
Organized & Unorganized	?

(*a*) Nature of Employment activities

(*b*) Nature of Social activities

(*c*) Nature of Production activities

(*d*) Nature of Political activities

33. If the workers in the image succeed in their demands, what might be a possible outcome for the factory? **1**

(*a*) The factory might increase automation to reduce labor costs.

(*b*) The factory might expand to increase production.

(*c*) The factory might close down due to increased operational costs.

(*d*) The factory might start exporting more goods.

34. What is the role of MNCs in the process of Globalisation? Identify the appropriate statements among the following options: **1**

(i) MNCs control foreign trade.

(ii) MNCs are involved in foreign investments.

(iii) MNCs promote isolation between countries.

(iv) MNCs facilitate the integration of production and markets across countries.

Choose the correct option:

(*a*) Statements (i) and (ii) are appropriate.

(*b*) Statements (i), (ii) and (iv) are appropriate.

(*c*) All the statements are appropriate.

(*d*) Only statement (iv) is appropriate

35. Suggest any two ways that the government can use to increase employment in the rural sector? **2**

36. "Banks are an efficient medium of exchange." Support the statement with arguments. **3**

37. How is the tertiary sector different from other sectors? Explain with examples. **3**

38A. How Self-Help Groups (SHGs) are important in rural society. Explain **5**

OR

38B. "Modern currency is accepted as a medium of exchange". Analyse the statement. **5**

MAP for Q. no. 9 (Section A) & Q. no. 17 (Section B)

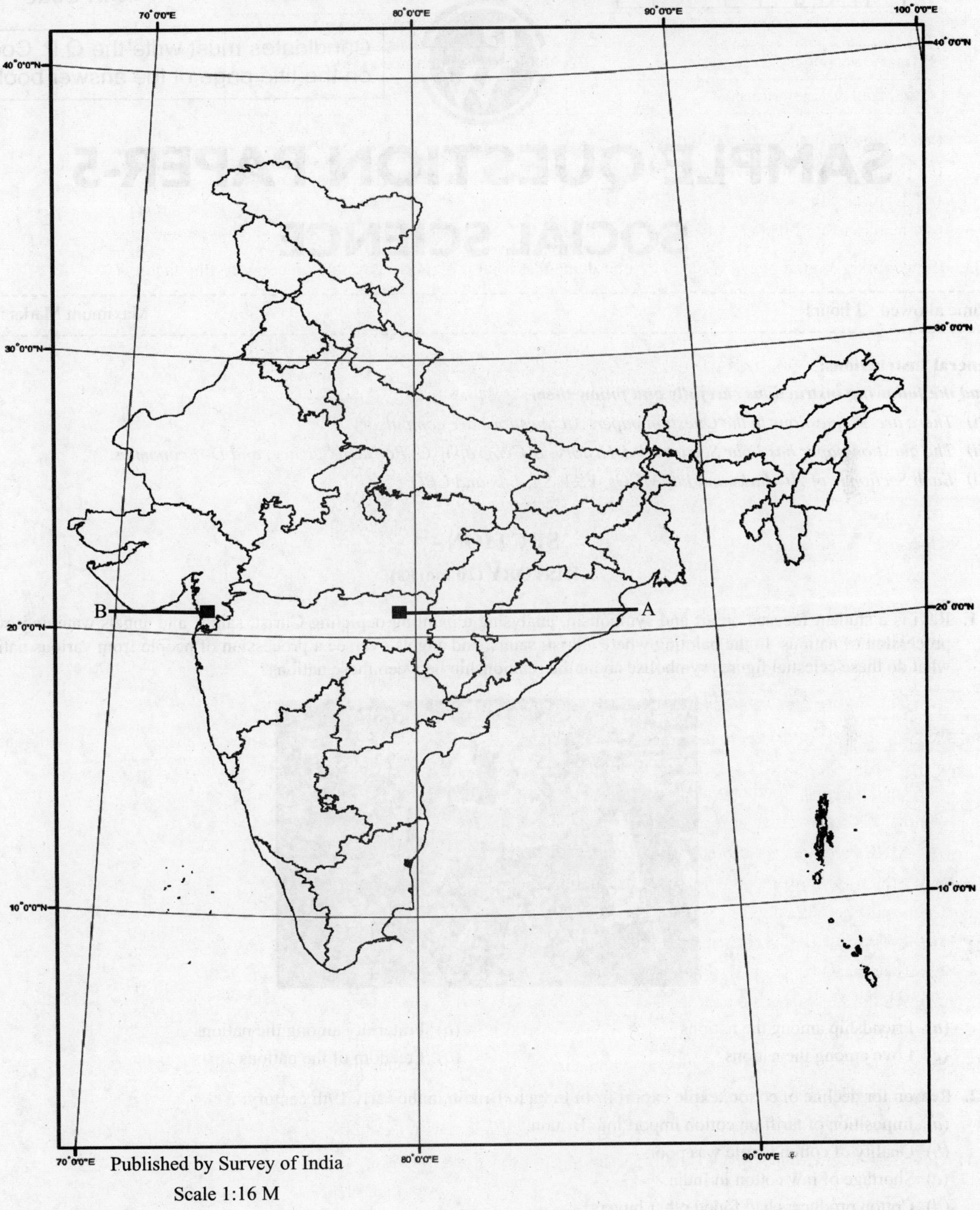

Roll No. | | | | | | | | |

Q.P. Code 05

Candidates must write the Q.P. Code on the title page of the answer book.

SAMPLE QUESTION PAPER-5

SOCIAL SCIENCE

Time allowed : 3 hours Maximum Marks : 80

General Instructions:

Read the following instructions carefully and follow them:

(i) There are 38 questions in the Question paper. All questions are compulsory.

(ii) The question paper has Four Sections – A-History, B-Geography C- Political Science, and D- Economics.

(iii) Each Section is of 20 Marks and has MCQs, VSA, SA, LAs and CBQ.

SECTION - A

HISTORY (20 marks)

1. Ravi is a student-focused on art and symbolism, analysing a painting depicting Christ, saints, and angels watching over a procession of nations. In the painting where Christ, saints, and angels oversee a procession of people from various nations, what do these celestial figures symbolise about the relationship between these nations? **1**

(*a*) Friendship among the nations (*b*) Fraternity among the nations

(*c*) Love among the nations (*d*) Freedom of the nations

2. Reason for decline of cotton textile export from India to Britain in the early 19th century: **1**

(*a*) Imposition of tariff on cotton import into Britain.

(*b*) Quality of cotton textile was poor.

(*c*) Shortage of raw cotton in India.

(*d*) Cotton producers had found other buyers.

3. The Indian masses willingly participated in the Civil Disobedience Movement despite the challenges faced during the Non-Cooperation Movement. Which of the following quotes BEST reflects the outlook of the masses? **1**

(*a*) 'The greatest glory in living lies not in never falling, but in rising every time we fall'

(*b*) 'An eye for an eye only ends up making the whole world blind'

(*c*) 'Injustice anywhere is a threat to justice everywhere'

(*d*) 'Obedience is the key to a peaceful society'

4. Match the **Column-I** with **Column-II** and choose the correct option from the following: **1**

	Column-I		Column-II
A.	Gita Govind	I.	B G Tilak
B.	Kesari	II.	Rammohan Roy
C.	Sambad Kaumudi	III.	Jaydev
D.	Chhote aur Bade ka Sawal	IV.	Kashibaba

Options:

(*a*) A-III, B-I, C-II, D-IV

(*b*) A-II, B-IV, C-III, D-I

(*c*) A-I, B-III, C-IV, D-II

(*d*) A-IV, B-II, C-I, D-III

5A. The First World War had ended with the defeat of Ottoman Turkey. There were rumors that a harsh peace treaty was going to be imposed on the Ottoman emperor—the spiritual head of the Islamic world (the Khalifa). To defend the Khalifa's temporal powers, a Khilafat Committee was formed in Bombay in March 1919. How did this event bring Muslims under the umbrella of a unified national movement? **2**

OR

5B. You are a historian tasked with creating an educational documentary on Mahatma Gandhi's Civil Disobedience Movement. One segment focuses on Gandhi's letter to Viceroy Irwin, dated January 31, 1930. Explain how Gandhi's demands in this letter addressed the interests of various classes in Indian society, such as peasants, industrialists, and workers. **2**

6. "The merchants and industrialists made a significant contribution to the Civil Disobedience Movement". In the light of the above statement, explain their role in the movement. **3**

7A. "Equality before law did not stand for universal suffrage in France after the revolution". Explain with suitable examples. **5**

OR

7B. Explain the conditions that were viewed as obstacles to economic exchange and growth by the new commercial classes. How did it end in 1834? **5**

8. Read the given text and answer the following questions: (1 + 1 + 2 = 4) **4**

Why Newspapers?

'Krishnaji Trimbuck Ranade inhabitant of Poona intends to publish a Newspaper in the Marathi Language with a view of affording useful information on every topic of local interest. It will be open for free discussion on subjects of general utility, scientific investigation and the speculations connected with the antiquities, statistics, curiosities, history and geography of the country and of the Deccan especially… the patronage and support of all interested in the diffusion of knowledge and Welfare of the People is earnestly solicited.' Bombay Telegraph and Courier, 6 January 1849 'The task of the native newspapers and political associations is identical to the role of the Opposition in the House of Commons in Parliament in England. That is of critically examining government policy to suggest improvements, by removing those parts that will not be to the benefit of the people, and also by ensuring speedy implementation. These associations ought to carefully study the particular issues, gather diverse relevant information on the nation as well as on what are the possible and desirable improvements, and this will surely earn it considerable influence.'

Native Opinion, 3 April 1870.

8.1. Analyse the primary objective proposed by Ranade for publishing Marathi Language newspaper.

8.2. Why did the Bombay Telegraph emphasize the role of newspaper in promoting welfare of Deccan region?

8.3. What were the key responsibilities attributed to native newspapers? Mention any two.

MAP SKILL-BASED QUESTION (2 Marks)

9. Two places **A** and **B** have been marked on the given outline map of India. **(1 + 1 = 2)**
Identify them and write their correct names on the lines drawn near them.

A. The place where Indian National Congress session was held in september, 1920.

B. The place where Mahatma Gandhi started first satyagraha.

SECTION - B

Geography (20 marks)

10. Two statements are given below. They are Assertion (A) and Reason (R) Read both the statements and choose the correct option. **1**

Assertion (A): Conservation of forests and wildlife is not essential for maintaining ecological balance.
Reason (R): Forests and wildlife provide essential ecosystem services such as carbon sequestration, soil conservation, water regulation, and climate regulation.

(*a*) Both, (A) and (R) are true and (R) is the correct explanation of (A)
(*b*) Both, (A) and (R) are true but (R) is not the correct explanation of (A)
(*c*) (A) is true but (R) is false.
(*d*) (A) is false but (R) is true.

11. Rajesh, a farmer in the northeastern region of India practices a traditional form of agriculture known as 'slash and burn'. He clears a new patch of forest every few years, cultivates it for a period, and then allows it to lie fallow to recover its fertility. How does Rajesh's method of farming impact the sustainability of his agricultural practices and the local ecosystem? **1**

(*a*) It enhances long-term soil fertility by continuous cultivation.
(*b*) It reduces the need for manual labour.
(*c*) It allows soil fertility to recover through natural processes when land is left fallow.
(*d*) It increases biodiversity through the introduction of new crops.

12. You are a consultant for an international coffee chain looking to source Arabica coffee from India due to its renowned quality. Your task is to identify the origin of Arabica coffee in India and determine the most suitable regions for its cultivation to ensure the best quality product for the chain. Which of the following statements accurately describes the historical introduction and current cultivation areas of Arabica coffee in India? **1**

(*a*) Arabica coffee was introduced from Brazil and is predominantly cultivated in Maharashtra, Gujarat, and Rajasthan.

(*b*) Arabica coffee was introduced from Ethiopia and is predominantly cultivated in Assam, West Bengal, and Odisha.

(*c*) Arabica coffee was introduced from Yemen and is predominantly cultivated in Karnataka, Kerala, and Tamil Nadu.

(*d*) Arabica coffee was introduced from Vietnam and is predominantly cultivated in Uttar Pradesh, Punjab, and Haryana.

13. Name any two fossil fuels used to generate thermal electricity. **2**

14A. Entrepreneur Meena is considering establishing a new industry, In Agrihub the area is known for its cotton production and skilled labour in traditional textile techniques. Meena envisions revitalizing the local textile industry by combining traditional skills with modern technology to cater to domestic and international markets. Alternatively, she is exploring the jute industry due to its export potential and success in neighbouring regions. What are the benefits and challenges Meena might face in developing a modernized cotton textile industry compared to starting a jute processing industry? **3**

OR

14B. In the town of Riverwood, which is situated near a large river and relies heavily on tourism and fishing, local leaders are concerned about the impact of a nearby power station on the river's health and the local economy. The power station is under pressure to implement sustainable practices that can reduce its environmental footprint while continuing to meet the energy demands of the growing population. Examine how the power station in Riverwood could implement the strategy of creating green belts and managing ash ponds to minimize its impact on the river's ecosystem. What are the expected benefits of these actions for the local community and environment? **3**

15A. Mr. Gautam, a city planner was tasked with addressing the water scarcity challenges in a rapidly urbanizing area that is also undergoing significant industrialization. The local government is considering expanding hydroelectric power facilities as part of the solution. Analyze the impact of industrialization and urbanization on water scarcity. Discuss the role of hydroelectric power in this context. **5**

OR

15B. Kushagra belongs to a rural family in arid Rajasthan. His community faces significant challenges in accessing clean water, primarily due to the region's dry climate and infrequent rainfall. The local government has introduced a rainwater harvesting project to help alleviate water scarcity. He and his family decided to implement this system in their home.

Explain how rainwater harvesting in Rajasthan adapts to its arid and semi-arid conditions and its impact on local households. **5**

16. Read the given text and answer the following questions: (1 + 2 + 1 = 4) **4**

Narmada Bachao Andolan or Save Narmada Movement is a Non-Governmental Organisation (NGO) that mobilized tribal people, farmers, environmentalists and human rights activists against the Sardar Sarovar Dam being built across the Narmada river in Gujarat. It originally focused on the environmental issues related to trees that would be submerged under the dam water. Recently it has re-focused the aim to enable poor citizens, especially the oustees (displaced people) to get full rehabilitation facilities from the government. People felt that their suffering would not be in vain and accepted the trauma of displacement believing in the promise of irrigated fields and plentiful harvests. So, often the survivors of Rihand told us that they accepted their sufferings as sacrifices for the sake of their nation. But now, after thirty bitter years of being adrift, their livelihood having even being more precarious, they keep asking: "Are we the only one chosen to make sacrifices for the nation?"

16.1. Why was the Sardar Sarovar Dam constructed?

16.2. Examine the tribal people's reasons for protesting.

16.3. Describe the issues that the "Save Narmada Movement" worked to resolve.

MAP SKILL-BASED QUESTION (3 Marks)

17. On the same outline map of India locate and label the following with suitable symbols: **1**

I. (*p*) The westernmost tidal port of India located in the Rann of Kachchh region.

OR

(*q*) The busiest port on the western coast, also the largest natural port in India.

II. Any two of the following: **(1 × 2 = 2)**

(*i*) The airport is located in the national capital of India.

(*ii*) The airport located in southern India, named after a former Prime Minister.

(*iii*) The longest dam in India, constructed on the Mahanadi River in Odisha, known for irrigation and flood control.

SECTION - C

POLITICAL SCIENCE (20 marks)

18. According to the infographic about party membership, which statement is correct about India's party membership trend from 1996 to 2004? **1**

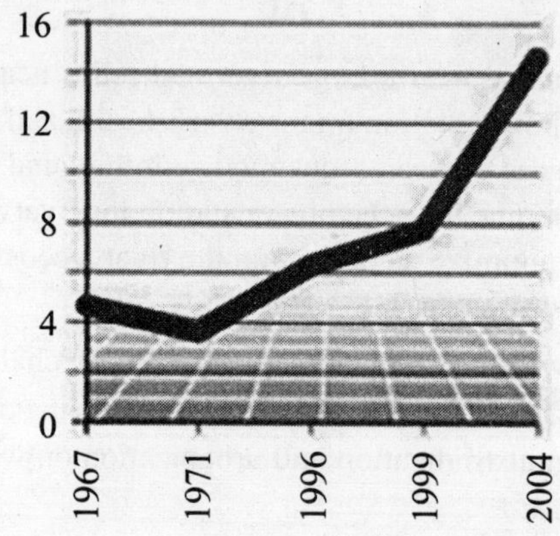

Fig. *Those who say they are member of a political party.*

(*a*) Party membership in India steadily declined.

(*b*) Party membership in India was constant throughout the years.

(*c*) Party membership in India increased.

(*d*) There is no available data for India's party membership between 1996 and 2004.

19. Analyse the map and answer the question that follows:

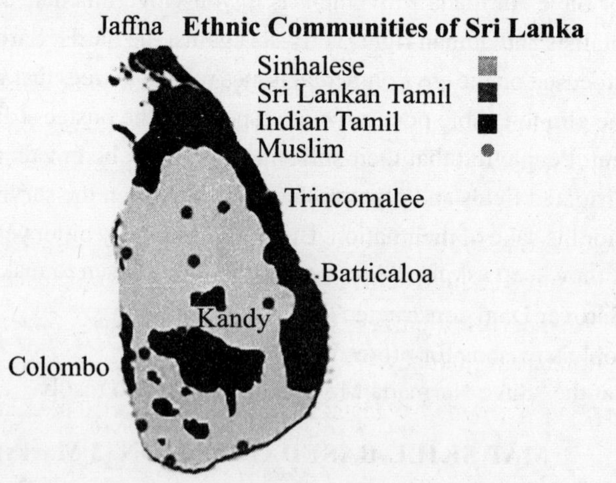

Which religion is followed by the majority in the Sri-Lanka? **1**

(*a*) Hinduism (*b*) Islam

(*c*) Buddhism (*d*) Christian

20. There are two statements marked as Assertion (A) and Reason (R). Mark your answer as per the codes provided below: **1**

Assertion (A): Women's political participation is crucial for achieving gender equality in society.

Reason (R): Women's perspectives and experiences are often different from men's, and their inclusion in decision-making processes can lead to more equitable policies

(*a*) Both A and R are true, and R is the correct explanation of A.

(*b*) Both A and R are true, but R is not the correct explanation of A.

(*c*) A is true, but R is false

(*d*) A is false, but R is true

21. The Constitution of India provides for a division of power between the Union and the States enumerated in three lists. Based on the division of subjects in the lists, Identify the ones that are correctly matched. **1**

(*i*) Defence and Banking - Union List

(*ii*) Police and Commerce - State list

(*iii*) Forest and Trade Unions - Concurrent list

(*iv*) Artificial intelligence - State list

Choose the correct option:

(*a*) (*i*) and (*ii*) (*b*) (*i*), (*ii*) and (*iii*) (*c*) (*i*), (*iii*) and (*iv*) (*d*) (*i*), (*ii*), (*iii*) and (*iv*)

22. Which outcome of democracy is most critically highlighted by the cartoon "Governmental Secrecy", and what does it suggest about the relationship between the government and its citizens? **1**

Governmental Secrecy

(*a*) The cartoon suggests that democracies are completely transparent, with no secrecy between the government and its citizens, ensuring full accountability.

(*b*) The cartoon indicates that democracies are highly efficient in sharing all information with citizens, thus eliminating any form of secrecy.

(*c*) The cartoon highlights that despite the principles of democracy, there is often a significant gap in transparency, with the government knowing much more about its citizens than the citizens know about governmental activities.

(*d*) The cartoon shows that in democracies, citizens have more information about the government than the government has about them, ensuring complete transparency.

23. What are the factors that have contributed to changes in the caste system in modern India? **1**

A. Urbanization

B. Occupational mobility

C. Growth of literacy and education

D. Weakening of the position of landlords in the villages

(*a*) Only A and B (*b*) A, B, and C (*c*) Only D (*d*) A, B, C, and D

24. A party has won the following percentage of seats in the 4 states where it has contested in the state legislative assembly election.

State	% of Votes Won	No of Seats Won
State A	19	10
State B	16	4
State C	35	42
State D	7	1

The party has not won any Lok Sabha seats.

(*i*) What type of political party will it be classified as? Why? **1**

(*ii*) Can it be classified as a national party? Justify your answer. **1**

25. In the fictitious democratic state of Lokapur, the election for the local Panchayat has brought several events into the limelight. One such issue is the auctioning of Panchayat positions to the highest bidder, as reported by the local news. This controversial practice has sparked a debate on the integrity of democratic processes at the grassroots level. Furthermore, the state has seen a remarkable election where over 1 million women have been elected to Panchayats, signaling a shift towards gender inclusivity in local governance. On the following developments in Lokapur, discuss their implications for the democratic process and local governance. **3**

26A. "Democracy promotes the dignity and freedom of the people." Justify the statement. **5**

OR

26B. "Democracy has failed to reduce economic inequality and poverty." Do you agree? Give arguments in support of your answer. **5**

27. Read the given text and answer the following questions: (1 + 1 + 2 = 4) **4**

Power sharing arrangements can also be seen in the way political parties, pressure groups and movements control or influence those in power. In a democracy, the citizens must have freedom to choose among various contenders for power. In contemporary democracies, this takes the form of competition among different parties. Such competition ensures that power does not remain in one hand. In the long run, power is shared among different political parties that represent different ideologies and social groups. Sometimes this kind of sharing can be direct, when two or more parties form an alliance to contest elections. If their alliance is elected, they form a coalition government and thus share power. In a democracy, we find interest groups such as those of traders, businessmen, industrialists, farmers and industrial workers. They also will have share in governmental power, either through participation in governmental committees or bringing influence on the decision-making process.

27.1. "Power sharing is an essential component of democracy". Support the statement with an example.

27.2. How does forming alliances show power-sharing?

27.3. How do political parties, pressure groups, and movements help restrict or influence those in positions of authority?

SECTION - D

ECONOMICS (20 marks)

28. Which of the following pairs is correctly matched? **1**

(*a*) Primary sector - Money lender

(*b*) Secondary sector - Priest

(*c*) Tertiary sector - Bank

(*d*) Manufacturing sector - Gardener

29. Look at the picture given below. What should not be the developmental goals for such an area? **1**

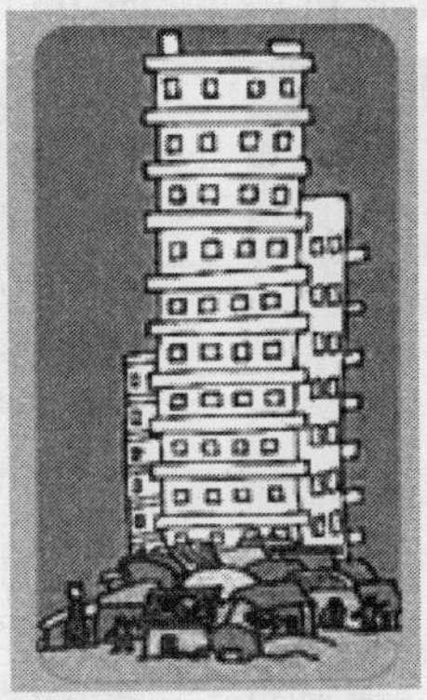

(*a*) Availability of loans for constructing pucca houses with their own toilets.

(*b*) Ownership of the MNCs built adjacent to the colony

(*c*) Availability of municipal services like water, electricity, and sanitation.

(*d*) Medical facilities like dispensaries in the locality.

30. Read the information given below and select the correct option. Rohan has taken a loan of ₹ 5 lakh from the bank to purchase a house at 12% rate of interest. He has to submit papers for the new house and his salary record to the bank. What is this process called? **1**

(*a*) Interest Rate (*b*) Collateral (*c*) Principal Amount (*d*) Installments

31. Globalisation is the increasing interconnectedness of the world through the flow of goods, services, capital, ideas, and people. Which of the following examples represents globalisation? **1**

(*a*) an online advertising portal for goods sold by local vendors run by the Indian government

(*b*) an IKEA store in Bengaluru selling products manufactured in China

(*c*) a traditional Vietnamese market selling handicrafts in Hanoi

(*d*) a Sunday market selling groceries produced locally

32. Imagine a scenario where the Indian government revises its policy to re-introduce tariffs on electronic goods to boost local manufacturing. As a result, international brands like Samsung and Apple face higher costs to sell their products in India, prompting them to consider setting up more manufacturing units within the country. What is likely the most immediate impact of the Indian government reintroducing tariffs on imported electronic goods? **1**

(*a*) Decrease in the variety of electronic goods available in Indian markets.

(*b*) Increase in the prices of imported electronic goods, making them less competitive.

(*c*) Increase in unemployment rates due to reduced imports.

(*d*) Decrease in the quality of electronic goods available.

33. Read the following data and select the appropriate option from the following. **1**

Educational Achievement of Rural Population of Uttar Pradesh		
Category	**Male**	**Female**
Literacy rate for the rural population	76%	54%
Literacy rate for rural children in the age group 10-14 years	90%	87%
Percentage of rural children aged 10-14 attending school	85%	82%

How much percentage of girls are not attending school?

(*a*) 82% (*b*) 15% (*c*) 13% (*d*) 18%

34. Observe the graph given below and answer the following question based on it:

Share of Sectors in Employment (%)

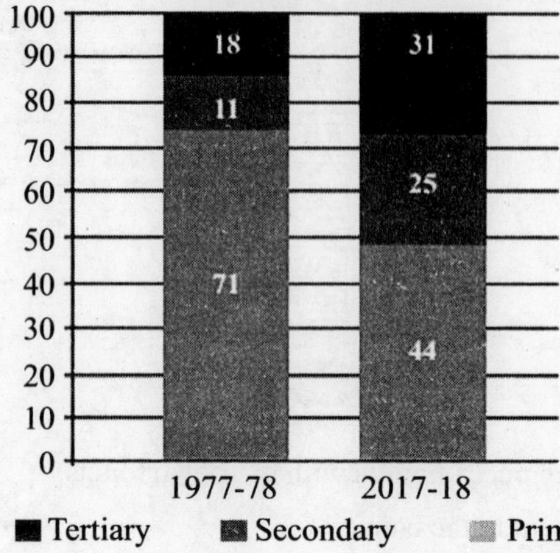

What can be inferred about the economic structure changes in India from 1977-78 to 2017-18? **1**

(*a*) The economy has become less diversified

(*b*) There is an increase in employment in high-skill sectors

(*c*) The economy has regressed to less productive sectors

(*d*) There has been no significant change in the economy

35. AutoTech, a large multinational corporation, has chosen Marina, a small coastal town in India, as the site for its new car manufacturing plant. This decision is influenced by several strategic benefits, such as access to international markets in Southeast Asia and Africa, the introduction of advanced technology, and the creation of job opportunities for the local population. Evaluate how the influx of foreign investment from AutoTech could transform the local economy of Marina. **2**

36. "All the services of the 'service sector' are not growing equally well." Evaluate the statement. **3**

37. Two families in a village—one wealthy and the other of modest means—both need to borrow money for agricultural activities. The wealthier family easily secures a loan from a formal banking institution, while the poorer family struggles to find a reliable lender and ends up borrowing from an informal source with higher interest rates. Analyze the reasons behind the disparity in access to formal sector credit between these two families. **3**

38A. Three friends from different states—Rohan from Haryana, Maya from Kerala, and Aman from Bihar—are discussing the progress of their respective home states. They consider factors like infant mortality rate, literacy rate, and net attendance ratio at the secondary stage. Each friend argues that their state is doing well in certain aspects while facing challenges in others others. Give a comparative analysis of these states on the basis of the factors- Infant mortality rate, literacy rate and net attendance ratio and overall development. **5**

Some comparative data on Haryana, Kerala and Bihar

State	Infant Mortality Rate per 1,000 live births (2018)	Literacy Rate % 2017-18	Net Attendance Ration (per 100 persons) secondary stage (age 14 and 15 years) 2017-18
Haryana	30	82	61
Kerala	7	94	83
Bihar	32	62	43

Source: Economic survey 2020-21, PA 157, National Sample Survey Organisation (Report No. 585). National statistical office, Government of India.

OR

38B. Kerala, with lower per capita income has a better human development ranking than Haryana. Hence, per capita income is not a useful criterion at all and should not be used to compare states. Do you agree? Give reasons in support of your answer. **5**

MAP for Q. no. 9 (Section A) & Q. no. 17 (Section B)

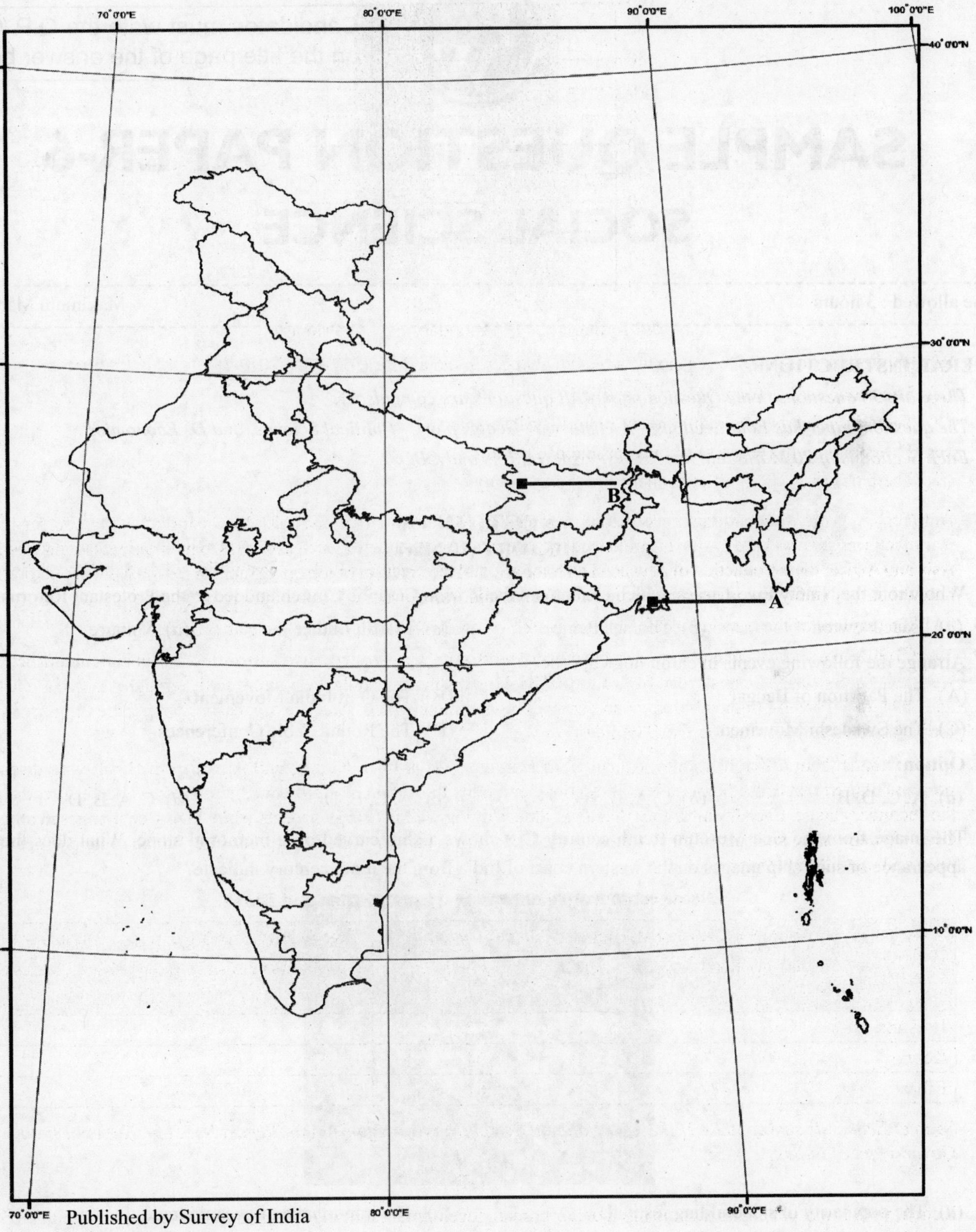

Published by Survey of India

Scale 1:16 M

Roll No. | | | | | | | | |

Q.P. Code 06

Candidates must write the Q.P. Code on the title page of the answer book.

SAMPLE QUESTION PAPER-6

SOCIAL SCIENCE

Time allowed : 3 hours Maximum Marks : 80

GENERAL INSTRUCTIONS:

(i) There are 38 questions in the Question paper. All questions are compulsory.

(ii) The question paper has Four Sections – A-History, B-Geography C- Political Science, and D- Economics.

(iii) Each Section is of 20 Marks and has MCQs, VSA, SA, LAs and CBQ.

SECTION - A
HISTORY (20 Marks)

1. Who wrote the Ninety Five Theses, which challenged the Roman Catholic Church and led to the Protestant Reformation? 1

(*a*) Isaac Newton (*b*) Thomas Paine (*c*) Martin Luther (*d*) Voltaire

2. Arrange the following events in chronological order: 1

(A) The Partition of Bengal (B) The Quit India Movement

(C) The Swadeshi Movement (D) The Round Table Conferences

Option:

(*a*) A, C, D, B (*b*) C, A, D, B (*c*) A, C, B, D (*d*) C, A, B, D

3. The image from the Goa Museum (tenth century CE) shows a ship carved on a memorial stone. What does the regular appearance of such ship images on the western coast of India from the ninth century indicate? 1

(*a*) The popularity of shipbuilding festivals (*b*) The importance of oceanic trade

(*c*) The decline of river transport (*d*) The use of ships only for warfare

4. Arrange the following in chronological order and choose the correct option: **1**

A. Napoleonic wars
B. The Treaty of Vienna
C. Greek Struggle for Independence
D. Slav Nationalism in Ottoman Empire

(*a*) (C), (B), (A) and (D) (*b*) (A), (B), (C) and (D) (*c*) (D), (C), (B) and (A) (*d*) (D), (B), (C) and (A)

5A. "Food offers many examples of long distance cultural exchange." Explain. **2**

OR

5B. Analyze food's role in the early stages of globalization using specific instances. **2**

6A. How had the Imperial State in China been the major producer of printed material for a long time? Explain with examples. **3**

OR

6B. How had the printing press created a new culture of reading in Europe? Explain with examples. **3**

7A. How did ideas of national unity in early nineteenth century Europe allied to the ideology of liberalism? Explain. **5**

OR

7B. How did Greek war of independence mobilise nationalist feelings among the educated elite across Europe? Explain. **5**

8. Read the given text and answer the following questions: (1 + 1 + 2 = 4) **4**

Nationalism spreads when people begin to believe that they are all part of the same nation when they discover some unity that binds them together. This sense of collective belonging came partly through the experience of united struggles. But there were also a variety of cultural processes through which nationalism captured people's imagination. History and fiction, folklore and songs, popular prints and symbols, all played a part in the making of nationalism. The identity of the nation is most often symbolised in a figure or image. This helps create an image with which people can identify the nation. It was in the twentieth century, with the growth of nationalism, that the identity of India came to be visually associated with the image of Bharat Mata.

8.1 Who portrayed Bharat Mata as an ascetic figure?

8.2 The French replaced the former royal standard with a new flag as a step to create a sense of collective identity among the French people. What similar steps did Indians take?

8.3 With reference to the context given above, acknowledge the contribution of Bankim Chandra Chattopadhyay in infusing the sense of nationalism.

MAP SKILL-BASED QUESTION (2 Marks)

9. Two places **A** and **B** have been marked on the given outline map of India. Identify them and write their correct names on the lines drawn near them. **(1 + 1 = 2)**

A. The place where Indian National Congress session was held in December, 1920.
B. The place associated with Cotton Mill Workers Satyagraha.

SECTION - B
GEOGRAPHY (20 Marks)

10. Which of the following types of erosion is most likely being shown in the given image?
(Hint: This erosion cuts deep channels or narrow valleys in the land after heavy rainfall.) **1**

(*a*) Sheet Erosion (*b*) Gully Erosion (*c*) Wind Erosion (*d*) None of the above

11. Match the **Column-I** with **Column-II** and choose the correct option from the following: **1**

Column-I (River)		**Column-II (Dam)**	
A.	Mahanadi	(I)	Sardar Sarovar
B.	Narmada	(II)	Hirakud
C.	Chambal	(III)	Salal
D.	Chenab	(IV)	Rana Pratap Sagar

(*a*) A-(IV), B-(III), C-(II), D-(I)
(*b*) A-(III), B-(IV), C-(I), D-(II)
(*c*) A-(II), B-(I), C-(IV), D-(III)
(*d*) A-(I), B-(II), C-(III), D-(IV)

12. In Mumbai, Maharashtra, Sunita observes that despite industrial advancement, the local river systems are heavily polluted. What is the most probable cause of this pollution? **1**

(*a*) Agricultural runoff
(*b*) Industrial waste
(*c*) Natural soil leaching
(*d*) Excessive rainfall

13. Lakshmi, a farmer in the coastal region of Odisha, notices the soil in her fields retains moisture well, aiding in paddy cultivation. Which type of soil is most likely found in her fields? **1**

(*a*) Black Soil
(*b*) Laterite Soil
(*c*) Alluvial Soil
(*d*) Arid Soil

14. Match the Column-I with Column-II and choose the correct option:
A geography teacher is explaining the distribution of soil types and theri agricultural uses in India to her class. **1**

Column-I (Soil Type)		**Column-II (Predominant Use)**	
A.	Black Soil	(I)	Tea and Coffee Plantation
B.	Alluvial Soil	(II)	Cotton Cultivation
C.	Red Soil	(III)	Rice and Wheat Cultivation
D.	Lateritc Soil	(IV)	Cashew Nut Cultivation

(*a*) A-(II), B-(III), C-(I), D-(IV)
(*b*) A-(II), B-(III), C-(IV), D-(I)
(*c*) A-(III), B-(II), C-(I), D-(IV)
(*d*) A-(II), B-(I), C-(III), D-(IV)

15. How does the presence of a wide variety of flora and fauna support human life and contribute significantly to essential services like food, water, air, and climate? **1**

(*a*) They provide food, water, and air quality regulation.
(*b*) They provide entertainment for humans.
(*c*) They are important for scientific research.
(*d*) They have no direct impact on human lives.

16. How do the specific geographical and climatic conditions of tropical and sub-tropical regions contribute to the successful cultivation of tea as an important beverage crop in India? **2**

17A. In the town of Neelkanth, there's a discussion about starting a new manufacturing project to boost local employment and economic growth. The town has access to a variety of raw materials, both agricultural and mineral. Local leaders, including Rohan and Amit, are debating whether to prioritize light industry or heavy industry for their new experience. They consider factors like local resources, capital investment, and the potential for export. The community is particularly interested in industries that could integrate well with the existing local agricultural base, yet could potentially transform into a key industry supplying materials to other sectors.
Evaluate the potential benefits and challenges Neelkanth would face if it chose to develop a heavy industry based on local mineral resources versus a light industry utilizing local agricultural products. Analyze which type of industry might be more sustainable in the long term and support the overall economic development of Neelkanth. **5**

OR

17B. Explain the reasons for concentration of iron and steel industries in and around Chotanagpur region. **5**

18. Read the given text and answer the following questions: (1 + 1 + 2 = 4) 4

The Jharia coal fire catastrophe is a severe environmental and humanitarian crisis affecting one of India's major coal-producing areas. For years, uncontrollable underground fires have been burning in Jharia, posing significant health and safety risks to the local population. The government has recognized the urgency of the situation and has decided to relocate the residents of Jharia to safer areas. This decision involves substantial financial support for the evacuation and resettlement process.

The primary hazards associated with coal mining in Jharia include these persistent underground fires, which release toxic fumes and contribute to air and soil pollution. These fires have made the area uninhabitable, causing numerous health issues among the residents, such as respiratory problems and skin diseases. Furthermore, the mining conditions in Jharia have been deemed unsafe due to inadequate safety standards. Reports indicate that over 50% of the coal-belt mines in the region do not meet the basic safety requirements, leading to frequent accidents and loss of lives.

In addition to the human and environmental toll, the financial implications for the coal industry are significant. The Supreme Court has imposed a fine of Rs 300 crore on a major coal-producing company for environmental damages. This penalty underscores the necessity for stricter environmental regulations and compliance. It also highlights the financial burden that coal companies face when failing to adhere to safety and environmental standards.

18.1 What immediate action has the government decided to take in response to the coal fire catastrophe in Jharia?

18.2 What are the primary hazards associated with coal mining in Jharia, as mentioned in the articles?

18.3 What financial penalties have been imposed on coal units, and what are the implications of these penalties?

MAP SKILL-BASED QUESTION (3 Marks)

19. On the same outline map of India locate and label the following with suitable symbols: 1

I. (*p*) The major sea port located in Tamil Nadu, known for handling cargo like salt, coal, and fertilizers.

OR

(*q*) The coal mines situated in Neyveli, which provide fuel to nearby thermal power stations.

II. Any two of the following: **(1 x 2 = 2)**

(*i*) Durg Iron Ore Mine

(*ii*) Paradip Sea Port

(*iii*) Mayurbhanj Iron Ore Mine

SECTION - C

POLITICAL SCIENCE (20 Marks)

20. *The central government and regional governments share responsibilities. The regional governments have specific powers to legislate on local matters, while the central government handles national issues.*

Which form of power-sharing is practiced in the above statement? 1

(*a*) Vertical division of power-sharing

(*b*) Community Government

(*c*) Harizontal division of power-sharing

(*d*) Coalition Government

21. We felt that democracy was better because it: 1

(*i*) Promotes equality among citizens;

(*ii*) Enhances the dignity of the individual

Which of the above statements given above is/are correct?

(*a*) (*i*) only (*b*) (*ii*) only (*c*) Both (*i*) and (*ii*) (*d*) Neither (*i*) nor (*ii*)

22. *A democratic government in a multicultural society has successfully managed to maintain peace and harmony among different ethnic groups through inclusive policies.*

What key democratic principle is being demonstrated here? 1

(*a*) Economic development. (*b*) Military control.

(c) Social diversity accommodation. (*d*) Political instability.

23. Sri Lanka emerged as an independent country in which year? **1**

(*a*) 1948 (*b*) 1950 (*c*) 1952 (*d*) 1954

24. Describe the positive impact of casteism with regard to political expression. **2**

25. State two key aspects that democracy must provide? **2**

26. "*The promotion of gender equality in educational opportunities leads to increased political participation by women.*"

(*i*) What does the statement imply about the relationship between education and political participation among women? **2**

(*ii*) How does the promotion of gender equality in education represent a shift in societal norms? **1**

27A. Discuss the functions performed by the political parties in India. **5**

OR

27B. Describe the role of opposition parties in a democracy. **5**

28. Read the given text and answer the following questions: (1 + 1 + 2 = 4) **4**

Decentralisation in India

This new system of local government is the largest experiment in democracy conducted anywhere in the world. There are now about 36 lakh elected representatives in the panchayats and municipalities, etc., all over the country. This number is bigger than the population of many countries in the world. Constitutional status for local government has helped to deepen democracy in our country. It has also increased women's representation and voice in our democracy. At the same time, there are many difficulties. While elections are held regularly of Panchayats and people participate enthusiastically in it but meetings of gram sabhas are not held regularly.

28.1 Why is Indian decentralization considered the largest experiment in democracy?

28.2 Analyze how the constitutional status of local government has helped to deepen democracy in India.

28.3 Explain any two steps taken by the Indian Government for decentralization.

SECTION - D

Economics (20 Marks)

29. Match the **Column-I** with **Column-II** and choose the correct option from the following: **1**

	Column-I (Category of Person)		Column-II (Developmental Goals/Aspirations)
A.	Landless rural labourers	(I)	Availability of other sources of irrigation
B.	Prosperous farmers from Punjab	(II)	More days of work and better wages
C.	Farmers who depend only on rain for growing crops	(III)	Low prices food grains and cheap inputs like seeds
D.	A rural woman from a land owning family	(IV)	Education of children in english medium schools and earning from land by giving on rent

(*a*) A-(III), B-(II), C-(I), D-(IV) (*b*) A-(II), B-(III), C-(I), D-(IV)

(*c*) A-(I), B-(III), C-(IV), D-(I) (*d*) A-(I), B-(III), C-(II), D-(IV)

30. Rani, a resident of a rural village, wants to start a small business of making handicrafts. However, she lacks the necessary funds to buy raw materials and tools. **1**

She hears about Self-Help Groups (SHGs) and microcredit from a friend.

What is the primary objective of Self-Help Groups (SHGs)?

(*a*) Providing free education to rural communities

(*b*) Empowering women through collective savings and credit

(*c*) Promoting large-scale agricultural production

(*d*) Distributing free food to the needy

31. Which of the following has helped the most in the spread of production of services? **1**

(*a*) Automobile Sector (*b*) Call Centres

(*c*) Information and Technology Sector (*d*) Manufacturing Industry

32. Which of the following states has the lowest percentage of total households demanding MGNREGA work? **1**

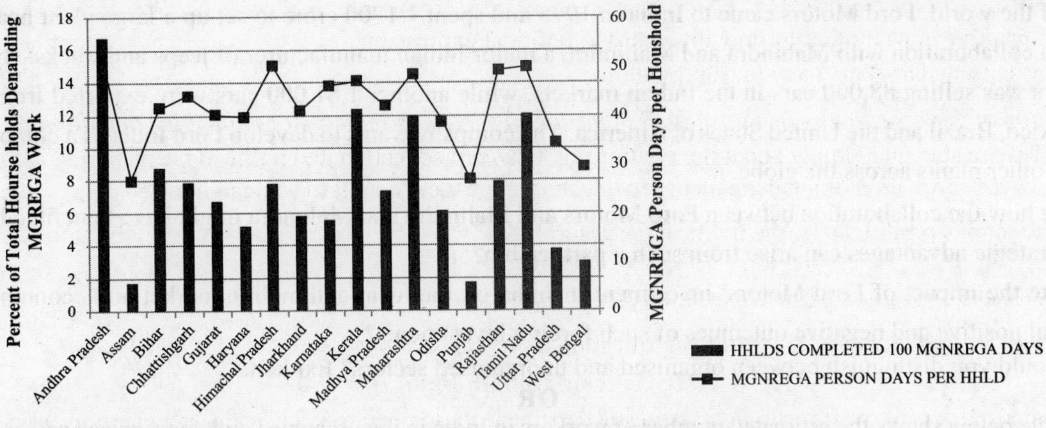

(*a*) Assam and West Bengal (*b*) Assam and Punjab

(*c*) Uttar Pradesh and West Bengal (*d*) Assam

33. ________ refers to some restrictions including tax on imports which government can use to increase or decrease foreign trade and to decide what kind of goods, how much of each, should come into the country. **1**

(*a*) Foreign Investment (*b*) Trade Barrier (*c*) Nationalisation (*d*) Liberalisation

34. Read the following data and answer the given question based on it: **1**

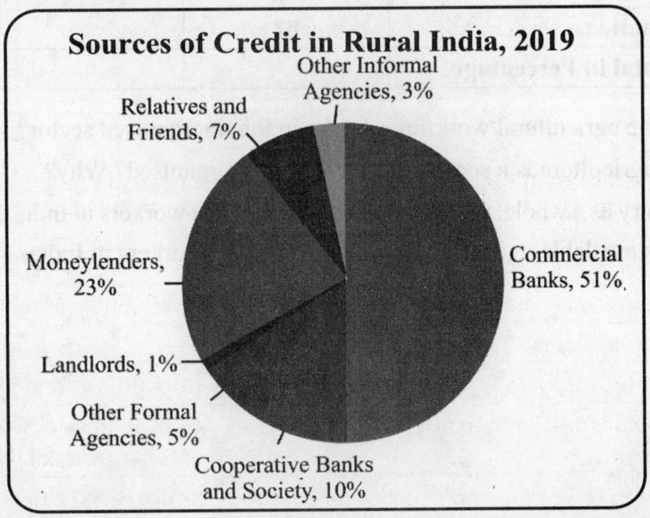

Which of the following best describes the reason why commercial banks are the largest source of credit in rural India?

(*a*) They provide the highest interest rates. (*b*) They offer easy access and lower interest rates.

(*c*) They have the smallest number of branches. (*d*) They are controlled by local landlords.

35. (*a*) Why do different persons have different notions of development? Which of the following explanations is more important and why? **3**

(*i*) Because people are different.

(*ii*) Because life situations of persons are different.

OR

(*b*) Why are developmental goals different for different people? Give examples to support your answer. **3**

36. In the wake of increasing financial irregularities reported in various small banks in India, a policy analyst at a leading think tank is tasked with assessing how the Indian government supervises the functioning of formal financial institutions to ensure their adherence to legal standards and protect the public interest. As a policy analyst, describe how the functioning of formal sources of loans, like banks and cooperatives, is supervised in India. Highlight the roles played by different regulatory bodies, such as the Reserve Bank of India (RBI), in maintaining oversight over these financial institutions. **3**

37. Ford Motors, an American company, is one of the world's largest automobile manufacturers with production spread over 26 countries of the world. Ford Motors came to India in 1995 and spent ₹ 1700 crore to set up a large plant near Chennai. This was done in collaboration with Mahindra and Mahindra, a major Indian manufacturer of jeeps and trucks. By the year 2017, Ford Motors was selling 88,000 cars in the Indian markets, while another 1,81,000 cars were exported from India to South Africa, Mexico, Brazil and the United States of America. The company wants to develop Ford India as a component supplying base for its other plants across the globe.

(*i*) Analyze how the collaboration between Ford Motors and Mahindra and Mahindra might have benefited both companies. What strategic advantages can arise from such a partnership? **1**

(*ii*) Evaluate the impact of Ford Motors' investment in India on the local automobile market and economy. What are the potential positive and negative outcomes of such foreign investments? **2**

38. (*a*) How would you distinguish between organised and unorganised sectors? Explain. **5**

OR

(*b*) The table below shows the estimated number of workers in India in the organised and unorganised sectors. Read the table carefully. Fill in the missing data and answer the questions that follow.

Workers In Different Sectors (In Millions)

Sector	Organised	Unorganised	Total
Primary	1		232
Secondary	41	74	115
Tertiary	40	88	128
Total	**82**		
Total in Percentage			**100%**

(*i*) What proportion of the agricultural workforce works in the unorganised sector? **1**

(*ii*) Do you believe that agriculture is a sector activity that is unorganised? Why? **2**

(*iii*) If we look at the country as a whole, we find that ——% of the workers in India are in the unorganised sector. Organised sector employment is available to only about ——% of the workers in India. **2**

Map for Q. no. 9 (Section A) & Q. no. 19 (Section B)

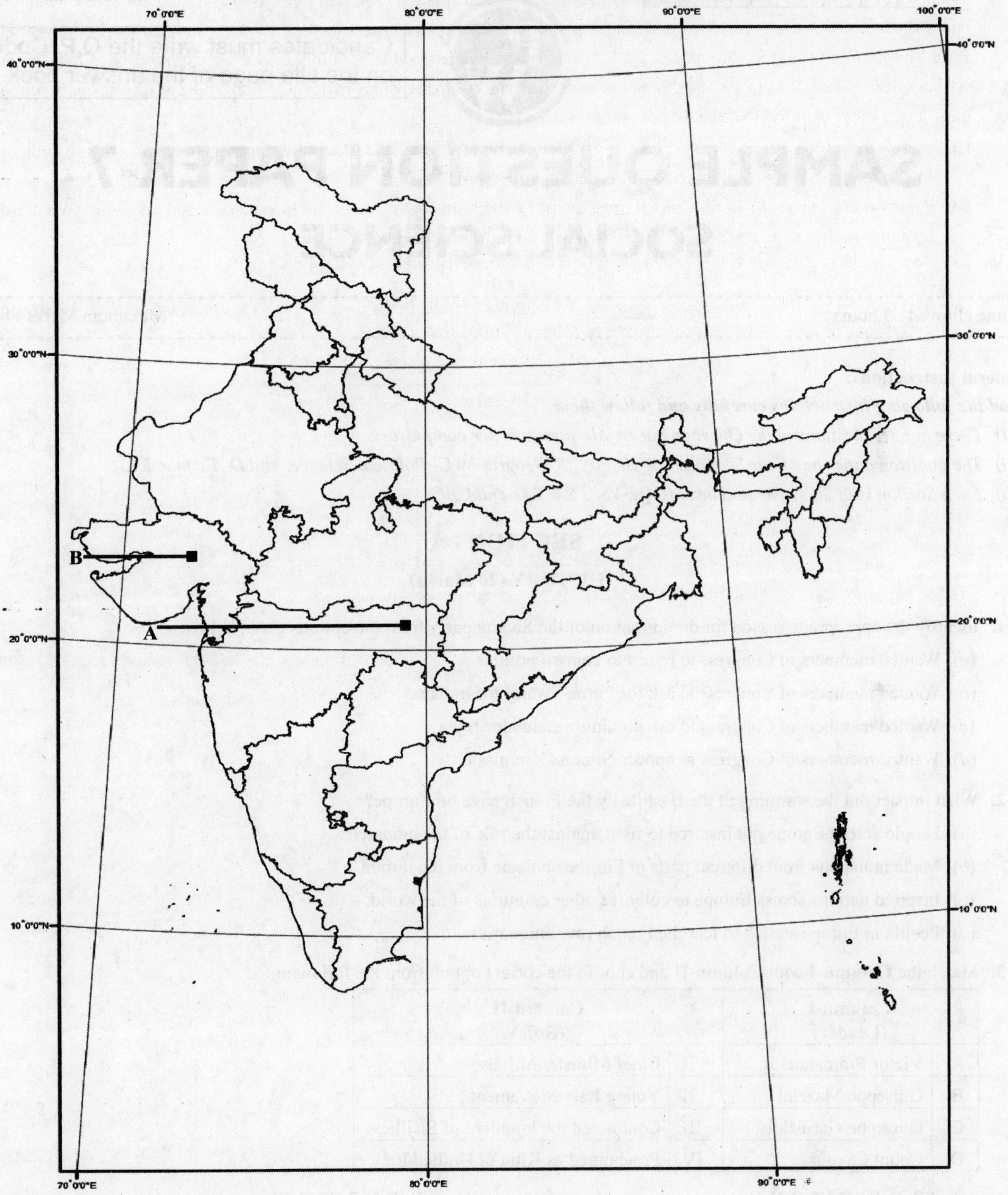

Roll No. | | | | | | | | |

Q.P. Code 07

Candidates must write the Q.P. Code on the title page of the answer book.

SAMPLE QUESTION PAPER-7

SOCIAL SCIENCE

Time allowed : 3 hours   Maximum Marks : 80

General Instructions:

Read the following instructions carefully and follow them:

(i) There are 38 questions in the Question paper. All questions are compulsory.

(ii) The question paper has Four Sections – A-History, B-Geography C- Political Science, and D- Economics.

(iii) Each Section is of 20 Marks and has MCQs, VSA, SA, LAs and CBQ.

SECTION - A

HISTORY (20 Marks)

1. Identify the appropriate reason for the formation of the Swaraj party from the options given below: 1

(*a*) Wanted members of Congress to return to council politics

(*b*) Wanted members of Congress to ask for Purna Swaraj for Indians

(*c*) Wanted members of Congress to ask dominion status for India

(*d*) Wanted members of Congress to oppose Simon Commission

2. What impact did the storming of the Bastille by the French have on Europe? 1

(*a*) People across Europe got inspired to fight against the rule of the monarch.

(*b*) Made monarchs from different parts of Europe abdicate from the throne.

(*c*) Inspired nations across Europe to colonize other countries of the world.

(*d*) People in Europe started to fear the French revolutionaries.

3. Match the **Column-I** with **Column-II** and choose the correct option from the following: 1

	Column-I (Leader)		Column-II (Role)
A.	Victor Emmanuel II	I.	Chief Minister of Italy
B.	Guiseppe Mazzini	II.	Young Italy Movement
C.	Guiseppe Garibaldi	III.	Conquered the kingdom of Sicillies
D.	Count Cavour	IV.	Proclaimed as King of Unified Italy

(*a*) A-I, B-IV, C-III, D-II

(*b*) A-II, B-I, C-IV, D-III

(*c*) A-IV, B-II, C-III, D-I

(*d*) A-I, B-IV, C-II, D-III

4. Look at the picture given below. Identify the name of the painter of this painting from the following options. **1**

(*a*) Raja Ravi Verma (*b*) Rabindra Nath Tagore

(*c*) Abanindranath Tagore (*d*) Samant Das Gupta

5A. Mention any two ways in which trade and cultural exchange took place across continents in the pre-modern world? **2**

OR

5B. "How did the introduction of new crops like potato impact people's lives in Europe during the pre-modern world? Give any two points." **2**

6A. "How did the spread of print culture in India contribute to the rise of nationalism? Explain with any three suitable examples." **3**

OR

6B. "The spread of print culture in India became an effective tool of resistance against colonial rule." Justify the statement with three suitable arguments or examples. **3**

7A. "Culture had played an important role in the development of nationalism in Europe during the 18th and 19th centuries". Support the statement with examples. **5**

OR

7B. Describe any three the steps taken by the French revolutionaries to create a sense of collective identity amongst the French people. **5**

8. Read the given text and answer the following questions: (1 + 1 + 2 = 4) **4**

Gutenberg was the son of a merchant and grew up on a large agricultural estate. From his childhood, he had seen wine and olive presses. Subsequently, he learnt the art of polishing stones, became a master goldsmith, and also acquired the expertise to create lead moulds used for making trinkets. Drawing on this knowledge, Gutenberg adapted existing technology to design his innovation. The olive press provided the model for the printing press, and moulds were used for casting the metal types for the letters of the alphabet. By 1448, Gutenberg perfected the system. The first book he printed was the Bible. About 180 copies were printed and it took three years to produce them. By the standards of the time, this was fast production. The new technology did not entirely displace the existing art of producing books by hand. In fact, printed books at first closely resembled the written manuscripts in appearance and layout. The metal letters imitated the ornamental handwritten styles. Borders were illuminated by hand with foliage and other patterns, and illustrations were painted. In the books printed for the rich, space for decoration was kept blank on the printed page. Each purchaser could choose the design and decide on the painting school that would do the illustrations.

8.1 What was the major drawback of new technology?

8.2 Which previous knowledge did Gutenberg draw on to design his innovation in the form of a printing press?

8.3 Write two features of the first book printed by Gutenberg.

MAP SKILL BASED QUESTIONS (2 Marks)

9. Two places **A** and **B** have been marked on the given outline map of India. Identify them and write their correct names on the lines drawn near them. **(1 + 1 = 2)**

A. The place where Indian National Congress session was held in December, 1920.

B. The place associated with calling off the Non-Cooperation Movement.

SECTION - B

Geography (20 Marks)

10. Considering the multi-purpose Sardar Sarovar Dam, which river's basin has been developed for irrigation, drinking water supply, and hydroelectric power generation under this project? **1**

(*a*) Ganga (*b*) Godavari (*c*) Mahanadi (*d*) Narmada

11. The image shows an indigenous irrigation technique that uses bamboo channels to transport water from hill springs to farms. In which Indian region is this eco-friendly method widely practised? **1**

(*a*) Western Ghats (*b*) Eastern Himalayas

(*c*) Western Rajasthan (*d*) Meghalaya

12. Read the following features of a soil and name the related soil: **1**

(*i*) It soil is ideal for growing cotton
(*ii*) Also called regur soil
(*iii*) Well known for its capacity to hold moisture.

(*a*) Black soil (*b*) Alluvial soil (*c*) Laterite soil (*d*) Red soil

13. The image shows a one-horned rhinoceros, an endangered species protected in its natural habitat. In which of the following Indian national parks is this animal primarily found? **1**

(*a*) Jim Corbett National Park (*b*) Kaziranga National Park

(*c*) Gir Forest National Park (*d*) Sunderbans National Park

14. Ankur, a resident from Rajasthan, decided to install a submerisble water pump in his house, capable of extracting groundwater from depths of 250-300 m. This practice of installign similar pumps is becoming increasingly popular across the state. Which of teh following will this growing practice MOST LIKELY lead to in the near future? **1**

(*a*) Decline in the groundwater quality

(*b*) Reduced monsoon water resources

(*c*) Increased number of waterborne diseases

(*d*) Water scarcity resulting from excessive utilization

15. In Bhakra – Nangal project water is being used for: **1**

(*i*) Hydel power production

(*ii*) Irrigation

(*iii*) Transportation

(*iv*) Cleaning

(*a*) (*i*) and (*iv*) (*b*) (*ii*) and (*i*)

(*c*) Only (*iii*) (*d*) Only (*ii*)

16. In what ways does excessive irrigation contribute to land degradation in Punjab? Explain any two factors. **2**

17A. Priya is preparing a presentation on India's economic strengths for her school's annual fest. While researching, she finds that manufacturing industries are called the "backbone of the economy."

Justify this statement by highlighting any five ways manufacturing supports India's economic development. **5**

OR

17B. Tanmay is preparing a research project on India's manufacturing strengths. While studying, he comes across data highlighting the vast scale of India's chemical industry.

Can you help Tanmay understand the present status of the chemical industry in India and its key features? **5**

18. Read the text carefully and answer the following questions: (1 + 2 + 1 = 4) **4**

In the 1960s and 1970s, conservationists demanded a national wildlife protection programme. The Indian Wildlife (Protection) Act was implemented in 1972, with various provisions for protecting habitats. An All-India list of protected species was also published. The thrust of the programme was towards protecting the remaining population of certain endangered species by banning hunting, giving legal protection to their habitats, and restricting trade in wildlife. Subsequently, central and many state governments established national parks and wildlife sanctuaries about which you have already studied. The central government also announced several projects for protecting specific animals, which were gravely threatened, including the tiger, the one-horned rhinoceros, the Kashmir stag or hangul, three types of crocodiles freshwater crocodile, saltwater crocodile and the Gharial, the Asiatic lion, and others. Most recently the Indian elephant, black buck (chinkara), the great Indian bustard (godawan) and the snow leopard, etc, have been given full or partial legal pro-tection against hunting and trade throughout India

18.1 What is the purpose of the Indian Wildlife (Protection) Act of 1972?

18.2 Name two specific animals that have been given full or partial legal protection under this Act.

18.3 How have central and state governments contributed to wildlife conservation since the implementation of the Wildlife Protection Act? Explain with an example.

MAP SKILL BASED QUESTIONS (3 Marks)

19. On the same outline map of India locate and label the following with suitable symbols: **1**

I. (*p*) The nuclear power plant located in Gujarat, near the Tapi River, known for producing atomic energy.

OR

(*q*) The western coastal major port in Karnataka that handles exports of iron ore and petroleum products.

II. Any two of the following: **(1 × 2 = 2)**

(*i*) Bailadila Iron Ore Mines

(*ii*) An International Airport in New Delhi

(*iii*) Kandla Sea Port

SECTION - C

POLITICAL SCIENCE (20 Marks)

20. Which of the following languages is recognized as the national language by the Constitution of India? **1**

(*a*) Hindi (*b*) English (*c*) Tamil (*d*) None of these

21. __________ reasons stress that power sharing will bring out better outcomes **1**

(*a*) Prudential (*b*) Moral (*c*) Economic (*d*) Social

22. '*In Goa, 7 powerful families are contesting 35% of the assembly seats*' states a headline in a recent newspaper article. **1**

Which challenge of political parties does it MOST LIKELY illustrate?

(*a*) Lack of internal democracy (*b*) Influence of money and muscle power

(*c*) Dynastic succession (*d*) Lack of Meaningful Choices

23. Which of the following statements accurately reflects the data on the percentage of women in national parliaments from the chart? **1**

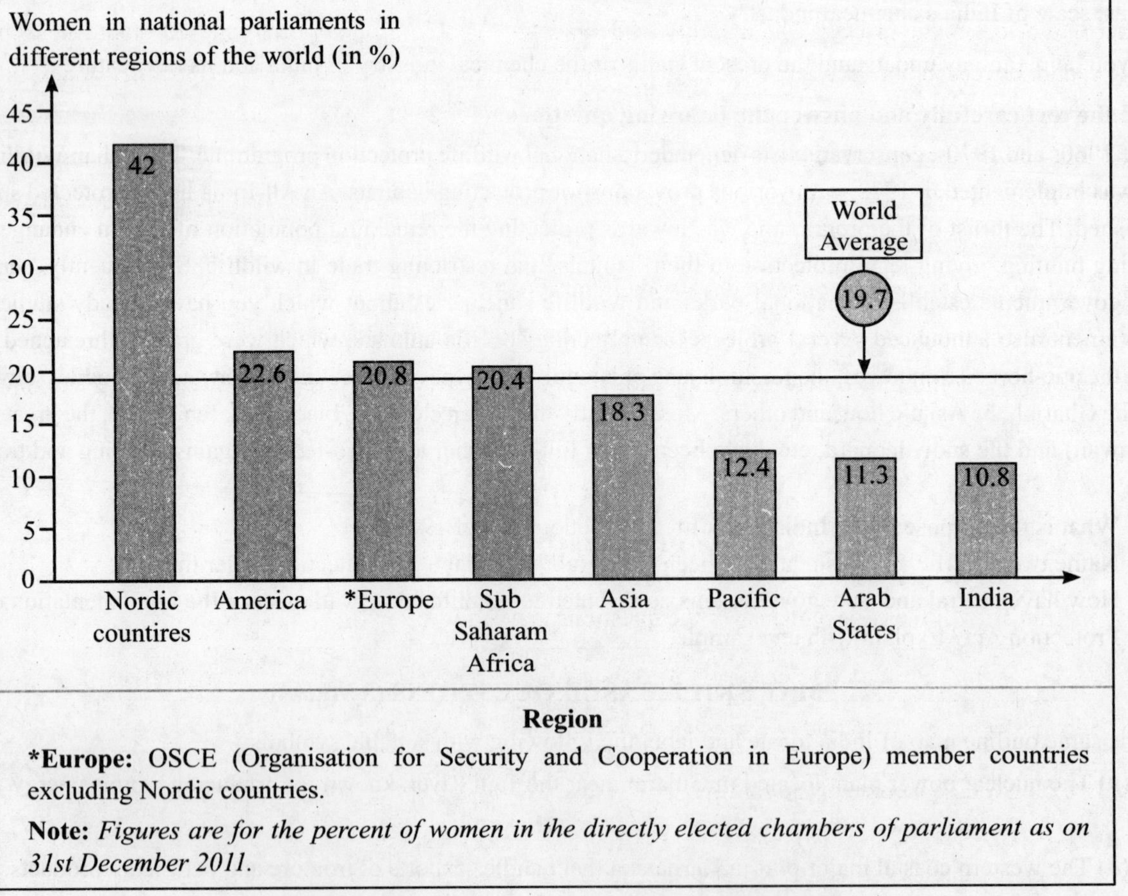

Region

***Europe:** OSCE (Organisation for Security and Cooperation in Europe) member countries excluding Nordic countries.

Note: *Figures are for the percent of women in the directly elected chambers of parliament as on 31st December 2011.*

(*i*) Europe (excluding Nordic countries) has a higher percentage of women in national parliaments compared to the Pacific region.

(*ii*) The world average percentage of women in national parliaments is above 20%.

(*iii*) Sub-Saharan Africa has a higher percentage of women in national parliaments than Asia.

(*iv*) The percentage of women in national parliaments in the Pacific region is the lowest among all regions listed.

(*a*) (*i*), (*ii*) and (*iii*)
(*b*) (*ii*) and (*iii*) only
(*c*) (*i*) and (*iii*) only
(*d*) (*i*), (*ii*), (*iii*) and (*iv*)

24. How do most democracies perform when it comes to providing fair elections? **2**

25. There are mainly two ways to form a federation. By considering all the clues identify the type of federation and give reasons to support your answer. **2**

Clue I: Very often, different constituent units of the federation have unequal powers.

Clue II: Some units are granted special powers

Clue III: The Central Government tends to be more powerful vis-à-vis the States.

26. Describe the nature of the Panchayati raj system in India. **3**

27A. Analyse how the participation of women in politics has evolved and its impact on society. **5**

OR

27B. Analyse the impact of the feminist movement on gender equality in India. **5**

28. Read the given text and answer the following questions: (1 + 1 + 2 = 4) **4**

If you consider all democracies and all dictatorships for the fifty years between 1950 and 2000, dictatorships have slightly higher rate of economic growth. The inability of democracy to achieve higher economic development worries us. But this alone cannot be reason to reject democracy. As economic development depends on several factors: country's population size, global situation, cooperation from other countries, economic priorities adopted by the country, etc. However, the difference in the rates of economic development between less developed countries with dictatorships and democracies is negligible. Overall, we cannot say that democracy is a guarantee of economic development. But we can expect democracy not to lag behind dictatorships in this respect.

28.1 What factors influence economic development in a country?

28.2 Can we conclude that democracy is not effective for economic development?

28.3 A country should opt. for dictatorships rather than democracy to ensure economic growth. Do you agree with this statement?

SECTION - D

ECONOMICS (20 Marks)

29. Study the statistics in the table and answer the questions that follows: **1**

₹	Member 1	Member 2	Member 3	Member 4
Income	15,000	6,000	8,000	9,000

Calculate the average income of the family:

(*a*) ₹950
(*b*) ₹9500
(*c*) ₹2500
(*d*) ₹3000

30. Megha has taken a loan of ₹ 5 Lakhs from the banks to purchase a house. The annual interest rate on the loan is 12 percent and the loan is to be repaid in 10 years in monthly installments. Megha had to submit to the bank, documents showing her employment records and salary before the bank agreed to give her the loan. The bank retained as collateral the papers of the new house, which will be returned to Megha only when she repays the entire loan with interest. **1**

From which sources of credit Megha has taken loan?

(*a*) Informal source
(*b*) Formal source
(*c*) Individual source
(*d*) None of the above

31. What is the primary factor that has stimulated the process of Globalisation? **1**

(I) Increase in foreign investment.
(II) Rise of trade barriers between countries.
(III) Rapid improvement in technology, especially in communication and transportation.
(IV) Decrease in multinational corporations' activities.

(*a*) Statements I and II are appropriate.
(*b*) Statements I, II and III are appropriate.
(*c*) All the statements are appropriate.
(*d*) Statement III is appropriate.

32. Ramesh, a small-scale farmer, needs a loan to buy seeds and fertilizers for the upcoming planting season. He decides to take a loan from a local money lender who offers the loan without any formal paperwork or collateral.

What potential risk does Ramesh face by taking a loan from the local moneylender? **1**

(*a*) The loan interest rate might be higher, leading to a larger debt burden if he fails to repay on time.
(*b*) The loan might come with government subsidies and lower interest rates.
(*c*) The loan repayment terms might be more flexible compared to bank loans.
(*d*) The moneylender might offer additional financial advice and support.

33. In a rural village, the majority of the population is engaged in agriculture. The villagers grow crops and raise livestock for their livelihood. There are a few small shops and a local craftsman who makes pottery. The village does not have any large industries or factories. **1**

Which sector of the economy is most dominant in this village?

(*a*) Primary Sector
(*b*) Secondary Sector
(*c*) Tertiary Sector
(*d*) Quaternary Sector

34. Which of the following is a significant impact of globalisation on the indian economy? **1**

(*a*) Decrease in competition among local producers.
(*b*) Improved access to international market for indian companies.
(*c*) Reduced foreign investment in india.
(*d*) Isolation of indian market from global trends.

35A. Apart from income which other things people look for growth and development. **3**

OR

35B. Write down some characteristics of development. **3**

36. Assess any three advantages of globalisation. **3**

37. Aman is a farmer who grows wheat. He wants to exchange his wheat for a pair of shoes. He meets Ravi, a shoemaker, but Ravi needs clothes, not wheat.

Based on this situation, answer the following:

(*i*) What kind of system is being used by Aman and Ravi? **1**
(*ii*) Mention any two limitations of this system. **2**

38A. What is organised and unorganised sector? The workers in the unorganised sector need protection on the following issues: wages, safety, and health. Explain with examples. **5**

OR

38B. Highlight five reasons for the importance of the tertiary sector in India. **5**

Map for Q. no. 9 (Section A) & Q. no. 19 (Section B)

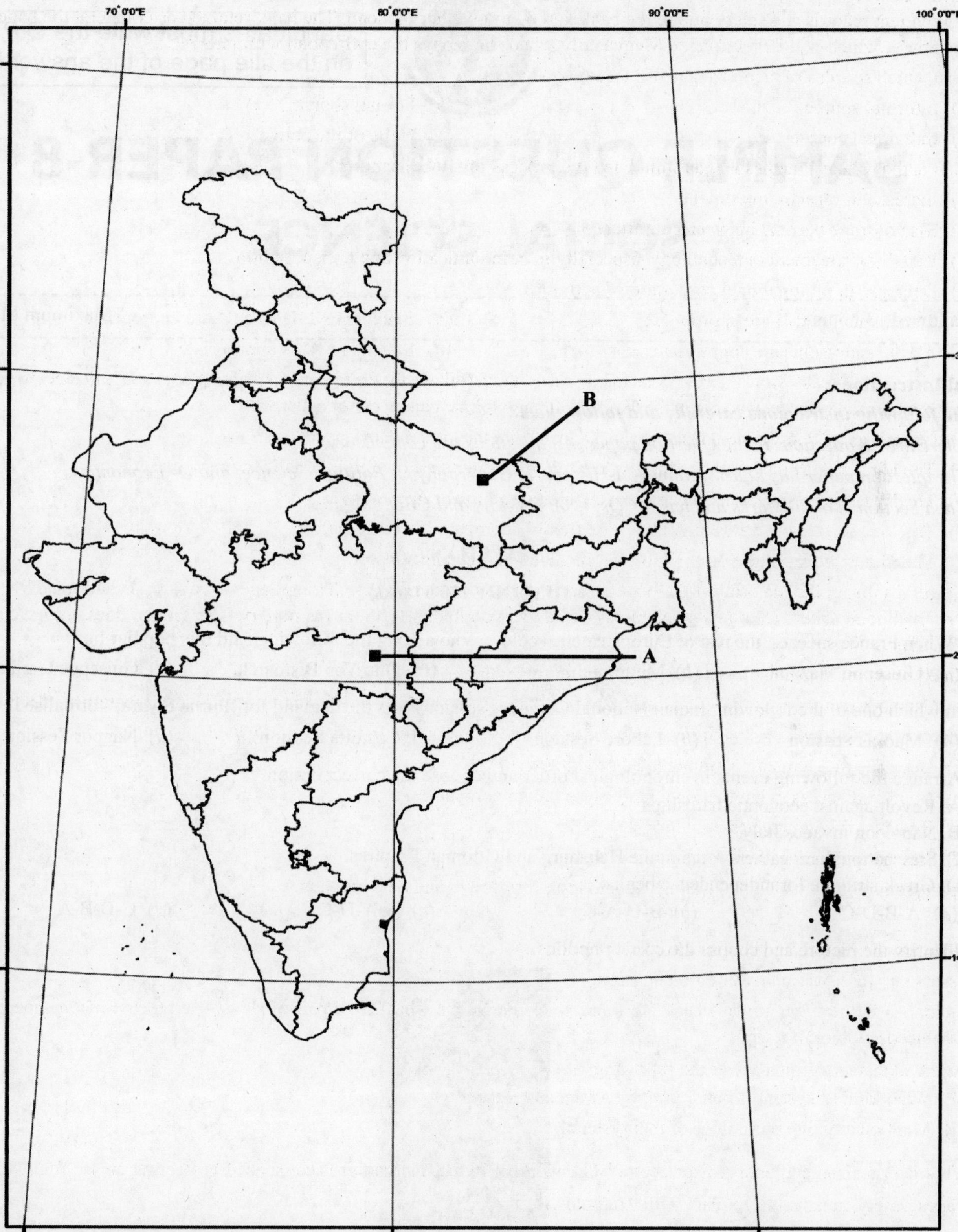

Published by Survey of India

Scale 1:16 M

Roll No. | | | | | | | | |

Q.P. Code 08

Candidates must write the Q.P. Code on the title page of the answer book.

SAMPLE QUESTION PAPER-8

SOCIAL SCIENCE

Time allowed : 3 hours | Maximum Marks : 80

General Instructions:

Read the following instructions carefully and follow them:

(i) There are 38 questions in the Question paper. All questions are compulsory.

(ii) The question paper has Four Sections – A-History, B-Geography C- Political Science, and D- Economics.

(iii) Each Section is of 20 Marks and has MCQs, VSA, SA, LAs and CBQ.

SECTION - A

HISTORY (20 Marks)

1. "When France sneezes, the rest of Europe catches cold". Who among the following said this popular line? 1

(*a*) Giuseppe Mazzini (*b*) Metternich (*c*) Otto Von Bismarck (*d*) Guiseppe Garibaldi

2. In which one of the following Indian National Congress sessions was the demand for 'Purna Swaraj' formalised? 1

(*a*) Madras Session (*b*) Lahore Session (*c*) Calcutta Session (*d*) Nagpur Session

3. Arrange the following events in chronological order and choose the correct option. 1

A. Revolt against economic hardships.
B. Napoleon invades Italy.
C. Slav nationalism gathers force in the Habsburg and Ottoman Empires.
D. Greek struggle for independence begins.

(*a*) A-B-D-C (*b*) B-D-A-C (*c*) B-A-D-C (*d*) C-D-B-A

4. Identify the picture and choose the correct options: 1

(*a*) Marianne (*b*) Bharat mata (*c*) Germania (*d*) Stellad 'itaalia'

5A. The strongest weapon used by the Spanish conqueror was not at all an ordinary military weapon. Justify the mentioned claim using two reasons. **2**

OR

5B. "Traders and travellers introduced new crops to the land they travelled". Give examples to support this statement. **2**

6. Why couldn't the production of handwritten manuscripts satisfy the ever increasing demand for books? Give any three reasons. **3**

7A. Identify the five methods the French Revolutionaries used to promote a sense of national unity among the French people. **5**

OR

7B. How had revolutionaries spread their ideas in many European States after 1815? Explain with examples. **5**

8. Read the given text and answer the following questions: (1 + 1 + 2 = 4) **4**

For centuries, silk and spices from China flowed into Europe through the silk route. In the eleventh century, Chinese paper reached Europe via the same route. Paper made possible the production of manuscripts, carefully written by scribes. Then, in 1295, Marco Polo, a great explorer, returned to Italy after many years of exploration in China.

China already had the technology of woodblock printing. Marco Polo brought this knowledge back with him. Now Italians began producing books with woodblocks, and soon the technology spread to other parts of Europe. Luxury editions were still handwritten on very expensive vellum, meant for aristocratic circles and rich monastic libraries which scoffed at printed books as cheap vulgarities. Merchants and students in the university towns bought the cheaper printed copies.

The production of handwritten manuscripts could not satisfy the ever-increasing demand for books. Copying was an expensive, laborious and time-consuming business. Manuscripts were fragile, awkward to handle, and could not be carried around or read easily. Their circulation, therefore, remained limited. With the growing demand for books, woodblock printing gradually became more and more popular.

8.1. Despite the introduction of print-culture, why were luxurious editions still handwritten?
8.2. Describe a drawback of handwritten manuscripts in comparison to printed material.
8.3. What was Marco Polo's contribution to print culture?

MAP SKILL-BASED QUESTION (2 Marks)

9. Two places **A** and **B** have been marked on the given outline map of India. Identify them and write their correct names on the lines drawn near them. **(1 + 1 = 2)**

A. The place where the Indian National Congress session was held in September, 1920.

B. The place associated with the Peasant Satyagraha.

SECTION-B

GEOGRAPHY (20 Marks)

10. In a hypothetical scenario, a large-scale mining project is planned in a region known for its rich biodiversity and tribal population. The project aims to extract valuable minerals, which would contribute significantly to the country's economy. However, it is likely to have adverse effects on the environment and the indigenous communities residing in the area. What should be the primary consideration when evaluating the feasibility of this mining project? **1**

(*a*) Economic benefits and revenue generation for the country
(*b*) Preservation of biodiversity and protection of indigenous rights
(*c*) Technological advancements and resource extraction efficiency
(*d*) Mitigating environmental impact through regulatory measures

11. There are two statements marked as Assertion (A) and Reason (R). Read the statements and choose the correct option. **1**

Assertion (A): Deforestation leads to a loss of biodiversity and disrupts the ecological balance.

Reason (R): Forests are home to a wide variety of plant and animal species, and their destruction results in habitat loss and species extinction.

(*a*) Both (A) and (R) are true, and (R) is the correct explanation of (A).
(*b*) Both (A) and (R) are true, but (R) is not the correct explanation of (A).
(*c*) (A) is true, but (R) is false.
(*d*) (A) is false, but (R) is true.

12. Which technique is shown in the image for conserving water? **1**

(*a*) Watershed (*b*) Rainwater harvesting (*c*) Rooftop saving (*d*) Saving water in umbrella

13. Mrs. Sharma, who is from southern state Tamil Nadu, wants to grow wheat or tea. Out of the two crops, which one can he grow in his state? Give any two reasons to support your response. **2**

14. Describe the locations where rice is grown in India. **3**

15A. Give examples to distinguish between metallic and non-metallic minerals. **5**

OR

15B. Name the non-metallic mineral which can split easily into thin sheets. Mention its uses. **5**

16. Read the given text and answer the following questions: (1 + 1 + 2 = 4) **4**

Water is a vital resource for all living beings. It is essential for various activities such as drinking, cooking, bathing, agriculture, and industry. However, the availability of clean and safe water is a major concern in many parts of the world. In India, the water crisis is a pressing issue, with many regions facing water scarcity and contamination. The main sources of water in India are rivers, lakes, ponds, and groundwater. Rivers are the primary source of freshwater, with the Ganga, Brahmaputra, and Yamuna being the major rivers. These rivers not only provide water for domestic use but also support agriculture and industry. Lakes and ponds are also important sources of water, especially in rural areas. Groundwater, obtained through wells and tube wells, is another significant source of water in India. However, the increasing population and rapid urbanization have put immense pressure on water resources. The demand for water has surpassed the available supply, leading to overexploitation and depletion of water sources. Moreover, pollution from industrial waste, sewage, and agricultural run-off has further worsened the quality of water, making it unfit for consumption. To address these challenges, it is crucial to adopt sustainable water management practices. This includes rainwater harvesting, water conservation, and efficient use of water resources. Government initiatives like the National Water Mission and Swachh Bharat Abhiyan aim to improve water availability and quality across the country. Additionally, public awareness and participation are essential for the success of these initiatives.

16.1 What are the main sources of water in India?
16.2 Why is the availability of clean and safe water a major concern in many parts of the world?
16.3 How can individuals contribute to sustainable water management?

MAP SKILL-BASED QUESTION (3 Marks)

17. On the same outline map of India locate and label the following with suitable symbols: **1**

I. (p) The cotton textile hub located on the western coast of India in Maharashtra, often called the "Manchester of India."

OR

(q) The city in Tamil Nadu known as the "Textile Capital of South India" for its thriving cotton industry.

II. Any two of the following: **(1 × 2 = 2)**
(*i*) Bhilai Steel Plant
(*ii*) Pune Software Technology Park
(*iii*) Hyderabad Software Technology Park

SECTION-C

POLITICAL SCIENCE (20 Marks)

18. What is the role of the highest court in a federal system? **1**

(*i*) Interpret the constitution only.

(*ii*) Resolve disputes between different government levels.

(*iii*) Legislate new laws.

(*a*) Only (*i*) (*b*) Only (*ii*) (*c*) (*i*) and (*ii*) only (*d*) (*i*), (*ii*) and (*iii*)

19. Which of the following statement is true regarding Belgium? **1**

Statement I: Belgium is a small country in United States, smaller in area than the state of Haryana.

Statement II: It has borders with France, the Netherlands, Germany and Luxembourg.

Statement III: In Belgium, some special laws require the support of a majority of members from each linguistic group.

Statement IV: Single community can make decisions unilaterally.

Options:

(*a*) Statement (II) and (III) are correct (*b*) Statement (I), (II), (III) and (IV) are correct

(*c*) Only Statement (IV) is correct (*d*) Statement (I) and (IV) are correct

20. Which of the following statements are correct regarding 'Holding together federation': **1**

A. A large country divides its power between constituent states and the national government.

B. The Central government tends to be more powerful vis-a-vis the States.

C. Constituent states have equal powers.

D. Constituent states have unequal powers.

Options:

(*a*) Only A (*b*) A and D (*c*) B and D (*d*) A, B, and D

21. Two statements are given below as Assertion (A) and Reason (R). Read the statements and choose the correct option. **1**

Statement-I: A multi-party system is better for democracy than a two-party system.

Statement-II: A multi-party system allows for a greater diversity of voices and perspectives to be represented in government.

Options:

(*a*) Both Statement-I and Statement-II are correct. (*b*) Both Statement-I and Statement-II are incorrect.

(*c*) Statement-I is correct & Statement-II is incorrect. (*d*) Statement-I is incorrect & Statement-II is correct.

22. Which of the following regarding the affidavit is correct? **1**

(*i*) A signed document submitted to an officer.

(*ii*) Contain details of his property and criminal cases pending against him

(*iii*) There is a system of checking if the information given by the candidate is correct

(*iv*) It is not mandatory for every candidate who contests election to file an affidavit.

Options:

(*a*) Only (*i*) (*b*) Only (*ii*) and (*iii*) (*c*) Only (*iii*) (*d*) Only (*i*) and (*ii*)

23. Match Column-I with Column-II and choose the correct option: **1**

	Column-I		Column-II
A.	A democratic government is a	(*i*)	improves the quality of decision making
B.	A democracy is attentive to the needs of	(*ii*)	legitimate government
C.	Democracy is considered a better form of government as it	(*iii*)	all citizens

Option:

(*a*) A-(*ii*), B-(*iii*), C-(*i*) (*b*) A-(*ii*), B-(*i*), C-(*iii*) (*c*) A-(*iii*), B-(*ii*), C-(*i*) (*d*) A-(*iii*), B-(*i*), C-(*ii*)

24. What are the three lists mentioned in the Indian constitution? **2**

25. "The concept of democracy is overwhelmingly supported throughout the world". Explain this claim. **3**

26A. "The existence of political parties is essential to a democracy". Examine the assertion. **5**

OR

26B. Describe any five measures to reform political parties in India. **5**

27. Read the given text and answer the following questions: (1 + 1 + 2 = 4) **4**

Communalism was and continues to be one of the major challenges to democracy in our country. The makers of our Constitution were aware of this challenge. That is why they chose the model of a secular state. This choice was reflected in several constitutional provisions. There is no official religion in the Indian state. Unlike the status of Buddhism in Sri Lanka, that of Islam in Pakistan, and that of Christianity in England, our Constitution does not give a special status to any religion. The Constitution provides to all individuals and communities the freedom to profess, practice, and propagate any religion, or not to follow any religion.

27.1 What is a secular state?

27.2 What measures have our constitutional framers taken to ensure secularism in our country?

27.3 How has India taken a different path than other nations like Sri Lanka, Pakistan, and England in the context of religion?

SECTION-D

ECONOMICS (20 Marks)

28. Rajesh is a farmer who grows vegetables. He needs to buy seeds and fertilizers for his farm but doesn't have any money at the moment. He decides to trade his vegetables directly with the shopkeeper who sells seeds and fertilizers. **1**

What problem does Rajesh face in this barter system, which would be solved by using money as a medium of exchange?

(*a*) Finding a shopkeeper who needs vegetables and is willing to exchange them for seeds and fertilizers.

(*b*) Ensuring the quality of the seeds and fertilizers he receives in exchange for his vegetables.

(*c*) Getting a discount on the seeds and fertilizers he needs.

(*d*) Transporting the vegetables to the shopkeeper's location.

29. ____________ aims at maintaining the quality of life of both the present and future generations. **1**

(*a*) Development

(*b*) Economic Growth

(*c*) Gross Development Product

(*d*) Sustainable Development

30. Study the data given below: **1**

Country	Total GDP	GDP Per Capita
United States	$25,462,700,000,000	$75,269
China	$17,963,200,000,000	$12,598

Source: https://www.worldometers.info/gdp/gdp-by-country/

Despite having a higher total Income than the United States, China has a lower per capita Income. What is the reason for this?

(*a*) United States has a more equitable distribution of income

(*b*) China has more rich people than the poor people

(*c*) China has a smaller population than United States

(*d*) China has a bigger population than United States

31. GDP is the total value of ________ produced during a particular year. **1**

(*a*) all goods and services

(*b*) all final goods and services

(*c*) all intermediate goods and services

(*d*) all intermediate and final goods and Services

32. Evaluate the impacts of opening foreign trade on the global economy by identifying the appropriate statements among the following options: **1**

Statement-I: The choice of goods in the markets increase.

Statement-II: Producers from two countries closely compete against each other despite the distance between their locations.

Statement-III: Foreign trade thus results in connecting the markets or integration of markets in different countries.

Statement-IV: The quality of the product gets better good.

Options:

(*a*) Statements-I and II are appropriate.

(*b*) Statements-I, II and III are appropriate.

(*c*) All the statements are appropriate.

(*d*) Only statement-IV is appropriate.

33. Globalisation has led to improvement in standard of living of- **1**

(*a*) All the people

(*b*) Persons in developed countries

(*c*) Workers in developing countries

(*d*) None of the above

34. Choose the correct option to fill in the blank

Removing barriers or restrictions on business and trade set by the government is called as ________ **1**

(*a*) Disinvestment

(*b*) Special economic zones

(*c*) Liberalisation

(*d*) Foreign direct investment

35. What is BMI? Your friend is 1.50 m tall and weighs 40 kg. Find out his BMI and comment on his report. **2**

36A. A worker in an urban region who was employed by a small manufacturer was recently fired and was later discovered selling electrical goods from a pushcart after being illegally paid, made to work overtime, and subjected to poor conditions at work. Examine how the government may best protect those employed in unorganised industries. **3**

OR

36B. According to the MGNREGA Act, Mr. Kishan, the head of the village, wished to increase employment possibilities to raise the income of his villagers. Please suggest any three activities that Mr. Kishan might start in his community **3**

37. How has globalisation impacted the employment conditions of workers in India? **3**

38A. A poor farmer borrowed money at a high rate of interest from a moneylender, and when he was unable to pay it back, he had to borrow money from another landlord to pay back the moneylender's interest. Mention what impact this might have on him.. **5**

OR

38B. "Self-help groups empower women and eradicate poverty." Support this statement with examples. **5**

Map for Q. no. 9 (Section A) & Q. no. 17 (Section B)

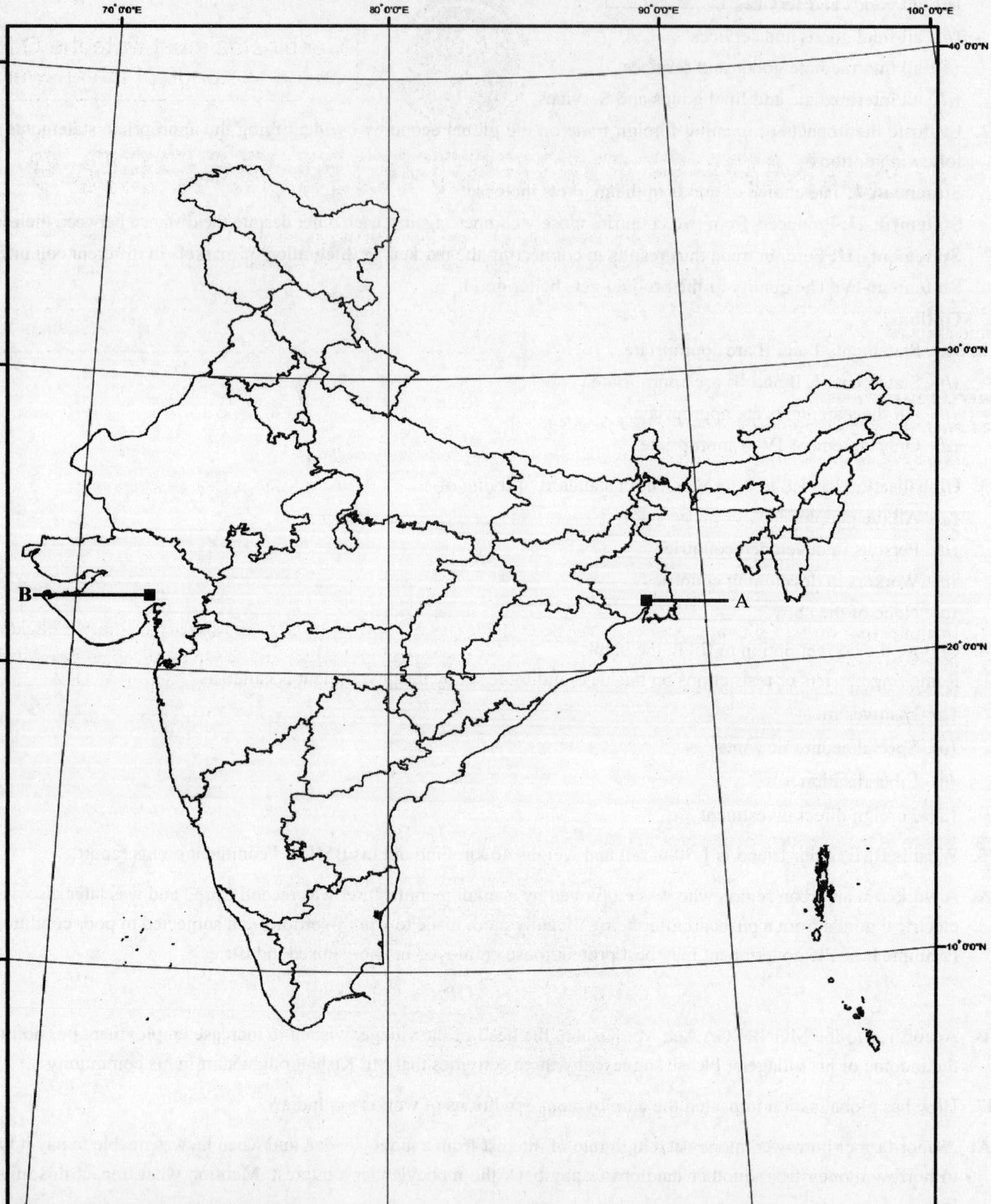

Published by Survey of India

Scale 1:16 M

Roll No. | | | | | | | | |

Q.P. Code 09

Candidates must write the Q.P. Code on the title page of the answer book.

SAMPLE QUESTION PAPER-9

SOCIAL SCIENCE

Time allowed : 3 hours   Maximum Marks : 80

General Instructions:

Read the following instructions carefully and follow them:

(i) There are 38 questions in the Question paper. All questions are compulsory.

(ii) The question paper has Four Sections – A-History, B-Geography C- Political Science, and D- Economics.

(iii) Each Section is of 20 Marks and has MCQs, VSA, SA, LAs, CBQ. and MBQ.

SECTION - A
HISTORY (20 Marks)

1. Imagine you are an economic analyst in the late 1920s, tasked with evaluating the impact of the worldwide economic depression on various sectors in India. Your focus is on the agricultural sector and the lives of Indian peasants during this period. What was the primary cause of these difficulties for Indian peasants during the late 1920s? **1**

(*a*) Increased agricultural prices and exports.
(*b*) Led to the establishment of the Swaraj Party.
(*c*) Caused agricultural prices to fall and exports to decline.
(*d*) Improved the economic condition of the countryside.

2. Which of the following option best signifies this caricature? **1**

(*a*) Otto Von Bismarck in the German Reichstag (Parliament)
(*b*) Victor Emmanuel II in the Italian Parliament
(*c*) Kaiser William II in the Prussian Parliament
(*d*) Napoleon Bonaparte in the French Parliament

3. Arrange the following statements in sequential order based on the events occurs **1**

A. Quit India movement was launched
B. Poona Pact was signed
C. Gandhi Irwin pact was signed.
D. Civil disobedience movement was launched

Options:

(*a*) (A),(B),(C) and (D)
(*b*) (D),(C),(B) and (A)
(*c*) (B),(A),(D) and(C)
(*d*) (A),(D), (C)and (B)

4. Given below is the painting 'Imperial Federation - Map of the World showing the extent of the British Empire in 1886'. Observe the painting and answer the question that follows: **1**

Which of the following elements depicted in the painting seem conflicting when presented together?

(*a*) The British soldiers and British colonies spread in both east and west

(*b*) The variety of animals and costumed figures depicting countries and their people

(*c*) Britannia, the personification of Britain, seated on top of the world and the words federation written at the top of the image

(*d*) The words 'freedom' and 'fraternity' written at the top and Atlas, depicting human labour, holding the world upon his shoulders

5A. Provide evidence to support the claim that the French Revolution was a turning point in European history. **2**

OR

5B. Analyze the impact of industrialisation on the development of nationalism in Europe? **2**

6. Thomas visits a city to observe Gutenberg's mechanical printing press. He notes the differences in the book production process, the cost, and the accessibility of books compared to traditional hand-copying methods. Based on Thomas's observations, Discuss the potential changes in the cost and accessibility of books due to the printing press. **3**

7A. Mention four main proposals with reference to the Non-Cooperation Movement as suggested by Mahatma Gandhi. **5**

OR

7B. Discuss the role of visual symbols and representations in shaping nationalist sentiments during the Indian independence movement. **5**

8. Read the given text and answer the following questions: (1 + 1 + 2 = 4) **4**

Source-1: Religious Reform and Public Debates

There were intense controversies between social and religious reformers and the Hindu orthodoxy over matters like widow immolation, monotheism, Brahmanical priesthood, and idolatry. in Bengal, as the debate developed, tracts and newspapers proliferated, circulating a variety of arguments.

Source-2: New Forms of Publication

New literary forms also entered the world of reading lyrics, short stories, essays about social and political matters. In different ways, they reinforced the new emphasis on human lives and intimate feelings, about the political and social rules that shaped such things.

Source-3: Women and Print

Since social reforms and novels had already created a great interest in women's lives and emotions, there was also an interest in what women would have to say about their own lives.

8.1 Evaluate how the print shaped the nature of the debate in the early nineteenth century in India.

8.2 To what extent do you agree that print opened up new worlds of experience and gave a vivid sense of the diversity of human lives?

8.3 To what extent did the print culture reflect a great interest in women's lives and emotions? Explain.

MAP SKILL-BASED QUESTION (2 Marks)

9. Two places **A** and **B** have been marked on the given outline map of India. Identify them and write their correct names on the lines drawn near them. **(1 + 1 = 2)**

A. The place where Indian National Congress session was held in 1927

B. The place where Gandhi ji started first Satyagraha.

SECTION - B

Geography (20 Marks)

10. In the fictional country of Greenlandia, excessive mining activities have led to severe land degradation. The government, with the help of environmental scientist Dr. Lila, is exploring ways to mitigate the negative impacts while continuing to meet economic needs. Dr. Lila suggests implementing stricter regulations on mining activities. Which of the following justifications best supports this policy from an environmental perspective? **1**

(*a*) It will increase government revenue through fines and penalties.

(*b*) It will protect biodiversity and prevent further loss of vegetation.

(*c*) It will encourage the use of alternative, sustainable resources.

(*d*) It will reduce the competition among mining companies.

11. Raj is a student who recently visited the Sutlej- Beas River basin for a school project. During his visit, he learned about the historical and modern purposes of dams. His group has been tasked to prepare a presentation that evaluates both the benefits and the environmental impact of dam construction.

Identify the correct statements based on the above scenario: **1**

Statement-I: The primary purpose of building dams in ancient India was for irrigation only.

Statement-II: Modern dams serve multiple purposes including recreation and inland navigation.

Statement-III: Jawaharlal Nehru referred to dams as the economic boosters of modern India.

Statement-IV: Dams have no impact on the natural flow and sedimentation of rivers.

(*a*) Statement-I & Statement-II are correct

(*b*) Statement-I & Statement-III are correct

(*c*) Statement-I & Statement-IV are correct

(*d*) Statement-I, II & III are correct

12. Read the following features of a soil and name the related soil: **1**

(*i*) This soil develop in areas of high temperature and heavy rainfall.

(*ii*) Humus content is low

(*iii*) Good for tea, coffee,cashew nut etc.

(*a*) Laterite soil

(*b*) Black soil

(*c*) Alluvial soil

(*d*) Red and yellow soil

13. You are an agricultural consultant advising a group of new farmers in the coastal region of Odisha. These farmers are eager to diversify their crops and are considering rice due to its popularity and market demand. Discuss the specific climatic conditions required for rice cultivation. **2**

14. Ananya, a research analyst at National Mineral Development Corporation (NMDC), is preparing a report on the impact of energy minerals on India's economy. Her research highlights the use of coal, uranium, and natural gas in various sectors such as power generation, manufacturing, and transportation. She observes that energy security is essential for industrial growth, employment generation, and GDP contribution.

Based on the above case, analyze how energy minerals contribute to India's economic development. Mention any three specific sectors where their role is crucial. **3**

15A. The Indian Ministry of Energy is developing a comprehensive energy strategy to address the growing demand for sustainable energy solutions. As part of this initiative, they are emphasizing the importance of non-conventional sources of energy. explain the significance of non-conventional sources of energy in India's energy strategy. discuss the different types of non-conventional energy sources along with their advantages. **5**

OR

15B. Lokesh is a consultant for a mining company tasked with evaluating a potential mining site. To make an informed decision, he needs to analyze the various modes of occurrence of minerals found at the site. Discuss the different ways minerals can occur in nature and explain how each mode of occurrence influences the mining methods and the economic viability of extracting these minerals. **5**

16. Read the given text and answer the following questions: (1 + 1 + 2 = 4) **4**

Manufacturing Industries

Manufacturing Industries not only help in modernizing agriculture, which forms the backbone of our economy, they also reduce the heavy dependence of people on agricultural income by providing them jobs in secondary and tertiary sectors. Industrial development is a pre-condition for eradication of unemployment and poverty from our country. This was the main philosophy behind public sector industries and joint sector ventures in India. It was also aimed at bringing down regional disparities by establishing industries in tribal and backward areas. Export of manufactured goods expands trade and commerce, and brings in much needed foreign exchange. Countries that transform their raw materials into a wide variety of finished goods of higher value are prosperous. India's prosperity lies in increasing and diversifying its manufacturing industries as quickly as possible. Agriculture and industry are not exclusive of each other. They move hand in hand. For instance, the agro-industries in India have given a major boost to agriculture by raising its productivity.

16.1 How do manufacturing industries help in modernizing agriculture in India?

16.2 Why is industrial development crucial for eradicating unemployment and poverty in India?

16.3 Explain how the relationship between agriculture and industry benefits both sectors in India.

MAP SKILL-BASED QUESTION (3 Marks)

17. On the same outline map of India, locate and label the following with suitable symbols: **1**

I. (*p*) The eastern state known as the largest producer of jute in India.

OR

(*q*) A neighboring state of West Bengal also produces jute.

II. Any two of the following: **(1 × 2 = 2)**

(*i*) The highest gravity dam in India located on the Sutlej River in Himachal Pradesh.

(*ii*) The dam built on the Chambal River in Rajasthan, important for irrigation and electricity.

(*iii*) A major multipurpose dam built on the Narmada River in Gujarat.

SECTION - C

POLITICAL SCIENCE (20 Marks)

18. A belief that the majority community should be able to rule a country in whichever way it wants, by disregarding the wishes and needs of the minority is called ____________. **1**

(*a*) Power Sharing

(*b*) Central Government

(*c*) Majoritarianism

(*d*) Community Government

19. *"Everything would come to an end if the legislative, executive, and judicial powers of government were to be exercised by the same person or authority."* *~Montesquieu, French jurist*

Which of the following is the BEST explanation of this quote? **1**

(*a*) All work in a country will stop in the absence of power-sharing.

(*b*) Separation of powers is needed to strengthen democracy.

(*c*) Governments can only function if powers are distributed.

(*d*) People cannot exist in a nation if powers are not divided.

20. There are two statements marked as Assertion (A) and Reason (R). Mark your answer as per the codes provided below: **1**

Assertion (A): Public expression of dissatisfaction with democracy shows the failure of the democracy.

Reason (R): When people express dissatisfaction with democracy, it shows that they have developed awareness and critical thinking skills to expect accountability from power holders, transforming them from subjects into citizens

(*a*) Both Assertion (A) and Reason (R) are the true and Reason (R) is a correct explanation of Assertion (A).

(*b*) Both Assertion (A) and Reason (R) are the true but Reason (R) is not a correct explanation of Assertion (A).

(*c*) Assertion (A) is true and Reason (R) is false.

(*d*) Assertion (A) is false and Reason (R) is true.

21. Match Column-I with Column-II and select the correct answer by using the codes given below: **1**

	Column-I		Column-II
A.	Power shared among different organs of government	(*i*)	Community government
B.	Power shared among governments at different levels	(*ii*)	Separation of powers
C.	Power shared by different social groups	(*iii*)	Coalition government
D.	Power shared by two or more political parties	(*iv*)	Federal government

(*a*) A-(*i*), B-(*iv*), C-(*ii*), D-(*iii*)

(*b*) A-(*iii*), B-(*i*), C-(*ii*), D-(*iv*)

(*c*) A-(*ii*), B-(*iv*), C-(*i*), D-(*iii*)

(*d*) A-(*iii*), B-(*ii*), C-(*i*), D-(*iv*)

22. Read the passage below.

Australia became a nation on 1 January 1901, when the British Parliament passed legislation enabling the six Australian colonies to collectively govern in their own right as the Commonwealth of Australia. It was a remarkable political accomplishment that had taken many years and several referenda to achieve. **1**

Source: Official website of the National Museum of Australia

From this, we can infer that Australia is an example of a ________.

(*a*) United democracy

(*b*) Unitary government

(*c*) 'Coming together' federation

(*d*) 'Holding together' federation

23. Analyze the data and answer the question that follows: 1

Inequality of Income in Selected Countries		
Name of the Countries	% Share of national income	
	Top 20%	Bottom 20%
South Africa	64.8	2.9
Brazil	63.0	2.6
Russia	53.7	4.4
USA	50.0	4.0
United Kingdom	45.0	6.0
Denmark	34.5	9.6
Hungary	34.4	10.0

***Fig:** Inequality of income in selected countries*

Which democratic country has a relatively more equitable income distribution?

(*a*) South Africa

(*b*) Russia

(*c*) United States

(*d*) Denmark

24. Based on the cartoon "The Rich Get Buff", what critical issue regarding economic growth and income distribution is highlighted? 1

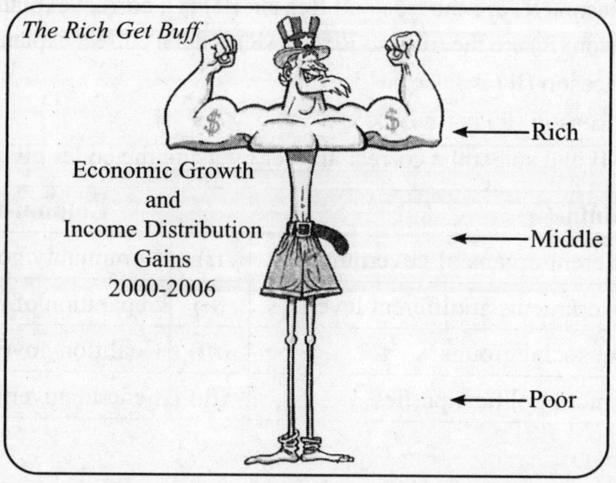

(*a*) The cartoon suggests that economic growth is evenly distributed across all social classes.

(*b*) The cartoon highlights the problem of income inequality, with the wealthy benefitting disproportionately from economic growth.

(*c*) The cartoon indicates that the middle class benefits the most from economic growth.

(*d*) The cartoon shows that economic growth primarily benefits the poor.

25. "*Democracies often struggle with economic inequalities, with a significant portion of wealth concentrated among a small segment of the population.*" 1

Which statement best captures the dilemma faced by democracies regarding economic inequality?

(*a*) Democracies are successful in eliminating economic inequalities among their citizens.

(*b*) In democracies, economic growth automatically leads to the equitable distribution of wealth among all citizens.

(*c*) Democracies face challenges in reducing economic disparities and ensuring equitable wealth distribution.

(*d*) Economic disparities do not exist in democracies due to their inherent principle of equality among citizens

26. Analyze the map and answer the question that follows:

(*a*) Identify an exception to the rule that most of the world's large countries are federations from the map. **1**

(*b*) Which is the largest federal country in the world? **1**

27. There are mainly two ways to form a federation. By considering all the clues identify the type of federation and give reasons to support your answer.

Clue I: Very often different constituent units of the federation have unequal powers.

Clue II: Some units are granted special powers

Clue III: The Central Government tends to be more powerful vis-a-vis the States. **2**

28. What changes occurred in Centre-State relations after 1990? What role did the Supreme Court play in this? **3**

29A. A research institute has been tasked with designing a framework to evaluate the performance of political parties in a democratic country. Discuss the key indicators that the institute should consider while designing this framework. **5**

OR

29B. Why is the lack of internal democracy within political parties considered a challenge to India's democracy? **5**

SECTION - D

ECONOMICS (20 Marks)

30. The following table shows the proportion of adults (aged 15-49 years) whose BMI is below normal (BMI <18.5 kg/m^2) in India. It is based on a survey of various states for the year 2015-16. Look at the table and answer the following questions. **1**

State	Male (%)	Female (%)
Kerala	8.5	10
Karnataka	17	21
Madhya Pradesh	28	28
All States	**20**	**23**

Which of the following states has the least female adults below normal BMI?

(*a*) Karnataka

(*b*) Kerala

(*c*) Madhya Pradesh

(*d*) All of the above

31. Besides banks, the other major source of cheap credit in rural areas are the cooperative societies (or cooperatives). Members of a cooperative pool their resources for cooperation in certain areas. There are several types of cooperatives possible such as farmers cooperatives, weavers cooperatives, industrial workers cooperatives, etc. Krishak Cooperative functions in a village not very far away from Sonpur. It has 2300 farmers as members. It accepts deposits from its members. With these deposits as collateral, the Cooperative has obtained a large loan from the bank. These funds are used to provide loans to members. Once these loans are repaid, another round of lending can take place. 1

Krishak Cooperative provides loans for the purchase of agricultural implements, loans for cultivation and agricultural trade, fishery loans, loans for construction of houses and for a variety of other expenses.

Why is Arun one of the few people in Sonpur to take a bank loan?

(*a*) Other people in the village prefer to borrow from moneylenders.
(*b*) Banks demand collateral which everyone cannot provide.
(*c*) Interest rates on bank loans are the same as the interest rates charged by traders.
(*d*) Bank loan have strict documentation requirements.

32. In the village of Econville, a local farmer, Mr.Arjun, grows wheat and sells it to a bakery, Mr.Sweet's Bakery, at ₹20 per kg. The bakery uses this wheat to make delicious biscuits, which are then sold in the local market at ₹80 per packet. Assume that there are no other production costs involved. Select among the following how should this transaction be reflected in the GDP? 1

(*a*) Include the value of both the wheat and biscuits separately to highlight all economic activities.
(*b*) Include only the value of the wheat, as it is the raw product and the basis of further production.
(*c*) Include only the value of biscuits, as it represents the final consumption goods.
(*d*) Exclude both values, as they do not contribute directly to the village's retail market.

33. A non-profit organization uses internet technology to launch a global campaign for environmental awareness. They use live streaming tools to conduct webinars and interactive sessions with participants from over 30 countries. How does internet technology specifically support global environmental campaigns? 1

(*a*) By allowing real-time monitoring of environmental changes only.
(*b*) By enabling high-definition video streaming of local issues globally.
(*c*) By facilitating interactive and educative sessions across different time zones.
(*d*) By limiting participation to environmental experts.

34. Priya, a college student, wanted to purchase a laptop for her studies. She applied for a loan at a nearby bank. The bank asked her for documents like her ID proof, address proof, and college admission letter. After verification, the bank approved her loan at a reasonable interest rate. 1

What does this case highlight?

(*a*) Banks provide loans to college students.
(*b*) Documentation is not necessary for obtaining loans.
(*c*) Formal sources of credit have certain eligibility criteria.
(*d*) College students should not buy laptops.

35A. Imagine you are an economic advisor in the planning commission of a developing country facing significant employment challenges, especially in the secondary and tertiary sectors. Your task is to analyze and present a detailed report during the next committee meeting on the impacts of inadequate job creation in these sectors. Discuss the impact of not having enough job creation in the secondary and tertiary sectors on employment. **3**

OR

35B. You are part of a policy analysis team in the Ministry of Finance. The team is tasked with evaluating the government's role in infrastructure development. Analyze why the government engages in activities such as constructing roads, and bridges, and providing irrigation systems, especially considering that these projects require substantial resources and coordination. **3**

36. Although averages are useful for comparing countries, do they also hide disparities? Explain the meaning of this statement. Support the statement with suitable arguments. **3**

37A. Consider a scenario where two small businesses operate in a bustling local market—one, a bakery specializing in artisan bread, and the other, a café offering gourmet coffee and sandwiches. They decide to collaborate to attract more customers. The bakery provides freshly baked bread to the cafe, which in turn, serves gourmet sandwiches made from this bread. How does the use of money, instead of bartering goods directly between the bakery and the café, enhance their business operations and economic activities within the market? Discuss the benefits of using money as a medium of exchange. **5**

OR

37B. A business owner decides to deposit the company's extra cash into a bank account at the beginning of the month. Explain how this action utilizes the concept of demand deposits and contributes to the business's financial management. **5**

38. Read the text carefully and answer the following questions: (1 + 1 + 2 = 4) **4**

Using IT in Globalisation

A news magazine published for London readers is to be designed and printed in Delhi. The text of the magazine is sent through the Internet to the Delhi office. The designers in the Delhi office get orders on how to design the magazine from the office in London using telecommunication facilities. The design is done on a computer. After printing, the magazines are sent by air to London. Even the payment of money for designing and printing from a bank in London to a bank in Delhi is done instantly through the Internet (e-banking)!

38.1 Explain the role of the internet in the design and printing process of the magazine described in the above case.

38.2 Write down IT tools speeding up the globalisation discussed in the above case.

38.3 Describe the significance of e-banking in the context of international transactions mentioned in the paragraph.

MAP for Q. no. 9 (Section A) & Q. no. 17 (Section B)

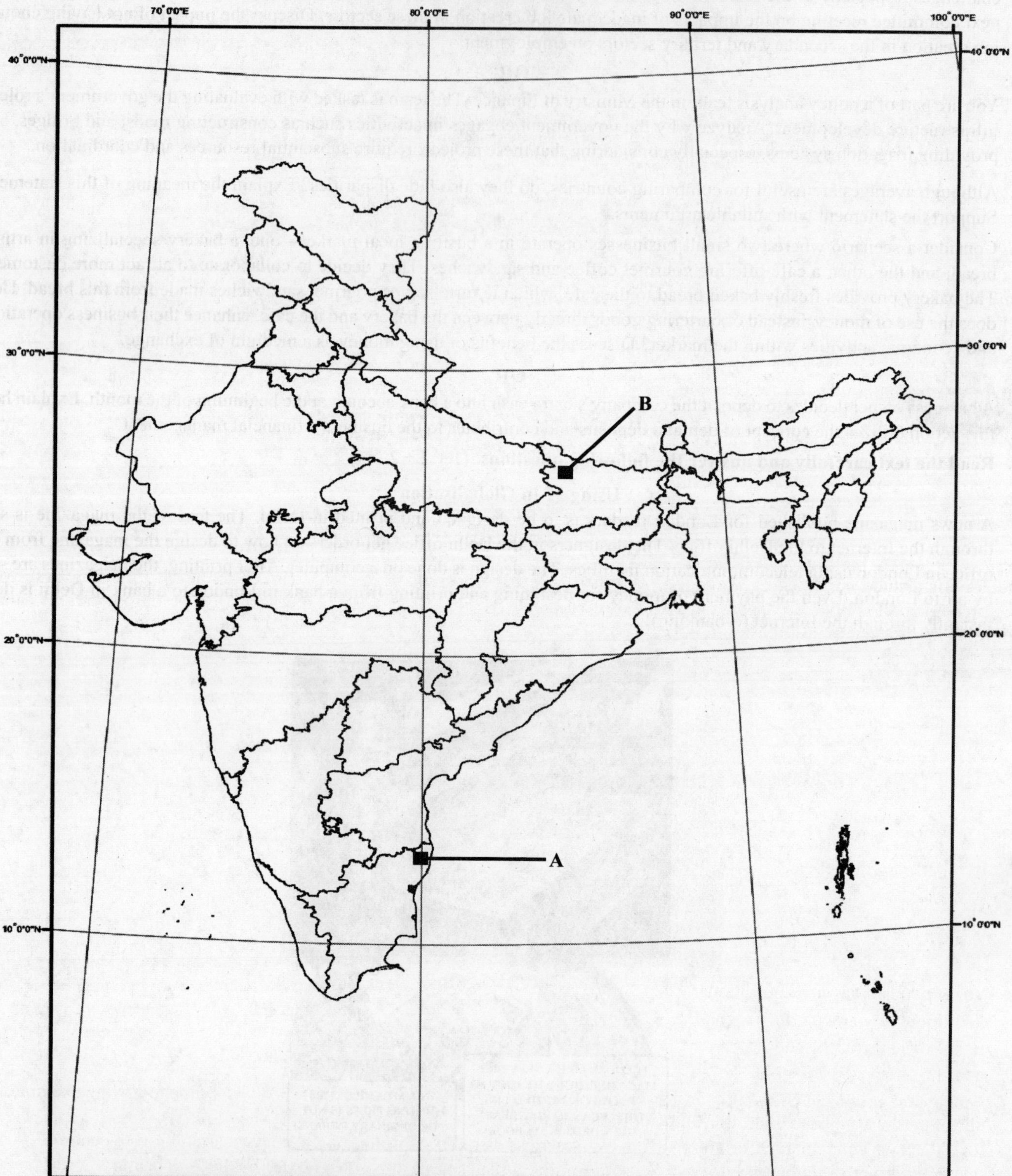

Published by Survey of India

Scale 1:16 M

Roll No. | | | | | | | |

Q.P. Code 10

Candidates must write the Q.P. Code on the title page of the answer book.

SAMPLE QUESTION PAPER-10
SOCIAL SCIENCE

Time allowed : 3 hours | Maximum Marks : 80

GENERAL INSTRUCTIONS:

(i) There are 38 questions in the Question paper. All questions are compulsory.

(ii) The question paper has Four Sections – A-History, B-Geography C- Political Science, and D- Economics.

(iii) Each Section is of 20 Marks and has MCQs, VSA, SA, LAs and CBQ.

SECTION-A

HISTORY (20 Marks)

1. Ravi is a student focused on art and symbolism, analyzing a painting depicting Christ, saints, and angels watching over a procession of nations. In the painting where Christ, saints, and angels oversee a procession of people from various nations, what do these celestial figures symbolize about the relationship between these nations? **1**

(*a*) Friendship among the nations
(*b*) Fraternity among the nations
(*c*) Love among the nations
(*d*) Freedom of the nations

2. Tracing the origins of common foods reveals the interconnection of different cultures. Which of the following examples best illustrates how global exploration and cultural exchange influenced culinary traditions? **1**

(*a*) Potatoes and tomatoes, originally from the Americas, became staples in European diets after the 16th century.
(*b*) Wheat, native to the Middle East, became a primary food source in North America by the 20th century.
(*c*) Rice, a staple in Asia, was introduced to Europe in the Middle Ages and replaced traditional grains.
(*d*) Corn, originally from Europe, was brought to Africa in the 19th century and became a major part of their diet.

3. Arrange the following events in the correct chronological order. 1

A. Coming of Simon Commission to India
B. Demand of Purna Swaraj in Lahore Session of INC
C. Government of India Act, 1919
D. Champaran Satyagraha

Options:

(*a*) (C), (B), (D), (A)
(*b*) (A), (B), (D), (C)
(*c*) (B), (C), (A), (D)
(*d*) (D), (C), (A), (B)

4. Read the following statements and select the correct options. 1

Statement-I: Gutenberg developed the printing press that time in the 1530, at Strasbourg.

Statement-II: The first book he printed with this technology was the Bible.

(*a*) Both Statement-I and Statement-II are correct.
(*b*) Both Statement-I and Statement-II are incorrect.
(*c*) Statement-I is correct & Statement-II is incorrect.
(*d*) Statement-I is incorrect & Statement-II is correct.

5A. Describe the events of the French Revolution which had influenced the people belonging to other parts of Europe. 2

OR

5B. Interpret the concept of 'liberalisation' in the field of economic sphere during the nineteenth century in Europe. 2

6A. You are an advisor to a medieval trade guild exploring new business opportunities along the Silk Routes. Prepare a detailed proposal highlighting how engaging in trade along these routes can benefit the guild economically and culturally. 3

OR

6B. "Explain how conquest, disease, and trade contributed to the shrinking of the pre-modern world in the sixteenth century. Give any three points." 3

7A. Explain the meaning and notion of 'Swaraj' as perceived by the Plantation Workers. How did they respond to the call of the Non-cooperation Movement? 5

OR

7B. Describe the spread of the Non-Cooperation Movement in the countryside. 5

8. Read the given text and answer the following questions: **(1 + 1 + 2 = 4)** 4

Source-1: Religious Reform and Public Debates

There were intense controversies between social and religious reformers and the Hindu orthodoxy over matters like widow immolation, monotheism, Brahmanical priesthood, and idolatry. in Bengal, as the debate developed, tracts and newspapers proliferated, circulating a variety of arguments.

Source-2: New Forms of Publication

New literary forms also entered the world of reading lyrics, short stories, essays about social and political matters. In different ways, they reinforced the new emphasis on human lives and intimate feelings, about the political and social rules that shaped such things.

Source-3: Women and Print

Since social reforms and novels had already created a great interest in women's lives and emotions, there was also an interest in what women would have to say about their own lives.

8.1 Evaluate how the print shaped the nature of the debate in the early nineteenth century in India.

8.2 To what extent do you agree that print opened up new worlds of experience and gave a vivid sense of the diversity of human lives?

8.3 To what extent did the print culture reflect a great interest in women's lives and emotions? Explain.

MAP SKILL-BASED QUESTION (2 Marks)

9. Two places **A** and **B** have been marked on the given outline map of India. Identify them and write their correct names on the lines drawn near them. **(1 + 1 = 2)**

A. The place where Indian National Congress session was held in September, 1920.

B. The place associated with Jallianwala Bagh massacre.

SECTION-B

GEOGRAPHY (20 Marks)

10. Which one of the following statements is not an argument in favour of multipurpose river projects? **1**

(*a*) Multi-purpose projects bring water to those areas which suffer from water scarcity.

(*b*) Multi-purpose projects by regulating water flow help to control floods.

(*c*) Multi-purpose projects lead to large scale displacements and loss of livelihood.

(*d*) Multi-purpose projects generate electricity for our industries and our homes.

11. Two statements are given below. They are Assertion (A) and Reason (R). Read both the statements and choose the correct option. **1**

Assertion (A): Resource planning is an easy process in India.

Reason (R): Resource planning involves the identification and inventory of resources across the regions of the country.

(*a*) Both, (A) and (R) are true and (R) is the correct explanation of (A)

(*b*) Both, (A) and (R) are true but (R) is not the correct explanation of (A)

(*c*) (A) is true but (R) is false

(*d*) (A) is false but (R) is true

12. Match Column-I with Column-II and choose the correct option from the following: **1**

	Column-I		Column-II
A.	Reserved Forests	(i)	forests are regarded as most valuable as far as the conservation of forest and wildlife resources.
B.	Protected Forests	(ii)	forest lands are protected from any further depletion.
C.	Unclassed Forests	(iii)	Other forests and wastelands belonging to both government and private individuals and communities.

Options:

(*a*) A-(i), B-(ii), C-(iii)
(*b*) A-(iii), B-(ii), C-(i)
(*c*) A-(i), B-(iii), C-(ii)
(*d*) A-(ii), B-(iii), C-(i)

13. "M" gave his friend clues about a type of soil that suits for growing cotton. Which of the following clues provided by "M" would be most useful in identifying the ideal type of soil? **1**

Clues:

(*i*) It is well-known for its capacity to hold moisture.

(*ii*) It turns yellow when it is hydrated.

(*iii*) It is rich in kankur and bhangar nodules.

(*iv*) It is a well-drained loamy soil.

(*a*) Clue (*i*) (*b*) Clue (*i*) and (*iii*) (*c*) Clue (*i*) and (*ii*) (*d*) Clue (*iv*)

14. Which of the following is the correct statement? **1**

(*a*) The famous Chipko movement in the Himalayas has not only successfully resisted deforestation in several areas.

(*b*) In India joint forest management (JFM) programme furnishes a good example for involving local communities in the management and restoration of degraded forests.

(*c*) The clear lesson from the dynamics of both environmental destruction and reconstruction in India is that local communities everywhere have to be involved in some kind of natural resource management.

(*d*) All of the above

15. Two statements are given below. They are Assertion (A) and Reason (R). Read both the statements and choose the correct option. **1**

Assertion (A): Water scarcity is a significant issue in both arid and non-arid regions around the world.

Reason (R): Unequal access to water and overuse in agriculture and industry contribute to water scarcity even in areas with sufficient rainfall.

(*a*) Both A and R are true, and R is the correct explanation of A.
(*b*) Both A and R are true, but R is not the correct explanation of A.
(*c*) A is true, but R is false
(*d*) A is false, but R is true.

16. You are an agricultural consultant advising a group of new farmers in the coastal region of Odisha. These farmers are eager to diversify their crops and are considering rice due to its popularity and market demand. Discuss the specific climatic conditions required for rice cultivation. **2**

17A. Lokesh is a consultant Tor a mining company tasked with evaluating a potential mining site. To make an informed decision, he needs to analyze the various modes of occurrence of minerals found at the site. Discuss the different wavs minerals can occur in nature and explain how each mode of occurrence influences the mining methods and the economic viability of extracting these minerals. **5**

OR

17B. Differentiate between metallic and non-metallic minerals with examples. **5**

18. Read the given text and answer the following questions: **(1 + 1 + 2 = 4)** **4**

A cooperative sugar mill has been established in the small town of Dharapuram in Tamil Nadu, significantly influencing the local economy and the lives of the sugarcane farmers. This mill not only processes sugarcane front local farms but also actively participates in community development through various sustainability and educational programs. The mill has become a central part of the town's economic landscape, employing many locals and contributing to infrastructure improvements. The integration of modern technology in the mill has enhanced production efficiency, leading to better pricing and market access for the farmers' produce. Additionally, the mill's presence has encouraged younger generations to consider careers in agriculture and agro-based industries, shifting perceptions about employment in these sectors.

18.1 How does the cooperative model of the sugar mill benefit the sugarcane farmers in Dharapuram?

18.2 What role does the sugar mill play in altering the employment landscape of Dharapuram?

18.3 Discuss the potential long-term impacts on agricultural practices in Dharapuram due to the mill's emphasis on sustainable farming techniques.

MAP SKILL-BASED QUESTION (3 Marks)

19. On the same outline map of India locate and label the following with suitable symbols: **1**

I. (*p*) The dam constructed on the Chenab River in Jammu & Kashmir for hydroelectric power generation.

OR

(*q*) The dam built across the Sutlej River in Himachal Pradesh, jointly serving irrigation and power needs.

II. Any two of the following: **(1 × 2 = 2)**

(*i*) Mayurbhanj Iron Ore Mine
(*ii*) Bokaro Coal Mine
(*iii*) Digboi Oil Fields

SECTION-C

POLITICAL SCIENCE (20 Marks)

20. Match Column-I with Column-II and choose the correct option from the following: **1**

	Column-I		Column-II
A.	Congress Party	I.	National Democratic Alliance
B.	Bharatiya Janata Party	II.	State party
C.	Communist Party of India (Marxist)	III.	United Progressive Alliance
D.	Telugu Desam Party	IV.	Left Front

(*a*) A-II, B-III, C-I, D-IV (*b*) A-III, B-I, C-IV, D-II (*c*) A-IV, B-III, C-I, D-II (*d*) A-II, B-IV, C-I, D-III

21. Analyze the data and answer the question that follows: **1**

Inequality of income in Selected Countries		
Name of the Countries	**% Share of national income**	
	Top 20%	**Bottom 20%**
South Africa	64.8	2.9
Brazil	63.0	2.6
Russia	53.7	4.4
USA	50.0	4.0
United Kingdom	45.0	6.0
Denmark	34.5	9.6
Hungary	34.4	10.0

Fig: Inequality of income in selected countries

Which democratic country has a relatively more equitable income distribution?

(*a*) South Africa (*b*) Russia (*c*) United States (*d*) Denmark

22. Subhash lobbies with various government offices to work specifically for the interests of the Scheduled Tribes. Which of the following parties is he MOST LIKELY to be associated with? **1**

(*a*) All-India Trinamool Congress

(*b*) Indian National Congress

(*c*) Communist Party of India

(*d*) Bahujan Samaj Party

23. Below is a cartoon created by Neelabh Banerjee, the renowned Indian cartoonist, illustrator, and comics artist. **1**

Source: asiapacific.unwomen.org

What is the cartoon trying to depict?

(*a*) The sexual division of labour in India

(*b*) Natural and unchangeable gender divisions

(*c*) Income-generating activities done by women in rural India

(*d*) The ability of men to contribute equally to domestic work as women

24. Study the map thoroughly and mention the languages that are dominantly present in Belgium. **2**

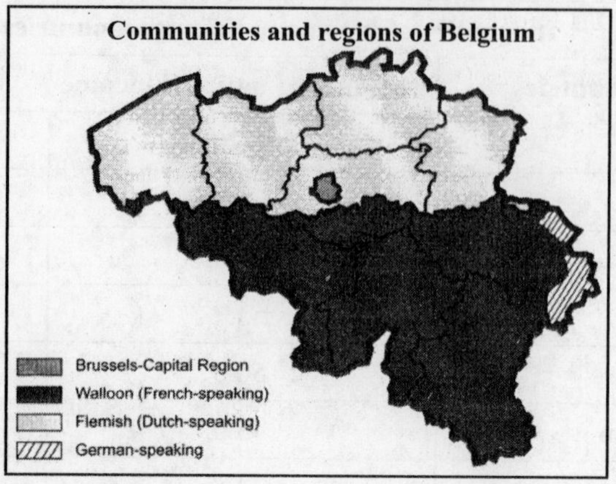

25. What were the demands of Sri Lankan Tamils? **2**

26. State two reasons to say that caste alone cannot determine election results in India. **3**

27A. "Democracy's ability to generate its own support is also its outcome and it cannot be ignored." Explain the statement. **5**

OR

27B. "Democracy promotes dignity and freedom of the people." Examine the statement. **5**

28. Read the given text and answer the following questions: (1 + 1 + 2 = 4) **4**

Language Diversity of India

How many languages do we have in India? The answer depends on how one counts it. The latest information that we have is from the Census of India held in 2011. This census recorded more than 1300 distinct languages, which people mentioned as their mother tongues. These languages were grouped under some major languages. For example, languages like Bhojpuri, Magadhi, Bundelkhandi, Chhattisgarhi, Rajasthani, and many others were grouped under 'Hindi.' Even after this grouping, the Census found 121 major languages. Of these, 22 languages are now included in the Eighth Schedule of the Indian Constitution and are therefore called 'Scheduled Languages.' Others are called 'non-scheduled languages.' In terms of languages, India is perhaps the most diverse country in the world.

28.1 Explain the importance of language diversity in India.

28.2 Differentiate between scheduled and non-scheduled languages.

28.3 'The fusion of languages has united the country into one cultural entity.' Explain the statement with an example.

SECTION-D

ECONOMICS (20 Marks)

29. Read the data given below and answer the question. **1**

Country	Gross National Income (GNI) per capita (2011 PPP $)	Life Expectancy at birth	Mean Years of Schooling of People aged 25 and above	HDI Rank in the world (2018)
Sri Lanka	11,899	76.6	11.2	78
India	6,951	67.7	6.5	134
Myanmar	4,038	67.3	6.5	144
Pakistan	5,374	66.4	4.4	164
Nepal	4,026	70.5	4.5	146
Bangladesh	6,511	73.7	7.4	129

Source : Human Development Report, 2023–24, United Nations Development Programme, New York.

Which of the following neighbouring countries has better performance in terms of human development than India?

(a) Bangladesh (b) Sri Lanka (c) Nepal (d) Pakistan

30. Read the following Assertion (A) and Reason (R). Answer these questions by selecting the appropriate option given below: **1**

Assertion (A): Kerala has a low Infant Mortality Rate.

Reason (R): Kerala has adequate provision of basic health and educational facilities.

(a) Both A and R are true and R is the correct explanation of A.

(b) Both A and R are true but R is not the correct explanation of A.

(c) A is true but R is false.

(d) A is false but R is true.

31. ________ refers to some restrictions including tax on imports which governments can use to increase or decrease foreign trade and to decide what kind of goods, how much of each, should come into the country. **1**

(a) Foreign Investment (b) Trade Barrier

(c) Nationalisation (d) Liberalisation

32. Assume there are four families in a locality. If the income of each family is ₹6,000, ₹4,000, ₹7,000 and ₹3,000 then find out the average income of the locality from the following options: **1**

Which sector does Ravi's work primarily fall under?

(a) ₹5,000 (b) ₹3,000 (c) ₹2,000 (d) ₹6,000

33. Priya, a college student, wanted to purchase a laptop for her studies. She applied for a loan at a nearby bank. The bank asked her for documents like her ID proof, address proof, and college admission letter. After verification, the bank approved her loan at a reasonable interest rate. What does this case highlight? **1**

(a) Banks provide loans to college students.

(b) Documentation is not necessary for obtaining loans.

(c) Formal sources of credit have certain eligibility criteria.

(d) College students should not buy laptops

34. Rajat is a small-scale entrepreneur who wants to expand his business by purchasing new machinery. He is considering borrowing money from formal credit institutions. How do formal credit institutions like commercial banks differ from informal sources of credit like moneylenders? **1**

(a) Formal institutions charge higher interest rates.

(b) Informal sources require collateral, while formal institutions do not.

(c) Formal institutions follow standardized procedures and charge lower interest rates.

(d) Informal sources offer larger loan amounts compared to formal institutions.

35. "MNCs have been a major force in the globalisation process connecting distant regions of the world." Justify the statement. **3**

36. Compare Tables "A" & "B" and answer the question given below.

Table-A

Share of Sectors in GDP in %			
Year	Tertiary	Secondary	Primary
1973-74	50	10	40
2013-14	68	21	11

Table-B

Share of Sectors in employment in %			
Year	Tertiary	Secondary	Primary
1977-78	18	11	71
2017-18	31	25	44

A remarkable fact about India is that while there has been a change in the share of the three sectors in GDP, a similar shift has not taken place in employment. Why didn't a similar shift out of the primary sector happen in the case of employment? Substantiate your answer. **3**

37. Sunil and Raman did their graduation from the same college. Sunil got employed in an unorganised sector and was not satisfied whereas Raman got employed in an organised sector and was happy and satisfied. Identify three reasons for Sunil's dissatisfaction as compared to Raman. **3**

38A. What is credit? How can it be both an asset and a debt trap? **5**

OR

38B. Consider a scenario where two small businesses operate in a bustling local market—one, a bakery specializing in artisan bread, and the other, a café offering gourmet coffee and sandwiches. They decide to collaborate to attract more customers. The bakery provides freshly baked bread to the cafe, which in turn, serves gourmet sandwiches made from this bread. How does the use of money, instead of bartering goods directly between the bakery and the cafe, enhance their business operations and economic activities within the market? Discuss the benefits of using money as a medium of exchange. **5**

Map for Q. no. 9 (Section A) & Q. no. 19 (Section B)

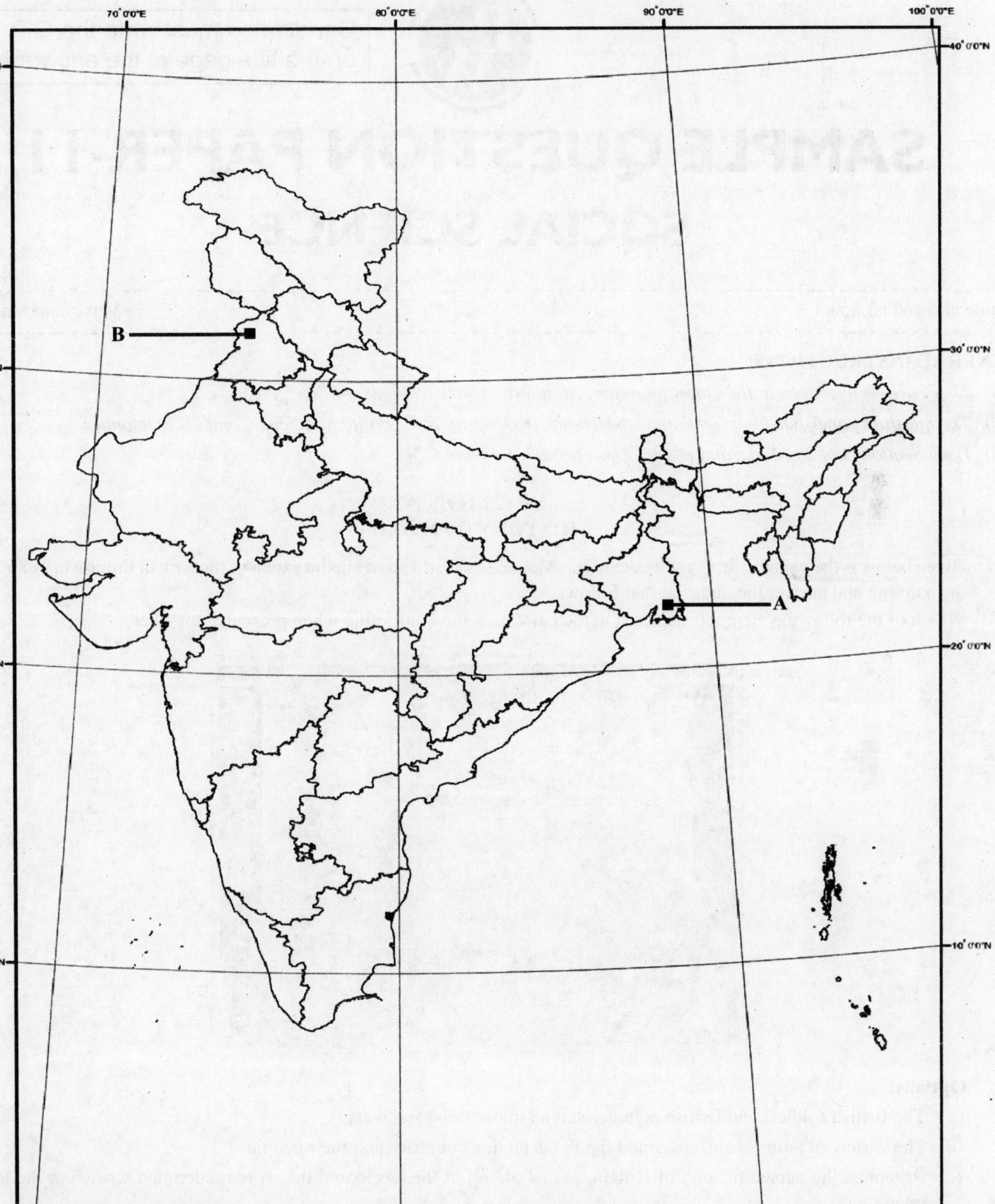

Published by Survey of India
Scale 1:16M

Roll No. | | | | | | | | |

Q.P. Code **11**

Candidates must write the Q.P. Code on the title page of the answer book.

SAMPLE QUESTION PAPER-11

SOCIAL SCIENCE

Time allowed : 3 hours — Maximum Marks : 80

GENERAL INSTRUCTIONS:

(i) There are 38 questions in the Question paper. All questions are compulsory.

(ii) The question paper has Four Sections – A-History, B-Geography C- Political Science, and D- Economics.

(iii) Each Section is of 20 Marks and has MCQs, VSA, SA, LAs and CBQ.

SECTION A
HISTORY (20 Marks)

1. Given below is the painting 'Imperial Federation - Map of the World showing the extent of the British Empire in 1886'. Observe the painting and answer the question that follows.

Which of the following elements depicted in the painting seem conflicting when presented together? **1**

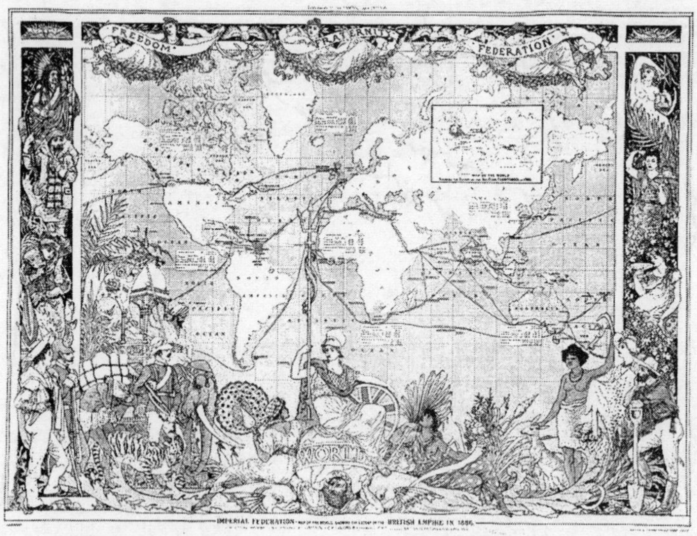

Options:

(*a*) The British soldiers and British colonies spread in both east and west

(*b*) The variety of animals and costumed figures depicting countries and their people

(*c*) Britannia, the personification of Britain, seated on top of the world and the words federation written at the top of the image

(*d*) The words 'freedom' and 'fraternity' written at the top and Atlas, depicting human labour, holding the world upon his shoulders

2. Arrange the following statements in sequential order: **1**

A. Mahatma Gandhi launched satyagraha in South Africa. B. Rowlatt act was passed

C. Champaran movement was launched. D. Jallianwala bagh massacre took place

Options:

(*a*) (A), (B), (C) and (D) (*b*) (A), (C), (B) and (D) (*c*) (D), (C), (B) and (A) (*d*) (C), (B), (D) and (A)

3. Read the following statements and select the correct options. **1**

Statement-I: Rajarama Mohan Roy wrote the Samachar chandrika.

Statement-II: Kashibaba published Chhote Aur Bade Ka Sawal.

(*a*) Both Statement-I and Statement-II are correct. (*b*) Both Statement-I and Statement-II are incorrect.

(*c*) Statement-I is correct & Statement-II is incorrect. (*d*) Statement-I is incorrect & Statement-II is correct.

4. The woodcut painting given below was created during the time when Indians were beginning to accept the idea of women's education in the late 19th century. **1**

Which of the following scenarios was the artist MOST LIKELY trying to portray in this art piece?

(*a*) Listening to music is the best way to spend one's free time

(*b*) Increasing popularity of the Western idea of marriage

(*c*) Challenging the conventional gender roles

(*d*) Pleasure is the ultimate goal of life

5A. What category of readers became important with the introduction of compulsory primary education in the late nineteenth century? **2**

OR

5B. Describe some of the new printed books which were sold by the pedlars in villages in eighteenth century Europe. **2**

6A. Sahil is researching the influence of the Napoleonic Code across various European regions once controlled by France. Explain how the implementation of this legal framework affected local legal systems, social hierarchies, and economic activities. **3**

OR

6B. "How did culture play an important role in shaping the idea of the nation in Europe during the nineteenth century? Support your answer with any three examples." **3**

7A. Explain the reasons behind Mahatma Gandhi's decision to withdraw the Non-Cooperation Movement in February 1922 and the formation of the Swaraj Party within the Congress. **5**

OR

7B. Explain the significance of the Salt March and the Civil Disobedience Movement as a shift from the Non-Cooperation Movement. **5**

8. Read the given text and answer the following questions: (1 + 1 + 2 = 4) **4**

Shanghai became the hub of the new print culture, catering to the Western-style schools. From hand printing, there was now a gradual shift to mechanical printing. Buddhist missionaries from China introduced hand-printing technology into Japan around AD 768-770. The oldest Japanese book, printed in AD 868, is the Buddhist Diamond Sutra containing six sheets of text and wood cut illustrations.

In the late eighteenth century, in the flourishing urban circles at Edo (later to be known as Tokyo), illustrated collections of paintings depicted an elegant urban culture, involving artists, courtesans, and teahouse gatherings. Libraries and bookstores were packed with hand-printed material of various types-books on women, musical instruments, calculations, tea ceremony, flower arrangements, proper etiquette, cooking and famous places.

8.1 Give the ancient name of Tokyo.

8.2 Name the center of the new print culture in China and describe it.

8.3 What is the name of the oldest printed book of Japan? Mention its features

MAP SKILL-BASED QUESTION (2 Marks)

9. Two places **A** and **B** have been marked on the given outline map of India. Identify them and write their correct names on the lines drawn near them **(1 + 1 = 2)**

(A) The place where Indian National Congress session was held in September 1920.

(B) The place associated with Jallianwala Bagh Massacre.

SECTION B

GEOGRAPHY (20 Marks)

10. Match **Column-I** with **Column-II** and choose the correct option from the following: **1**

	Column-I (Projects)		Column-II (Activities)
A.	Bhakra-Nangal Project	I.	Hydel power production and irrigation
B.	Hirakud Project	II.	Conservation of water with flood control
C.	Sardar Sarovar Dam	III.	Irrigation facilities in drought-prone areas
D.	Krishna-Godavari Project	IV.	Inter-state water dispute over water diversion

Choose the correct combination:

(*a*) A-I, B-II, C-III, D-IV (*b*) A-III, B-I, C-IV, D-II (*c*) A-IV, B-III, C-II, D-I (*d*) A-II, B-IV, C-I, D-III

11. Which of the following options represent a potential cause of depletion of flora and fauna? **1**

(*a*) Over-harvesting resources such as timber and wildlife.

(*b*) Polluting the environment with chemicals and waste.

(*c*) Destroying natural habitats through deforestation and urbanization.

(*d*) All of the above.

12. Read the following statements and select the correct options. **1**

Statement-I: Biotic resources are the resources which have life.

Statement-II: Abiotic resources are the resources which do not have life.

Options:

(*a*) Both Statement-I and Statement-II are correct.

(*b*) Both Statement-I and Statement-II are incorrect.

(*c*) Statement-I is correct & Statement-II is incorrect.

(*d*) Statement-I is incorrect & Statement-II is correct.

13. Mr. Sharma, a geography teacher, discusses with his class how Jharkhand, rich in mineral resources, faces environmental challenges. **1**

What would he the most sustainable way to mitigate the environmental impact while continuing mining in Jharkhand?

(*a*) Increasing the area of open pit mines
(*b*) Implementing stricter environmental regulations
(*c*) Encouraging the export of raw minerals
(*d*) Reducing the overall extraction of minerals

14. Priya, a student from Jharkhand, noticed significant environmental changes due to mining activities around her hometown. Given this situation, which of the following is the most likely impact of mining on her region? **1**

(*a*) Increase in agricultural productivity
(*b*) Enhancement of local biodiversity
(*c*) Increase in land degradation
(*d*) Improvement in air quality

15. A farmer named Rajesh is considering expanding his crop production to include maize on his farm near the Ganges River. He is aware that temperature and soil type are critical for the success of the crop. Given the typical conditions in this region during the growing season and the characteristics of soil, w hich of the following options should Rajesh choose for the best maize cultivation? **1**

(*a*) 10°C to 15°C in sandy soil
(*b*) 21 °C to 27°C in old alluvial soil
(*c*) 30°C to 35°C in clayey soil
(*d*) 18°C to 24°C in loamy soil

16. "Agriculture and industry move hand in hand." Support the statement with examples. **2**

17A. The Indian Ministry of Energy is developing a comprehensive energy strategy to address the growing demand for sustainable energy solutions. As part of this initiative, they are emphasizing the importance of non-conventional sources of energy, explain the significance of non-conventional sources of energy in India's energy strategy, discuss the different types of non-conventional energy sources alone with their advantages. **5**

OR

17B. Explain with examples the significance of the usage of non-conventional sources of energy for the country. **5**

18. Read the given text and answer the following questions: (1 + 1 + 2 = 4) **4**

The textile industry holds a unique position in India's economy, significantly contributing to industrial production, employment, and foreign exchange earnings. It is self-reliant and complete in the value chain from raw material to high-value products. Key industries based on agricultural raw materials include cotton, jute, silk, woollen textiles, sugar, and edible oil.

In ancient India, cotton textiles were made with hand spinning and handloom weaving. Post-18th century, power looms were introduced. The first successful textile mill in Mumbai was established in 1854. During the colonial period, traditional industries struggled against mill-made cloth from England. The cotton textile industry initially thrived in Maharashtra and Gujarat due to raw cotton availability, market access, transport facilities, labor, and a moist climate.

This industry supports agriculture, providing livelihoods to farmers, workers in ginning, spinning, weaving, dyeing, designing, packaging, tailoring, and sewing. It also drives demand for chemicals, dyes, packaging materials, and engineering works.

18.1 Name some industries which are based on agricultural raw materials?

18.2 What is the process of making cotton in textile industry?

18.3 In which places the earlier stages of cotton textile industry was concentrated

MAP SKILL-BASED QUESTION (3 Marks)

19. On the same outline map of India locate and label the following with suitable symbols: **1**

I. (p) The major dam built on the Krishna River in Telangana, contributing to both irrigation and hydel power.

OR

(q) The dam built across the Tungabhadra River, a tributary of Krishna, providing irrigation to Karnataka and Andhra Pradesh.

II. Any two of the following: **(1 × 2 = 2)**

(i) Namrup Thermal Power Plant

(ii) Tarapur Nuclear Plant

(iii) Haldia Sea Port

SECTION C

POLITICAL SCIENCE (20 Marks)

20. __________ provides that equal wages should be paid to equal work. **1**

(*a*) Equal Wages Act, 1977 (*b*) Equal Remuneration Act, 1976

(*c*) Wages act 1980 (*d*) Equal Income Act. 1978

21. Which of the following statements accurately describes a "community government"? **1**

(*i*) 'Community government' is elected by people belonging to one language community – Dutch, French and German-speaking – no matter where they live.

(*ii*) This government has the power regarding cultural, educational and language-related issues.

(*iii*) This government has the power regarding economical, educational and language-related issues.

(*iv*) 'Community government' is elected by people belonging to one language community – Dutch, Spanish and German-speaking – no matter where they live.

(*a*) Only (*i*) (*b*) Only (*iii*) (*c*) Only (*iv*) (*d*) Both (*i*) and (*ii*)

22. *'The Parliament cannot change the sharing of power between the Union government and the state governments on its own. Any change to it has to be first passed by both the Houses of Parliament with at least a two-thirds majority.'*

Which feature of federalism does the above statement adhere to? **1**

(*a*) Different tiers of the government have their own jurisdiction in specific matters of legislation, taxation, and administration.

(*b*) Changes in the fundamental provisions of the constitution require the consent of both levels of government.

(*c*) The union government has the final power to settle any dispute between the different levels of government.

(*d*) The jurisdictions of the tiers of government are specified in the constitution

23. Match the **Column-I** with **Column-II** and select the correct answer by using the codes given below **1**

	Column-I		Column-II
A.	Power shared among different organs of government	I.	Community government
B.	Power shared among governments at different levels	II.	Separation of powers
C.	Power shared by different social groups	III.	Coalition government
D.	Power shared by two or more political parties	IV.	Federal government

(*a*) A-I, B-IV, C-II, D-III

(*b*) A-III, B-I, C-II, D-IV

(*c*) A-II, B-IV, C-I, D-III

(*d*) A-III, B-II, C-I, D-IV

24. *"In Belgium, a unique power-sharing model was established to accommodate the diverse linguistic and regional communities, promoting stability and unity within the country."*

What does the above statement illustrate about the relationship between power-sharing and national unity? **2**

25. Mention different aspects of life in which women are discriminated against or disadvantaged in India. **2**

26. What is the main difference between a federal form of government and a unitary one? Explain with examples. **3**

27A. Analyze the Bahujan Samaj Party's (BSP) ideological roots and its impact on the party's political approach and performance in the 2019 Lok Sabha elections. **5**

OR

27B. Define the term 'Political Party'. Explain the need of political parties in India. **5**

28. Read the given text and answer the following questions: (1 + 1 + 2 = 4) **4**

In substantive terms, it may be reasonable to expect from democracy a government that is attentive to the needs and demands of the people and is largely free of corruption. The record of democracies is not impressive on these two counts. Democracies often frustrate the needs of the people and often ignore the demands of a majority of its population. The routine tales of corruption are enough to convince us that democracy is not free of this evil. At the same time, there is nothing to show that non-democracies are less corrupt or more sensitive to the people.

28.1 Explain any one key impact of corruption on democratic governance.
28.2 How does the reality of democracy differ from the general expectations of democracy?
28.3 Discuss the role of transparency in addressing corruption in a democracy.

SECTION D

ECONOMICS (20 marks)

29. The following table shows the proportion of adults (aged 15 - 49 years) whose BMI is below normal (BMI < 18.5 kg/m^2) in India. It is based on a survey of various states for the year 2015-16.

State	Male (%)	Female (%)
Kerala	8.5	10
Karnataka	17	21
Madhya Pradesh	28	28
All States	**20**	**23**

Source: National Family Health Survey-4

Which of the following states has the maximum male adults below normal BMI? **1**

(*a*) Kerala
(*b*) Karnataka
(*c*) Madhya Pradesh
(*d*) Both Kerala and Karnataka

30. Two statements are given below. They are Assertion (A) and Reason (R). Read both the statements and choose the correct option: **1**

Assertion (A): India is classified as a low middle-income country by the World Bank.
Reason (R): In 2023, India's per capita income was US$ 10030 per annum, which falls within the low middle-income category.
Options:
(*a*) Both (A) and (R) are true and (R) is the correct explanation of (A).
(*b*) Both (A) and (R) are true but (R) is not the correct explanation of (A).
(*c*) (A) is true but (R) is false.
(*d*) (A) is false but (R) is true.

31. Krishak Cooperative functions in a village not very far away from Sonpur. It has 2300 farmers as members. It accepts deposits from its members. With these deposits as collateral, the Cooperative has obtained a large loan from the bank. These funds are used to provide loans to members. Once these loans are repaid, another round of lending can take place.

Krishak Cooperative provides loans for the purchase of agricultural implements, loans for cultivation and agricultural trade, fishery loans, loans for construction of houses and for a variety of other expenses.

What is the purpose of Krishak Cooperative obtaining a large loan from the Bank? **1**

(*a*) To make profit for the cooperative
(*b*) To provide grants to its members
(*c*) To invest in other business
(*d*) To provide loans to its members.

32. Two statements are given below. They are Assertion (A) and Reason (R). Read both the statements and choose the correct option: **1**

Assertion (A): The service sector is the fastest-growing sector in the Indian economy.
Reason (R): The demand for services such as healthcare, education, and IT has increased due to rising incomes and changing lifestyles.
(*a*) Both (A) and (R) are true, and (R) is the correct explanation of (A).
(*b*) Both (A) and (R) are true, but (R) is not the correct explanation of (A).
(*c*) (A) is true, but (R) is false
(*d*) (A) is false, but (R) is true.

33. How did liberalisation impact foreign trade and investment in India? **1**

(I) Liberalisation removed government restrictions on foreign trade.

(II) Liberalisation increased barriers to foreign investments.

(III) Liberalisation promoted the protection of domestic producers.

(IV) Liberalisation allowed businesses more freedom in making decisions about imports and exports.

Options:

(*a*) Statements-I and II are appropriate.

(*b*) Statements-I, II, and III are appropriate.

(*c*) All the statements are appropriate.

(*d*) Only statement-I and IV are appropriate.

34. The integration and interconnection among the economies of different countries are called ______. **1**

(*a*) Privatisation (*b*) Liberalisation (*c*) Globalisation (*d*) Social Welfare

35A. How is the tertiary sector different from other sectors? Illustrate with a few examples. **3**

OR

35B. What do you understand by disguised unemployment? Explain with an example each from the urban and rural areas. **3**

36A. Assess any three advantages of globalization. **3**

OR

35B. How does foreign trade lead to the integration of markets across countries? Explain with an example other than those given here. **3**

37. Rani works as a helper at a tea stall. She has no fixed salary, no paid leave, and can be removed any day without notice. Her friend Suman works in a bank, gets a monthly salary, medical benefits, and job security.

Based on the situation above, answer the following: Do you think Rani is being exploited in the unorganised sector? Give reasons to support your answer. **3**

38A. A farmer has borrowed money from a money lender at a high rate of interest, as he could not pay the interest, he was forced to borrow from another landlord to settle the amount for the interest borrowed to the money lender.

State the consequences he may face in this situation. **5**

OR

38B. "In India, about 80 percent of farmers are small farmers, who need credit for cultivation." Analyse this statement and answer the following question: **5**

(*i*) Why might banks be unwilling to lend to small Farmers?

(*ii*) What are the other sources from which the small farmers can borrow?

(*iii*) Explain with an example how the terms of credit can be unfavorable for the small farmer.

(*iv*) Suggest some ways by which small farmers can get cheap credit.

(*v*) How can government policies support small farmers in accessing credit?

Map for Q. no. 9 (Section A) & Q. no. 19 (Section B)

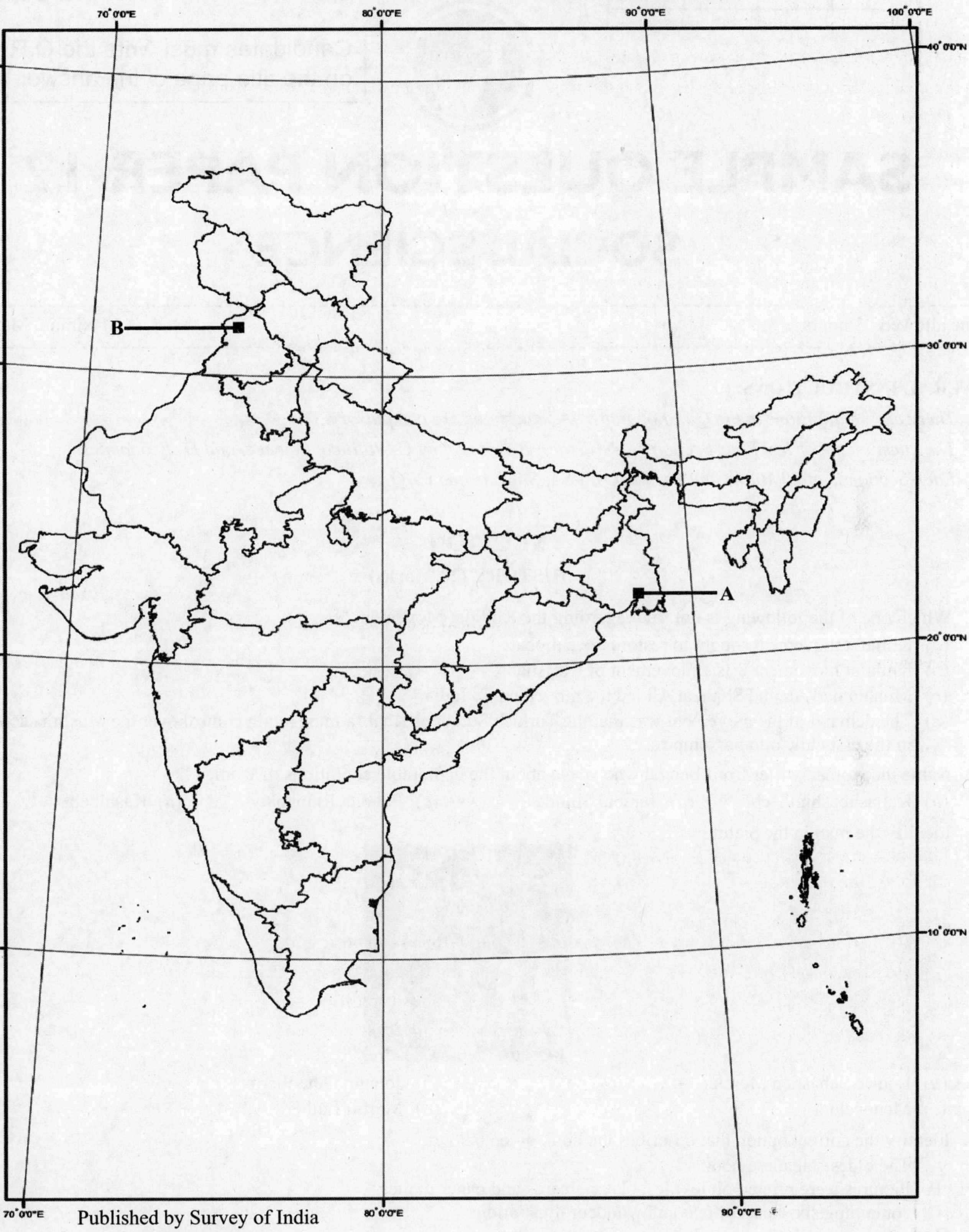

Published by Survey of India
Scale 1:16M

Roll No. | | | | | | | | | Q.P. Code **12**

Candidates must write the Q.P. Code on the title page of the answer book.

SAMPLE QUESTION PAPER-12

SOCIAL SCIENCE

Time allowed : 3 hours   Maximum Marks : 80

GENERAL INSTRUCTIONS:

(i) *There are 38 questions in the Question paper. All questions are compulsory.*

(ii) *The question paper has Four Sections – A-History, B-Geography C- Political Science, and D- Economics.*

(iii) *Each Section is of 20 Marks and has MCQs, VSA, SA, LAs and CBQ.*

SECTION - A

HISTORY (20 Marks)

1. Which one of the following is not true regarding the Khilafat Movement? **1**

(*a*) Khilafat movement sought to restore the caliphate

(*b*) Khilafat movement was a movement of Christians.

(*c*) Muhammad Ali and Shaukat Ali led the movement in India.

(*d*) The demand of the movement was that the Turkish Sultan or Khalifa must retain control over the Muslim sacred places in the erstwhile ottoman empire.

2. Name the woman writer from Bengal who wrote about the deplorable conditions of women **1**

(*a*) Kailashbashini Debi (*b*) Tarabai Shinde (*c*) Pandita Ramabai (*d*) Kashibaba

3. Identify the man in the picture **1**

(*a*) Louise Sebastian Mercier (*b*) Johann Gutenberg

(*c*) Menocchio (*d*) Martin Luther

4. Identify the correct option that describes the book given below. **1**

A. The oldest Japanese book

B. Pictures were printed on textiles, playing cards and paper money

C. containing six sheets of text and woodcut illustrations

Options:

(*a*) Buddhist Diamond Sutra (*b*) The Jikji (*c*) Chapbooks (*d*) Bible

5. Evaluate the relationship between the two statements regarding the role of industrialisation in the unification and strengthening of Germany. 1

Statement I: Industrialisation was essential for the economic strengthening of newly unified nations like Germany.

Statement II: The unification of Germany under Bismarck's leadership utilized industrialisation to consolidate state power and modernise the military.

Options:

(*a*) Both statements are false.

(*b*) Statement I is true, Statement II is false.

(*c*) Statement I is false, Statement II is true.

(*d*) Both statements are true.

6. You are part of a cultural delegation visiting cities along the ancient Silk Routes. Prepare a presentation detailing how historical globalisation through these routes influenced the spread of religions such as Christianity, Islam, and Buddhism. 2

7A. What were the reactions of the local populations to the French rule in the conquered territories? 3

OR

7B. Provide evidence to support the claim that the rise of nationalism in Europe was influenced by multiple factors. 3

8. "Analyze how Friedrich's views reflect the ideology of liberalism in the context of national unity. 3

9A. What were the demands put forward by Gandhiji in his letter dated 31 January 1930 to Viceroy? What was the object and importance of Salt March? 5

OR

9B. "Dalits participation in the civil disobedience movement was therefore limited". Justify the statement. 5

MAP SKILL-BASED QUESTION (2 Marks)

10. Two places **A** and **B** have been marked on the given political outline map of India. Identify them and write their correct names on the lines drawn near them: **(1 + 1 = 2)**

(A) The place where the Indian National Congress session was held in December 1920.

(B) The place where Jallianwala Bagh massacre took place.

SECTION - B

GEOGRAPHY (20 Marks)

11. Identify the soil with the help of following features: 1

(*i*) Consists of sand, silt and clay

(*ii*) Very fertile

(*iii*) Most suitable for cultivation of sugarcane, paddy and wheat.

Options:

(*a*) laterite soil (*b*) Alluvial soil (*c*) Regur soil (*d*) Arid soil

12. Match Column-I with Column-II and choose the correct option from the following: 1

	Column-I		Column-II
A.	Heavy Industries	(i)	Iron and steel
B.	Private Sector	(ii)	TISCO, Bajaj Auto Ltd.
C.	Small-Scale Industry	(iii)	Investment more than rupees 1 crore
D.	Large Scale Industry	(iv)	Maximum investment upto rupees 1 crore

Options:

(*a*) A-(i), B-(ii), C-(iv), D-(iii)

(*b*) A-(ii), B-(iii), C-(i), D-(iv)

(*c*) A-(iii), B-(i), C-(ii), D-(iv)

(*d*) A-(iv), B-(iii), C-(ii), D-(i)

13. "Black soil is also called 'regur soil' and is known for its capacity to hold moisture, making it ideal for growing cotton." Read the following features of the soil and choose the correct option: **1**

I. Ideal for growing cotton
II. Also called regur soil
III. Found in the northern plains
IV. Well known for its capacity to hold moisture

Options:

(*a*) Only I, II and IV are correct.
(*b*) Only II, III and IV are correct.
(*c*) Only I, II and III are correct.
(*d*) Only I, III and IV are correct.

14A. What do you understand by Rat-hole mining? **2**

OR

14B. What are two types of iron ore? **2**

15. Describe how communities have conserved and protected forests and wildlife in India. **3**

16A. Describe the factors that are responsible for the various objections against the multipurpose projects. **5**

OR

16B. How is rainwater harvesting carried out in semi-arid regions of Rajasthan? Explain. **5**

17. Read the given text and answer the following questions: (1 + 1 + 2 = 4) **4**

Agriculture is the backbone of many economies around the world. It involves the cultivation of crops and the rearing of animals for food, fiber, and other products. Agriculture can be broadly classified into two categories: subsistence agriculture and commercial agriculture. Subsistence agriculture is characterized by small-scale farming, where farmers produce crops and raise animals primarily for their own consumption. This type of agriculture is prevalent in rural areas and often relies on traditional farming methods. On the other hand, commercial agriculture is focused on producing crops and livestock for sale in the market. It involves large-scale farming operations, the use of modern technology, and specialized farming practices. Commercial agriculture plays a vital role in meeting the food demands of a growing population and contributes significantly to the economy through exports and employment generation.

17.1 What are the two categories of agriculture mentioned in the passage?
17.2 How does commercial agriculture contribute to the economy?
17.3 How does commercial agriculture differ from subsistence agriculture?

MAP SKILL-BASED QUESTION (3 Marks)

18. On the same outline map of India locate and label the following with suitable symbols: **1**

I. (*p*) The iron and steel plant located in Karnataka, known for being one of the largest steel producers in South India.

OR

(*q*) The steel plant situated in Tamil Nadu, contributing to the development of southern India's industrial base.

II. Any two of the following: **(1 x 2 = 2)**

(*i*) An International Airport Amritsar
(*ii*) The state which is the largest producer of rice in India and known for the fertile deltaic region.
(*iii*) The leading producer of sugarcane in the northern plains of India.

SECTION - C

POLITICAL SCIENCE (20 Marks)

19. When power is shared among different organs of government it is called as _______ distribution of power **1**

(*a*) vertical (*b*) horizontal (*c*) political (*d*) parliamentary

20. Who grants authority to both sets of government in a federal form of government? **1**

(*a*) Centre (*b*) Parliament (*c*) Constitution (*d*) President

21. Identify the most appropriate reason for low proportion of women in highly paid jobs: **1**

(*a*) Matriarchal society
(*b*) Gender discrimination
(*c*) Low literacy rates among women
(*d*) Absence of respect for women

22. Studies on political and social inequalities in democracy show that: **1**

(*a*) democracy and development go together
(*b*) inequalities exist in democracies
(*c*) inequalities do not exist under a dictatorship
(*d*) dictatorship is better than democracy.

23. Two statements are given as Assertion (A) and Reason (R). Read the statements and select the correct option: **1**

Assertion (A): Economic growth and development is not a desirable outcome of democracy.

Reason (R): Democracy provides a conducive environment for economic growth & development.

Options:

(*a*) Both A and R are true and R is the correct explanation of A.
(*b*) Both A and R are true, but R is not the correct explanation of A.
(*c*) A is true, but R is false.
(*d*) A is false, but R is true.

24. Which was not the provision in Belgian Constitution? **1**

(*a*) Constitution prescribes that the number of Dutch and French-speaking ministers shall be equal in central government.
(*b*) Some special laws require the support of majority of members from each linguistic group.
(*c*) Brussels has a separate government in which both communities have equal representation.
(*d*) The community government has no power regarding cultural, educational and language related issues.

25. Discuss the state of women's political participation in India in comparison to the global average. **2**

26. State any three differences between the local government before and after the Constitutional amendment in 1992. **3**

27A. Describe the challenges faced by the Political Parties in Indian democracy. **5**

OR

27B. Describe the features of Bharatiya Janata Party with special reference to its ideals. **5**

28. Read the given text and answer the following questions: (1 + 1 + 2 = 4) **4**

Power is shared among different organs of government, such as the legislature, executive and judiciary. We call it horizontal distribution of power because it allows different organs of government placed at the same level to exercise different powers. Such a separation ensures that none of the organs can exercise unlimited power. Each organ checks the others. This results in a balance of power among various institutions. In a democracy, even though ministers and government officials exercise power, they are responsible to the Parliament or State Assemblies. Similarly, although judges are appointed by the executive, they can check the functioning of executive or laws made by the legislatures. This arrangement is called a system of checks and balances. Power can be shared among governments at different levels as well – a general government for the entire country and governments at the provincial or regional level. Such a general government for the entire country is usually called federal government. In India, we refer to it as the Central or Union Government. The governments at the provincial or regional level are called by different names in different countries. In India, we call them State Governments. The same principle can be extended to levels of government lower than the State government, such as the municipality and panchayat. This division of powers involving higher and lower levels of government is called vertical division of power.

28.1 What is the difference between horizontal division of power and vertical division of power?

28.2 What is the purpose of the system of checks and balances in a democracy?

28.3 How does the system of checks and balances work in India's democracy?

SECTION - D

ECONOMICS (20 Marks)

29. Why was National Income considered as the most important criterion for assessing the development of a country? **1**

(*a*) It was the most convenient way of assessing the development of the country
(*b*) The countries with small population could also be included
(*c*) Greater income will enable people to fulfill all their needs
(*d*) All of the above

30. Find the odd one out. **1**

(*a*) Liberalisation
(*b*) Privatisation
(*c*) Globalisation
(*d*) Authorisation

31. Read the data given below and answer the question. **1**

State	Per Capita Income (2018-19 in Rs)	Literacy Rate (%) 2017-18	Infant Mortality Rate per 1,000 live births (2018)	Net Attendance Ratio (age 14 and 15 years) 2017-18
Haryana	2,36,147	82	30	61
Kerala	2,04,105	94	7	83
Bihar	40,982	62	32	43

On the basis of the above information- The state with highest per capita income is........, The state with the lowest literacy rate is......., The state with the lowest infant mortality rate is........., and The state with the highest net attendance ratio for the secondary stage is......... respectively.

(*a*) Haryana, Kerala, Kerala, Bihar
(*b*) Bihar, Kerala, Kerala, Haryana
(*c*) Haryana, Bihar, Kerala, Kerala
(*d*) Bihar, Haryana, Kerala, Kerala

32. Shyam has to make preparations for next year's cultivation of the field. He wants to purchase a tractor for which he has to take a loan. He does not have a collateral. From which source of credit will he borrow the money? **1**

(*a*) Bank (*b*) Cooperative (*c*) Moneylender (*d*) None

33. Choose the correct option: **1**

Globalisation, by connecting countries, shall result in

(*a*) Lesser competition among producers (*b*) Greater competition among producers
(*c*) No change in competition among producers (*d*) None of these

34. Which of the following is an economic consequence of globalisation? **1**

(*a*) Preservation of local industries and traditional practices.
(*b*) Increased income inequality between different countries.
(*c*) Strengthening of national boundaries and isolationism.
(*d*) Promotion of self-sufficiency and reduced reliance on imports.

35. Why should intermediate goods not be included to know the total production in a sector? **2**

36. Suggest ways to create more employment avenues in urban areas. **3**

37A. Explain three terms of credit. How do these differ in different cases? **5**

OR

37B. Why is it necessary that banks and cooperatives increase their lending in rural areas? Explain. **5**

38. Read the source given below and answer the questions that follow: (1 + 1 + 2 = 4) **4**

For comparing countries, their income is considered to be one of the most important attributes. Countries with higher income are more developed than others with less income. This is based on the understanding that more income means more of all things that human beings need. Whatever people like, and should have, they will be able to get with greater income. So, greater income itself is considered to be one important goal. Now, what is the income of a country? Intuitively, the income of the country is the income of all the residents of the country. This gives us the total income of the country. However, for comparison between countries, total income is not such an useful measure. Since, countries have different populations, paring total income will not tell us what an average person is likely to earn. Are people in one country better off than others in a different country? Hence, we compare the average income which is the total income of the country divided by its total population. The average income is also called per capita income. In World Development Reports, brought out by the World Bank, this criterion is used in classifying countries. Countries with per capita income of US$ 49,300 per annum and above in 2019, are called high income or rich countries and those with per capita income of US$ 2500 or less are called low-income countries. The rich countries, excluding countries of. Middle East and certain other small countries are generally called developed countries.

38.1 Explain the significance of per capita Income.

38.2 What are the classifications of countries based on per capita income?

38.3 Which entity is responsible for determining these classifications?

Map for Q. no. 10 (Section A) & Q. no. 18 (Section B)

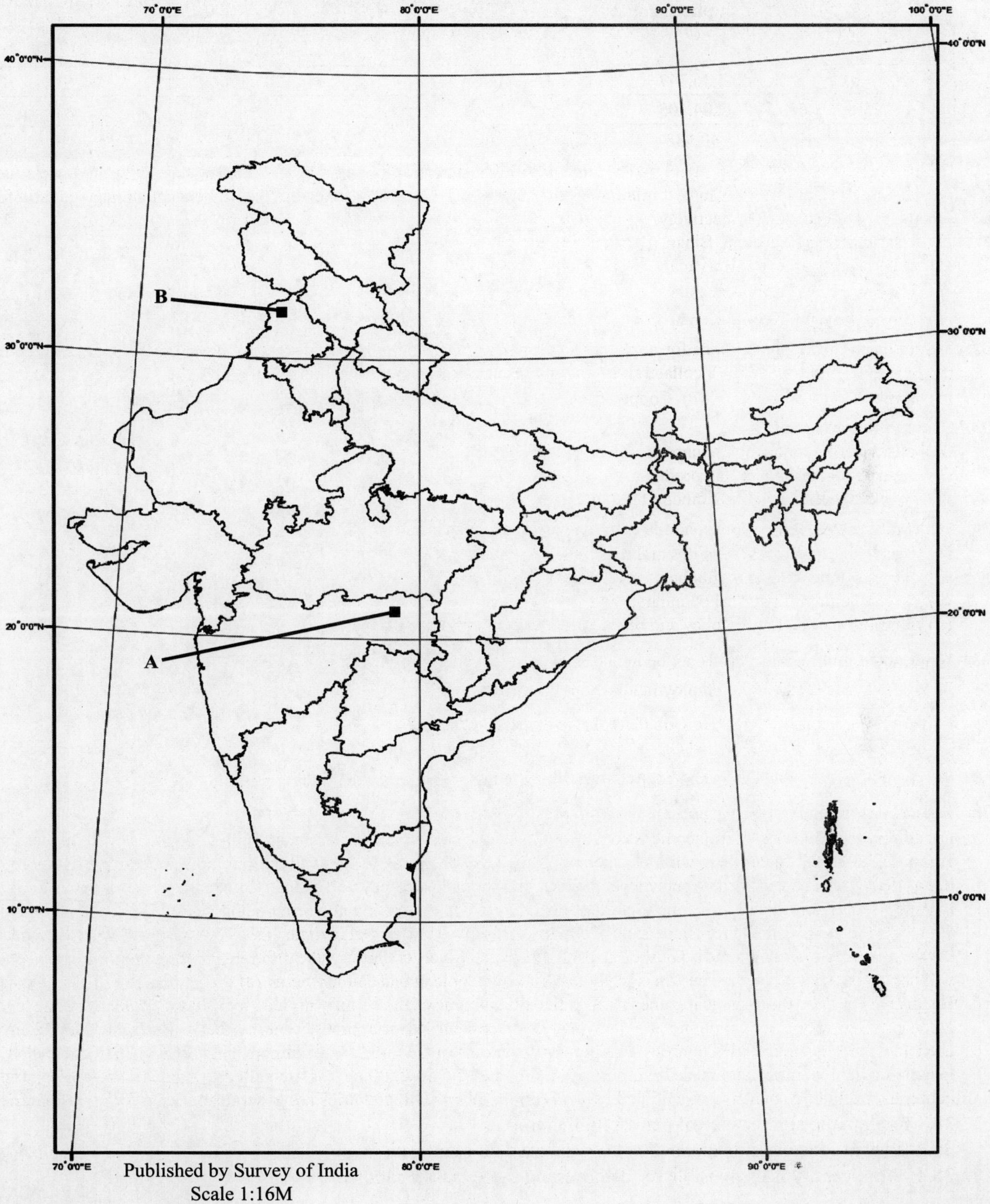

Published by Survey of India
Scale 1:16M

EXPLANATIONS

SAMPLE QUESTION PAPER-I

(Explanations)

Revision Time : 8 Min

SECTION - A

HISTORY (20 Marks)

Marking Scheme (Ques 1-5) 5 Min

☞ Each question carries 1 mark.

1. (*a*) The primary aim of the Non-Cooperation Movement, led by Mahatma Gandhi, was to achieve complete independence from British rule. ***(1 M)***

2. (*a*) The Frankfurt Parliament was an assembly of German states' representatives held in 1848-1849.Its primary aim was to create a unified German nation with a constitution and democratic governance. ***(1 M)***

3. (*a*) A. Khilafat movement - Jan. 1921

C. Chauri Chaura - 1922

D.Ambedkar establishes depressed classes association- 1930

B. Second round table conference- Dec. 1931 ***(1 M)***

4. (*d*) J L Nehru : Oudh Kisan Sabha ***(1 M)***

5. (*d*) Italy was divided into seven states, of which only one, Sardinia-Piedmont, was ruled by an Italian princely house ***(1 M)***

6. **Marking Scheme** 6 Min

☞ Define about Silk Routes ***(1 M)***

☞ Define missionary Movements ***(1 M)***

The following statement in the context of the pre-modern world as follows;

(*i*) **Silk Routes:** These ancient trade routes linked Asia with Europe and Africa, carrying not only goods like silk and spices but also cultural ideas and religions such as Buddhism and Christianity.

(*ii*) **Missionary Movements:** Alongside traders, Christian missionaries and Muslim preachers traveled these routes, spreading their faiths and fostering cultural interactions across continents.

7A. **Marking Scheme** 6 Min

☞ Preservation of traditional institutions ***(1 M)***

☞ Modernization to strengthen tradition ***(1 M)***

Two beliefs of conservatism that emerged after 1815 were:

(*i*) Established and traditional institutions of state and society like monarchy, the Church, property and family should be preserved.

(*ii*) They believed in the modernization of the traditional institution to strengthen them, rather than returning to the society of pre-revolutionary days.

OR

7B. **Marking Scheme** 6 Min

☞ Leadership by educated middle class ***(1 M)***

☞ Composition of the group ***(1 M)***

The liberal-nationalist revolutions during the 1830-1848 period led by these:

(*i*) The liberal-nationalist revolutions were led by the educated middle-class elite.

(*ii*) This group included professors, school teachers, clerks, and members of the commercial middle classes.

8A. **Marking Scheme** 14 Min

☞ **Active Resistance:** Non-violent but firm resistance to injustice ***(1 M)***

☞ **Truth (Satya):** Upholding and seeking truth in all actions ***(1 M)***

☞ **Non-Violence (Ahimsa):** Changing the oppressor's heart through love and patience ***(1 M)***

☞ **Self-Sacrifice:** Willingness to suffer without retaliation ***(1 M)***

☞ **Moral High Ground:** Creating pressure by showing justice and dignity in action ***(1 M)***

Principles of Satyagraha as explained by Mahatma Gandhi:

(*i*) **Active Resistance:** Satyagraha is not passive but involves active, non-violent resistance to injustice. It requires courage and strength, not submission.

(*ii*) **Truth (Satya):** The power of satyagraha lies in the adherence to truth. Gandhi emphasized the need to search for and uphold truth in every action.

(*iii*) **Non-Violence (Ahimsa):** Satyagraha is based on non-violence. It seeks to win over the oppressor through love and patience, appealing to their conscience.

(*iv*) **Self-Sacrifice:** A satyagrahi must be willing to endure suffering without retaliation. The goal is to transform the oppressor's heart, not to defeat them through force.

(*v*) **Moral High Ground:** Satyagraha aims to create moral pressure on the oppressor by demonstrating the justice of the cause and the dignity of the resisters.

OR

8B. **Marking Scheme** *14 Min*

- **Colonial forest laws** restricted tribal access to forests in the Gudem Hills, affecting fuelwood collection, grazing, and livelihood. ***(1 M)***
- **Forced begar (unpaid labour)** was imposed by the British for road building, causing resentment among tribals. ***(1 M)***
- **Denial of traditional rights** and the threat to their lifestyle and cultural practices led to growing unrest. ***(1 M)***
- **Alluri Sitaram Raju's leadership** inspired the tribals with his charisma, belief in justice, divine powers, and partial support for Gandhism. ***(1 M)***
- **Under Raju's leadership, tribals launched guerrilla attacks** on British forces and police stations from 1922 to 1924. ***(1 M)***

Causes of the Rampa Rebellion:

(*i*) The British closed forest areas in the Gudem Hills, which prevented tribal people from collecting fuelwood, grazing cattle, or using forest resources, affecting their livelihood.

(*ii*) The government forced the tribals to do begar (unpaid labour) for building roads, which increased their anger and frustration.

(*iii*) Tribals felt that their traditional rights were being denied, and their way of life was under threat due to harsh colonial forest laws.

(*iv*) Alluri Sitaram Raju emerged as a charismatic leader, inspiring people with his claims of divine powers and support for Gandhiji's movement, though he believed in armed struggle.

(*v*) The tribals, under Raju's leadership, attacked police stations and officials, starting a guerrilla war from 1922 to 1924, which became a symbol of tribal resistance.

9. **Marking Scheme** *10 Min*

- **9.1.** Define picketing liquor shops ***(1 M)***
- **9.2.** About the Non-Cooperation-Khilafat Movement ***(1 M)***
- **9.3.** Any two valid reasons for the slowdown of the movement in cities ***(2 M)***

9.1 Picketing is a form of demonstration or protest by which people block the entrance to a shop, factory, or office.

9.2 The Non-Cooperation-Khilafat movement began in January 1921. The movement started with the middle-class participation in the cities.

9.3 The movement in the cities gradually slowed down for a variety of reasons: Khadi being expensive was unaffordable was poor people, lack of alternative Indian institutions posed a problem in boycotting British institutions.

10. Marked on the map. ***(2 M)***

SECTION - B

GEOGRAPHY (20 Marks)

11.(*a*) **Marking Scheme (Ques 11-13)** *3 Min*

- Each question carries 1 mark.

Location: Situated on the Sutlej River in Himachal Pradesh and Punjab.

Purpose: The dam serves multiple purposes, including irrigation, hydroelectric power generation, flood control, and water supply.

Significance: It is one of the largest and most important multipurpose projects in India, providing significant benefits for agriculture, energy, and water management. ***(1 M)***

12. (*c*) **Location:** Situated in Assam, India.

Significance: Kaziranga is renowned for its population of the one-horned rhinoceros.

Conservation Efforts: The Park has been a dedicated site for the preservation and protection of the one-horned rhinoceros, making it one of the key areas for rhinoceros' conservation globally. ***(1 M)***

13. (*c*) Based on the provided image, the land-use category that has increased from 1960 to 2014 is:

Forest The percentage of forest land has increased from **18.11% in 1960-61** to **23.3% in 2014-15**, as indicated by the pie charts. ***(1 M)***

14. **Marking Scheme** ⏰ *6 Min*

☞ Should mention agriculture providing raw materials to industries. ***(1 M)***
☞ Should explain how plantation crops (e.g., tea, coffee) are processed in factories, showing direct agriculture-industry link ***(1 M)***

Agriculture and industry are closely linked, as seen through the following examples:

(*i*) **Raw Material Supply:** Agriculture provides raw materials for various industries; for instance, cotton farming supports the textile industry, and sugarcane cultivation is crucial for the sugar industry.

(*ii*) **Plantation and Industry:** Plantation agriculture, like tea and coffee, integrates with industry as these crops are processed in factories before reaching the market, illustrating a direct link between farming and industrial activities.

Nailing the Right Answer

- Mention specific examples where agriculture provides raw materials to industries, such as cotton for textiles and sugarcane for the sugar industry.
- Highlight how plantation crops like tea and coffee are processed in factories, showing the direct connection between agriculture and industrial processes.

15. **Marking Scheme** ⏰ *8 Min*

☞ Mention that agriculture provides livelihood to a large population, especially in rural India ***(1 M)***
☞ Should include that agriculture plays a substantial role in contributing to India's Gross Domestic Product ***(1 M)***
☞ Explain that agriculture supplies raw materials to industries (e.g., textiles, food processing), aiding industrial growth ***(1 M)***

Significance of Agriculture in the Indian Economy:

(*i*) **Employment Generation:** Agriculture employs a significant portion of the Indian population, especially in rural areas, providing livelihoods to millions.

(*ii*) **Contribution to GDP:** It contributes substantially to India's GDP, supporting economic growth and development.

(*iii*) **Raw Material Supply:** Agriculture supplies essential raw materials to various industries, such as textiles and food processing, driving industrial growth and stability.

16A. **Marking Scheme** ⏰ *13 Min*

(for both metallic and non-metallic sides are correctly mentioned for each aspect.) (½ mark if only one side (either metallic or non-metallic) is correctly stated.)
☞ Composition ***(1 M)***
☞ Examples ***(1 M)***
☞ Luster ***(1 M)***
☞ Conductivity ***(1 M)***
☞ Uses ***(1 M)***

Differences between Metallic and Non-Metallic Minerals:

	Aspect	Metallic Minerals	Non-Metallic Minerals
(*i*)	**Composition**	Contain metal elements in their chemical composition.	Do not contain metal elements in their chemical composition.
(*ii*)	**Examples**	Iron, copper, bauxite, manganese.	Limestone, mica, gypsum, coal.
(*iii*)	**Luster**	Exhibit a shiny or metallic luster.	Exhibit a non-metallic, dull luster.
(*iv*)	**Conductivity**	Good conductors of heat and electricity.	Poor conductors of heat and electricity.
(*v*)	**Uses**	Used in construction, manufacturing, electronics.	Used in construction, agriculture, industrial processes.

OR

16B. **Marking Scheme** ⏰ *13 Min*

☞ Construction Sector and give clearly linked examples names. ***(1 M)***
☞ Energy Sector and provide correct minerals (e.g., coal, uranium) used in electricity generation. ***(1 M)***
☞ Manufacturing Sector with give specific minerals (e.g., iron, copper, aluminium) with their industrial use. ***(1 M)***
☞ Agriculture Sector with Clearly linked examples of minerals. ***(1 M)***
☞ Technology & Space Sector Rare earth minerals exact use. ***(1 M)***

Minerals are essential to human life, integral to everything from basic infrastructure to advanced technology, which are as follows:

(*i*) **Construction:** Minerals like limestone, clay, and gypsum are fundamental for constructing buildings, bridges, and roads, demonstrating their essential role in infrastructure development.

(*ii*) **Energy Production:** Coal, uranium, and thorium are used for energy production, highlighting their critical role in generating electricity and supporting industrial and domestic activities.

(*iii*) **Manufacturing:** Iron, copper, and aluminium are used extensively in the manufacturing of automobiles, appliances, and electronics, showcasing their utility in various industries.

(*iv*) **Agriculture:** Minerals such as phosphate, potash, and lime are used to make fertilizers, which are crucial for agriculture, ensuring food production and food security.

(*v*) **Technology and Space:** Rare earth elements and other minerals are vital for producing high-tech electronics, batteries, and even spacecraft, indicating their significance in advancing technology and exploration.

Nailing the Right Answer

- ❐ Provide examples of how minerals are essential in different sectors, such as construction (limestone, clay), energy production (coal, uranium), and manufacturing (iron, copper).
- ❐ Highlight the importance of minerals in advanced technology and agriculture, such as rare earth elements for electronics and phosphate for fertilizers, showing their broad impact on modern life

17. **Marking Scheme** ⏰ *10 Min*

☞ **17.1** Any one well-explained point related to the question. ***(1 M)***

☞ **17.2** Any two correct factual roles of the Act clearly,brief ***(1 M)***

☞ **17.3** Both time-period efforts are clearly compared At least one valid point for each period is correctly mentioned (1 Mark for each point) ***(2 M)***

17.1 Conserving forests and wildlife preserve biodiversity, sustains ecosystems, supports life, maintains water, air quality, and aids agriculture.

17.2 The Indian Wildlife (Protection) Act of 1972 protects endangered species by banning hunting, securing habitats, restricting wildlife trade, and establishing national parks and sanctuaries for conservation.

17.3 In the 1960s and 1970s, conservation measures focused on legal protection and creating sanctuaries Recent efforts emphasize targeted species protection projects and advanced enforcement techniques, including technology and community involvement.

18. **Marking Scheme** ⏰ *3 Min*

Section I: Locate and Label (any one)

(p) Tehri Dam – in Uttarakhand ***(1 M)***

OR

(q) Rana Pratap Sagar Dam- in Rajasthan.

Section II: Any two of the following ***(1 × 2 = 2 M)***

(i) Narora Nuclear Power Plant – Uttar Pradesh

(ii) International Airport in Chennai – Meenambakkam Airport, Tamil Nadu

(iii) International Airport in Mumbai – Chhatrapati Shivaji Maharaj International Airport, Maharashtra

Marked on the map.

SECTION - C

POLITICAL SCIENCE (20 Marks)

Marking Scheme (Ques 19-24) ⏰ *6 Min*

☞ Each question carries 1 mark.

19. (*a*) Buddhists ***(1 M)***

20. (*a*) Majoritarianism emphasizes the dominance of the majority community, while Power sharing emphasizes the sharing of power among different groups. ***(1 M)***

21. (*d*) In poor countries, the rate of economic growth under dictatorships and democracies is negligible and not drastic. ***(1 M)***

22. (*d*) Between 1970 and 1993, Belgium amended their constitution four times to work out an arrangement enabling everyone to live together within the same country. ***(1 M)***

23. (*b*) It is free of corruption ***(1 M)***

24. (*a*) Both the given statements are correct. ***(1 M)***

25. **Marking Scheme** ⏰ *6 Min*

- ☞ **Trend in Governance:** Identify the direction of change in the governance structure based on S1 and S2. ***(1 M)***
- ☞ **Commitment to Federalism:** Explain how this trend supports local-level decision-making. ***(1 M)***

(*i*) These statements indicate a growing trend of decentralization in India, where power and decision-making are increasingly being transferred to local levels.

(*ii*) This shift reflects India's strong commitment to federalism and promotes local-level governance by enabling decisions to be made as close to the people as possible.

26. **Marking Scheme** ⏰ *7 Min*

- ☞ **Social Practice:** Mention ongoing caste-based social preferences in society. ***(1 M)***
- ☞ **Legal and Social Discrimination:** State the continued existence of caste-based discrimination despite legal bans. ***(1 M)***
- ☞ **Economic Inequality:** Explain economic disparity among caste groups. ***(1 M)***

The Statement that says "Caste inequality are still prevalent in India" is true because:

(*i*) Even today, most people marry within their own caste or tribe.

(*ii*) Discrimination based on caste, including untouchability has not ended completely, despite constitutional prohibition.

(*iii*) On the economic front as well, the proportion of people living below the poverty line is highest among the Scheduled Tribes and lowest among the 'upper' castes.

Topper's Explanation ***(CBSE, 2019)***

Caste inequalities are still prevalent in India. This statement can be justified by the following →

(i) Although the constitution has prohibited caste discrimination; it is still practised in parts of the country.

(ii) People still now marry within the same caste.

(iii) The decades of advantages and disadvantages are ~~followed~~ felt even today.

(iv) People who earlier had access to education have done very well in accessing modern education. But people who did not have access to education or were prohibited, have lagged behind.

(v) The economic status still now follow the caste hierarchies – the upper class the best off, the lower caste the worst and the OBCs in between

27A. **Marking Scheme** ⏰ *14 Min*

- ☞ **Core Principle:** Mention political equality as a fundamental principle of democracy. ***(1 M)***
- ☞ **Equal Voting Rights:** Explain the concept of one person, one vote, one value. ***(1 M)***
- ☞ **Universal Equality:** Highlight that each individual's voice holds equal weight regardless of background. ***(1 M)***
- ☞ **Representative Nature:** Explain how elections reflect the will of the people equally ***(1 M)***
- ☞ **Inclusive Governance:** Mention how the system ensures all voices are heard fairly and equally. ***(1 M)***

The statement "Democratic systems are based on political equality" stands true because:

(*i*) Political equality is the fundamental principle of democracy, which says all individuals have equal rights and say in the democratic process and decision-making.

(*ii*) In a democracy, every citizen gets one vote, and each vote has equal value, ensuring that no one has more influence over the government than anyone else.

(*iii*) This core concept ensures that each person's voice holds equal weight, regardless of their social, economic, or cultural background.

(*iv*) In democracies, political equality is fundamental, ensuring that elected representatives are chosen by the people, for the people, reflecting the collective will and preferences of all the people.

(*v*) This principle promotes inclusiveness and fairness, ensuring that all voices, regardless of any other discriminatory factor, are heard and considered equally in the political process.

OR

27B. **Marking Scheme** ⏰ *14 Min*

- ☞ **Equal Participation:** Mention that democracy ensures equal voting and participation rights for all castes. ***(1 M)***
- ☞ **Political Representation:** Explain how marginalized castes can influence laws and policies through elected leaders. ***(1 M)***

☞ **Platform for Equality:** State how democracy promotes dignity and provides a platform to resist caste-based discrimination. *(1 M)*
☞ **Mechanism for Reform:** Acknowledge democracy's role in gradually addressing inequalities. *(1 M)*
☞ **Amplifying Marginalized Voices:** Highlight how democracy enables previously ignored voices to be heard and valued. *(1 M)*

In India, democracy has played a significant role in strengthened the claims of disadvantaged and discriminated castes in the following ways:

(*i*) It gives everyone, no matter their caste, an equal chance to vote, share their opinions, and choose their leaders.

(*ii*) This helps make sure that even those from lower castes can have a say in how the country is run and what laws are made through the representative elected by them.

(*iii*) Democracy also pushes for treating everyone with respect and gives a platform for fighting against unfair treatment based on caste.

(*iv*) While there are still issues and inequalities that exist, democracy offers a way to challenge and slowly change these problems.

(*v*) It's about giving everyone a fair chance and making sure that all voices, especially those that have been ignored in the past, are heard and valued.

28. **Marking Scheme** ⏰ *10 Min*

28.1 Functions of Political Parties *(1 M)*
28.2 Reason to persuade people about their policies *(1 M)*
28.3 ☞ Identify the method political parties use tosecure support for their policies. *(1 M)* ☞ Explain how gaining support enables them to implement policies effectively. *(1 M)*

28.1 The main functions of a political party are to contest elections, hold power in the government, agree on policies and programs for society to promote the collective good.

28.2 Political parties try to persuade people about their policies because they aim to show why their policies are better than other and seek to gain popular support and form government through elections.

28.3 (*i*) Political parties seek to implement their policies by winning popular support through elections.

(*ii*) By gaining the trust and votes of the people, they can achieve the power needed to put their policies into action.

SECTION - D

ECONOMICS (20 Marks)

Marking Scheme (Ques 29-34) ⏰ *8 Min*

☞ Each question carries 1 mark.

29. (*d*) Let the income of fourth family = x

therefore,

Total income of all four families = 4,000 + 7,000 + 3,000 + x = 14,000 + x

Average per capita income of the all four families

$$= \frac{\text{Total income of all four families}}{\text{No. of families}}$$

$$5{,}000 = \frac{14{,}000 + x}{4}$$

20,000 = 14,000 + x, x = 6,000

Income of the fourth family = ₹ 6,000 *(1 M)*

30. (*b*) Bank primarily use the major portion of deposits to extend loans to various borrowers, which helps in generating profit through interest payments. *(1 M)*

31. (*c*) A-(ii), B-(iv), C-(i), D-(iii) *(1 M)*

32. (*a*) Primary Sector *(1 M)*

33. (*a*) Statement-(*iii*) is false as India is not the cheapest manufacturing location, China is the cheapest location. Statement-iv is also false as India lies in Asia continent and it is not close to the markets in the US and Europe. *(1 M)*

34. (*b*) Taking a loan from a Self-Help Group (SHG) *(1 M)*

35A. **Marking Scheme** ⏰ *6 Min*

☞ Definition of open unemployment and disguised unemployment *(1 M)*
☞ Distinction on the basis of visibility *(1 M)*
☞ Distinction on the basis of output/production *(1 M)*

Basis	Open Unemployment	Disguised Unemployment
Definition	When people who are willing to work and have the ability to work do not get any job, it is called open unemployment.	When more people are working in a job than actually needed, it is called disguised unemployment. Even if some of them stop working, the work will still continue.

Visibility	It is clearly visible — people are not working at all.	It is not clearly visible — people appear to be working.
Output/ Production	No work means no production.	Extra people do not increase production.

OR

35B. Marking Scheme ⏰ *6 Min*

- ☞ Development of agriculture and industry increases demand for support services (like transport, storage, etc.) ***(1 M)***
- ☞ Rise in income increases demand for services like tourism, shopping, etc. ***(1 M)***
- ☞ Basic services like education, health, banking, and transport are in demand ***(1 M)***

Tertiary sector or service sector plays a very significant role and its importance is rising day by day:

(*i*) As incomes of the people rise, people spend more on services like tourism, shopping, and entertainment.

(*ii*) Tertiary sector has become the largest producer in India because various kinds of Services such as hospitals, educational institutions, post and telegraph services, police stations, courts, village administrative offices, transport, banks, insurance companies, etc. are required.

(*iii*) Even development of agriculture and industry leads to the development of services such as transport, trade and storage, etc.

36. Marking Scheme ⏰ *7 Min*

- ☞ Effectiveness ***(1 M)***
- ☞ Job Creation ***(1 M)***
- ☞ Community Development ***(1 M)***

Foreign investment has improved the standard of living in Araville in the following ways:

(*i*) **Enhanced Product Availability:** Foreign investment introduces a variety of products, improving consumer choice and satisfaction, thus potentially raising living standards.

(*ii*) **Job Creation:** Multinationals often bring job opportunities in various sectors, boosting employment and income levels in Araville.

(*iii*) **Community Development:** To distribute benefits equitably, the government could implement policies ensuring multinationals invest in local infrastructure and community programs.

37. Marking Scheme ⏰ *7 Min*

- ☞ Calculation ***(1 M)***
- ☞ Bar Diagram ***(1 M)***
- ☞ Conclusion/Observation ***(1 M)***

(*i*)

In 2000	In 2013
Primary sector = 22.22%	Primary sector = 13.94%
Secondary sector = 20.73%	Secondary sector = 18.70%
Tertiary sector = 57.04%	Tertiary sector = 67.36%

(*ii*)

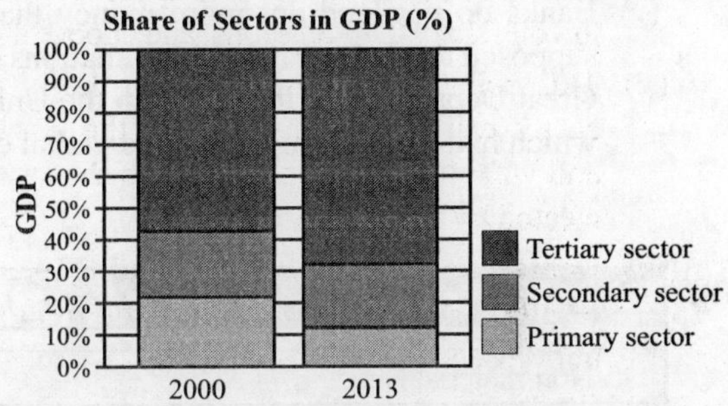

(*iii*) The conclusion can be drawn from the bar graph is that the share of the tertiary sector in the GDP has increased by 10%, while that of the primary sector has halved approx. The secondary sector has grown by about 2%.

Nailing the Right Answer

- ❒ Use proper units while calculating shares (%).
- ❒ Analyze trends and make clear conclusions from the graph.
- ❒ Highlight any significant shifts in sector contributions.
- ❒ Ensure accurate calculations and insightful interpretations for maximum marks.

38A. Marking Scheme ⏰ *15 Min*

- ☞ Bank regulation through reserve monitoring ***(1 M)***
- ☞ Promotes financial inclusion and fair lending ***(1 M)***
- ☞ Transparency and reporting obligation ***(1 M)***
- ☞ Reason for supervision – promoting equitable growth ***(1 M)***
- ☞ Preventing economic instability and protecting economy ***(1 M)***

RBI supervises the functioning of banks in the following ways:

(*i*) The Reserve Bank of India keeps track of how much money banks lend out as well as how much cash they maintain.

(*ii*) It also ensures that banks make loans to small cultivators, small-scale industries, and small borrowers, rather than just profiteering businesses.

(*iii*) Banks are required to submit information to the RBI on the amounts loaned, to whom, and at what interest rates regularly.

(*iv*) This monitoring is required to ensure that equality is maintained in the financial sector and that small businesses have an environment to grow.

(*v*) Banks do not lend out more money than they are supposed to, as this can lead to situations such as the Great Depression of the 1930s in the United States, which had a major impact on the global economy.

OR

38B.

Marking Scheme	⏰ ***15 Min***
☞ Non-material Needs	***(1 M)***
☞ Public Services	***(1 M)***
☞ Natural Resources	***(1 M)***
☞ Time and Health	***(1 M)***
☞ Social Status	***(1 M)***

The statement "Money cannot buy all the goods and services that you may need to live well" means:

(*i*) **Non-material Needs:** Money cannot buy emotional well-being, happiness, love, and personal relationships which are essential for a fulfilling life.

(*ii*) **Public Services:** Many public services like clean air, water, and safety are provided by the government and cannot be bought directly.

(*iii*) **Natural Resources:** Certain natural resources and environmental quality cannot be purchased, such as a pollution-free environment.

(*iv*) **Time and Health:** Money cannot buy time, health, or life. While money can access healthcare, it cannot guarantee health or longevity.

(*v*) **Social Status:** Respect, reputation, and social standing cannot be bought. These are earned through behavior and interactions within society.

Topper's Explanation ***(CBSE, 2020)***

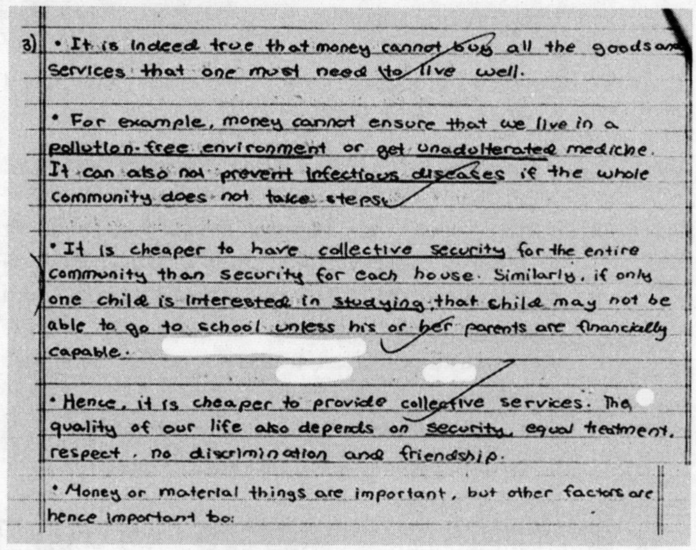
3) • It is indeed true that money cannot buy all the goods and services that one must need to live well.

• For example, money cannot ensure that we live in a pollution-free environment or get unadulterated medicine. It can also not prevent infectious diseases if the whole community does not take steps.

• It is cheaper to have collective security for the entire community than security for each house. Similarly, if only one child is interested in studying, that child may not be able to go to school unless his or her parents are financially capable.

• Hence, it is cheaper to provide collective services. The quality of our life also depends on security, equal treatment, respect, no discrimination and friendship.

• Money or material things are important, but other factors are hence important too.

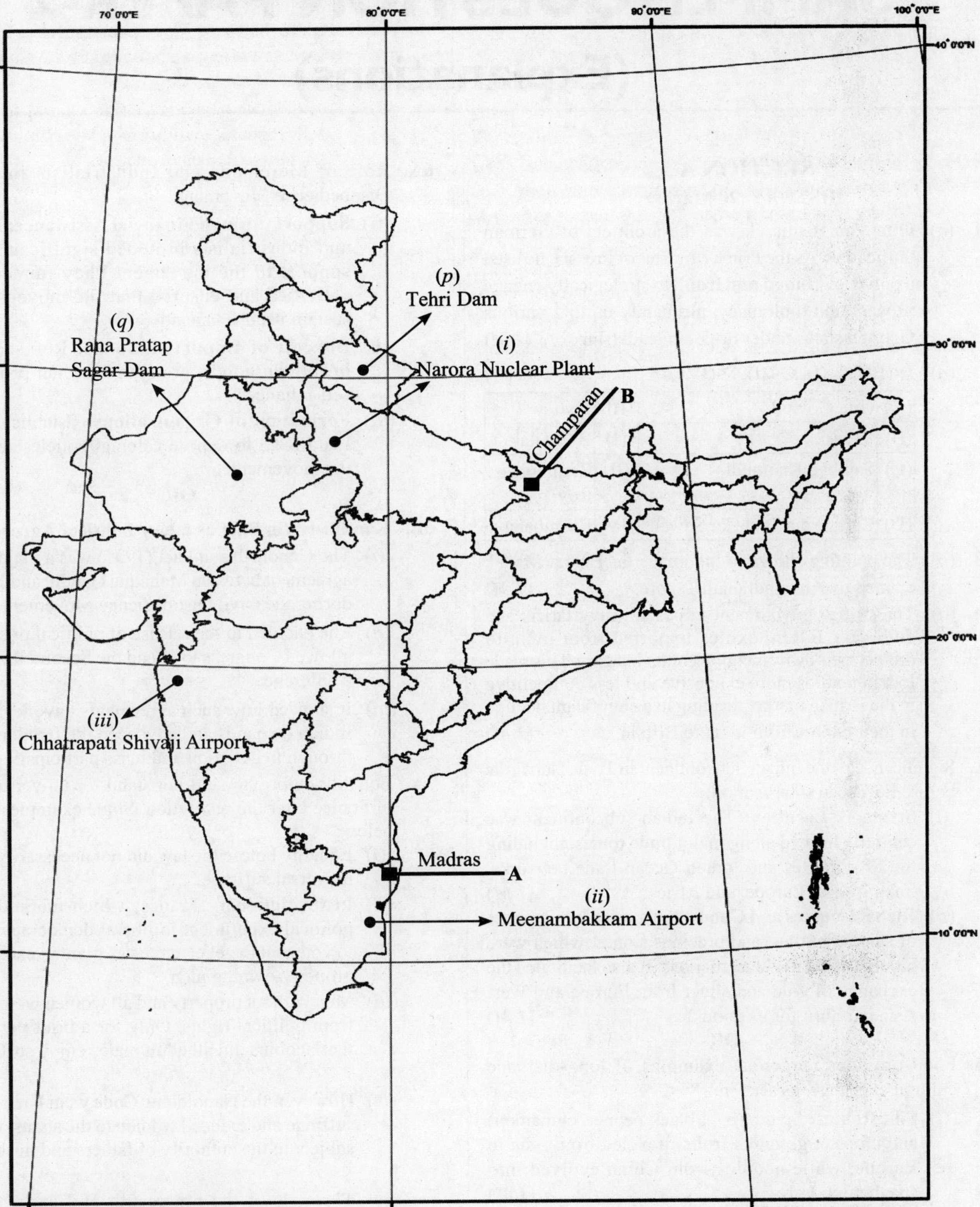

Published by Survey of India

Scale 1:16 M

SAMPLE QUESTION PAPER-2

(Explanations)

SECTION A

HISTORY (20 Marks)

1. (*a*) Otto Von Bismarck was the architect of German unification. As the Prime Minister of Prussia, he used a policy of **"blood and iron"** to strategically engage in wars and diplomacy, ultimately uniting various German states under Prussian leadership. ***(1 M)***

2. (*a*) A-(III), B-(I), C-(II), D-(IV) ***(1 M)***

(A)	Gita Govind	(III)	Jaydev
(B)	Kesari	(I)	B G Tilak
(C)	Sambad Kaumudi	(II)	Rammohan Roy
(D)	Chhote aur Bade ka Sawal	(IV)	Kashibaba

3. (*b*) The painting shown in the image is "Bharat Mata", created by Abanindranath Tagore. ***(1 M)***

4. (*a*) The British government imposed heavy tariffs and duties on cotton textiles imported from India to protect their own emerging cotton industry. This made Indian textiles more expensive and less competitive in the British market, leading to a significant decline in their export from India to Britain. ***(1 M)***

5A. Significance of the Indian Subcontinent in Trade Networks before European Intervention:

(*i*) **Strategic Location:** The Indian subcontinent was centrally located along major trade routes, including the Silk Routes and Indian Ocean trade networks, linking Asia, Europe, and Africa. ***(1 M)***

(*ii*) **Rich Resources and Goods:** India was a key exporter of spices, textiles, and precious stones, which were highly valued in global markets. It also facilitated the exchange of gold and silver from Europe and West Asia in return for its goods. ***(1 M)***

OR

5B. Food provides numerous examples of long-distance cultural exchange, as seen in:

(*i*) **Silk Routes:** Spices (e.g., black pepper, cinnamon) and crops (e.g., citrus fruits) traveled from Asia to Europe, while noodles from China evolved into spaghetti in Italy ***(1 M)***

(*ii*) **Columbian Exchange:** Potatoes, tomatoes, and chillies from the Americas were introduced globally, transforming diets in Europe and Asia. ***(1 M)***

6A. Role of Merchants and Industrialists in the Civil Disobedience Movement:

(*i*) **Support through Financial Assistance:** Merchants and industrialists provided significant financial support to the movement.They funded various activities and ensured that the movement could sustain itself financially. ***(1 M)***

(*ii*) **Boycott of Imported Goods:** Refused to trade in foreign goods, promoting Indian products and self-reliance. ***(1 M)***

(*iii*) **Formation of Organizations:** Established groups like FICCI to oppose colonial policies and support the movement. ***(1 M)***

OR

6B. Gandhi-Irwin Pact as a Key Political Agreement:

(*i*) The Gandhi-Irwin Pact (1931) was a major political agreement between Mahatma Gandhi and Lord Irwin during the Civil Disobedience Movement. ***(1 M)***

(*ii*) The pact led to the release of political prisoners and allowed Congress to attend the Second Round Table Conference. ***(1 M)***

(*iii*) It showed how such agreements gave legitimacy to Indian demands and advanced the freedom struggle through negotiation and mass participation. ***(1 M)***

7A. Equality before law did not stand for universal suffrage in France after the revolution. Some examples are given below:

(*i*) Equality before the law did not necessarily stand for universal suffrage. ***(1 M)***

(*ii*) In revolutionary France, which marked the first political experiment in liberal democracy, the right to vote and to get elected was granted exclusively to property-owning men. ***(1 M)***

(*iii*) Men without property and all women were excluded from political rights. Only for a brief period under the Jacobins did all adult males enjoy suffrage. ***(1 M)***

(*iv*) However, the Napoleonic Code went back to limited suffrage and reduced women to the status of a minor, subject to the authority of fathers and husbands. ***(1 M)***

(*v*) Throughout the nineteenth and early twentieth centuries women and non-propertied men organised opposition movements demanding equal political rights. ***(1 M)***

OR

7B. The conditions which were viewed as obstacles to economic exchange and growth by the new commerical classes are:

(*i*) There was absence of freedom of markets. **(*1 M*)**

(*ii*) State imposed various restrictions on the movement of goods and capital. **(*1 M*)**

(*iii*) Presence of large numbers of states created problems as each had its own currency, and weights and measures. **(*1 M*)**

(*iv*) Duties were often levied according to the weight or measurement of the goods. As each region had its own system of weights and measures, this involved time-consuming calculation. **(*1 M*)**

(*v*) In 1834, a customs union or zollverein was formed at the initiative of Prussia and joined by most of the German states. **(*1 M*)**

8. 8.1 The primary objective of Ranade for publishing a Marathi language newspaper was to provide useful information on various local interest topics and promote the diffusion of knowledge and welfare among the people. **(*1 M*)**

8.2 The Bombay Telegraph emphasized the role of the newspaper to provide useful information on local interests, promoting knowledge and welfare in the Deccan region. **(*1 M*)**

8.3 The key responsibilities attributed to native newspapers were:

(*a*) Critically examining government policies to suggest necessary improvements and remove any detrimental aspects, ensuring that the changes benefit the public. **(*1 M*)**

(*b*) Conducting thorough research on various issues to gather diverse and relevant information, which would help in influencing public opinion and possibly policy decisions through informed debates and discussions. **(*1 M*)**

9. (*a*) Marked on the map. **(*2 M*)**

SECTION-B
GEOGRAPHY (20 Marks)

10. (*d*) Conservation of forests and wildlife is crucial for maintaining ecological balance because they offer ecosystem services like carbon sequestration and water regulation, contrary to the assertion that it's not essential. **(*1 M*)**

11. (*b*) Maize is used both as food and fodder. It is a Kharif crop requiring a temperature between 21°C to 27°C. It grows well in old alluvial soil. Modern inputs have increased its production. **(*1 M*)**

12. (*a*) Alluvial soil can be classified based on its age into old alluvial soil (Bangar) and new alluvial soil (Khadar). Bangar is the older, more weathered soil found away from the riverbeds, while Khadar is the newer, more fertile soil found closer to the riverbanks. **(*1 M*)**

13. (*b*) Grown in Nilgiri Hills; Loamy, well-drained, slightly acidic soil. **(*1 M*)**

14. (*c*) Joint Forest Management involves local communities in forest care, offering them benefits like non-timber products from protected areas. **(*1 M*)**

15. (*a*) Mining in Odisha causes deforestation and topsoil loss, leading to severe land degradation, especially in iron ore and bauxite regions. **(*1 M*)**

16. The main resources for generating atomic or nuclear power in India are:

(*i*) Uranium: Sourced from mines in Jharkhand and the Aravalli ranges of Rajasthan. **(*½ M*)**

(*ii*) Thorium: Abundant in the Monazite sands of Kerala. **(*½ M*)**

Significance: Uranium and Thorium are crucial for generating nuclear power, providing a stable and sustainable energy source, and reducing reliance on fossil fuels. **(*1 M*)**

17A. The impact of industrialization and urbanization on water scarcity and the role of hydroelectric power can be understood by the following points:

(*i*) **Urbanization increases water demand:** Higher population densities in urban areas significantly boost domestic water needs, straining existing supplies and depleting groundwater levels. **(*1 M*)**

(*ii*) **Industrial water consumption:** Industries near urban centers consume vast water amounts and often pollute local water sources, worsening water scarcity. **(*1 M*)**

(*iii*) **Water quality degradation:** Urban and industrial waste contaminates water resources, reducing the availability of clean water for consumption and agriculture. **(*1 M*)**

(*iv*) **Role of hydroelectric power:** Hydroelectric projects manage water by storing it in reservoirs for power generation and supply during droughts, but disrupt natural water flows and ecosystems. **(*1 M*)**

(*v*) **Environmental and social trade-offs:** While providing renewable energy and aiding water management, hydroelectric facilities can cause environmental damage and community displacement. **(*1 M*)**

OR

17B. The adaptability of rainwater harvesting to arid and semi-arid conditions and its impact can be understood by the following points:

(*i*) **Customized Collection Systems:** In arid Rajasthan, families often construct rooftop rainwater harvesting systems where rainwater from roofs is channeled through pipes into underground tanks or **'tankas'** for storage. Other structures like **khadins** and **Johads** are also used in rain water harvesting. ***(1 M)***

(*ii*) **Long-term Storage:** These underground 'tankas' are specifically designed to store water for long periods, ensuring a reliable supply during the prolonged dry seasons typical of the region. ***(1 M)***

(*iii*) **Improving Water Quality:** Stored rainwater is generally cleaner and safer for consumption compared to the often saline or fluoride-contaminated groundwater in Rajasthan. ***(1 M)***

(*iv*) **Reducing Dependence:** By harvesting rainwater, families reduce their dependence on distant water sources and erratic government supply, gaining autonomy over their water needs. ***(1 M)***

(*v*) **Enhancing Livelihoods:** Access to consistent water supplies supports home gardening and small-scale agriculture, improving food security and family income. ***(1 M)***

Nailing the Right Answer

- **Structure and Examples:** Clearly mention the types of traditional structures used for rainwater harvesting (e.g., Kunds, Tankas, Johads) and their specific functions.
- **Community Efforts and Maintenance:** Highlight the role of community efforts in constructing and maintaining these structures, ensuring sustainable water supply.

18. 18.1 The Sardar Sarovar Dam was constructed with the objective of securing irrigation and power. ***(1 M)***

18.2 The tribal people's protest was motivated by the massive displacement and loss of livelihood. ***(1 M)***

18.3 Initially focused on environmental concerns, such as submerged trees and ecosystems. ***(1 M)***

Later aimed to ensure proper rehabilitation for displaced individuals, securing their livelihoods and rights. ***(1 M)***

19. Marked on the map. ***(3 M)***

SECTION - C

POLITICAL SCIENCE (20 Marks)

20. (*c*) A-(I), B-(IV), C-(II), D-(III) ***(1 M)***

21. (*a*) Self-explanatory ***(1 M)***

22. (*b*) (ii) and (iii) ***(1 M)***

23. (*b*) According to our Indian constitution, subjects that do not fall into any of the three lists and subjects that came up after the constitution was made are called the Residuary subjects, and, the Union Government has the power to legislate on these subjects. ***(1 M)***

24. A political party is a group of people who come together to contest elections and hold power in the government. ***(1 M)***

Two key Components of a political party are:

(*i*) **Leaders:** Make major decisions and guide the overall direction of the party. ***(½ M)***

(*ii*) **Active members:** Support daily operations and campaign activities of the party. ***(½ M)***

25. (*i*) **Meaning:** Subjects that do not fall in any of the three lists or subjects that come up after the constitution was made are known as residuary subjects. ***(1 M)***

(*ii*) **Jurisdiction:** According to the Indian Constitution, the Union government has the power to legislate on these residuary subjects. ***(1 M)***

26. (*i*) **Changes in Centre-State Relations:** After 1990, the rise of regional parties and coalition governments at the Centre significantly improved Centre-State relations. States gained more respect and autonomy, and a culture of power-sharing emerged. ***(1½ M)***

(*ii*) **Role of Supreme Court:** The Supreme Court passed a judgment that made it difficult for the central government to dismiss state governments arbitrarily, thus strengthening federal power sharing and respect for state autonomy. ***(1½ M)***

27A. The statement is true, democracy is much superior to any other form of government in promoting dignity and freedom of individuals because: **(Any five)**

(*i*) **Equality and Respect:** Democracy ensures that every individual is treated equally and with respect, unlike any other form of government where individuals' freedoms can be suppressed. ***(1 M)***

(*ii*) **Legal and Moral Recognition:** Democratic societies legally and morally recognize the dignity and freedom of every individual. ***(1 M)***

(*iii*) **Self-expression and Participation:** Democracies allow individuals to express themselves freely and participate in the governance process, promoting freedom and dignity. ***(1 M)*** (*iv*) **Non-discrimination:** Democratic systems aim to eliminate discrimination and promote equality, ensuring that all individuals, regardless of their background, religion, and gender, have the opportunity to live with dignity. **(*1 M*)**

(*v*) **Gender equality:** Most societies are male-dominated and women do not get equal chances and respectful positions. In democracies, equal respect and treatment for women is ensured. **(*1 M*)**

(*vi*) **Addressing Social Inequality:** Democracies recognized the claims of the backward and disadvantaged sections of society and they are granted equal status and opportunity to enable them to live their life in a more dignified way. **(*1 M*)**

Topper's Explanation ***(CBSE, 2018)***

32) • All people want to be treated with dignity and respect. Conflicts arise when people feel that they are not being treated with respect.

• However, the passion for dignity and respect is the basis of democracy. Democracies all over the world have realized this, at least in principle.

• It is not a simple matter to realize all people are equal, especially in societies that have been built on the basis of Subordination and oppression, since centuries.

• For example, the dignity of women. Women all around the world have started several campaigns to be treated with respect. It has become easier for them to wage a struggle in democracy as disrespect of women lacks its legal and its moral foundations.

• Similarly, democracy has helped strengthen the claims of various disadvantaged and discriminated against castes. It has helped them, as in democratic India today, untouchability is unexpectable, legally and morally as well.

OR

27B. Yes, I agree. While democracies promote political equality, ensuring that everyone has an equal say in electing their leaders, they have not been very successful in reducing economic disparities. **(*1 M*)**

Here are some example to support my stand:

(*i*) In democratic countries like South Africa and Brazil, the top 20 percent of people take away more than 60 percent of the national income, leaving less than 3 percent for the bottom 20 percent population. **(*1 M*)**

(*ii*) In India, the poor constitute a large proportion of our voters. Yet democratically elected governments do not appear to be as keen to address the question of poverty as you would expect them to. **(*1 M*)**

(*iii*) In many democracies, the number of poor people is very high. Their incomes have been declining. Sometimes they find it difficult to meet their basic needs in life. **(*1 M*)**

(*iv*) In Bangladesh, more than half of its population lives in poverty. People in several poor countries are now dependent on the rich countries even for food supplies. **(*1 M*)**

28. 28.1 A clear example supporting power sharing in democracy is Belgium's power-sharing model. Belgium faced ethnic tensions between Dutch-speaking and French-speaking communities. Power-sharing ensured no single group dominates and prevented conflict, showing how power-sharing is crucial for democracy. **(*1 M*)**

28.2 When political parties form alliances, they share power by working together to make decisions. This helps them govern more fairly because they consider different views and needs, making sure no single group has all the control. **(*1 M*)**

28.3 Political parties influence authority by competing in elections, ensuring no single party controls power. Pressure groups, representing various social and economic interests, influence policy decisions and participate in government committees. Movements bring societal issues to the forefront, impacting decision-making and holding authorities accountable. **(*2 M*)**

SECTION-D

ECONOMICS (20 Marks)

29. (*b*) Collateral is an asset which is a property of a borrower of loan such as – land, building, livestock, deposits with bank etc. **(*1 M*)**

30. (*b*) an IKEA store in Bengaluru selling products manufactured in China **(*1 M*)**

31. (*c*) In GDP calculations, it is crucial to consider only the value of final goods and services to avoid double counting. The wheat used by Mr. Sweet's Bakery is an intermediate good, as it is further processed into biscuits, which are then sold to consumers. Hence, only the value of the biscuits should be included in the GDP, as they represent the final product available for consumption. **(*1 M*)**

32. (*a*) In the process of globalisation:

(*i*) Barriers are removed by the government.

(*ii*) Foreign companies are allowed to set up factories.

(*iii*) It has enabled all the companies (domestic MNCs) to increase investments and foreign trade. **(*1 M*)**

33. (*d*) The percentage of rural children is 10-14 attending school, includes those students who are therefore, 100 – 82 = 18% of the respondents (because we are only asked about the girls) **(1 M)**

34. (*c*) In the initial stage of development, People were more engaged in agriculture and related activities i.e., the primary sector. **(1 M)**

35. The statement "All the services of the 'service sector' are not growing equally well" can be evaluated as follows:

(*i*) **Growth Variation:** Some service sector areas, like IT, grow rapidly, while smaller services, like local shops, grow slowly. **(1 M)**

(*ii*) **Skill Demand:** High-tech services expand quickly; basic services lag due to lower demand and support. **(1 M)**

(*iii*) **Tech Impact:** Technology enhances sectors like finance but leaves traditional services behind. **(1 M)**

36. The disparity in the share of formal sector credit between wealthier and poorer households can be attributed to several factors:

(*i*) Richer households have more assets to use as collateral, making it easier for them to secure loans from formal sources. **(1 M)**

(*ii*) They have better documentation and credit histories, enhancing their trustworthiness in the eyes of formal institutions. **(1 M)**

(*iii*) Poorer households lack collateral and proper documentation, leading them to depend on informal sources. **(1 M)**

37. The advantages of globalisation are as follows:

(*i*) **Access to New Markets:** Globalisation provides business units with the opportunity to expand into new markets, globally reach buyers, and increase revenue. **(1 M)**

(*ii*) **Spread of knowledge and technology:** Globalisation spreads knowledge among buyers and sellers and it brings the latest technology globally. The MNCs use inputs with the latest technologies. **(1 M)**

(*iii*) **Promotes economic growth:** Globalisation promotes economic growth by distributing resources more efficiently and also indirectly through complementary reforms in terms of capital and financial development. **(1 M)**

38A. India should focus on the following points to become a developed country:

(*i*) It should make provision for accommodating all its existing able people in jobs who are willing and able to do but unable to get a suitable job. **(1 M)**

(*ii*) It should reduce the gap between rich and poor people. **(1 M)**

(*iii*) The government should make provisions for making the country self-reliant by providing skill education to all. **(1 M)**

(*iv*) Primary health and education must be accessible to all evenly in the remote parts of the country. **(1 M)**

(*v*) The government should encourage small-scale industries and cottage industries by giving cheaper credit and training to those who are willing to be an entrepreneur. **(1 M)**

OR

38B. I don't agree with the statement that per capita income is not at all a useful criterion to compare states. **(1 M)**

Here's why,

(*i*) Per capita income measures the average money people earn; it's useful but doesn't tell the whole story. **(1 M)**

(*ii*) Kerala's better ranking in human development means it does well in health and education, despite lower per capita income. **(1 M)**

(*iii*) So, per capita income is a good start but we should also look at how healthy and educated people are to really understand development. **(1 M)**

(*iv*) Development is about more than money; it's about quality of life too. Both income and human development factors are important to compare how well different states are doing. **(1 M)**

Mistakes 101 : What not to do!

- ❑ Students may focus only on Kerala's health/ education achievements and ignore the importance of income.
- ❑ Just comparing the two states without explaining the larger idea of development doesn't fully answer the question.

Map for Q. no. 9 (Section A) & Q. no. 19 (Section B)

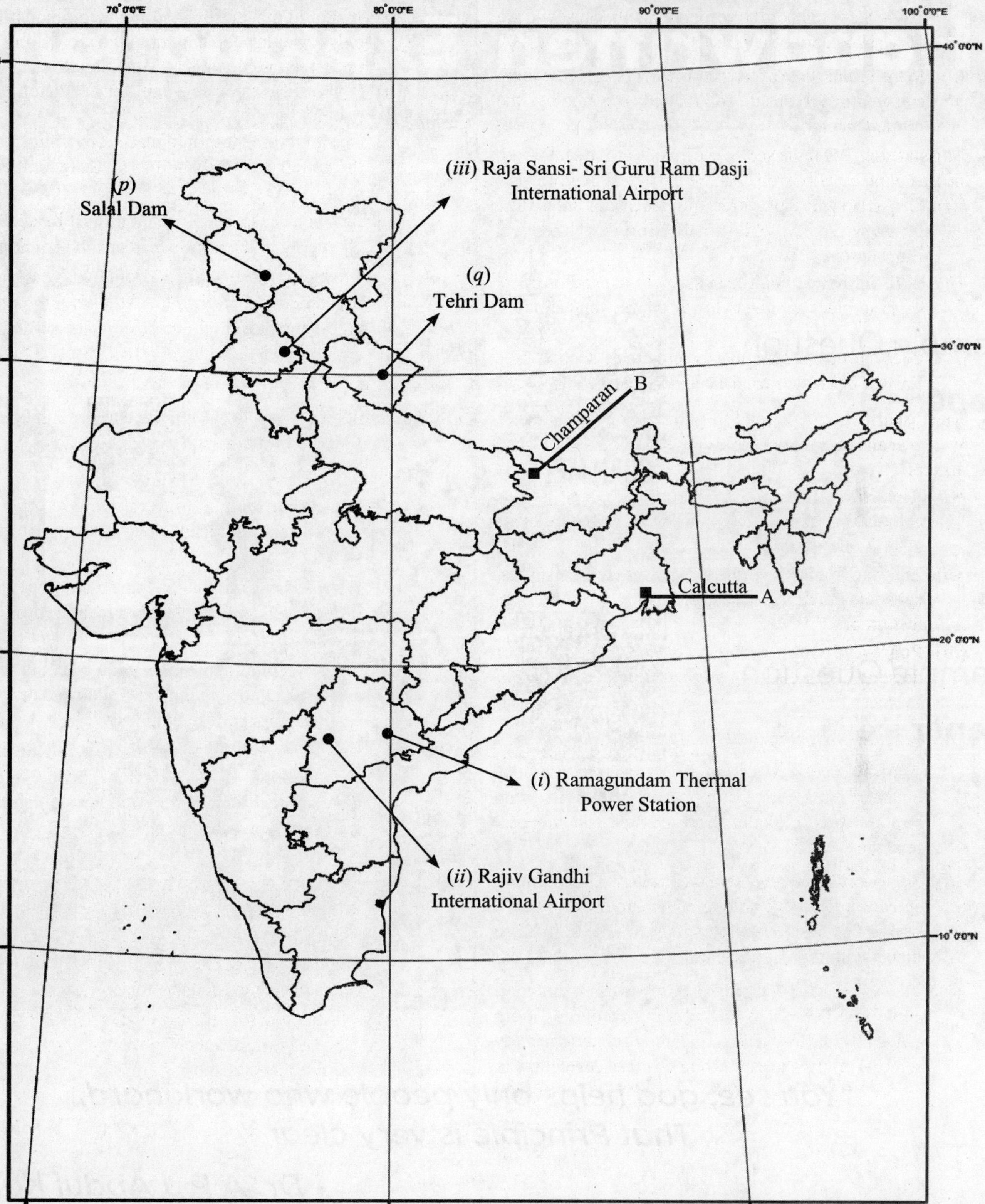

Published by Survey of India
Scale 1:16M

Handwritten Explanations

Sample Question
Paper - 3

SCAN ME!

Sample Question
Paper - 4

SCAN ME!

*"You see, god helps only people who work hard.
That Principle is very clear."*

- Dr. A P J Abdul Kalam

SAMPLE QUESTION PAPER-5 (Explanations)

Revision Time : 8 Min

SECTION - A

HISTORY (20 Marks)

Marking Scheme (Ques 1-4) — *4 Min*

☞ Each question carries 1 mark.

1. (*b*) The celestial figures, including Christ and angels, overseeing the scene symbolise fraternity among the nations. This artistic choice reflects a divine endorsement of unity and brotherhood across different peoples and cultures, suggesting a harmonious global community underpinned by mutual support and solidarity. *(1 M)*

2. (*a*) The British government imposed heavy tariffs and duties on cotton textiles imported from India to protect their own emerging cotton industry. This made Indian textiles more expensive and less competitive in the British market, leading to a significant decline in their export from India to Britain. *(1 M)*

3. (*a*) This quote encapsulates the spirit of resilience and determination shown by the Indian masses in continuing their fight for independence, undeterred by the difficulties and failures they faced during the Non-Cooperation Movement. *(1 M)*

4. (*a*) A-(*iii*), B-(*i*), C-(*ii*), D-(*iv*) *(1 M)*

5A. **Marking Scheme** — *6 Min*

Elaborate two ways the Khilafat Movement contributed to a unified national movement:

☞ Discussion between Muhammad Ali, Shaukat Ali, and Gandhi for united mass action *(1 M)*

☞ Decision at the Calcutta session for non-cooperation for Khilafat and swaraj *(1 M)*

The Khilafat Movement played a crucial role in bringing Muslims under the umbrella of a unified national movement in these ways:

(*i*) A young generation of Muslim leaders like the brothers Muhammad Ali and Shaukat Ali began discussing with Mahatma Gandhi the possibility of united mass action on the issue.

(*ii*) At the Calcutta session of the Congress in September 1920, he convinced other leaders of the need to start a non-cooperation movement in support of Khilafat as well as for swaraj.

OR

5B. **Marking Scheme** — *6 Min*

Elaborate on two key aspects of Gandhi's demands:

☞ General and specific nature of the demands *(1 M)*

☞ Inclusivity of the demands for uniting various social classes *(1 M)*

Gandhi's Demands:

(*i*) **General and Specific Demands:** Gandhi's letter included eleven demands, some of general interest and others specific to different classes like industrialists and peasants.

(*ii*) **Inclusivity:** By making the demands wide-ranging, Gandhi aimed to ensure that all classes within Indian society could identify with them and unite in the campaign.

6. **Marking Scheme** — *8 Min*

Mention three roles of Merchants and Industrialists in the Civil Disobedience Movement.

☞ **Support through Financial Assistance:** Providing funds to sustain the movement *(1 M)*

☞ **Boycott of Imported Goods:** Promoting self-reliance by refusing to trade in foreign goods *(1 M)*

☞ **Formation of Organisations:** Establishing groups like FICCI to oppose colonial policies. *(1 M)*

Role of Merchants and Industrialists in the Civil Disobedience Movement:

(*i*) **Support through Financial Assistance:** Merchants and industrialists provided significant financial support to the movement.They funded various activities and ensured that the movement could sustain itself financially.

(*ii*) **Boycott of Imported Goods:** Refused to trade in foreign goods, promoting Indian products and self-reliance.

(*iii*) **Formation of Organizations:** Established groups like FICCI to oppose colonial policies and support the movement.

7A.

Marking Scheme ⏰ *13 Min*

Mention five points related to universal suffrage and political rights after the French Revolution:
☞ Universal suffrage not guaranteed under equality before the law *(1 M)*
☞ Voting rights for property-owning men in revolutionary France *(1 M)*
☞ Exclusion of women and men without property from political rights *(1 M)*
☞ Return to limited suffrage and restrictions under the Napoleonic Code *(1 M)*
☞ Movements by women and non-propertied men for political rights *(1 M)*

Equality before law did not stand for universal suffrage in France after the revolution. Some examples are given below:

(*i*) Equality before the law did not necessarily stand for universal suffrage.

(*ii*) In revolutionary France, which marked the first political experiment in liberal democracy, the right to vote and to get elected was granted exclusively to property-owning men.

(*iii*) Men without property and all women were excluded from political rights. Only for a brief period under the Jacobins did all adult males enjoy suffrage.

(*iv*) However, the Napoleonic Code went back to limited suffrage and reduced women to the status of a minor, subject to the authority of fathers and husbands.

(*v*) Throughout the nineteenth and early twentieth centuries women and non-propertied men organised opposition movements demanding equal political rights.

OR

7B.

Marking Scheme ⏰ *13 Min*

Mention five conditions viewed as obstacles to economic exchange by the new commercial classes:
☞ Absence of freedom of markets *(1 M)*
☞ State restrictions on movement of goods and capital *(1 M)*
☞ Multiple currencies, weights, and measures *(1 M)*
☞ Duties based on weight or measurement, causing delays *(1 M)*
☞ Formation of the customs union/zollverein in 1834 *(1 M)*

The conditions which were viewed as obstacles to economic exchange and growth by the new commerical classes are:

(*i*) There was absence of freedom of markets.

(*ii*) State imposed various restrictions on the movement of goods and capital.

(*iii*) Presence of large numbers of states created problems as each had its own currency, and weights and measures.

(*iv*) Duties were often levied according to the weight or measurement of the goods. As each region had its own system of weights and measures, this involved time-consuming calculation.

(*v*) In 1834, a customs union or zollverein was formed at the initiative of Prussia and joined by most of the German states.

8.

Marking Scheme ⏰ *10 Min*

(*i*) The objective to publish a Marathi Language newspaper. *(1 M)*
(*ii*) Reason for emphasizing the role of newspaper in promoting the welfare of the Deccan region *(1 M)*
(*iii*) Elaborate two key responsibilities of native newspapers: ☞ Critically examining government policies for public benefit *(1 M)* ☞ Researching to influence public opinion and policy *(1 M)*

8.1. The primary objective of Ranade for publishing a Marathi language newspaper was to provide useful information on various local interest topics and promote the diffusion of knowledge and welfare among the people.

8.2. The Bombay Telegraph emphasized the role of the newspaper to provide useful information on local interests, promoting knowledge and welfare in the Deccan region.

8.3. The key responsibilities attributed to native newspapers were:

(*a*) Critically examining government policies to suggest necessary improvements and remove any detrimental aspects, ensuring that the changes benefit the public.

(*b*) Conducting thorough research on various issues to gather diverse and relevant information, which would help in influencing public opinion and possibly policy decisions through informed debates and discussions.

MAP SKILL-BASED QUESTION

9. **Marking Scheme** 2 Min

A. Calcutta	*(1 M)*
B. Champaran	*(1 M)*

SECTION - B

GEOGRAPHY (20 Marks)

Marking Scheme (Ques 10-12) 3 Min

- Each question carries 1 mark.

10. (*d*) Conservation of forests and wildlife is crucial for maintaining ecological balance because they offer ecosystem services like carbon sequestration and water regulation, contrary to the assertion that it's not essential.

11. (*c*) The 'Slash and burn' agriculture method adopted by Rajesh involves clearing land for cultivation and then moving on to allow the land to regenerate. This practice relates to sustainability as it gives time for **natural processes to restore soil fertility**, although it may not be sustainable in the long term without additional land management practices.

12. (*c*) Arabica coffee, known globally for its superior quality was first brought to India from Yemen. It thrives in the Nilgiri regions of Karnataka, Kerala, and Tamil Nadu, where the climatic conditions are ideal for cultivating this variety.

13. **Marking Scheme** 6 Min

Name two fossil fuels used to generate thermal electricity.

Mention of fossil fuel: Coal	*(1 M)*
Mention of fossil fuel: Natural gas	*(1 M)*

Two fossil fuels used to generate thermal electricity are coal and natural gas.

(*i*) Coal is burned to produce steam, which drives turbine generators. Widely used to generate thermal electricity in India.

(*ii*) Natural gas is combusted in gas turbines or boilers to generate electricity. Both are primary energy sources.

14A. **Marking Scheme** 8 Min

Discuss one implication of each event:

Identification of Benefits for Both Cotton Textile and Jute Processing Industry	*(1½ M)*
Identification of Challenges for Both Cotton Textile and Jute Processing Industry	*(1½ M)*

Benefits and Challenges in Developing Cotton Textile Industry vs. Jute Processing Industry:

(*i*) **Cotton Textile Industry:**

Benefit: Utilizes local skilled labour and traditional textile techniques.

Challenge: High initial investment for modernizing facilities.

(*ii*) **Jute Processing Industry:**

Benefit: High export potential due to eco-friendly products.

Challenge: Requires expertise in jute processing which might be lacking locally.

OR

14B. **Marking Scheme** 8 Min

Identification of Green Belt Creation with explanation	*(1 M)*
Identification of Ash Pond Management with an explanation	*(1 M)*
Benefits for the local community and environment	*(½ + ½ M)*

The implementation of green belts and ash pond management at the Riverwood power station:

(*i*) **Green Belt Creation:** Plant trees and vegetation around the power station to act as a natural barrier, reducing soil erosion and water pollution.

(*ii*) **Ash Pond Management:** Securely contain ash in lined ponds to prevent leaching into the river, safeguarding water quality.

The expected benefits of these actions for the local community and environment are:

(*iii*) **Benefits for the local community and environment:** Green belts provide habitats for local wildlife, enhancing biodiversity around the river area and improving River health boosting tourism and fishing, which is crucial for the local economy.

15A. **Marking Scheme** 13 Min

Mention five points analyzing the impact of industrialization and urbanization on water scarcity.

Urbanization increases water demand.	*(1 M)*
Industrial water consumption worsens water scarcity.	*(1 M)*
Water quality degradation due to waste from industries and urban areas.	*(1 M)*
Role of hydroelectric power in water management.	*(1 M)*
Environmental and social trade-offs of hydroelectric power.	*(1 M)*

The impact of industrialization and urbanization on water scarcity and the role of hydroelectric power can be understood by the following points:

(*i*) **Urbanization increases water demand:** Higher population densities in urban areas significantly boost domestic water needs, straining existing supplies and depleting groundwater levels.

(*ii*) **Industrial water consumption:** Industries near urban centers consume vast water amounts and often pollute local water sources, worsening water scarcity.

(*iii*) **Water quality degradation:** Urban and industrial waste contaminates water resources, reducing the availability of clean water for consumption and agriculture.

(*iv*) **Role of hydroelectric power:** Hydroelectric projects manage water by storing it in reservoirs for power generation and supply during droughts, but disrupt natural water flows and ecosystems.

(*v*) **Environmental and social trade-offs:** While providing renewable energy and aiding water management, hydroelectric facilities can cause environmental damage and community displacement.

OR

15B. **Marking Scheme** — 13 Min

Mention five points about how rainwater harvesting adapts to arid and semi-arid conditions and its impact.	
☞ Customized Collection Systems like rooftop harvesting and tanks.	(1 M)
☞ Long-term storage through underground 'tankas'.	(1 M)
☞ Improving water quality through stored rainwater.	(1 M)
☞ Reducing dependence on distant water sources.	(1 M)
☞ Enhancing livelihoods by supporting home gardening and food security.	(1 M)

The adaptability of rainwater harvesting to arid and semi-arid conditions and its impact can be understood by the following points:

(*i*) **Customized Collection Systems:** In arid Rajasthan, families often construct rooftop rainwater harvesting systems where rainwater from roofs is channeled through pipes into underground tanks or **'tankas'** for storage. Other structures like **khadins** and **Johads** are also used in rain water harvesting.

(*ii*) **Long-term Storage:** These underground 'tankas' are specifically designed to store water for long periods, ensuring a reliable supply during the prolonged dry seasons typical of the region.

(*iii*) **Improving Water Quality:** Stored rainwater is generally cleaner and safer for consumption compared to the often saline or fluoride-contaminated groundwater in Rajasthan.

(*iv*) **Reducing Dependence:** By harvesting rainwater, families reduce their dependence on distant water sources and erratic government supply, gaining autonomy over their water needs.

(*v*) **Enhancing Livelihoods:** Access to consistent water supplies supports home gardening and small-scale agriculture, improving food security and family income.

Nailing the Right Answer

❒ **Structure and Examples:** Clearly mention the types of traditional structures used for rainwater harvesting (e.g., Kunds, Tankas, Johads) and their specific functions.

❒ **Community Efforts and Maintenance**: Highlight the role of community efforts in constructing and maintaining these structures, ensuring sustainable water supply.

16. **Marking Scheme** — 10 Min

(*i*)	Reason for constructing Sardar Sarovar Dam	(1 M)
(*ii*)	Reason for protest from the tribal population.	(1 M)
(*iii*)	Environmental Concerns and Rehabilitation Efforts: • Initial focus on environmental concerns. • Later focus on rehabilitation efforts.	 (1 M) (1 M)

16.1. The Sardar Sarovar Dam was constructed with the objective of securing irrigation and power.

16.2. The tribal people's protest was motivated by the massive displacement and loss of livelihood.

16.3. Initially focused on environmental concerns, such as submerged trees and ecosystems.

Later aimed to ensure proper rehabilitation for displaced individuals, securing their livelihoods and rights.

MAP SKILL-BASED QUESTION

17. **Marking Scheme** 3 Min

I. (*p*) Kandla Port – Gujarat (*1 M*)

OR

(*q*) Mumbai Port – Maharashtra (*1 M*)

Any two of the following:

II. (*i*) Indira Gandhi International Airport – Delhi (*1 M*)

(*ii*) Rajiv Gandhi International Airport – Hyderabad (*1 M*)

(*iii*) Hirakud Dam – Odisha (*1 M*)

SECTION C

POLITICAL SCIENCE (20 marks)

Marking Scheme (Ques 18-23) 6 Min

☞ Each question carries 1 mark.

18. (*c*) The graph shows a steady rise in the percentage of people who said they were members of a political party from 1996 to 2004. Between 1999 and 2004, the graph indicates a sharp upward trend, signifying an increase in party membership. (*1 M*)

19. (*c*) In Sri Lanka, the major social groups are the Sinhala-speakers, and most of the Sinhala-speaking people are Buddhists, which makes option (*c*) correct(*1 M*)

20. (*a*) Self-explanatory. (*1 M*)

21. (*b*) According to our Indian constitution, subjects that do not fall into any of the three lists and subjects that came up after the constitution was made are called the Residuary subjects, and, the Union Government has the power to legislate on these subjects. (*1 M*)

22. (*c*) The cartoon "Governmental Secrecy" illustrates the disparity between the amount of information the government holds about its citizens and the limited information citizens have about government operations. This highlights a critical challenge in democracies related to transparency and accountability. (*1 M*)

23. (*d*) A, B, C and D (*1 M*)

24. **Marking Scheme** 6 Min

☞ Type of political party + reason (*½+ ½ M*)

☞ Justify whether the party can be classified as a national party. (*1 M*)

(*i*) It will be recognized as a state party in States A, B, and C. This is because it has won 6% of votes and 2 seats in the state legislative assembly elections in those states.

(*ii*) The party cannot be classified as a national party even though it has won more than 6% of votes in four state assembly elections, as the party has not won any Lok Sabha seats.

25. **Marking Scheme** 8 Min

Discuss one implication of each event:

☞ **Auctioning of Panchayat Positions:** Undermines democratic essence and favors financial power. (*1½ M*)

☞ **One Million Elected Women in Panchayats:** Promotes gender balance and new perspectives in governance. (*1½ M*)

The implications of the events are as follows:

(*i*) **The auctioning of panchayat positions:** The auctioning of Panchayat positions undermines the essence of democracy which is based on fair and free elections. It could lead to governance by those with financial power rather than by those with the welfare of the people in mind.

(*ii*) **One million elected women in panchayats:** The election of a large number of women to the Panchayats is a positive development, fostering gender balance and potentially bringing new perspectives to local governance that can address women's issues more effectively.

26. **Marking Scheme** 13 Min

Mention in five points how democracy promotes dignity and freedom of the people:

☞ Equality and Respect (*1 M*)

☞ Legal and Moral Recognition (*1 M*)

☞ Self-expression and Participation (*1 M*)

☞ Non-discrimination (*1 M*)

☞ Addressing Social Inequality (*1 M*)

(A) Democracy is much superior to any other form of government in promoting the dignity and freedom of individuals because: **(Any Five)**

(*i*) **Ensures Equality and Respect:** Democracy ensures that everyone is treated equally and with respect, unlike any other form of government where individuals' freedoms can be suppressed.

(*ii*) **Legal and Moral Recognition:** Democratic societies legally and morally recognize the dignity and freedom of every individual.

(*iii*) **Self-expression and Participation:** Democracies allow individuals to express themselves freely and participate in the governance process, promoting freedom and dignity.

(*iv*) **Non-discrimination:** Democratic systems aim to eliminate discrimination and promote equality, ensuring that all individuals, regardless of their background, religion, and gender, have the opportunity to live with dignity.

(*v*) **Gender equality:** Most societies are male-dominated and women do not get equal chances and respectful positions. In democracies, equal respect and treatment for women is ensured.

(*vi*) **Addressing Social Inequality:** Democracies recognize the claims of the backward and disadvantaged sections of society and are granted equal status and opportunity to enable them to live their lives more dignifiedly.

OR

Marking Scheme *13 Min*

- Your stance on whether democracy has failed to reduce economic inequality and poverty. ***(1 M)***
- Provide supporting arguments or examples to justify your stance.

  Economic disparity in South Africa and Brazil ***(1 M)***

  Poverty in India and government response ***(1 M)***

  High poverty levels in many democracies ***(1 M)***

  Dependency on rich countries in Bangladesh ***(1 M)***

(B) Yes, I agree. While democracies promote political equality, ensuring that everyone has an equal say in electing their leaders, they have not been very successful in reducing economic disparities.

Here are some example to support my stand:

(*i*) In democratic countries like South Africa and Brazil, the top 20 percent of people take away more than 60 percent of the national income, leaving less than 3 percent for the bottom 20 percent population.

(*ii*) In India, the poor constitute a large proportion of our voters. Yet democratically elected governments do not appear to be as keen to address the question of poverty as you would expect them to.

(*iii*) In many democracies, the number of poor people is very high. Their incomes have been declining. Sometimes they find it difficult to meet their basic needs in life.

(*iv*) In Bangladesh, more than half of its population lives in poverty. People in several poor countries are now dependent on the rich countries even for food supplies.

27. **Marking Scheme** *10 Min*

(*i*) Example supporting power sharing in democracy ***(1 M)***

(*ii*) Explaining how forming alliances shows power-sharing. ***(1 M)***

(*iii*) Explain the role of political parties, pressure groups, and movements in influencing authority:
- **Role of Political Parties:** Competing in elections to balance power. ***(1 M)***
- **Role of Pressure Groups and Movements:** Influencing policy and highlighting societal issues. ***(1 M)***

27.1 A clear example supporting power sharing in democracy is Belgium's power-sharing model. Belgium faced ethnic tensions between Dutch-speaking and French-speaking communities. Power-sharing ensured no single group dominates and prevented conflict, showing how power-sharing is crucial for democracy.

27.2 When political parties form alliances, they share power by working together to make decisions. This helps them govern more fairly because they consider different views and needs, making sure no single group has all the control.

27.3 (*a*) Political parties influence authority by competing in elections, ensuring no single party controls power and thus preventing authoritarian rule.

(*b*) Pressure groups, representing various social and economic interests, influence policy decisions and participate in government committees. Movements bring societal issues to the forefront, impacting decision-making and holding authorities accountable.

SECTION-D

ECONOMICS (20 Marks)

Marking Scheme (Ques 28-34) 7 Min
☞ Each question carries 1 mark.

28. (*c*) Tertiary sector - Bank *(1 M)*

29. (*b*) Ownership of the MNCs built adjacent to the colony *(1 M)*

30. (*b*) Collateral is an asset which is a property of a borrower of loan such as – land, building, livestock, deposits with bank etc. *(1 M)*

31. (*b*) an IKEA store in Bengaluru selling products manufactured in China *(1 M)*

32. (*b*) Reintroducing tariffs on imported electronics would make these goods more expensive than locally manufactured ones, potentially reducing their competitiveness in the Indian market and encouraging companies to consider local production to avoid tariffs. *(1 M)*

33. (*d*) The percentage of rural children is 10-14 attending school, includes those students who are therefore, 100 – 82 = 18% of the respondents (because we are only asked about the girls) *(1 M)*

34. (*b*) An increase in tertiary sector employment suggests a shift towards more skilled and knowledge-based activities, reflecting economic sophistication. *(1 M)*

35.

Marking Scheme 6 Min	
Explain any two key impacts of AutoTech's investment on Marina's economy.	
☞ Job Creation	*(1 M)*
☞ Skill Development	*(1 M)*
☞ Economic Growth	*(1 M)*

The transformative impact of AutoTech's foreign investment on Marina's economy through these key aspects: **(Any two)**

(*i*) **Job Creation:** AutoTech's plant will provide numerous jobs, reducing unemployment and boosting local incomes.

(*ii*) **Skill Development:** Introducing advanced technologies and training programs will enhance the skills of local workers.

(*iii*) **Economic Growth:** Increased economic activity from manufacturing and exports will stimulate further development in Marina.

36.

Marking Scheme 7 Min	
Evaluate the statement on the uneven growth of the service sector.	
☞ Explain the growth variation in various services.	*(1 M)*
☞ Impact of demand on high-tech services and on basic services.	*(1 M)*
☞ Role of technology in enhancements of various fields.	*(1 M)*

The statement "All the services of the 'service sector' are not growing equally well" can be evaluated as follows:

(*i*) **Growth Variation:** Some service sector areas, like IT, grow rapidly, while smaller services, like local shops, grow slowly.

(*ii*) **Skill Demand:** High-tech services expand quickly; basic services lag due to lower demand and support.

(*iii*) **Tech Impact:** Technology enhances sectors like finance but leaves traditional services behind.

37.

Marking Scheme 7 Min	
Explain reasons for the disparity in formal sector credit access between wealthier and poorer households.	
☞ Collateral Advantage	*(1 M)*
☞ Better Documentation	*(1 M)*
☞ Lack of Collateral in Poorer Households	*(1 M)*

The disparity in the share of formal sector credit between wealthier and poorer households can attributed to several factors:

(*i*) Richer households have more assets to use as collateral, making it easier for them to secure loans from formal sources.

(*ii*) They have better documentation and credit histories, enhancing their trustworthiness in the eyes of formal institutions.

(*iii*) Poorer households lack collateral and proper documentation, leading them to depend on informal sources.

38A.

Marking Scheme	16 Min
Discuss the development indicators for Haryana, Kerala, and Bihar.	
☞ Comparison of Infant Mortality Rate (IMR)	*(1 M)*
☞ Literacy rate comparison among these states.	*(1 M)*
☞ Net Attendance ratio of these countries.	*(1 M)*
☞ Conclusion on Overall Development	*(1 M)*
☞ Impact on state policies	*(1 M)*

In a discussion about the development status of Haryana, Kerala, and Bihar, considering factors like infant mortality rate, literacy rate, and net attendance ratio:

(*i*) **Infant Mortality Rate (IMR):** Kerala has the lowest IMR, indicating better health facilities. Lower IMR in Kerala reflects superior healthcare, while higher IMR in Haryana and Bihar suggests health services need improvement.

(*ii*) **Literacy Rate:** Kerala's literacy rate is highest, suggesting better education policies. High literacy in Kerala aligns with strong education systems; lower rates in Haryana and Bihar point to areas for educational development.

(*iii*) **Net Attendance Ratio:** Kerala also leads in secondary-stage attendance, while Bihar lags. Kerala's higher attendance indicates successful education retention, which determines Bihar's need for educational employment initiatives.

(*iv*) **Overall Development:**

❑ **Conclusion:** Kerala excels in both health and education, Haryana has moderate success, and Bihar requires significant advancement in these sectors.

❑ **Implications:** These indicators influence state policies on health and education, directing focus on infrastructure, accessibility, and quality of services.

OR

38B.

Marking Scheme	16 Min
(A) Opinion on given statement.	*(1 M)*
(B) Provide supporting arguments or examples to justify your stance.	
☞ Per Capita Income Insight	*(1 M)*
☞ Kerala's human development ranking.	*(1 M)*
☞ Comprehensive View	*(1 M)*
☞ Importance of quality of life.	*(1 M)*

I don't agree with the statement that per capita income is not at all a useful criterion to compare states. Here's why,

(*i*) Per capita income measures the average money people earn; it's useful but doesn't tell the whole story.

(*ii*) Kerala's better ranking in human development means it does well in health and education, despite lower per capita income.

(*iii*) So, per capita income is a good start but we should also look at how healthy and educated people are to really understand development.

(*iv*) Development is about more than money; it's about quality of life too. Both income and human development factors are important to compare how well different states are doing.

Mistakes 101 : What not to do!

Overemphasis on per capital income. Students may focus solely on per capital income as a criterion for comparing states, overlooking other important factors like human development, health, and education.

MAP for Q. no. 9 (Section A) & Q. no. 17 (Section B)

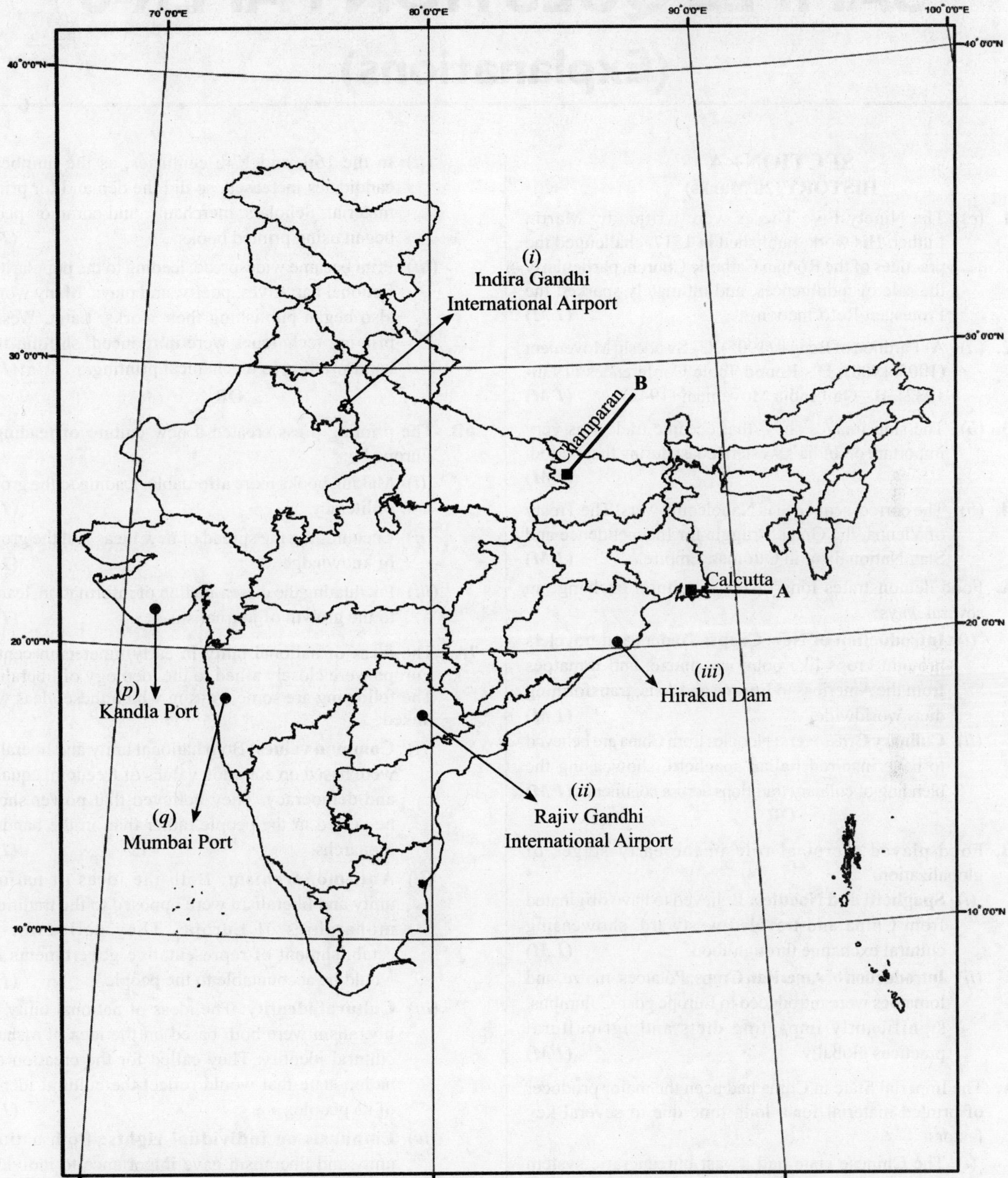

Published by Survey of India

Scale 1:16 M

SAMPLE QUESTION PAPER-6
(Explanations)

SECTION - A
HISTORY (20 Marks)

1. (*c*) The Ninety-Five Theses were written by Martin Luther. His work, published in 1517, challenged the practices of the Roman Catholic Church, particularly the sale of indulgences, and ultimately sparked the Protestant Reformation. ***(1 M)***

2. (*a*) A - Partition of Bengal (1905), C - Swadeshi Movement (1905-1908), D - Round Table Conferences (1930-1932), B - Quit India Movement (1942) ***(1 M)***

3. (*b*) The ship images show that oceanic trade was very important on India's western coast during that period. ***(1 M)***

4. (*b*) The correct sequence is Napoleonic wars, The Treaty of Vienna, the Greet Struggle for Independence and Slav Nationalism in Ottoman Empire. ***(1 M)***

5A. Food demonstrates long-distance cultural exchange in several ways:

(*i*) **Introduction of New Crops:** Traders and travelers brought crops like potatoes, maize, and tomatoes from the Americas to Europe and Asia, transforming diets worldwide. ***(1 M)***

(*ii*) **Culinary Crossovers:** Noodles from China are believed to have inspired Italian spaghetti, showcasing the blending of culinary traditions across continents. ***(1 M)***

OR

5B. Food played a crucial role in the early stages of globalization:

(*i*) **Spaghetti and Noodles:** Believed to have originated from China and traveled westward, showcasing cultural exchange through food. ***(1 M)***

(*ii*) **Introduction of American Crops:** Potatoes, maize, and tomatoes were introduced to Europe post-Columbus, significantly impacting diets and agricultural practices globally. ***(1 M)***

6A. The Imperial State in China had been the major producer of printed material for a long time due to several key factors:

(*i*) The Chinese state had a vast bureaucratic system that recruited officials through civil service exams. Large numbers of textbooks were printed under state sponsorship to prepare candidates. ***(1 M)***

(*ii*) In the 16th and 17th centuries, as the number of candidates increased, so did the demand for printed material. Scholars, merchants, and common people began using printed books. ***(1 M)***

(*iii*) Print became widespread, leading to the popularity of fictional narratives, poetry, and plays. Many women also began publishing their works. Later, Western printing techniques were introduced, shifting from hand-printing to mechanical printing. ***(1 M)***

OR

6B. The printing press created a new culture of reading in Europe by:

(*i*) Making books more affordable, leading to the growth of literacy. ***(1 M)***

(*ii*) Encouraging the spread of new ideas and the growth of knowledge. ***(1 M)***

(*iii*) Facilitating the dissemination of information, leading to the growth of journalism. ***(1 M)***

7A. The ideas of national unity in early nineteenth century Europe were closely allied to the ideology of liberalism. The following are some ways in which these ideas were linked:

(*i*) **Common values:** Both national unity and liberalism were based on common values of freedom, equality, and democracy. They believed that power should be vested in the people rather than in the hands of monarchs. ***(1 M)***

(*ii*) **Anti-monarchism:** Both the ideas of national unity and liberalism were opposed to the traditional monarchies of Europe. They called for the establishment of representative governments that would be accountable to the people. ***(1 M)***

(*iii*) **Cultural identity:** The ideas of national unity and liberalism were both based on the idea of a shared cultural identity. They called for the creation of a nation-state that would reflect the cultural identity of its people. ***(1 M)***

(*iv*) **Emphasis on individual rights:** Both national unity and liberalism gave importance to individual rights. They believed that individual should have the freedom to live their lives as they wished, free from government interference. ***(1 M)*** (*v*) **Emphasis on education:** Both national unity and liberalism emphasized the importance of education. They believed that education was essential for the development of a modern nation-state. ***(1 M)***

OR

7B. The Greek War of Independence mobilized nationalist feelings among the educated elite across Europe in the following ways:

(*i*) **Symbol of hope:** The Greek War of Independence was seen as a symbol of hope for the liberation of other oppressed nations and peoples in Europe. This inspired nationalist feelings among the educated elite across Europe. ***(1¼ M)***

(*ii*) **Media coverage:** The war was widely covered by the media in Europe, which helped to spread awareness about the struggle for independence among the educated elite. ***(1¼ M)***

(*iii*) **Inspiration for other nationalist movements:** The success of the Greek War of Independence inspired other nationalist movements across Europe, as it demonstrated that a small nation could successfully fight for its independence against a larger and more powerful empire. ***(1¼ M)***

(*iv*) **Significance of the war:** The Greek War of Independence was significant in that it helped to mobilize nationalist feelings among the educated elite across Europe and inspired other nationalist movements. It also showed that a small nation could successfully fight for its independence against a larger and more powerful empire. ***(1¼ M)***

8. 8.1 Abanindranath Tagore, a prominent artist of the Bengal School of Art, is credited with portraying Bharat Mata as an ascetic figure. ***(1 M)***

8.2 Indians adopted the image of Bharat Mata to symbolise the nation, fostering unity and a sense of belonging among the people. ***(1 M)***

8.3 Contribution of Bankim Chandra Chattopadhyay in Infusing the Sense of Nationalism:

(a) **Creation of "Vande Mataram":** Bankim Chandra Chattopadhyay composed the patriotic song "Vande Mataram" in his novel Anandamath. This song became a powerful tool in the Indian freedom struggle ***(1 M)***

(b) **Bharat Mata Symbolism:** He depicted India as "Bharat Mata" (Mother India) in Anandamath. This personification of the nation fostered a strong emotional connection among Indians. ***(1 M)***

9. Marked on the map. ***(2 M)***

SECTION - B
GEOGRAPHY (20 Marks)

10. (*b*) The image depicts a deep, narrow channel formed by running water. This type of erosion is known as gully erosion.

Gully erosion occurs when water accumulates and rapidly flows in narrow channels during or after heavy rains, cutting deep and narrow grooves in the soil. This process results in the formation of gullies, which are clearly visible in the provided image. ***(1 M)***

11. (*c*) A-(II), B-(I), C-(IV), D-(III) ***(1 M)***

12. (*b*) Industrial advancement often leads to the discharge of industrial waste into river systems, causing significant pollution in urban areas like Mumbai. ***(1 M)***

13. (*c*) Alluvial soil, found in coastal regions and river plains, retains moisture well, making it ideal for paddy cultivation in areas like Odisha. ***(1 M)***

14. (*b*) A-(II), B-(III), C-(IV), D-(I) ***(1 M)***

15. (*a*) They provide food, water, and air quality regulation. ***(1 M)***

16. Tea requires tropical and sub-tropical climates with deep, fertile, well-drained soil rich in humus. ***(1 M)***

Climate: Tea prefers **warm and humid climates** with well-distributed rainfall. Ideal temperatures range from **15°C to 30°C** and Higher altitudes (around **1,000 - 2,000 meters above sea level**) are favourable for quality tea production. ***(1 M)***

Nailing the Right Answer

- Crop and Climate: Clearly state the beverage crop (Tea) and the required tropical/sub-tropical climate with well-distributed rainfall.
- Mention the need for deep, fertile, well-drained soil rich in humus, and specify the ideal temperature range (15°C to 30°C) and higher altitudes for quality production.

17A. The impact of heavy versus light industry in Neelkanth involves considering several key factors:

(*i*) **Resource Utilization:** Heavy industry leverages local minerals, boosting the economy but requiring large investments. The light industry uses renewable agricultural resources, promoting sustainability. ***(1 M)***

(*ii*) **Environmental Impact:** Heavy industry may increase pollution and energy use, necessitating robust environmental controls. Conversely, the light industry typically has a smaller environmental footprint. ***(1 M)*** (*iii*) **Economic Stability:** Heavy industry might be vulnerable to global economic shifts, whereas light industry linked to daily consumer needs offers more stability. **(*1 M*)**

(*iv*) **Employment Opportunities:** Heavy industry creates specialized, high-paying jobs but may exclude unskilled locals. The light industry provides broader employment, suiting the existing workforce's skills. **(*1 M*)**

(*v*) **Sustainability and Growth:** Light industry, integrating with agriculture, enhances long-term sustainability, supporting local farmers and adapting to market and regulatory changes. **(*1 M*)**

OR

17B. Chotanagpur region is the hub of many iron and steel plants because:

(*i*) Iron and steel industry requires iron ore, coal, limestone and manganese which are available in close proximity. **(*1 M*)**

(*ii*) Good network of roads and railway facilites that leads to the movement of raw materials to iron and steel plants. **(*1 M*)**

(*iii*) Rivers provide the cheapest means of inland water transport for iron and steel goods. **(*1 M*)**

(*iv*) Nearness to the city of Kolkata provides huge market, banking, insurance and financial services for iron and steel plants. **(*1 M*)**

(*v*) Availability of cheap labour from Bihar, West Bengal, Jharkhand and Chhatttisgarh. Hence due to these locational advantages iron and steel plants like Jamshedpur, Durgapur, Burnpur, Bokaro and Rourkela are confined to the Chotanagpur region **(*1 M*)**

Topper's Explanation **(*CBSE, 2017*)**

20 The reasons for the concentration of iron and steel industries in and around the Chotanagpur plateau are—

(i) Availibility of iron ore
The region is close to the iron mines, thus the raw material can be easily transported to the industries

(ii) Proximity of other raw material
Limestone and coking coal is also readily and easily available for production

(iii) Good transport system.
The region is well connected through railways as well as roadways facilitating easy transportation of the raw material as well as the distribution of finished products.

(iv) Availibility of labour
Cheap and skilled labour is easily available for the states of Uttar Pradesh, Bihar and Jharkhand.

(V) Port facilities
Kolkata port nearby facilitates the export of the finished goods

(vi) The industry has immense scope for development in the home market.

18. 18.1 The government has decided to evacuate and shift the residents of Jharia due to the uncontrollable underground fires. They have sanctioned funds to support the relocation process. **(*1 M*)**

18.2 The primary hazards include uncontrollable underground fires, unsafe mining conditions, and inadequate safety standards. These hazards have led to the loss of lives and significant health risks for the residents and workers. **(*1 M*)**

18.3 The Supreme Court has imposed a fine of Rs 300 crore on a major coal-producing company for causing environmental damage. **(*1 M*)**

This penalty is in addition to other financial liabilities, emphasizing the need for stricter environmental compliance and the potential financial burden on coal companies for failing to adhere to regulations. **(*1 M*)**

19. Marked on the Map **(*3 M*)**

SECTION - C
POLITICAL SCIENCE (20 Marks)

20. (*a*) The statement describes a form of power-sharing where power is divided between different levels of government, such as central and regional governments, which is characteristic of vertical power-sharing. **(*1 M*)**

21. (*c*) Both (i) and (ii) **(*1 M*)**

22. (*c*) Social diversity accommodation. **(*1 M*)**

23. (*a*) Sri Lanka emerged as an independent country in 1948. **(*1 M*)**

24. The positive impact of casteism regarding political expression includes the following:

(*i*) **Representation and Decision Making:** It enables marginalized groups to access decision-making bodies, promoting their representation and ensuring their voices are heard in governance and policy-making. **(*1 M*)** (*ii*) **Improved Access to Resources and Opportunities:** Political mobilization around caste issues has helped disadvantaged groups, gain better access to essential resources like land, education, and job opportunities. This has improved their economic conditions and social standing. ***(1 M)***

25. The two key aspects that democracy must provide are:

(*i*) **Right to Choose Rulers:** Democracy must ensure that people can elect their leaders through free and fair elections, reflecting the will of the citizens. ***(1 M)***

(*ii*) **Accountability and Responsiveness:** Democracy must create a government accountable to citizens and responsive to their needs. ***(1 M)***

26. (*i*) The statement implies that there is a direct relationship between increased educational opportunities for women and their enhanced participation in political processes. ***(1 M)***

(*ii*) As education levels increase among women, they gain more knowledge, skills, and confidence, which empower them to engage more actively in politics either as voters, candidates, or in any other political roles. ***(1 M)***

(*iii*) Promoting gender equality in education suggests a societal move towards valuing and utilizing the potential of women equally in public spheres, including politics, which historically have been male-dominated domains. ***(1 M)***

27A. In india, political parties play several crucial roles ensuring the system functions smoothly and effectively. Here are the key functions:

(*i*) **Contest Elections:** Political parties select candidates and contest elections. For example, in India, parties like the BJP and Congress put forward candidates to compete in elections. ***(1 M)***

(*ii*) **Policy Making:** Parties propose different policies and programs. Voters choose from these during elections. ***(1 M)***

(*iii*) **Forming and Running Governments:** The party that wins the majority forms the government and makes policy decisions. ***(1 M)***

(*iv*) **Opposition Role:** Parties that do not win form the opposition, critiquing and providing alternatives to the government's policies. ***(1 M)***

(*v*) **Access to Government:** Political parties often act as intermediaries between the government and the people, making it easier for citizens to get their issues addressed. ***(1 M)***

OR

27B. Opposition parties play a very crucial role in a democracy. Following are the some functions which makes it very crucial for democracy:

(*i*) **Critiquing Government Policies:** Opposition parties critically evaluate and challenge the policies and actions of the ruling party, ensuring checks and balances. ***(1 M)***

(*ii*) **Mobilizing Public Opinion:** They mobilize public opinion against policies they disagree with, raising awareness and influencing public discourse. ***(1 M)***

(*iii*) **Ensuring Accountability:** By questioning and challenging the ruling party, opposition parties prevent misuse of power and corruption, and hold the government accountable for its decisions and actions. ***(1 M)***

(*iv*) **Policy Influence:** Through debates and discussions, opposition parties can influence policy-making, ensuring that multiple perspectives are considered. ***(1 M)***

(*v*) **Providing Alternatives:** Opposition parties present alternative policies and visions for governance, offering voters a choice during elections and contributing to the democratic process. ***(1 M)***

28. 28.1 Indian decentralization is considered the largest experiment in democracy because it involves about 36 lakh elected representatives, more than the population of many countries, reflecting massive democratic engagement. ***(1 M)***

28.2. Granting constitutional status to local governments in India has significantly deepened democracy by ensuring regular elections, expanding women's participation, and enabling direct local decision-making, thus enhancing democratic engagement at the grassroots level. ***(1 M)***

28.3. The Indian Government has implemented several measures to encourage decentralization:

(*i*) **Amendment of the Constitution in 1992:** This amendment made it mandatory to hold regular elections for local government bodies like panchayats and municipalities. It also ensured the reservation of seats for the Scheduled Castes, the Scheduled Tribes, and women to ensure their representation. ***(1 M)***

(*ii*) **Power and Revenue Sharing:** The state governments must share some powers and revenue with local bodies. This change aims to empower local bodies to manage and resolve local issues more effectively. ***(1 M)***

SECTION - D
ECONOMICS (20 Marks)

29. (*b*) A-(II), B-(III), C-(I), D-(IV) ***(1 M)***

30. (*b*) Empowering women through collective savings and credit ***(1 M)***

31. (*c*) The IT sector has helped the most in the spread of the production of services. IT sector services include email, mobile phones, satellite, voice mail etc. **(*1 M*)**

32. (*b*) In Assam and Punjab, less than 2 percent of total households demanding MGNREGA work. **(*1 M*)**

33. (*b*) Trade Barrier refers to some restrictions including tax on imports which governments can use to increase or decrease foreign trade and to decide what kind of goods, how much of each, should come into the country. **(*1 M*)**

34. (*b*) Commercial banks offer lower interest rates and easier access compared to informal sources, making them the largest source of credit. **(*1 M*)**

35. (*a*) (*ii*) Different persons have different notions of development. This is because the life situations of people are different. **(*1 M*)**

- The development goals of a girl from a rich urban family will differ from a farmer in Rajasthan. It is because their conditions, lifestyle, and status are very different from each other. **(*1 M*)**
- People's goals depend on their present condition. Over a period of time, if the conditions or situations change, then automatically the goals of a person will also change. **(*1 M*)**

OR

(*b*) Development or progress may have a different meaning for different individuals. Each individual has his/her own notion/perception of development.**(*1 M*)**

(*i*) People seek things that are most important for them, i.e., things which they feel can fulfill their aspirations or desires. **(*1 M*)**

(*ii*) For example, development for a farmer might be proper irrigation facilities, high yield, higher prices for their crop yield, etc. **(*1 M*)**

36. The role of RBI can be understood by the following points:

(*i*) **Regulatory Body:** The Reserve Bank of India (RBI) primarily regulates banks and non-banking financial companies (NBFCs), ensuring adherence to financial standards and ethical lending practices. RBI ensures that banks maintain a minimum cash balance. **(*1 M*)**

(*ii*) **Auditing:** Regular audits are conducted to examine the financial health and integrity of lending institutions, ensuring transparency and accountability. **(*1 M*)**

(*iii*) **Consumer Protection:** The RBI monitors lenders to protect consumers from unfair practices, providing mechanisms to address complaints and disputes effectively. **(*1 M*)**

37. (*ii*) Collaboration with Mahindra provides Ford Motors access to local resources and market, while Mahindra benefits from Ford's global reach, shared technology, and financial risk mitigation. **(*1 M*)**

(*iii*) Impact of Ford Motors' Investment:

(*a*) **Positives:** economic growth, job creation, technological advancement, and increased export revenue. **(*1 M*)**

(*b*) **Negatives:** local competition, potential environmental impact, and economic dependency on MNCs. **(*1 M*)**

38. (*a*) Difference between organised sector and unorganised sector are: **(Each point carries 1 Mark)**

Basis	Organised Sector	Unorganised Sector
Term of employment	The term of employment is regular.	The term of employment is irregular.
Rules and Regulation of Govt.	It has to follow the rules and regulations of government.	It has rules but they don't follow the government's rules and regulations.
Job Security	Workers enjoy the security of employment.	Workers have no fixed employment.
Remuneration	Workers of this sector get paid during holidays, leave and overtime for more work etc.	Workers don't get paid for holidays or leave. And in case of less work they may be asked to leave their job.
Other benefits	Workers enjoy the other benefits like medical facilities etc.	Workers are not supposed to enjoy other benefits.

OR

(*b*) (*i*) If we assume primary sector includes only agricultural workforce, we can determine the population of unorganised primary sector. No. of unorganised agricultural workforce = 232 – 1 = 231 Millions **(*1 M*)**

(*ii*) Yes, I believe that India's agriculture is an unorganised sector activity for the following reasons:

- ❑ The majority of agricultural employees are not paid on a regular basis.
- ❑ This industry deals with the issue of underemployment. **(*2 M*)**

(*iii*) Percentage of workers in unorganised sector

$$= \frac{(231 + 74 + 88)}{(232 + 115 + 128)} \times 100 = \frac{393}{475} \times 100$$

$= 82.74\%$

Percentage of workers in organized sector

$$= \frac{82}{475} \times 100 = 17.26\%$$ **(*2 M*)**

Map for Q. no. 9 (Section A) & Q. no. 19 (Section B)

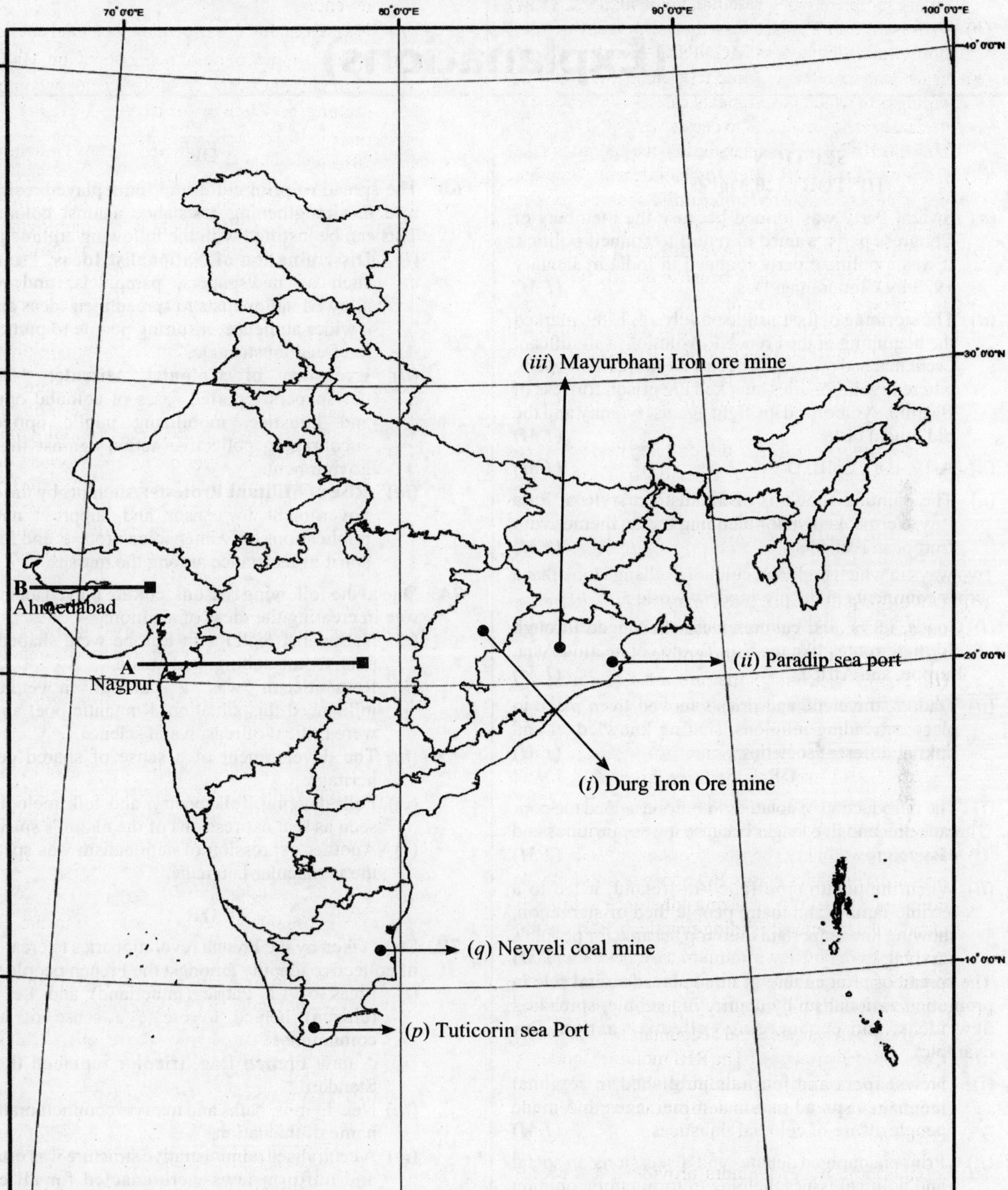

Published by Survey of India
Scale 1:16M

SAMPLE QUESTION PAPER-7
(Explanations)

SECTION - A
HISTORY (20 Marks)

1. (*a*) Swaraj Party was formed because the members of Congress party wanted to return to council politics. It was a political party founded in India in January 1923 by Chittaranjan Das. **(*1 M*)**

2. (*a*) The storming of the Bastille on July 14, 1789, marked the beginning of the French Revolution, a significant event that had profound effects on Europe. This event, where revolutionaries attacked the prison fortress of Bastille, symbolized the fight against tyranny and the old feudal order. **(*1 M*)**

3. (*a*) A-IV, B-II, C-III, D-I **(*1 M*)**

4. (*a*) The painting shown is in the distinct style of Raja Ravi Verma, known for blending Indian themes with European realism. **(*1 M*)**

5A. Two ways in which trade and cultural exchange took place across continents in the pre-modern world are:

(*i*) Goods, ideas, and cultures were exchanged through old trade routes like the Silk Route connecting Asia, Europe, and Africa. **(*1 M*)**

(*ii*) Traders, travelers, and priests moved from place to place, spreading religions, sharing knowledge, and linking different societies. **(*1 M*)**

OR

5B. (*i*) The introduction of potatoes in Europe helped the poor eat better and live longer because it was nutritious and easy to grow. **(*1 M*)**

(*ii*) When the potato crop failed in Ireland, it led to a terrible famine and many people died of starvation, showing how important this crop became for people's survival. **(*1 M*)**

6A. The spread of print culture in India played a vital role in promoting nationalism by connecting people, spreading new ideas, and encouraging collective action. For example:

(*i*) Newspapers and journals published in regional languages spread nationalist messages and made people aware of colonial injustices. **(*1 M*)**

(*ii*) Print encouraged debates and discussions on social and political issues, helping to form public opinion against British rule. **(*1 M*)**

(*iii*) Nationalist leaders used pamphlets, tracts, and books to inspire people, promote reforms, and unite different communities in the freedom movement. **(*1 M*)**

OR

6B. The spread of print culture in India played a significant role in strengthening resistance against colonial rule. This can be justified with the following arguments:

(*i*) **Dissemination of Nationalist Ideas:** Print media, such as newspapers, pamphlets, and journals, allowed nationalists to spread their ideas and reach a wider audience, inspiring people to participate in the freedom struggle. **(*1 M*)**

(*ii*) **Exposure of Colonial Misrule:** Nationalist newspapers reported cases of colonial oppression and injustice, mobilizing public opinion and encouraging collective action against the British government. **(*1 M*)**

(*iii*) **Rise of Militant Protests:** Attempts by the colonial government to censor and suppress nationalist publications only intensified protests and fueled the spirit of resistance among the masses. **(*1 M*)**

7A. Due to the following reasons, culture played an important role in creating the ideas of a nation:

(*i*) Nationalist feelings in Europe were shaped by art, poetry, storytelling, and music. **(*1 M*)**

(*ii*) Romanticism was a cultural movement that influenced this situation. Romantic poet and artists were critical of reason and science. **(*1 M*)**

(*iii*) The development of a sense of shared collective heritage. **(*1 M*)**

(*iv*) Folk dancing, folk poetry, and folk melodies were seen as real expressions of the nation's spirit. **(*1 M*)**

(*v*) Another expression of nationalism was speaking in the vernacular language. **(*1 M*)**

OR

7B. Steps taken by the French revolutionaries to create a sense of collective identity amongst the French people were

(*i*) Ideas of La Patrie (fatherland) and Le Citoyen (citizen) helped to create a sense of a united community. **(*1 M*)**

(*ii*) A new French flag, tricolor replaced the Royal Standard. **(*1 M*)**

(*iii*) New hymns, oaths and martyrs commemorated in the name of the nation. **(*1 M*)**

(*iv*) A centralised administrative structure was established and uniform laws were enacted for all citizens. French was promoted as a common language of the nation. **(*1 M*)**

(*v*) The Estates General was elected by a group of active citizens and was renamed the National Assembly. **(*1 M*)**

8. **8.1** Printed books initially resembled handwritten manuseripts, requiring manual decoration and illustration which slowed down production and maintained some reliance on tranditional book. **(1 M)**

8.2 In his childhood, Gutenberg had seen wine and olive presses. He also learnt the art of polishing stones, became a master goldsmith and acquired the expertise to create lead moulds used for making trinkets that helped him to design his new printing press. **(1 M)**

8.3 Main features of the printed Bible are as follows:

(*a*) It closely resembled the written manuscripts in appearance and layout. **(1 M)**

(*b*) Borders of the Bible were illuminated by hand with foliage and other patterns. **(1 M)**

9. Marked on Map **(2 M)**

SECTION - B

GEOGRAPHY (20 Marks)

10. (*d*) The Sardar Sarovar Dam has been built over the Narmada River in Gujarat. It is one of the largest water resource projects in India, covering four states: Maharashtra, Madhya Pradesh, Gujarat, and Rajastha **(1 M)**

11. (*d*) The bamboo drip irrigation system is a traditional method of irrigation used in Meghalaya. It involves using bamboo pipes to divert perennial springs on the hilltops to lower reaches by gravity, which is an efficient way of water management in hilly regions. **(1 M)**

12. (*a*) Black soil, also known as regur soil, is ideal for growing cotton and is well known for its capacity to hold moisture. This type of soil is prevalent in the Deccan trap region, covering areas like Maharashtra, Saurashtra, Malwa, Madhya Pradesh, and Chhattisgarh **(1 M)**

13. (*b*) Kaziranga National Park, Assam is renowned for its significant population of the one-horned rhinoceros. It was designated a UNESCO World Heritage site in 1985. **(1 M)**

14. (*d*) Installing deep submersible pumps causes excessive utilization of groundwater, leading to declining water tables and aquifer depletion. This unsustainable practice will MOST LIKELY result in (*d*) water scarcity in Rajasthan. **(1 M)**

15. (*b*) The Bhakra–Nangal project uses water primarily for (*ii*) irrigation and (*i*) hydel power production, supporting agriculture and electricity generation across northern India. It is not used for transportation or cleaning **(1 M)**

16. Over-irrigation leads to land degradation in Punjab mainly due to waterlogging and soil salinity.

(*i*) Waterlogging: Over-irrigation in Punjab leads to waterlogging, which reduces soil acration and negatively affects crop growth. **(1 M)**

(*ii*) Soil Salinity: Excessive irrigation increases soil salinty, making the land infertile and unsuitable for agriculture, contributing to land degradation. **(1 M)**

17A. The manufacturing industry significantly contributes to India's economy through various means:

(*i*) **Modernizes Agriculture:** It provides machinery, fertilizers, and technology, enhancing agricultural productivity and efficiency. **(1 M)**

(*ii*) **Generates Employment:** Creates jobs in the secondary and tertiary sectors, helping reduce unemployment and poverty. **(1 M)**

(*iii*) **Reduces Regional Disparities:** Establishes industries in backward and tribal areas, helping bridge regional economic gaps and promoting balanced development. **(1 M)**

(*iv*) **Boosts Trade and Commerce:** Exporting manufactured goods increases foreign exchange, which is vital for economic growth and stability. **(1 M)**

(*v*) **Supports Agriculture:** Agro-based industries utilize agricultural produce, adding value and creating a symbiotic relationship between agriculture and industry. **(1 M)**

Nailing the Right Answer

- **Sectoral Contributions:** Highlight how the manufacturing industry modernizes agriculture and generates employment, improving productivity and reducing poverty.
- **Economic and Regional Impact:** Mention its role in reducing regional disparities by establishing industries in backward areas and boosting trade through exports, which enhances foreign exchange and economic stability.

OR

17B. The chemical manufacturing industry in India is currently positioned as follows:

(*i*) **Growth and Diversification:** The industry is rapidly expanding and diversifying, encompassing both large-scale and small-scale units. **(1 M)**

(*ii*) **Inorganic Chemicals:** Produces sulfuric acid, nitric acid, alkalies, soda ash, and caustic soda, used in fertilizers, synthetic fibers, plastics, adhesives, paints, and dyes. **(1 M)**

(*iii*) **Organic Chemicals:** Produces petrochemicals used in manufacturing synthetic fibers, rubber, plastics, dye-stuffs, drugs, and pharmaceuticals. **(1 M)**

(*iv*) **Strategic Location:** The industry is strategically located near oil refineries and petrochemical plants, facilitating efficient production and distribution. **(1 M)** (*v*) **Economic Impact:** The chemical manufacturing industry significantly contributes to India's economy by generating employment and enhancing industrial output. **(*1 M*)**

Nailing the Right Answer

- ❒ Mention the industry's rapid growth and diversification, including the production of both inorganic and organic chemicals.
- ❒ Highlight the strategic location near oil refineries and petrochemical plants, and its significant contribution to employment and industrial output.

18. 18.1 The purpose of the Indian Wildlife (Protection) Act of 1972 is to protect habitats, ban hunting, provide legal protection to endangered species, and restrict trade in wildlife. **(*1 M*)**

18.2 Two specific animals given protection under this Act are the tiger and the one-horned rhinoceros. **(*1 M*)**

18.3 Central and state governments have established national parks and wildlife sanctuaries. For example, Project Tiger was launched to protect tigers, leading to the creation of tiger reserves across India to increase their population and habitat protection. **(*2 M*)**

19. Marked on Map. **(*3 M*)**

SECTION - C

POLITICAL SCIENCE (20 Marks)

20. (*d*) The constitution of India does not designate any language as the ''national language". **(*1 M*)**

21. (*a*) Prudential reasons are the parctical reason for making decisions. In the context of power-sharing, it means supporting power-sharing because it can lead to better outcomes like less conflicts, more stability and keep the country running smoothly. **(*1 M*)**

22. (*c*) This headline is a classic example of dynastic succession, where political power stays within certain families, limiting chances for others and undermining the democratic process within parties **(*1 M*)**

23. (*c*) Statement (*ii*) is incorrect because the world average percentage of women in national parliaments is 19.7%, which is less than 20% and statement (iv) is incorrect because the percentage of women in national parliaments in the Indian region is the lowest among all regions listed. **(*1 M*)**

24. Most democracies ensure fair elections by holding regular, free, and open elections. However, they often struggle to provide equal chances for all candidates and maintain transparency. Despite these challenges, democracies typically perform better than non-democratic regimes in ensuring fairness. **(*2 M*)**

25. (*i*) There are two main ways to form a federation– coming-together federations and holding-together federations. The above clues refer to the holding together federations. **(*1 M*)**

(*ii*) In holding together federations, the central government tends to be more powerful, and constituent units often have unequal powers, and some may have special powers as well to protect their cultural heritage. **(*1 M*)**

26. Nature of the Panchayati Raj System in India:

(*i*) **Three-tier structure:** Comprises Gram Panchayats (village level), Panchayat Samitis (block level), and Zilla Parishads (district level). **(*1 M*)**

(*ii*) **Decentralisation:** Empowers local governance by transferring administrative and financial responsibilities to the grassroots level. **(*1 M*)**

(*iii*) **Democratic participation:** Facilitates direct involvement of the people in decision-making through regular elections and Gram Sabha meetings.. **(*1 M*)**

Topper's Explanation ***(CBSE, 2020)***

- Every village or group of villages has a gram panchayat which consists of several ward members [panch] and a president [sarpanch]. It is elected by all the adult ward members living in that ward.
- It is under the supervision of the gram sabha which consists of the adult members of that population who meet a few times a year to discuss the performance of the gram sabha and the annual budget.
- A few Gram Sabhas form a Panchayat Samiti or Block or Mandal elected by all the Panchayat members in that area.
- A few Panchayat Samitis constitute the Zilla Parishad which consists of MLAs, members of legislative assemblies, and other ministers.
- Zilla Parishad chairperson is the political head of Zilla Parishad.

27A. (*i*) **Historical Exclusion:** Traditionally, women were excluded from political roles as they were seen mainly as caregivers. This limited their public and political participation. **(*1 M*)**

(*ii*) **Feminist Movements:** Over time, feminist movements globally fought for women's rights, including the right to vote and hold public office, leading to gradual inclusion in politics. **(*1 M*)**

(*iii*) **Legal and Social Progress:** Laws and policies, like reservation of seats in local bodies in India, have encouraged women's participation. **(*1 M*)**

(*iv*) **Challenges Persist:** Despite progress, women's representation in legislative bodies remains low compared to men. Women in politics face underrepresentation in higher strata of power. **(*1 M*)**

(*v*) **Impact on Society:** Female political participation has led to more attention to women's issues and gender equality, highlighting the need for diverse perspectives in governance for balanced and inclusive development. **(*1 M*)**

OR

27B. The feminist movements had a great impact on gender equality in India. This can be understood with the help of the following points:

(*i*) **Raising Awareness:** The feminist movement has played a crucial role in highlighting the issues of gender inequality and discrimination against women in various areas of life. *(1 M)*

(*ii*) **Legislative Reforms:** It has led to significant legislative changes aimed at improving the status of women, including laws related to dowry, domestic violence, and equal pay for equal work. *(1 M)*

(*iii*) **Education and Employment:** Feminist movement has contributed to increased access to education and employment opportunities for women, challenging traditional roles and stereotypes. *(1 M)*

(*iv*) **Political Representation:** The movement has pushed for greater political representation for women, leading to policy changes like reserving seats for women in local government bodies. *(1 M)*

(*v*) **Conclusion:** The feminist movement has had a significant impact on gender equality in India, influencing society's attitudes, laws, and policy decisions towards a more equitable treatment of women. *(1 M)*

28. 28.1 Economic development in a country is influenced by various factors such as the country's population size, the global situation, cooperation from other countries, and the economic priorities adopted by the country. *(1 M)*

28.2 No, we cannot conclude that democracy is not effective for economic development because the difference is negligible and economic development depends upon various factors besides government type like population size, government policies etc. *(1 M)*

28.3 No, I don't agree because the difference in the rates of economic development between dictatorships and democracies is negligible. When we find such difference in the rates of economic growth between the countries under dictatorship and democracy, it is better to prefer democracy as it has several other positive outcomes which are not present under dictatorships. *(2 M)*

SECTION - D

ECONOMICS (20 marks)

29. (*b*) Average Income of the family:

= 15,000 + 6,000 + 8,000 + 9,000

Sum of Incomes = 38,000

Average = Sum of members/No. of members

$= \frac{38,000}{4} = 9,500$ *(1 M)*

30. (*b*) Megha has taken a loan from a "formal source" of credit, which is a bank. *(1 M)*

31. (*d*) Statement (*iii*) accurately identifies rapid technological advancements, especially in communication and transportation, as a primary factor that has stimulated the process of globalisation. *(1 M)*

32. (*a*) The loan interest rate might be higher, leading to a larger debt burden if he fails to repay on time. *(1 M)*

33. (*a*) Primary sector *(1 M)*

34. (*b*) Improved access to international markets for indian companies. *(1 M)*

35A. Apart from income, other things people look for growth and development are:

(*i*) **Equal Treatment:** This means everyone gets the same chance to succeed, no matter who they are. It makes things fair and lets everyone have a go at doing well. *(1 M)*

(*ii*) **Freedom:** It means being able to make your own choices. It lets people follow their dreams and come up with new ideas, making life better for themselves and others. *(1 M)*

(*iii*) **Security:** Feeling safe where you live and work is important. They also value job security, a good working environment, and the time to be with family, which all contribute significantly to their overall growth and development. *(1 M)*

OR

35B. The characteristics of development are: **(Any Three)**

(*i*) **Development is a Continuous process:** It is a continuous process that creates growth and brings in progress and positive change. *(1 M)*

(*ii*) **Income as an essential component:** It is the most important component of development, but along with income, people also seek equal treatment, good health, peace, literacy, job security, etc. *(1 M)*

(*iii*) **Mixed goals:** For development, people look at mixed goals such as freedom, money, equal opportunity, etc. *(1 M)*

(*iv*) **Conflicting goals:** Development for one may not be developed for another. It may be destructive for others. *(1 M)*

36. Advantages of Globalisation:

(*i*) **Economic Growth:** Globalisation boosts economic growth by increasing trade and investment flows. *(1 M)*

(*ii*) **Technology Transfer:** It facilitates the transfer of technology and innovation across countries. *(1 M)*

(*iii*) **Consumer Benefits:** Consumers enjoy a wider variety of goods and services at lower prices due to increased competition. *(1 M)*

37. (*i*) Aman and Ravi are using a **barter system,** where goods are exchanged directly without using money.

(*ii*) Two limitations of this system are:

- **Lack of double coincidence of wants** – Aman wants shoes, but Ravi doesn't want wheat. **(*1 M*)**
- **Difficulty in fixing the value of goods** like wheat and shoes for a fair exchange. **(*1 M*)**

38A. Organised Sectors are placed with secured work, regular terms, and benefits like leave, pension, etc. follow government laws. E.g. Government jobs. **(*1 M*)**

Unorganised sectors are those sectors which are jobs without security rules not followed. E.g. Street vendors, and small traders, etc. **(*1 M*)**

Workers in the unorganised sector often face numerous challenges:

(*i*) **Wages:** They receive low and irregular wages. For example, a daily wage laborer might earn less than the minimum wage, without any overtime pay or benefits. **(*1 M*)**

(*ii*) **Safety:** Unorganised sector workers often work in hazardous conditions without proper safety measures. For example, construction workers frequently lack helmets, gloves, and harnesses, leading to accidents and injuries. **(*1 M*)**

(*iii*) **Health:** They do not have access to health benefits or insurance. For instance, a street vendor lacks medical leave or health insurance, making it difficult to afford medical care. **(*1 M*)**

Nailing the Right Answer

- Provide examples of government policies or initiatives aimed at protecting.
- Discuss the economic implications of neglecting the issuss of wages, safety & health in the unorganised sector.

OR

38B. The tertiary sector is important in India for several reasons:

(*i*) **Service Provision:** The tertiary sector provides essential services like healthcare, education, and banking, which are crucial for the development of the country. **(*1 M*)**

(*ii*) **Economic Contribution:** It significantly contributes to India's GDP. For instance, IT services have boosted the economy by providing software solutions worldwide. **(*1 M*)**

(*iii*) **Employment Generation:** It creates numerous job opportunities. For example, the tourism industry employs millions in hotels, travel agencies, and tour operations. **(*1 M*)**

(*iv*) **Infrastructure Support:** The sector supports infrastructure development through transport, communication, and trade services, facilitating primary and secondary sector growth. **(*1 M*)**

(*v*) **Rising Incomes:** Increased demand for services such as retail, entertainment, and personal services reflects higher income levels and urbanization, driving economic progress. **(*1 M*)**

Topper's Explanation ***(CBSE, 2019)***

The importance of the tertiary sector in India can be reasoned as follows.

(i) ~~India~~
(ii) The tertiary sector contributes significantly to the country's GDP

(iii) It provides employment to a large number of people with one-third of the women employed.

(iv) It brings much of the needed foreign exchange in the country.

(v) the government provides basic services like education, health care, transport etc. which falls under the tertiary sector.

(vi) It creates new opportunities like those related to information and communication technology.

(vii) It provides aid to the development of the primary and tertiary sectors by creating new services like transport and storage.

(viii) Tertiary sector also includes other facilities and services like doctors, teachers, engineers to play a major in the society.

Map for Q. no. 9 (Section A) & Q. no. 19 (Section B)

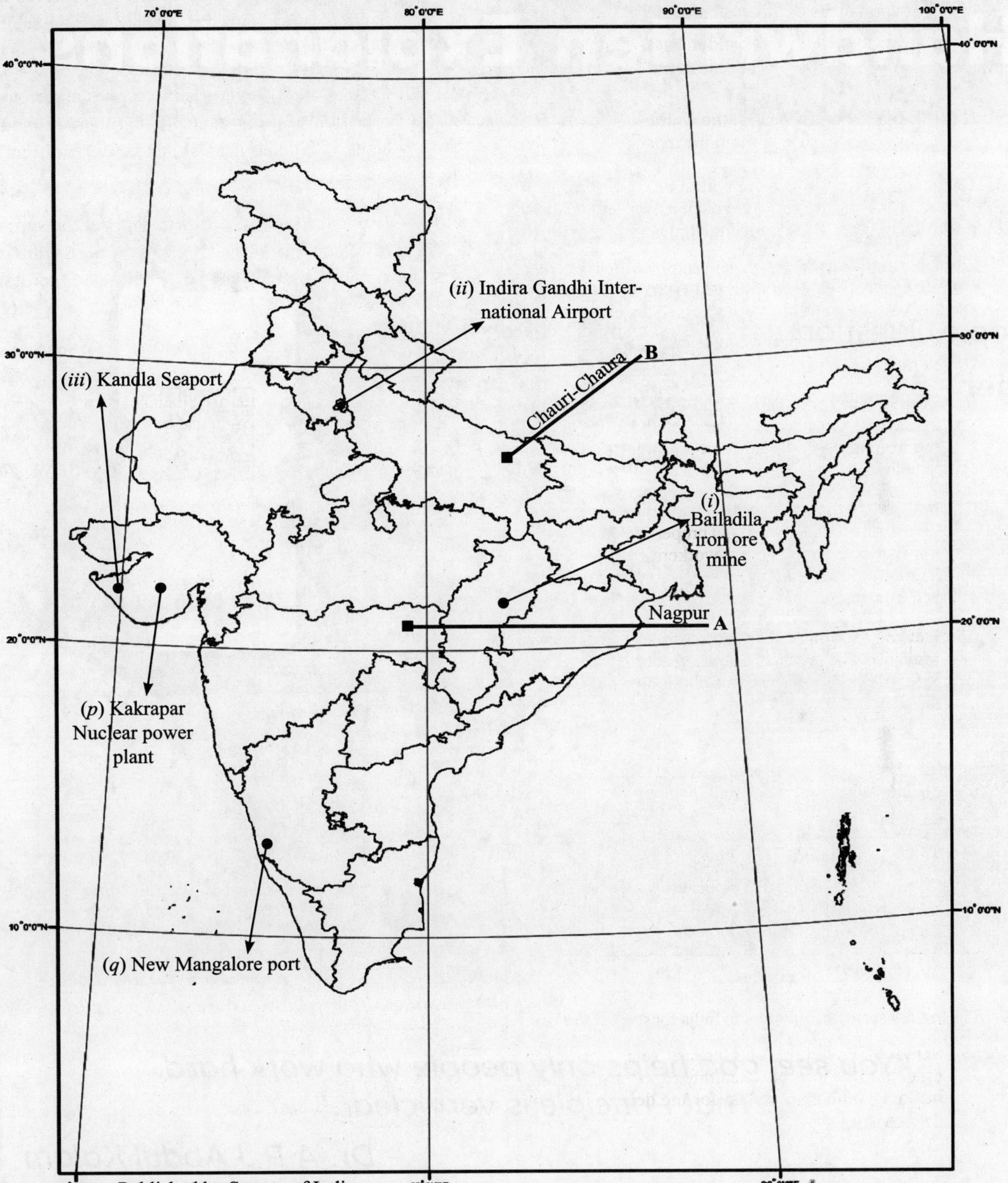

Published by Survey of India

Scale 1:16 M

Handwritten Explanations

Sample Question

Paper - 8

SCAN ME!

"You see, god helps only people who work hard.
That Principle is very clear."

- Dr. A P J Abdul Kalam

SAMPLE QUESTION PAPER-9
(Explanations)

SECTION - A

HISTORY (20 Marks)

Marking Scheme (Ques 1-4) *4 Min*

☞ Each question carries 1 mark.

1. (*c*) The worldwide economic depression led to a fall in agricultural prices and a decline in exports, causing significant economic hardship for Indian peasants who found it difficult to sell their harvests and pay their revenue. ***(1 M)***

2. (*a*) In the given image, Bismarck is having hunter in his hand which shows how his subordinates were afraid of Bismarck when he became autocratic during assemblies. ***(1 M)***

3. (*b*) D. Civil disobedience movement was launched: 1930

C. Gandhi Irwin pact was signed: 1931

B. Poona Pact was signed: 1932

A. Quit India movement was launched: 1942 ***(1 M)***

4. (*d*) The words 'freedom' and 'fraternity' written at the top and Atlas, depicting human labour, holding the world upon his shoulders. ***(1 M)***

5A. **Marking Scheme** *6 Min*

Mention two aspects to describe how the French Revolution was a turning point in European history.

☞ **End of Monarchy:** Introduction of democracy and revolutionary movements ***(1 M)***

☞ **Social and Political Transformations:** Fundamental reshaping of European society ***(1 M)***

The French Revolution was a turning point in European history in below aspects;

(*i*) The French Revolution ended monarchy, heralding democracy in Europe, inspiring revolutionary movements across the continent.

(*ii*) It induced profound social and political transformations,reshaping European society fundamentally.

OR

5B. **Marking Scheme** *6 Min*

Mention two impacts of industrialization on the development of nationalism in Europe

☞ **Growth of New Social Classes:** Highlight the emergence of new social groups ***(1 M)***

☞ **Economic Integration:** Explain the role of economic unity in promoting nationalism ***(1 M)***

The impact of industrialisation on the development of nationalism in Europe can be analyzed as follows:

(*i*) **Growth of New Social Classes:** Industrialisation led to the rise of new social groups like the working class and middle class, fostering ideas of national unity and identity among the educated middle classes.

(*ii*) **Economic Integration:** Increased industrial production and trade promoted the idea of a unified economic territory, which was crucial for the nationalist movements seeking to abolish aristocratic privileges and establish national unity.

6. **Marking Scheme** *8 Min*

Mention three points to describe the impact of the printing press:

☞ **Reduced Cost of Production:** Gutenberg press lowered book costs ***(1 M)***

☞ **Increased Book Production:** Mass production significantly boosted supply ***(1 M)***

☞ **Wider Accessibility:** Books became affordable and more accessible ***(1 M)***

The potential changes in the cost and accessibility of books due to the printing press as follows:

(*i*) **Reduced Cost of Production:** The Gutenberg press significantly reduced the time and labor needed to produce books, lowering the cost per book compared to traditional hand-copying methods.

(*ii*) **Increased Book Production:** The efficiency of the printing press allowed for the mass production of books. For instance, by the second half of the 15th century, 20 million copies of printed books were available, drastically increasing the supply.

(*iii*) **Wider Accessibility:** Books became more affordable and widely available, enabling more people, including commoners and students, to access and own books.

7A. **Marking Scheme** *13 Min*

Mention main proposals suggested by Mahatma Gandhi with reference to the Non-Cooperation Movement:
☞ **Surrender of Titles:** Mention the symbolic rejection of British authority *(1¼ M)*
☞ **Boycott of Civil Services and Institutions:** Emphasize non-cooperation in government institutions *(1¼ M)*
☞ **Refusal to Attend Official Functions:** Highlight the protest against colonial rule *(1¼ M)*
☞ **Boycott of Foreign Goods:** Discuss the promotion of Swadeshi and economic undermining of the British *(1¼ M)*

The four main proposals suggested by Mahatma Gandhi with reference to the Non-Coöperation Movement:

(*i*) **Surrender of Titles:** Gandhiji proposed that Indians should surrender the titles and honors awarded by the British government. This was a symbolic act to show the rejection of British authority and recognition.

(*ii*) **Boycott of Civil Services and Institutions:** He suggested the boycott of government schools, colleges, law courts, and other institutions to show non-cooperation with the British administration. This included resigning from civil services, army, and police positions.

(*iii*) **Refusal to Attend Official Functions:** Indians were urged not to participate in any official functions or ceremonies held by the British government, as a mark of protest against colonial rule.

(*iv*) **Boycott of Foreign Goods:** He called for the boycott of foreign goods and promotion of swadeshi (home-grown) products. This aimed at economically undermining the British while promoting Indian industries.

OR

7B. **Marking Scheme** *13 Min*

Mention the role of visual symbols in shaping nationalist sentiments during the Indian Independence Movement.
☞ **Bharat Mata:** Depiction of India as a mother goddess. *(1¼ M)*
☞ **National Flags:** Symbols of unity and self-reliance *(1¼ M)*
☞ **Folklore and Songs:** Revival of traditional culture *(1¼ M)*
☞ **Popular Prints and Symbols:** Mobilising people *(1¼ M)*

Role of Visual Symbols and Representations in Shaping Nationalist Sentiments During the Indian Independence Movement:

(*i*) **Bharat Mata:** The image of Bharat Mata, created by Abanindranath Tagore, portrayed India as a mother goddess. This image symbolized the nation's identity and evoked patriotic sentiments among the masses.

(*ii*) **National Flags:** The tricolour flag designed during the Swadeshi Movement had symbols representing unity among the provinces and religious communities of India. The Swaraj flag, with a spinning wheel at the center, represented Gandhian ideals of self-reliance.

(*iii*) **Folklore and Songs:** Nationalist leaders collected and promoted folk tales, songs, and legends. This revival of traditional culture helped instill a sense of pride and unity among Indians.

(*iv*) **Popular Prints and Symbols:** Visual representations of leaders and symbols, such as Jawaharlal Nehru holding Bharat Mata, reinforced the idea of sacrifice and dedication to the motherland. These visuals played a crucial role in mobilizing people.

8. **Marking Scheme** *10 Min*

(*i*) Impact of print culture in early 19th-century in India. *(1 M)*
(*ii*) How does print introduce diversity and new literary experiences? *(1 M)*
(*iii*) Highlighting Interest in Women's Lives: ☞ Description of how print culture sparked curiosity through social reforms. *(1 M)* ☞ Emphasis on women's roles and emotions highlighted through literary forms *(1 M)*

8.1 The print culture in the early nineteenth century in India shaped the nature of the debate by providing a platform for social and religious reformers to express their opinions and ideas. It allowed for the circulation of various arguments and tracts, which helped to spread awareness and promote discussion.

8.2 Print opened up a new world of experience and gave a vivid sense of diversity of human lives by introducing new literary forms such as lyrics, short stories, and essays about social and political matters.

8.3 The print culture greatly reflected an interest in women's lives and emotions by:

(*a*) Sparking curiosity about women's experiences and perspectives through social reforms and novels.

(*b*) Emphasizing human lives and intimate feelings with new literary forms, such as essays and short stories, further highlighting women's roles and emotions in society.

9. Marked on the Map. ***(2 M)***

SECTION - B

GEOGRAPHY (20 Marks)

Marking Scheme (Ques 10-12) 3 Min

☞ Each question carries 1 mark.

10. (*b*) Stricter mining regulations primarily aim to protect the environment by preserving biodiversity and preventing vegetation loss.

11. (*a*) Statement III is incorrect as Jawaharlal Nehru referred to dams as the 'temples of modern India'. Statement IV is incorrect as Dams affect the natural flow and can cause excessive sedimentation.

12. (*a*) Laterite soil develops in areas with high temperature and heavy rainfall. It is characterized by low humus content and is suitable for growing tea, coffee, and cashew nuts.

13. **Marking Scheme** 6 Min

Mention any two climatic conditions required for rice cultivation in coastal Odisha:

☞ **High Temperature:** Warm climate with temperatures above 25°C. ***(1 M)***

☞ **Abundant Water:** Water-intensive crop, effective water source utilization. ***(1 M)***

☞ **High Humidity:** High humidity levels with over 100 cm annual rainfall. ***(1 M)***

To cultivate rice successfully in the coastal region of Odisha, the following climatic conditions are considered: **(Any two)**

(*i*) **High Temperature:** Rice cultivation requires a warm climate with temperatures typically above 25°C. This is vital for germination and growth.

(*ii*) **Abundant Water:** Rice is a water-intensive crop. The coastal regions should utilize their proximity to water sources effectively, ensuring adequate flooding of rice paddies.

(*iii*) **High Humidity:** The area should have high humidity levels, ideally coupled with an annual rainfall of over 100 cm. In regions with less rainfall, irrigation methods may be necessary.

14. **Marking Scheme** 8 Min

Mention three points about the role of energy minerals and India's economic development:

☞ Mentions coal/uranium and explains their use in generating electricity ***(1 M)***

☞ Explains use of energy minerals in running factory machines, production etc. ***(1 M)***

☞ Mentions natural gas in vehicles/reducing imports/GDP/employment etc. ***(1 M)***

Energy minerals play a key role in India's progress by supporting industries, generating employment, and boosting the economy. Their importance can be seen in the following sectors:

(*i*) **Power Generation:** Coal and uranium are used to produce electricity, which powers homes, schools, hospitals, and factories.

(*ii*) **Manufacturing:** These minerals run machines in factories producing steel, cement, and other goods needed for development.

(*iii*) **Transport and Economy:** Natural gas fuels vehicles and helps reduce oil imports, supporting energy security and economic growth..

15A. **Marking Scheme** 13 Min

Mention point-wise about non-conventional energy sources:

☞ Significance of non-conventional energy in India's strategy. ***(1 M)***

☞ Explain any four types of non-conventional energy ***(2 M)***

☞ Mention key advantages ***(1 M)***

☞ Summary on sustainability and energy security. ***(1 M)***

Significance in Energy Strategy: Non-conventional sources like solar, wind, tidal and geothermal are vital for sustainable energy development, reducing dependency on finite fossil fuels.

Types of Non-Conventional Energy Sources:

(*i*) **Solar Energy:** Abundant in India, reduces reliance on traditional fuels, and provides clean energy.

(*ii*) **Wind Energy:** Effective in coastal regions, provides renewable and clean power.

(iii) **Biogas:** Converts organic waste into energy, improving waste management and providing a renewable source.

(iv) **Geothermal Energy:** Utilizes Earth's internal heat, providing a stable and sustainable energy source.

Advantages: They lower greenhouse gas emissions, create jobs, reduce energy costs, and support rural development.

Significance: Non-conventional sources are essential for sustainable development, reducing dependency on finite fossil fuels, and ensuring energy security.

OR

15B.

Marking Scheme	*13 Min*
Mention five points about minerals' occurrence and their effect on mining methods and economic viability:	
☞ Igneous and Metamorphic Rocks	*(1 M)*
☞ Sedimentary Rocks	*(1 M)*
☞ Residual Deposits	*(1 M)*
☞ Alluvial Deposits	*(1 M)*
☞ Ocean Water	*(1 M)*

Minerals occur in nature in several ways, affecting the mining methods and economic viability of extraction:

(i) **Igneous and Metamorphic Rocks:** Minerals in cracks, crevices, and faults (veins and lodes) require drilling and blasting, useful for minerals like tin and copper. Economically viable for high-concentration minerals like tin and copper.

(ii) **Sedimentary Rocks:** Minerals like coal and gypsum in beds or layers are mined through surface mining, such as strip mining or open pit mining, which is Cost-effective but can cause significant environmental impact. Common for coal and gypsum.

(iii) **Residual Deposits:** Minerals like bauxite, from decomposed surface rocks, are extracted via open-cast mining, making it economically viable.

(iv) **Alluvial Deposits:** Minerals like gold in valley floors and hill bases are extracted through placer mining, a cost-effective and less environmentally damaging method.

(v) **Ocean Water:** Extracting minerals like salt and magnesium through evaporation is viable for minerals abundant in seawater.

16.

Marking Scheme	*10 Min*
(i) Explain how manufacturing industries modernize agriculture.	*(1 M)*
(ii) The importance of industrial development for reducing unemployment and poverty.	*(1 M)*
(iii) Symbiotic Relationship Between Agriculture and Industry:	
☞ Explanation of how agro-industries boost agricultural productivity by providing inputs and technology	*(1 M)*
☞ Discussion on how agriculture supplies raw materials to industries for growth and development	*(1 M)*

16.1 Manufacturing industries help in modernizing agriculture by providing machinery, tools, and fertilizers, which enhance productivity and efficiency in agricultural practices.

16.2 Industrial development is crucial for eradicating unemployment and poverty as it creates jobs in secondary and tertiary sectors, reducing the heavy dependence on agricultural income.

16.3 The relationship between agriculture and industry is symbiotic. Agro-industries boost agricultural productivity by providing modern inputs and technology, while agriculture supplies raw materials to industries, ensuring their sustained growth and development.

17. Marked on Map. *(3 M)*

SECTION - C

POLITICAL SCIENCE (20 Marks)

Marking Scheme (Ques 18-25)	*8 Min*
☞ Each question carries 1 mark.	

18. (c) Majoritarianism refers to a system where the majority community enforces its will over the entire population, often disregarding the rights and concerns of minority communities. This approach undermines democratic principles of equality and inclusive governance *(1 M)*

19. (b) Montesquieu's quote emphasizes the importance of separating the legislative, executive, and judicial powers to prevent the concentration of authority in one entity, which is crucial for maintaining a democratic system and preventing tyranny. *(1 M)*

20. (d) Public expression of dissatisfaction with democracy shows the success of the democracy because when people express dissatisfaction with democracy, it shows that they have developed awareness and critical thinking skills to expect accountability from power holders, transferring them from subjects into citizens. *(1 M)*

21. (c) A-(ii), B-(iv), C-(i), D-(iii) *(1 M)*

22. (*c*) Australia is an example of a 'coming together' federation where independent states (colonies) voluntarily unite to form a federation, sharing sovereignty while retaining individual autonomy. ***(1 M)***

23. (*d*) Denmark has a more equitable income distribution, with the top 20% earning 34.5% and the bottom 20% earning 9.6% of the national income, indicating a relatively fairer income distribution. ***(1 M)***

24. (*b*) The cartoon "The Rich Get Buff" shows that rich people benefit a lot more from economic growth than middle and lower-class people. It highlights the problem of income inequality. ***(1 M)***

25. (*c*) Democracies face challenges in reducing economic disparities and ensuring equitable wealth distribution. ***(1 M)***

26.

Marking Scheme — 6 Min

☞ An exception to the trend of large countries being federations. ***(1 M)***
☞ Largest federal country globally. ***(1 M)***

(*a*) China is a large country highlighted on the map in white, indicating it does not have a federal system but rather a unitary system. This makes it an exception to the general trend where most large countries are federations.

(*b*) Russia is the largest country in the world by land area and is shown on the map as having a federal political system, making it the largest federal country globally.

27.

Marking Scheme — 6 Min

Identify the type of federation and provide reasoning.
☞ **Types of Federation** ***(1 M)***
☞ **Reason** ***(1 M)***

(*i*) There are two main ways to form a federation: coming together federations and holding together federations. The above clues refer to the Holding together federations.

(*ii*) In holding together federations, the Central government tends to be more powerful and constituent units often have unequal powers, and some may have special powers as well to protect their cultural heritage.

28.

Marking Scheme — 8 Min

☞ **Changes in Centre-State Relations:** Discuss the impact of regional parties and coalition governments. **(1½ M)**
☞ **Role of Supreme Court:** Explain how the Supreme Court's judgment strengthened state autonomy. **(1½ M)**

(*i*) **Changes in Centre-State Relations:** After 1990, the rise of regional parties and coalition governments at the Centre significantly improved Centre-State relations. States gained more respect, autonomy, and a culture of power-sharing emerged.

(*ii*) **Role of Supreme Court:** The Supreme Court passed a judgment that made it difficult for the central government to dismiss state governments arbitrarily, thus strengthening federal power sharing and respect for state autonomy.

29A.

Marking Scheme — 15 Min

Describe five indicators to evaluate the performance of political parties in a democracy.
☞ **Electoral Success:** Importance of electoral performance. ***(1 M)***
☞ **Policy Implementation:** Role in translating promises into action. ***(1 M)***
☞ **Internal Democracy:** Importance of internal party processes. ***(1 M)***
☞ **Transparency and Accountability:** Role of openness in party operations. ***(1 M)***
☞ **Inclusiveness or Responsiveness:** Measure of representing social groups or addressing public needs. ***(1 M)***

The key indicators that the institute should consider to evaluate the performance of political parties in a democratic country are: **(Any five)**

(*i*) **Electoral Success:** High electoral performance indicates strong public support and legitimacy.

(*ii*) **Policy Implementation:** Evaluating how well a party translates its manifesto promises into actual policies and actions once in power.

(*iii*) **Internal Democracy:** Assessing the degree of internal democracy within the party, such as how candidates are selected and how decisions are made.

(*iv*) **Transparency and Accountability:** The extent to which a party is transparent in its operations and accountable to its members and the public.

(*v*) **Inclusiveness:** Measuring the extent to which a party includes and represents various social groups, including minorities and marginalized communities.

(*vi*) **Responsiveness:** Evaluate how responsive a party is to the needs and demands of the public. This includes the party's ability to address public concerns and adapt to changing circumstances.

OR

29B.

Marking Scheme — 15 Min

Explain the challenges posed by the lack of internal democracy within political parties.
☞ **Loss of Public Trust:** Impact on people's faith in democracy. *(1 M)*
☞ **Risk of Political Instability:** Potential for factionalism. *(1 M)*
☞ **Risk of Authoritarian Rule:** Centralization of power. *(1 M)*
☞ **Ineffective Decision-Making:** Issues with top-level decisions. *(1 M)*
☞ **Weakened Democracy:** Overall impact on democratic effectiveness. *(1 M)*

The lack of internal democracy within the political party is considered a challenge to India's democracy because:

(*i*) **Loss of Public Trust:** People might lose faith in democracy if they see that parties aren't fair internally. This can reduce participation and trust in the democratic process.

(*ii*) **Risk of Political instability:** A persistent lack of internal democracy can lead to factionalism, where dissatisfied members may break away to form their own parties.

(*iii*) **Risk of Authoritarian Rule:** When power is concentrated in the hands of a few, it can lead to authoritarian behavior where leaders might ignore democratic norms and rule as they want.

(*iv*) **Ineffective Decision-Making:** Decisions made by a small group of top leaders may not reflect the needs and desires of the larger membership or electorate, leading to ineffective policies and a potential loss of voter support.

(*v*) **Weakened Democracy:** These factors can collectively weaken the effectiveness and stability of India's democracy, impacting its overall function.

SECTION - D

ECONOMICS (20 Marks)

Marking Scheme (Ques 30-34) — 6 Min

☞ Each question carries 1 mark.

30. (*b*) Kerala *(1 M)*

31. (*b*) Arun is one of the few people in sonpur to take a bank loan because banks demand collateral which everyone cannot provide. This requirement of collateral makes it difficult for many villagers to access bank loans, leading them to prefer money lenders higher despite interest eates. *(1 M)*

32. (*c*) In GDP calculations, it is crucial to consider only the value of final goods and services to avoid double counting. The wheat used by Mr. Sweet's Bakery is an intermediate good, as it is further processed into biscuits, which are then sold to consumers. Hence, only the value of the biscuits should be included in the GDP, as they represent the final product available for consumption. *(1 M)*

33. (*c*) Internet technology supports global environmental campaigns by enabling interactive and educative sessions that can engage participants globally despite different time zones, enhancing the campaign's reach and impact. *(1 M)*

34. (*c*) Formal sources of credit have certain eligibility criteria *(1 M)*

35A.

Marking Scheme — 6 Min

Mention three points about the impact of less job creation in secondary and tertiary sectors:
☞ Significant growth in industrial output and services without corresponding employment growth. *(1 M)*
☞ Tertiary sector's production rose significantly, but employment growth was much smaller. *(1 M)*
☞ Continued reliance on the primary sector for employment, despite its smaller GDP contribution. *(1 M)*

The impact of less job creation in secondary and tertiary sectors of employment can be understood by the following points:

(*i*) Despite significant growth in industrial output and services, employment growth in these sectors have not kept pace, leading to a skewed employment scenario.

(*ii*) The tertiary sector's production rose by 14 times, but employment only rose five times, indicating a mismatch in job creation.

(*iii*) This led to continued reliance on the primary sector for employment, despite its smaller contribution to GDP.

OR

35B. **Marking Scheme** ⏰ *6 Min*

Mention three reasons why the government engages in certain activities:

- ☞ **Necessity for Large Investments:** The government invests where the private sector cannot. *(1 M)*
- ☞ **Collection Challenge:** Difficulty in gathering funds from numerous users. *(1 M)*
- ☞ **Accessibility:** Ensuring essential facilities are available to all citizens. *(1 M)*

The government engages in such activities because of the following reasons:

(*i*) **Necessity for Large Investments:** These activities require substantial financial resources, often exceeding the private sector's capabilities. So, the government invests in such activities.

(*ii*) **Collection Challenge:** It is difficult to gather funds from numerous users of these services.

(*iii*) **Accessibility:** It should be ensured that essential facilities like roads and bridges are available to all citizens. The government takes responsibility for such activities to ensure the availability of such essential facilities.

36. **Marking Scheme** ⏰ *6 Min*

Mention three points about the limitations of using averages for comparison:

- ☞ Averages do not indicate a rising standard of living. *(1 M)*
- ☞ Averages do not show how equally or unevenly income is distributed. *(1 M)*
- ☞ Averages do not provide information regarding the Human Development Index (HDI), like infant mortality rate or literacy rate. *(1 M)*

Averages are useful for comparison but still hide disparities means that the average of everything gives us the mean value for comparison but,

(*i*) It does not indicate a rising standard of living as average income only measures quantitative aspects.

(*ii*) It does not tell us how equally or evenly income is distributed.

(*iii*) It does not give information regarding the human development index such as infant mortality rate, literacy rate, etc.

Topper's Explanation

Average income hide disparities. This can be proved by the following.

(i) Average income hide disparities in case there is no equitable distribution of income.

For example if a small population have a very high income, the total income as well as the average income rises thus hiding disparities about the actual situation

(ii) They average income donot indicate rising standards of living as development depends on non-materialistic factors like freedom, equality, respect, justice etc.

(iii) Average income donot tell us about the HDI as it depends on health and educational status also.

37A. **Marking Scheme** ⏰ *15 Min*

Mention four points about the role of money as a medium of exchange:

- ☞ Money as a medium of exchange changes transactions *(1¼ M)*
- ☞ Facilitates transactions through common value measure *(1¼ M)*
- ☞ Enhances economic activities and market efficiency *(1¼ M)*
- ☞ Example of shoe manufacturer case *(1¼ M)*

The role of money and its benefits of using as a medium of exchange can be understood by the following points:

(*i*) Money, as a medium of exchange, fundamentally changes how transactions are conducted, moving beyond the restrictive barter system.

(*ii*) It facilitates transactions by providing a common value measure, making trade more straightforward and allowing for the specialization of labour.

(*iii*) Economic activities are enhanced as money increases market efficiency, expands trade opportunities, and encourages investment and savings.

(*iv*) The case of the shoe manufacturer illustrates how money enables producers to easily convert their goods into a widely accepted medium, which can then be used to purchase diverse commodities.

OR

37B.

Marking Scheme	15 Min
Mention five points about the benefits of Demand Deposits:	
☞ Security of funds	*(1 M)*
☞ High liquidity/Accessibility	*(1 M)*
☞ Interest Earnings	*(1 M)*
☞ Helps with cash flow management	*(1 M)*
☞ Facilitates smoother transactions	*(1 M)*

Demand deposits are bank account deposits that can be withdrawn on demand. It is beneficial in several ways:

(*i*) **Safety of Funds:** Depositing cash into a bank account safeguards the money against theft or loss, providing security and peace of mind for the business owner.

(*ii*) **Accessibility:** Demand deposits allow for high liquidity, meaning funds can be withdrawn or transferred quickly and easily when needed, without significant processing delays.

(*iii*) **Interest Earnings:** While typically lower than other investment forms, demand deposits often earn some interest, contributing to increased earnings for the business over time.

(*iv*) **Cash Flow Management:** Managing cash flows effectively is critical for any business. Having funds in a bank account enables better tracking and management of cash flows.

(*v*) **Facilitating Transactions:** With cash deposited in a bank, a business can utilize various payment methods such as checks, wire transfers, and online payments, facilitating smoother business transactions.

38.

Marking Scheme	10 Min
(*i*) Role of the Internet in communication and file transfer.	*(1 M)*
(*ii*) key components for enabling digital communication.	*(1 M)*
(*iii*) Elaborate two points about e-banking:	
☞ Secure and Instant Transactions	*(1 M)*
☞ Efficient Fund Transfer for Services	*(1 M)*

38.1 The internet plays a crucial role in enabling instantaneous communication and file transfer between the London office and the Delhi office.

38.2 Telecommunication, internet and computer.

38.3 E-banking enables secure and instant financial transactions across borders. In this scenario, it allows the London office to swiftly transfer funds to the Delhi office for the services rendered, eliminating the delays and complexities associated with traditional banking methods.

Mistakes 101 : What not to do!

- ❒ Not providing specific examples or details of how the internet facilitates communication and file transfer between offices.
- ❒ Failing to explain how e-banking enhances security and efficiency in international transactions, such as encryption methods or real-time fund transfers.

Map for Q. no. 9 (Section A) & Q. no. 17 (Section B)

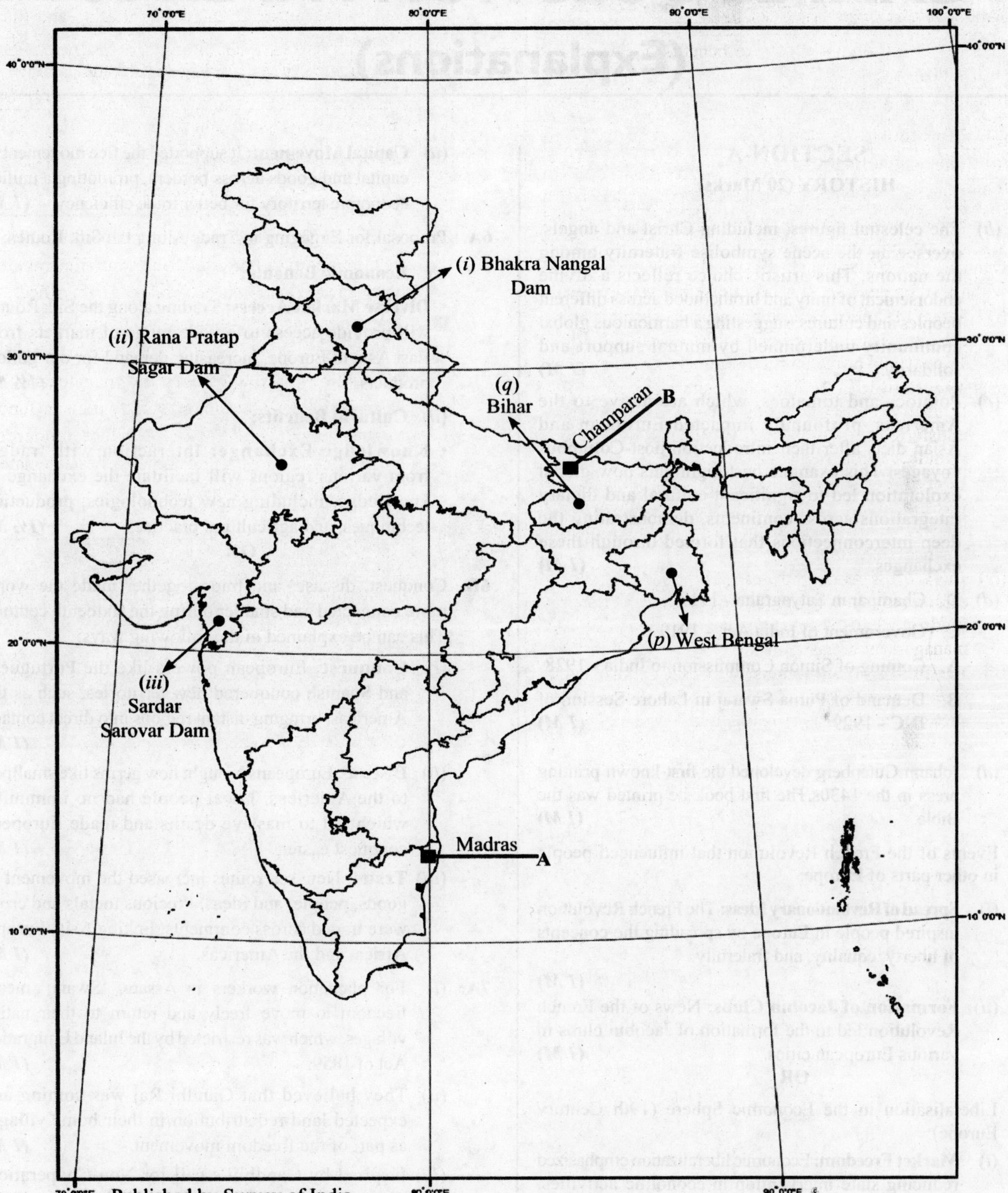

Published by Survey of India

Scale 1:16 M

SAMPLE QUESTION PAPER-10
(Explanations)

SECTION-A
HISTORY (20 Marks)

1. (*b*) The celestial figures, including Christ and angels, overseeing the scene symbolise fraternity among the nations. This artistic choice reflects a divine endorsement of unity and brotherhood across different peoples and cultures, suggesting a harmonious global community underpinned by mutual support and solidarity. ***(1 M)***

2. (*c*) Potatoes and tomatoes, which are native to the Americas, profoundly impacted European and Asian diets after their introduction post-Columbus voyages. This example best highlights how global exploration led to significant cultural and dietary integrations across continents, demonstrating the deep interconnections that formed through these exchanges. ***(1 M)***

3. (*d*) D. Champaran Satyagraha - 1917

C. Government of India Act, - 1919

A. Coming of Simon Commission to India - 1928

B. Demand of Purna Swaraj in Lahore Session of INC - 1929 ***(1 M)***

4. (*d*) Johann Gutenberg developed the first-known printing press in the 1430s.The first book he printed was the Bible. ***(1 M)***

5A. Events of the French Revolution that influenced people in other parts of Europe:

(*i*) **Spread of Revolutionary Ideas:** The French Revolution inspired people in Europe by spreading the concepts of liberty, equality, and fraternity. ***(1 M)***

(*ii*) **Formation of Jacobin Clubs:** News of the French Revolution led to the formation of Jacobin clubs in various European cities. ***(1 M)***

OR

5B. Liberalisation in the Economic Sphere (19th Century Europe):

(*i*) **Market Freedom:** Economic liberalization emphasized reducing state intervention in economic activities, advocating for free trade and the removal of customs barriers. ***(1 M)***

(*ii*) **Capital Movement:** It supported the free movement of capital and goods across borders, promoting a unified economic territory for better trade efficiency. ***(1 M)***

6A. Proposal for Engaging in Trade Along the Silk Routes:

(*i*) **Economic Benefits:**

- **Diverse Market Access:** Trading along the Silk Routes will provide access to a wide range of markets from East Asia to Europe, increasing demand for our guild's products. ***(1½ M)***

(*ii*) **Cultural Benefits:**

- **Knowledge Exchange:** Interaction with traders from various regions will facilitate the exchange of knowledge, including new technologies, production techniques, and agricultural practices. ***(1½ M)***

OR

6B. Conquest, disease, and trade together made the world more connected and smaller during the sixteenth century. This can be explained in the following ways:

(*i*) **Conquest:** European powers like the Portuguese and Spanish conquered new territories, such as the Americas, bringing distant regions into direct contact. ***(1 M)***

(*ii*) **Disease:** Europeans brought new germs like smallpox to the Americas. Local people had no immunity, which led to massive deaths and made European conquest easier. ***(1 M)***

(*iii*) **Trade:** New sea routes increased the movement of goods, people, and ideas. Precious metals and crops were traded across continents, linking Asia, Europe, Africa, and the Americas. ***(1 M)***

7A. (*i*) For plantation workers in Assam, 'Swaraj' meant freedom to move freely and return to their native villages, which was restricted by the Inland Emigration Act of 1859. ***(1 M)***

(*ii*) They believed that Gandhi Raj was coming and expected land redistribution in their home villages as part of the freedom movement. ***(1 M)***

(*iii*) Inspired by Gandhiji's call for Non-Cooperation, thousands of workers left the tea plantations without permission and started heading home. ***(1 M)*** (*iv*) Their journey remained incomplete as they were stopped by railway and steamer strikes, and were brutally beaten up by the police. **(1 M)**

(*v*) Plantation workers' idea of Swaraj was thus deeply emotional and rooted in their personal struggles, rather than political goals defined by the Congress. **(1 M)**

OR

7B. The spread of Non-Cooperation Movement in the countryside:

(*i*) In Awadh, peasants led by Baba Ramchandra revolted against high rents and forced labor, organizing nai-dhobi bandhs. **(1 M)**

(*ii*) The Oudh Kisan Sabha formed under Jawaharlal Nehru, mobilizing over 300 village branches by October 1920. **(1 M)**

(*iii*) In the Gudem Hills of Andhra Pradesh, Alluri Sitaram Raju led tribals in guerrilla warfare against oppressive forest laws, linking their struggle with Gandhiji's movement. **(1 M)**

(*iv*) Assam's plantation workers left plantations, believing Gandhi Raj would provide land and freedom. **(1 M)**

(*v*) These diverse groups, interpreting swaraj as freedom from economic and social oppression, united under the Non-Cooperation Movement, significantly impacting rural India by merging local struggles with the broader national movement against British rule. **(1 M)**

8. 8.1. Indian decentralisation is considered the largest experiment in democracy because it involves about 36 lakh elected representatives, more than the population of many countries, reflecting massive democratic engagement. **(1 M)**

8.2. Granting constitutional status to local governments in India has significantly deepened democracy by ensuring regular elections, and enabling direct local decision-making, thus enhancing democratic engagement at the grassroots level. **(1 M)**

8.3. The two steps taken by the Indian Government for decentralization are:

(*a*) In 1992, the Indian Government amended the Constitution to mandate regular elections for local governments, reserve seats for SCs, STs, OBCs, and women **(1 M)**

(*b*) States are required to share powers and revenue with local government bodies. This change aims to empower local bodies to manage and resolve local issues more effectively. **(1 M)**

9. Marked on map. **(2 M)**

SECTION-B

GEOGRAPHY (20 Marks)

10. (*c*) While multipurpose river projects provide water, control floods, and generate electricity, they also cause large-scale community displacements and livelihood loss, making this a critical concern against such projects. **(1 M)**

11. (*d*) Resource planning in India is challenging due to its diverse geography and population, while the necessity of identifying resources adds complexity to the process. **(1 M)**

12. (*a*) A-(i), B-(ii), C-(iii) **(1 M)**

13. (*a*) The ideal type of soil for growing cotton is black soil, which is known for its capacity to hold moisture. This characteristic is crucial for cotton cultivation as it requires soil that can retain moisture well.

The other clues do not specifically point to black soil. Clue (ii) refers to yellow soil, clue (iii) does not describe black soil accurately, and clue (iv) describes loamy soil, which is not specifically ideal for cotton. **(1 M)**

14. (*d*) All of the above **(1 M)**

15. (*a*) Both A and R are true, and R is the correct explanation of A. **(1 M)**

16. To cultivate rice successfully in the coastal region of Odisha, the following climatic conditions are considered: (Any two)

(*i*) **High Temperature:** Rice cultivation requires a warm climate with temperatures typically above 25°C. This is vital for germination and growth. **(1 M)**

(*ii*) **Abundant Water:** Rice is a water-intensive crop. The coastal regions should utilize their proximity to water sources effectively, ensuring adequate flooding of rice paddies. **(1 M)**

(*iii*) **High Humidity:** The area should have high humidity levels, ideally coupled with an annual rainfall of over 100 cm. In regions with less rainfall, irrigation methods may be necessary. **(1 M)**

17A. Minerals occur in nature in several ways, affecting the mining methods and economic viability of extraction:

(*i*) **Igneous and Metamorphic Rocks:** Minerals in cracks, crevices, and faults (veins and lodes) require drilling and blasting, useful for minerals like tin and copper. Economically viable for high-concentration minerals like tin and copper. **(1 M)**

(*ii*) **Sedimentary Rocks:** Minerals like coal and gypsum in beds or layers are mined through surface mining, such as strip mining or open-pit mining, which arc Cost-effective but can cause significant environmental impact. Common for coal and gypsum. **(1 M)** (*iii*) **Residual Deposits:** Minerals like bauxite, from decomposed surface rocks, are extracted via open-cast mining, making it economically viable. ***(1 M)***

(*iv*) **Alluvial Deposits:** Minerals like gold in valley floors and hill bases are extracted through placer mining, a cost-effective and less environmentally damaging method. ***(1 M)***

(*v*) **Ocean Water:** Extracting minerals like salt and magnesium through evaporation is viable for minerals abundant in seawater. ***(1 M)***

OR

17B. (Each point carries 1 M)

Base	Meaning Minerals	Non-Metallic Minerals
Meaning	Minerals that contain metal in raw form and arc generally hard substances.	Minerals that do not contain metals and encompass a vast range of minerals with diverse properties.
Conductivity	Good conductors of electricity' and heat.	Poor conductors of electricity and heat.
Luster	Possess a shiny or metallic luster.	Do not exhibit a metallic luster; appearance can be dull, glassy, or pearly.
Examples	Iron ore (used in steel making), bauxite (used in aluminum production), copper (used in electrical wires).	Mica (used in electrical insulators), gypsum (used in plaster and drywall), limestone (used in cement production).
Economic Use	Mainly used in the manufacturing of machinery, vehicles, and construction materials.	Used in industries like construction, agriculture, pharmaceuticals, and cosmetics.

18. 18.1. The cooperative model ensures farmers have direct stakes in the mill's profits, leading to fairer pricing for their sugarcane and shared decision-making in mill operations. ***(1 M)***

18.2 The mill creates diverse job opportunities, from agricultural processing to administrative roles, reducing dependency on seasonal agricultural work. ***(1 M)***

18.3 Long-term impacts may include increased adoption of sustainable farming, improved crop yields, and better soil health, contributing to environmental sustainability and economic resilience. ***(2 M)***

19. Marked on the map ***(3 M)***

SECTION C

POLITICAL SCIENCE (20 Marks)

20. (*b*) 1-C, 2-A, 3-D, 4-B ***(1 M)***

21. (*d*) Denmark has a more equitable income distribution, with the top 20% earning 34.5% and the bottom 20% earning 9.6% of the national income, indicating a relatively fairer income distribution than other countries. ***(1 M)***

22. (*d*) The Bahujan Samaj Party (BSP) is primarily focused on representing the interests of marginalized communities, including Scheduled Tribes, Scheduled Castes, and Other Backward Classes. This makes it the most likely party for Subhash to be associated with. ***(1 M)***

23. (*a*) The sexual division of labour in India ***(1 M)***

24. According to the map, in Belgium:

(i) The dominant languages are Dutch and French. ***(1 M)***

(ii) Dutch is spoken by the majority in the Flemish region. Whereas French is spoken by a large population in the Wallonia region. ***(1 M)***

25. The demands of Sri Lankan Tamils were:

(*i*) Recognition of Tamil as an official language. ***(½ M)***

(*ii*) Provision of regional autonomy. ***(½ M)***

(*iii*) Equality of opportunity in securing education and jobs. ***(½ M)***

(*iv*) An independent Tamil Eelam (state) in northern and Eastern parts of Sri Lanka. ***(½ M)***

26. Caste cannot solely determine election results in India because:

(*i*) No parliamentary constituency in the country has a clear majority of one single caste. So, the party needs to win the confidence of more than one caste and community to win elections. ***(1 M)***

(*ii*) Urbanization, education, and economic status influence voter behavior more significantly in many areas, reducing the impact of caste alone. ***(1 M)***

(*iii*) Voters are becoming more issue-oriented rather than caste-oriented, prioritizing performance, leadership, quality, governance and development issues over caste identity ***(1 M)***

27A. The statement "Democracy's ability to generate its own support is also its outcome and it cannot be ignored." signifies that:

(*i*) People naturally value democratic principles and choose democracy over other forms of government. ***(1 M)*** (*ii*) This preference is evident globally. People in various countries, regardless of whether they live in democratic or non-democratic regimes, tend to support the idea of democracy. **(*1 M*)**

(*iii*) People believe in having a government elected by them and feel that democracy suits their country. It reflects people's belief in democracy as a fair and just method of governance. **(*1 M*)**

(*iv*) Even when individuals criticize their democratic systems or express dissatisfaction with certain aspects, their engagement and demands for improvement further validate democracy's significance. **(*1 M*)**

(*v*) This continuous cycle of support, critique, and evolution underlines democracy's capacity to sustain and enhance itself. **(*1 M*)**

OR

27B. The statement stands true. Democracy stands much superior to any other form of government in promoting dignity and freedom of the individual because: **(Any five)**

(*i*) **Equality and Respect:** The passion for respect and freedom are the basis of democracy. This principle is universally recognized. **(*1 M*)**

(*ii*) **Legal and Moral Recognition:** Democratic societies legally and morally recognize the dignity and freedom of every individual, providing a framework for protecting these rights. **(*1 M*)**

(*iii*) **Claims of the backward:** Democracies recognise the claims of the backward and disadvantaged sections of society and they are granted equal status and opportunity **(*1 M*)**

(*iv*) **Non-discrimination:** Democratic systems aim to eliminate discrimination ensuring that all individuals, regardless of their background, have the opportunity to live with dignity. **(*1 M*)**

(*v*) **No gender bias:** Most societies are male-dominated and women do not get equal chances. In democracies, equal respect and treatment of women have been accepted. **(*1 M*)**

(*vi*) **Self-expression and Participation:** Individuals are allowed to express themselves freely and participate in the governance process which proves democracy provides freedom **(*1 M*)**

Topper's Explanation ***(CBSE, 2017)***

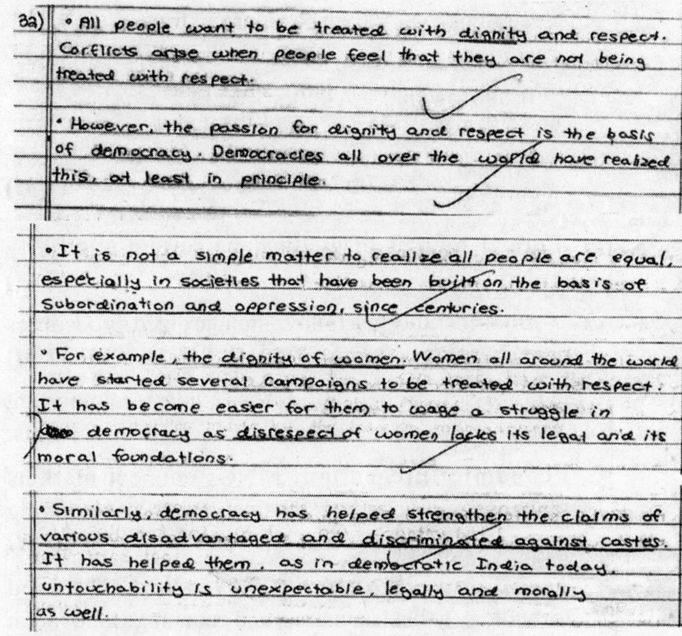
32) • All people want to be treated with dignity and respect. Conflicts arise when people feel that they are not being treated with respect.

• However, the passion for dignity and respect is the basis of democracy. Democracies all over the world have realized this, at least in principle.

• It is not a simple matter to realize all people are equal, especially in societies that have been built on the basis of subordination and oppression, since centuries.

• For example, the dignity of women. Women all around the world have started several campaigns to be treated with respect. It has become easier for them to wage a struggle in democracy as disrespect of women lacks its legal and its moral foundations.

• Similarly, democracy has helped strengthen the claims of various disadvantaged and discriminated against castes. It has helped them, as in democratic India today, untouchability is unexpectable, legally and morally as well.

28.1 India's language diversity makes its culture rich and diverse. It helps people from different backgrounds respect each other's culture, encourage cultural exchange, and respect all communities. **(*1 M*)**

28.2 Scheduled Languages are those that are included in the Eighth Schedule of the Indian Constitution, comprising 22 major languages. Non-scheduled languages, on the other hand, refer to languages not included in the Eighth Schedule. **(*1 M*)**

28.3 The fusion of languages in India promotes cultural unity. For example-using languages like Hindi and English across India helps in bringing people together, even though they may speak different local languages. This shows how languages can help unite a country. **(*2 M*)**

SECTION-D

ECONOMICS (2O Marks)

29. (*b*) Sri Lanka **(*1 M*)**

30. (*a*) Kerala's low Infant Mortality Rate is indeed due to the adequate provision of basic health and educational facilities. The availability and accessibility of these facilities ensure better healthcare and education, contributing significantly to lower infant mortality rates in the state. **(*1 M*)**

31. (*b*) Trade barrier refers to some restrictions including tax on imports which governments can use to increase or decrease foreign trade and to decide what kind of goods, how much of each, should come into the country. **(*1 M*)**

32. (*a*) Average Income of the locality

$$= \frac{\text{Total Income of All families}}{\text{No. of families in locality}} \text{ or } \frac{\text{Total Income}}{\text{Total Population}}$$

$$= \frac{6,000+4,000+7,000+3,000}{4}$$

$$= \frac{20,000}{4} = ₹5,000$$ **(1 M)**

33. (*c*) Formal sources of credit have certain eligibility criteria **(1 M)**

34. (*c*) Formal institutions follow standardized procedures and charge lower interest rates. **(1 M)**

35. In the process of globalisation, MNCs play an important role. Its role can be understood with the following points:

- **Economic Integration:** MNCs connect markets globally by investing across countries, and merging economies of the world. **(1 M)**
- **Technology Transfer:** They bring advanced technology to host countries, and encourage innovation and skills development. The globalisation process is sped up in this way. **(1 M)**
- **Job Creation:** MNCs establish operations worldwide in different countries and as a result create employment opportunities for the people residing in those countries. Therefore, MNCs reduce the problem of unemployment. **(1 M)**

36. A substantial shift in employment in the primary Sector has not happened because of the following reasons:

(*i*) **Insufficient Job Creation:** Not enough jobs were created in the secondary and tertiary sectors to absorb the surplus labor from the primary sector. **(1 M)**

(*ii*) **Underemployment in Agriculture:** Many workers in agriculture are underemployed, indicating they can leave without impacting production significantly. **(1 M)**

(*iii*) **Imbalance in Sector Contribution:** Industrial and service sectors' output increased significantly, but job growth did not match. Many remain in the primary sector, despite its lower GDP contribution, while secondary and tertiary sectors are underemployed relative to their output. **(1 M)**

37. Reasons for Sunil's dissatisfaction as compared to Raman are:

(*i*) **Lack of Job Security:** Sunil worked in the unorganised sector where jobs are not secure and workers can be removed without any notice. **(1 M)**

(*ii*) **No Employment Benefits:** He did not receive benefits like paid leave, medical facilities, provident fund, or pension. **(1 M)**

(*iii*) **Poor Working Conditions:** Sunil had long working hours with low and irregular wages, and no protection under labour laws. **(1 M)**

38A. Credit is an agreement where the lender provides money or goods to the borrower with a promise of future payment.

Example: Salim, a shoe manufacturer, took credit to buy raw materials and later repaid it after selling shoes. **(1 M)**

Credit as an asset and a debt trap can be:

(*i*) Helpful in growth: If used for productive work, credit helps increase income and improve life. **(1 M)**

(*ii*) Risky in loss: If the borrower faces a loss (like crop failure), it becomes hard to repay. **(1 M)**

(iii) Debt trap: Swapna's case, crop failure led to inability to repay, pushing her into a debt trap. When unable to repay, the borrower takes new loans, leading to a cycle of debt. **(1 M)**

(iv) Final outcome: So, credit is an asset if income increases, but a debt trap if losses happen. **(1 M)**

OR

38B. The ways money helps the bakery and café work together are:

(*i*) They don't need to exchange goods directly. It saves time and avoids the need for both to want each other's product at the same time. **(1 M)**

(*ii*) Payments become simple and flexible. The café can pay for bread later, and the bakery can use that money for other needs. **(1 M)**

The benefits of using money as a medium of exchange in the market are:

(*i*) Trade becomes wider – They can buy or sell from many people, not just each other. **(1 M)**

(*ii*) Saves and invests easily – People can save and invest money for future needs. **(1 M)**

(*iii*) Faster business – Money speeds up transactions and helps in keeping proper records. **(1 M)**

Nailing the Right Answer

- ❑ Define credit as a loan with future repayment. Use Salim's case to show gain (asset) and Swapna's to show loss (debt trap). Explain how credit helps when used productively, but harms when repayment fails, leading to a debt cycle.
- ❑ State that money removes double coincidence of wants. Explain it as a medium of exchange. Highlight benefits like flexible payments, faster trade, and wider markets. Mention how money improves efficiency and record-keeping in business.

Map for Q. no. 9 (Section A) & Q. no. 19 (Section B)

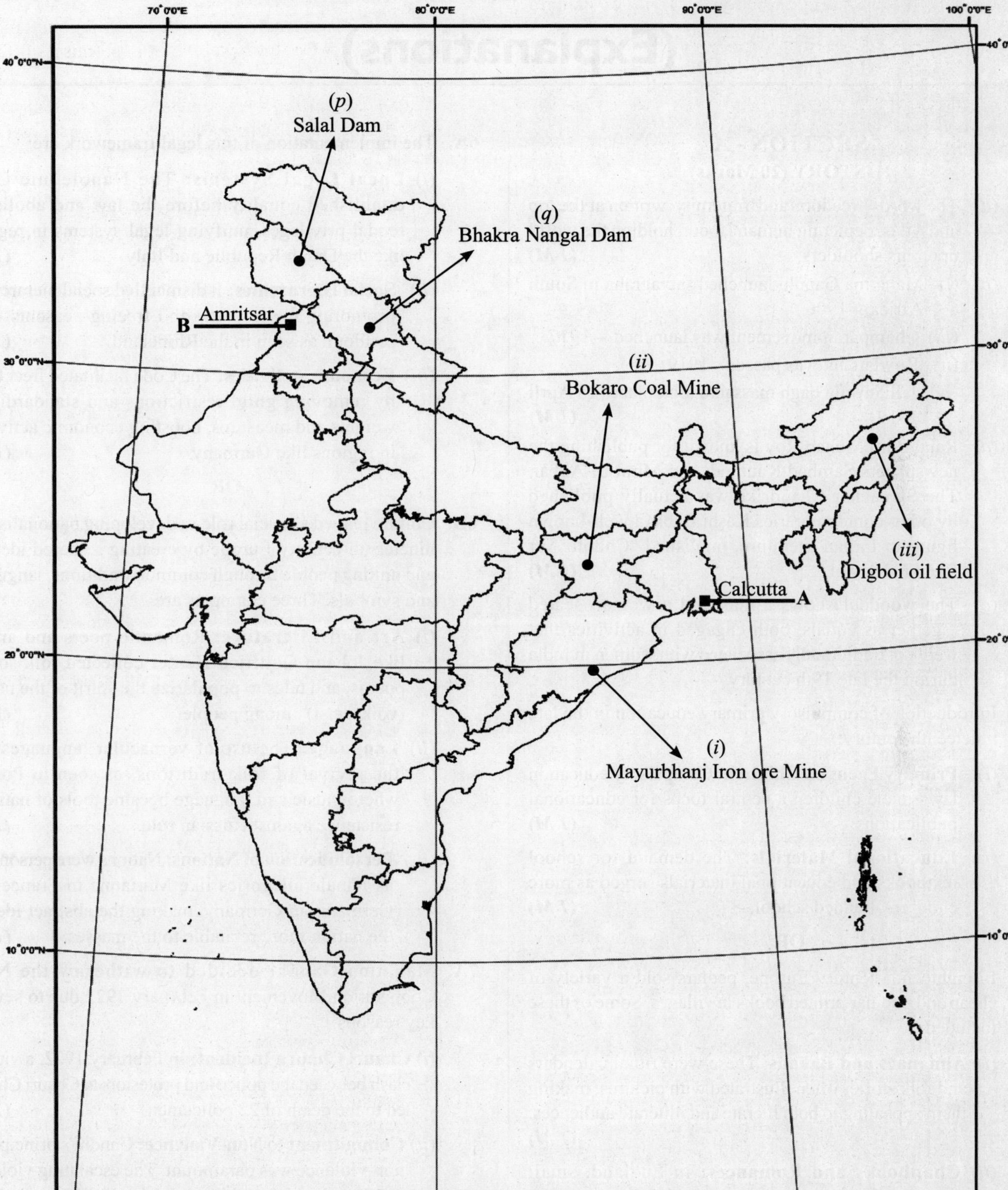

Published by Survey of India
Scale 1:16M

SAMPLE QUESTION PAPER-11
(Explanations)

SECTION - A
HISTORY (20 Marks)

1. (*d*) The words 'freedom' and 'fraternity' written at the top and Atlas, depicting human labour, holding the world upon his shoulders. ***(1 M)***

2. (*b*) (*i*) Mahatma Gandhi launched satyagraha in South Africa. - 1906

(*iii*) Champaran movement was launched. - 1917

(*ii*) Rowlatt act was passed - 1919

(*iv*) Jallianwala bagh massacre took place- 13 April 1919 ***(1 M)***

3. (*d*) Raja, Ram Mohan Roy is known for publishing the newspapers Sambad Kaumudi and Mirat-ul-Akbar. The Samachar Chandrika was actually published by other contemporaries.Kashi Baba, a well-known figure in Indian literature, published "Chhote Aur Bade Ka Sawal." ***(1 M)***

4. (*c*) The woodcut shows a man and a woman seated together as equals, both engaged in activities that were not traditionally associated with women in India during the late 19th century.

5A. Introduction of compulsory primary education in the late nineteenth century:

(*i*) **Primary Focus on Children:** Compulsory education laws made children a central focus for educational publications. ***(1 M)***

(*ii*) **Educational Materials:** The demand for school textbooks and educational materials surged as more children attended school. ***(1 M)***

OR

5B. In eighteenth-century Europe, pedlars sold a variety of cheap and popular printed books in villages. Some of these included:

(*i*) **Almanacs and Ballads**: These were ritual calendars and folk stories often illustrated with pictures, making them appealing to both literate and illiterate audiences. ***(1 M)***

(*ii*) **Chapbooks and Romances:** In England, small books called chapbooks were sold for a penny by chapmen. In France, similar low-priced books called Bibliothèque Bleue were common. ***(1 M)***

6A. The implementation of this legal framework are:

(*i*) **Local Legal Systems:** The Napoleonic Code established equality before the law and abolished feudal privileges, unifying legal systems in regions like the Dutch Republic and Italy. ***(1 M)***

(*ii*) **Social Hierarchies:** It dismantled social hierarchies, promoting meritocracy and freeing peasants from serfdom, as seen in the Rhineland. ***(1 M)***

(*iii*) **Economic Activities:** The Code facilitated freer trade by removing guild restrictions and standardizing weights and measures, boosting economic activities in regions like Germany. ***(1 M)***

OR

6B. Culture played a crucial role in developing nationalism in nineteenth-century Europe by creating a shared identity and uniting people through common traditions, language, and symbols. Three examples are:

(*i*) **Art and Literature:** Romantic poets and artists like Johann Gottfried Herder collected folk songs, poems, and tales to popularize the spirit of the nation (volksgeist) among people. ***(1 M)***

(*ii*) **Language:** The use of vernacular languages and the revival of folk traditions, as seen in Poland where music and language became tools of national resistance against Russian rule. ***(1 M)***

(*iii*) **Personification of Nations:** Nations were personified as female allegories like Marianne in France and Germania in Germany, making the abstract idea of the nation more relatable to the masses. ***(1 M)***

7A. Mahatma Gandhi decided to withdraw the Non-Cooperation Movement in February 1922 due to several key reasons:

(*i*) **Chauri Chaura Incident:** In February 1922, a violent clash between the police and protestors at Chauri Chaura led to the death of 22 policemen. ***(1 M)***

(*ii*) **Commitment to Non-Violence:** Gandhi's principle of non-violence was paramount. The escalating violence conflicted with his philosophy, leading him to halt the movement to maintain discipline among his followers. ***(1 M)*** (*iii*) **Reassessment of Strategy:** Gandhi felt that the Indian masses needed better training in nonviolent resistance before resuming any mass struggle, necessitating a pause in the movement. **(*1 M*)**

(*iv*) **Internal Dissent within Congress:** Some Congress leaders, including C.R. Das and Motilal Nehru, were weary of continuous mass movements and sought to engage in legislative politics. **(*1 M*)**

(*v*) **Formation of Swaraj Party:** In response to the withdrawal, C.R. Das and Motilal Nehru formed the Swaraj Party within Congress in 1923 to contest elections and obstruct colonial governance from within the legislative councils. **(*1 M*)**

OR

7B. The Salt March and the Civil Disobedience Movement marked a significant shift from the Non-Cooperation Movement due to:

(*i*) **Symbolic Protest:** The Salt March (12 March 1930) symbolized defiance against British authority by making salt, a basic necessity, from seawater. **(*1 M*)**

(*ii*) **Wider Participation:** This movement included a broader range of social groups like peasants, tribals, women, and workers, enhancing nationalistic fervor. **(*1 M*)**

(*iii*) **Breaking Colonial Laws:** Encouraged active breaking of colonial laws, directly challenging British rule. **(*1 M*)**

(*iv*) **Economic Impact:** Boycotts of foreign goods, picketing liquor shops, and non-payment of taxes aimed to economically weaker British interests. **(*1 M*)**

(*v*) **Repression and Response:** British repression led to arrests and violence, but the movement's persistence showed the growing determination and resilience of Indians against colonial rule. **(*1 M*)**

8. 8.1. The ancient name of Tokyo was Edo. It was originally a small fishing village named Edo and became the seat of the Tokugawa shogunate, effectively becoming the de facto capital of Japan **(*1 M*)**

8.2. Shanghai became the hub of the new print culture, catering to the Western-style schools. There was gradual shift from hand printing to mechanical printing. **(*1 M*)**

8.3. (*a*) The oldest printed book of Japan is the buddhist Diamond Sutra, printed in AD 868. **(*1 M*)**

(*b*) It contains six sheets of text and woodcut illustrations. **(*1 M*)**

9. Marked on map. **(*2 M*)**

SECTION - B

GEOGRAPHY (20 Marks)

10. (*a*) 1-A, 2-B, 3-C, 4-D **(*1 M*)**

1. Bhakra-Nangal Project - (A) Hydel power production and irrigation
2. Hirakud Project - (B) Conservation of water with flood control
3. Sardar Sarovar Dam - (C) Irrigation facilities in drought-prone areas
4. Krishna-Godavari Project - (D) Inter-state water dispute over water diversion

11. (*d*) **Over-harvesting**: Reduces species populations.

Pollution: Poisons and degrades habitats.

Habitat destruction: Causes loss of homes for species. **(*1 M*)**

12. (*a*) Statement-I is correct because **biotic resources** are those that have life, such as plants and animals.

Statement-II is correct because **abiotic resources** are non-living resources, such as minerals, water, and air. **(*1 M*)**

13. (*b*) Stricter regulations ensure sustainable mining practices, reduce environmental damage, and help balance resource extraction with conservation. **(*1 M*)**

14. (*c*) Mining activities often lead to land degradation by removing vegetation, disrupting soil structure, and causing erosion, which negatively impacts the environment and reduces land quality in the region. **(*1 M*)**

15. (*b*) Maize requires a temperature range of 21°C to 27°C for optimal growth, and it grows well in old alluvial soil, which offers adequate nutrients and water retention for the crop. **(*1 M*)**

16. Agriculture and industry are closely linked, as seen through the following examples:

(*i*) **Raw Material Supply:** Agriculture provides raw materials for various industries; for instance, cotton farming supports the textile industry, and sugarcane cultivation is crucial for the sugar industry. **(*1 M*)**

(*ii*) **Plantation and Industry:** Plantation agriculture, like tea and coffee, integrates with industry as these crops are processed in factories before reaching the market, illustrating a direct link between farming and industrial activities, **(*1 M*)**

17A. Significance in Energy Strategy: Non-conventional sources like solar, wind, tidal, and geothermal are vital for sustainable energy development, reducing dependency on finite fossil fuels. **(*1 M*)**

Types of Non-Conventional Energy Sources: *(Any four)*

(*i*) **Solar Energy:** Abundant in India, reduces reliance on traditional fuels, and provides clean energy. *(½ M)*

(*ii*) **Wind Energy:** Effective in coastal regions, provides renewable and clean power. *(½ M)*

(*iii*) **Biogas:** Converts organic waste into energy, improving waste management and providing a renewable source. *(½ M)*

(*iv*) **Geothermal Energy:** Utilizes Earth's internal heat, providing a stable and sustainable energy source. *(½ M)*

(*v*) **Tidal Energy:** Harnesses Ocean tides, offering a predictable and renewable energy source. *(½ M)*

Advantages: They lower greenhouse gas emissions, create jobs, reduce energy costs, and support rural development. *(1 M)*

Significance: Non-conventional sources arc essential for sustainable development, reducing dependency on finite fossil fuels, and ensuring energy security. *(1 M)*

OR

17B. The significance of using non-conventional sources of energy for a country includes:

(*i*) **Renewable Energy:** Non-conventional sources like solar and wind arc abundant and sustainable, reducing dependency on finite fossil fuels. *(1 M)*

(*ii*) **Environmental Benefits:** They emit fewer pollutants,reducing greenhouse gas emissions and combating climate change. *(1 M)*

(*iii*) **Economic Advantages:** Creates jobs in renewable energy sectors and lowers energy costs over time due to technological advancements. *(1 M)*

(*iv*) **Energy Security:** Diversifies energy supply, reducing a country's vulnerability to energy price volatility and supply disruptions. *(1 M)*

(*v*) **Rural Development:** Solar and wind projects can provide power to remote areas, improving living conditions and reducing urban migration. *(1 M)*

18. **18.1** Industries based on agricultural raw materials include cotton, jute, silk, woollen textiles, sugar, and edible oil. *(1 M)*

18.2 The process includes ginning (separating fibers), spinning (making yarn), weaving/knitting (making fabric), and dyeing/designing (adding patterns). *(1 M)*

18.3 The early cotton textile industry thrived in Maharashtra and Gujarat due to the availability of raw cotton, market access, transport facilities, labor, and a moist climate. The first successful textile mill was established in Mumbai in 1854. *(2 M)*

19. Marked on map. *(3 M)*

SECTION - C

POLITICAL SCIENCE (20 Marks)

20. (*b*) The Equal Remuneration Act, 1976 provides that equal wages should be paid to equal work. However in almost all areas of work, from sports and cinema to factories and fields, women are paid less than men, even when both do the same work. *(1 M)*

21. (*d*) The statement (*iii*) is incorrect because community governments in Belgium do not handle economic issues. Statement (*iv*) is incorrect primarily due to the inclusion of the "Spanish-speaking" community, which does not exist as a recognized community in Belgium. The recognized language communities are Dutch, French, and German-speaking, not Spanish. *(1 M)*

22. (*b*) Changes in the fundamental provisions of the constitution require the consent of both levels of government. *(1 M)*

23. (*c*) A-(ii), B-(iv), C-(i), D-(iii) *(1 M)*

24. (i) The statement illustrates that power-sharing can strengthen national unity by acknowledging and respecting the diversity within a country. *(1 M)*

(ii) Involving various groups in governance reduces conflicts and fosters cooperation because no single group can dominate others, and all people feel respected and valued. *(1 M)*

25. In India, women are discriminated against and disadvantaged in the following ways: **(Any two)**

- They are not provided with adequate education. Thus, the literacy rate among women is only 54 percent compared with 76 percent among men. *(1 M)*
- In almost all areas of work, from sports and cinema to factories and fields, women are paid less than men, even when both do exactly the same work. *(1 M)*
- In many parts of India parents prefer to have sons, and due to the preference for the boy child, girl child aborted before she is born in many parts of the country. *(1 M)*
- On average an Indian woman works one hour more than an average man every day. Yet much of her work is not paid and therefore often not valued. *(1 M)*

26. The differences between the federal form of government and unitary form of government are:

(Each point carries *1 M*)

Criteria	Federal Form of government	Unitary Form of government
Power Distribution	Powers are divided between the central government and state/provincial governments.	All powers are centralised in the national government.
Relationship Between Levels	Central and state/provincial governments operate independently.	Sub-national units (if any) are subordinate to the central government.
Constitutional Structure	The Constitution allocates powers to both levels of government.	The Constitution may not provide for power sharing; central authority holds ultimate power.

27A. (*i*) **Foundation and Ideology:** The Bahujan Samaj Party (BSP) was formed in 1984 by Kanshi Ram, aiming to represent the 'Bahujan Samaj' which includes Dalits, adivasis, OBCs, and religious minorities. ***(1 M)***

(*ii*) **Inspirational Figures:** The BSP draws inspiration from social reformers like Sahu Maharaj, Mahatma Phule, Periyar Ramaswami Naicker, and Dr. B.R. Ambedkar. ***(1 M)***

(*iii*) **Political Strategy:** The party focuses on the welfare of Dalits and oppressed people, advocating for their rights and better living conditions through political representation. ***(1 M)***

(*iv*) **Political influence:** In Uttar Pradesh, the BSP has a strong base and has governed multiple times. Besides Uttar Pradesh, BSP has a substantial presence in states like Madhya Pradesh, Chhattisgarh, Uttarakhand, Delhi, and Punjab, demonstrating significant political influence. ***(1 M)***

(*v*) **Performance in Lok Sabha:** In the 2019 Lok Sabha elections, it secured 10 seat, reflecting its sustained appeal among voters. ***(1 M)***

OR

27B. Political Party: A political party is a group of people who come together because they share similar ideas about how a country should be governed. They work together to contest elections and try to win and form the government. ***(1 M)***

Need for Political Parties in India:

(*i*) **Ensure representation:** Political parties ensure that different groups and individuals have a voice in the government. They represent the interests of various sections of society ***(1 M)***

(*ii*) **Present Policies and Leaders:** Political parties give people choices in elections. They present different policies and leaders, offering voters options on who should govern. ***(1 M)***

(*iii*) **Raise Public Concerns:** They bring people's issues to the government. By raising public concerns in legislative bodies, parties ensure that the government considers various perspectives. ***(1 M)***

(*iv*) **Ensure accountable government:** Political parties keep a check on the government's actions and decisions. Through debates and votes, they shape legislation and oversee government actions. ***(1 M)***

Topper's Explanation ***(CBSE, 2017)***

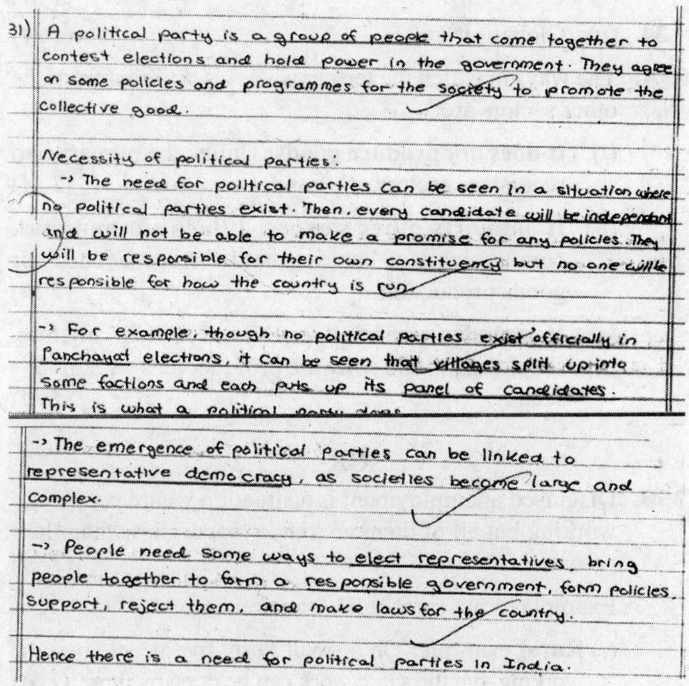

31) A political party is a group of people that come together to contest elections and hold power in the government. They agree on some policies and programmes for the society to promote the collective good.

Necessity of political parties:

-> The need for political parties can be seen in a situation where no political parties exist. Then, every candidate will be independent and will not be able to make a promise for any policies. They will be responsible for their own constituency but no one will be responsible for how the country is run.

-> For example, though no political parties exist officially in Panchayat elections, it can be seen that villages split up into some factions and each puts up its panel of candidates. This is what a political party does.

-> The emergence of political parties can be linked to representative democracy, as societies become large and complex.

-> People need some ways to elect representatives, bring people together to form a responsible government, form policies, support, reject them, and make laws for the country.

Hence there is a need for political parties in India.

28.

28.1 Corruption in democratic governance erodes public trust. When people see leaders misusing power for personal gain, they lose faith in the system, leading to less public participation and weaker democratic processes. ***(1 M)***

28.2 The reality of democracy is different from the expectation because we expect fairness and responsiveness from the democracy, but corruption and neglect of public needs show that these ideals are not always met in practice. ***(1 M)***

28.3 Transparency help fight corruption in a democracy. Laws like the Right to Information Act allow citizens to check government actions. This makes officials more careful and honest, as they know their actions are being watched. **(2 M)**

SECTION - D

ECONOMICS (20 Marks)

29. (*c*) Madhya Pradesh **(1 M)**

30. (*a*) India comes in the category of low middle income countries as its per capita income in 2023 was just about US$ 10030 per annum. **(1 M)**

31. (*d*) To provide loans to its members. **(1 M)**

32. (*a*) The service sector has been growing rapidly in India due to rising incomes, urbanisation, and changing lifestyles. This has led to an increase in demand for services such as healthcare, education, IT, and tourism. **(1 M)**

33. (*d*) Removing barriers or restrictions set by the government is what is known as liberalisation. **(1 M)**

34. (*c*) Globalisation **(1 M)**

35A. The ways in which the tertiary sector is different from the other sectors are:

(*i*) **It does not produce goods:** Unlike the primary and secondary sectors, it provides services. **(1 M)**

(*ii*) **It supports other sectors:** It helps in transport, communication, banking, and storage needed for goods production. **(1 M)**

(*iii*) **It includes essential services:** Teachers, doctors, shopkeepers, and software professionals work in this sector. **(1 M)**

OR

35B. Disguised unemployment is a situation where people are working but all of them are made to work less than their potential. **(1 M)**

Examples from rural and urban areas are:

(*i*) **Rural example:** On a small farm, five people may be working, but the same work can be done by three. **(1 M)**

(*ii*) **Urban example:** In a family-run shop, three members may be helping, though only one is actually needed for the work. **(1 M)**

36A. Globalisation offers several advantages, such as:

(*i*) **Increased Market Access:** Enables producers to sell internationally, boosting sales and profits. **(1 M)**

(*ii*) **Technological Advancement:** Facilitates transfer of advanced technology, enhancing production efficiency and innovation. **(1 M)**

(*iii*) **Employment Opportunities:** Creates numerous jobs as MNCs establish operations in developing countries, boosting local economies and standards of living. **(1 M)**

Topper's Explanation ***(CBSE, 2018)***

10. The advantages of globalisation are

(i) It has allowed the producers to reach beyond their domestic market. They can sell their services and goods in the markets of other countries besides their own country.

(ii) It has increased the choice of products for the consumers especially the well-off section of the society.

(iii) It has improved the quality of product due to increased competition. Also the price of similar goods tend to equilise in different markets.

OR

36B. Foreign trade leads to the integration of markets across countries. The following reasons illustrate how this happens:

(*i*) **Increased Market Access:** Foreign trade allows producers to sell in international markets, expanding their reach beyond domestic boundaries. **(1 M)**

(*ii*) **Price Equalization:** Similar goods' prices in different countries become comparable, promoting competition. **(1 M)**

(*iii*) **Example:** Indian spices sold in European markets create competition with local spices, integrating both markets and providing consumers with diverse choices at competitive prices. **(1 M)**

37. Yes, Rani is being exploited in the unorganised sector. The reasons are:

(*i*) **No job security** – Rani can be asked to leave her job at any time without prior notice. **(1 M)**

(*ii*) **Lack of benefits** – She does not receive paid leave, health benefits, or provident fund like workers in the organised sector. **(1 M)**

(*iii*) **Low and uncertain wages** – Her income is not fixed and depends on daily availability of work, making her financially unstable. **(1 M)**

38A. The Farmer has fallen into a **"Debt trap"**, He is in a situation where he will not be able to **repay the debt** incurred because the Informal sector was the source of credit opted for by the farmer. **(1 M)**

He may face the following Consequences:

(*i*) The farmer may face **endless harassment and physical harm** from the men sent by the money lender. **(1 M)** (*ii*) He will not be able to make regular interest payments or repay the full amount borrowed. This could lead to significant stress and anxiety, as well as potential physical injuries. ***(1 M)***

(*iii*) Borrowing from another **landlord to repay** the original loan may create a cycle of debt for the farmer particularly if the interest rates on the second loan are also high. ***(1 M)***

(*iv*) The farmer may experience **personal consequences**, such as mental stress, anxiety, and depression due to the **constant pressure** of **repayments** and **harassment** from the lenders. ***(1 M)***

Mistakes 101 : What not to do!

Lack of elaboration on the role of credit in development. The answer should provide specific examples and explanations to support the role of credit in various sectors of the economy, such as agriculture, entrepreneurship, and small-scale industries.

OR

38B. "In India, about 80 percent of farmers are small farmers, who need credit for cultivation" The following reasons are:

(*i*) Banks might be unwilling to lend to **small farmers** due to the high **risk** of **non-repayment**. Small farmers often **lack collateral** and have **irregular incomes**, making them more susceptible to **crop failures** and **market fluctuations**. ***(1 M)***

(*ii*) Small farmers can borrow from **local moneylenders, agricultural cooperatives, friends and relatives,** and **microfinance institutions**. They can also access credit through self-help groups **(SHGs)** and **government schemes**. ***(1 M)***

(*iii*) An example of unfavorable credit terms is when a **moneylender** charges high **interest rates** like 5% per month. For instance, borrowing **₹. 10,000** for six months could result in a repayment of **₹. 13,000**, leading to a debt trap. ***(1 M)***

(*iv*) Small farmers can get **cheap credit** by forming self-help groups **(SHGs)**, accessing **government schemes** like **Kisan Credit Card (KCC)**, and borrowing from **cooperative banks** and **microfinance institutions**. ***(1 M)***

(*v*) Government policies can support small farmers by providing **subsidized loans, crop insurance schemes,** and establishing **rural banks** and **cooperative societies** for easier access to **affordable credit**.***(1M)***

Nailing the Right Answer

- Address the high risk of non-repayment as a key reason for banks unwilingness to lend to small farmers.
- Highlight diverse sources of credit for small farmers, including local moneylenders, cooperatives and government schemes.

Map for Q. no. 9 (Section A) & Q. no. 19 (Section B)

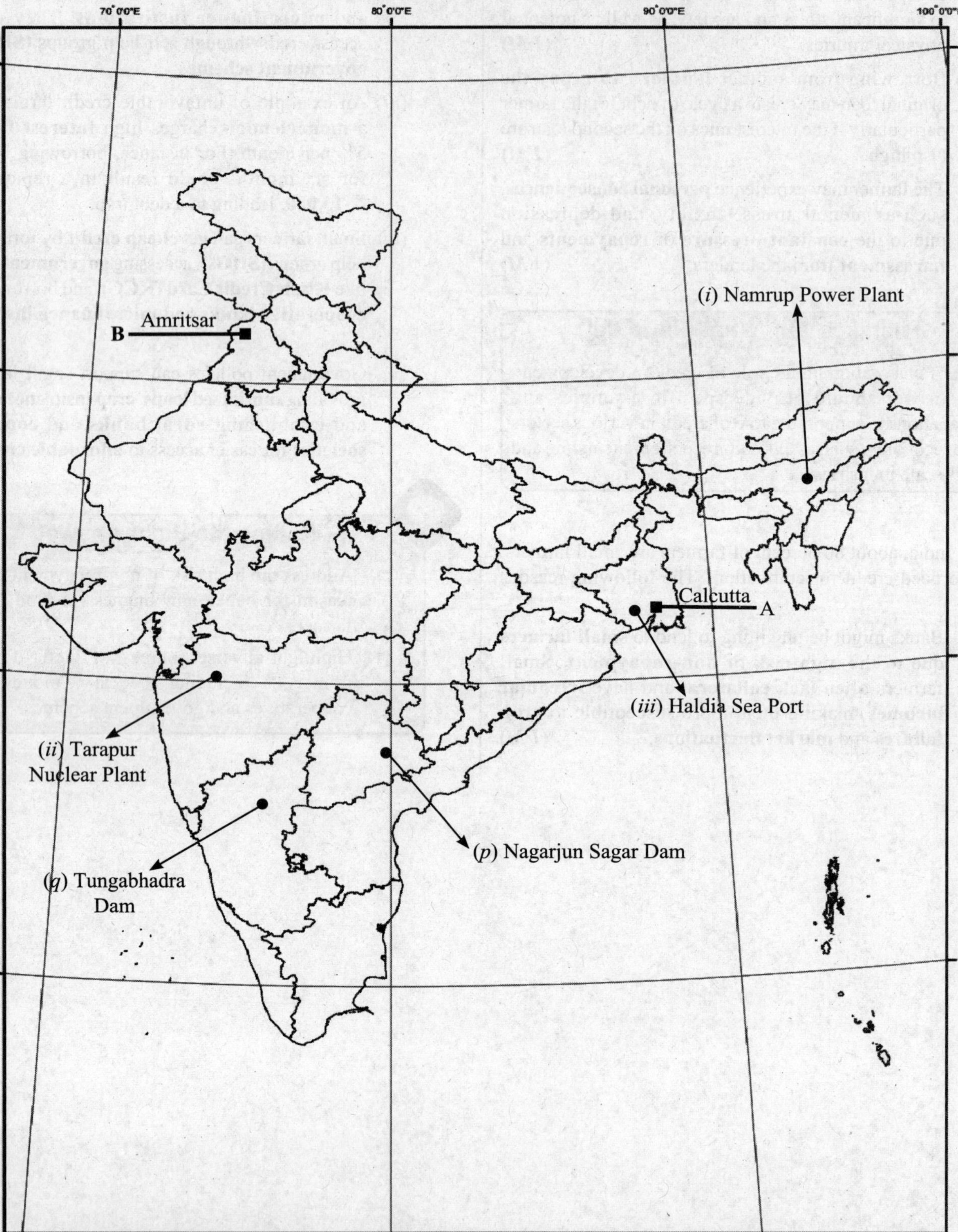

Published by Survey of India
Scale 1:16M

Handwritten Explanations

Sample Question
Paper - 12

SCAN ME!

"The future depends on what we do in the present."
– Mahatma Gandhi

CBSE SAMPLE QUESTION PAPER

(Issued by CBSE on 30th July, 2025)

Class-X Session: 2025-26

SOCIAL SCIENCE (087)

Time allowed : 3 hours | Maximum Marks : 80

General Instructions:

Read the following instructions carefully and follow them:

(i) There are 38 questions in the Question paper. All questions are compulsory.

(ii) The question paper has Four Sections – A-History, B-Geography C- Political Science, and D- Economics.

(iii) Each Section is of 20 Marks and has MCQs, VSA, SA, LAs and CBQ.

(iv) Very Short Answer Type Questions (VSA), carry 2 Marks each. Answers to each question should not exceed 40 words.

(v) Short Answer Type Questions (SA), carry 3 Marks each. Answers to each question should not exceed 60 words.

(vi) Long answer type questions (LA), carry 5 Marks each. Answers to each question should not exceed 120 words.

(vii) There are case based questions (CBQ) with three sub questions and are of 4 Marks each. Answers to each question should not exceed 100 words.

(viii) The map-based questions, carry 5 Marks with two parts- Q10. In Section A-History (2 Marks) and Q18. In Section B -Geography (3 Marks)

(ix) There is no overall choice in the question paper. However, an internal choice has been provided in few questions. Only one of the choices in such questions must be attempted.

SECTION - A

HISTORY (20 Marks)

1. Match the following and Choose the correct option: 1

Column - I		Column - II	
A	Frederic Sorrieu	1	Torch of enlightenments
B.	Statue of Liberty	2	Shattered remains of absolutist Institutions
C.	Foreground in front of the Statue of Liberty	3	Democratic and Social Republics
D	Sorrieu's utopian vision.	4	French Artist

(*a*) A-4, B-1, C-2, D-3 (*b*) A-2, B-4, C-4, D-1 (*c*) A-1, B-2, C-4, D-3 (*d*) A-4, B-1, C-3, D-4

Ans. (*a*) A-4, B-1, C-2, D-3

2. Identify and name the leader shown in the picture given below: - **1**

Source-India and the Contemporary World-II, NCERT

(*a*) Lala Lajpat Rai (*b*) Bal Gangadhar Tilak
(*c*) Gopal Krishan Gokhale (*d*) Raja Rammohan Roy

Ans. (*b*) Bal Gangadhar Tilak

3. Thousands of people fled Europe for America in the 19th century due to - **1**

(*a*) Widespread poverty and deadly diseases (*b*) Frequent famines and poor living conditions
(*c*) Continuous wars and political instability. (*d*) Harsh climate and repeated natural disasters.

Ans. (*a*) Widespread poverty and deadly diseases

4. Louise-Sebastien Mercier proclaimed "Tremble, therefore, tyrants of the world! Tremble before the virtual writer!" Who are referred to as the tyrants in this context?: **1**

(*a*) Educated classes who wanted to change the society (*b*) Absolutist institutions like monarchy and church
(*c*) Authors of the new books (*d*) Printing press

Ans. (*b*) Absolutist institutions like monarchy and church

5A. "The Silk route was a good example of vibrant pre-modern trade and cultural links between distant parts of the world." Explain the statement with any two examples. **2**

Ans. (*i*) Chinese pottery, textiles and spices from India and Southeast Asia also travelled the same route. In return, precious metals - gold and silver - flowed from Europe to Asia.

(*ii*) Trade and cultural exchange went hand in hand. Buddhism from India spread in several directions through intersecting points on the silk routes.

(*iii*) Early Christian missionaries travelled this route to reach Asia and Muslim preachers took the same route a few centuries later. *(Any 2 points)*

OR

5B. 'Sometimes the new crops could make the difference between life and death.'. Explain the statement. **2**

Ans. (*i*) Sometimes new crops like potatoes could make the difference between life and death. It was with the introduction of the humble potato that Europe's poor began to eat well, eat better and live longer.

(*ii*) Ireland's poor peasants became so dependent on potatoes that when the potato crop was destroyed by disease in the mid-1840s, hundreds of thousands of peasants died of starvation

6A. 'A variety of cultural processes played an important role in developing a sense of nationalism in India'. Support the statement with suitable examples. **3**

Ans. (*i*) **Figure or Image** – The identity of India came to be visually associated with the image of Bharat Mata. This image was created by Bankim Chandra Chattopadhyay. Rabindranath Tagore painted his famous image of Bharat Mata. In this painting, Bharat Mata is portrayed as an ascetic figure; she is calm, composed, divine and spiritual.

(*ii*) **Songs** – Bankim Chandra Chattopadhyay wrote 'VandeMataram' as a hymn to the motherland. It was included in his novel Anandmath and widely sung during the Swadeshi Movement in Bengal.

(*iii*) **Folklore** – Indian folklore was revived. In late-nineteenth-century India, nationalists began recording folk tales sung by bards and they toured villages to gather folk songs and legends. These tales gave a true picture of traditional culture. It helped to restore a sense of pride in our past. In Bengal, Rabindranath Tagore himself began collecting ballads, nursery rhymes and myths, and led the movement for folk revival. In Madras, Natesa Sastri published a massive four-volume collection of Tamil folk tales, The Folklore of Southern India.

(*iv*) **Flag**

(*a*) During the Swadeshi movement in Bengal, a tricolour flag (red, green and yellow) was designed. It had eight lotuses representing eight provinces of British India, and a crescent moon, representing Hindus and Muslims.

(*b*) By 1921, Gandhiji had designed the Swaraj flag. It was again a tricolour (red, green and white) and had a spinning wheel in the centre, representing the Gandhian ideal of self-help. Carrying the flag, holding it aloft, during marches became a symbol of defiance.

(*v*) **Re – interpretation of History** – Indians began looking into the past to discover India's great achievements. They wrote about art and architecture, Science and Maths, religion and culture, law, philosophy etc. Indians were asked to take pride in India's great achievements in the past and struggle to change the miserable conditions of life under British rule.

*(Any **three** points to be considered)*

OR

6B. Salt March 'became an effective tool of resistance against colonialism.' Justify the statement with suitable arguments. **3**

Ans. (*i*) Salt became an effective tool of resistance against colonialism because of the following reasons: Gandhiji found in salt a powerful bond that would unite the nations as it – was consumed by all rich and poor alike.

(*ii*) Gandhiji's letter to Viceroy Irwin stated eleven demands. Most of them were of general interest but the most stirring was to abolish the salt tax imposed by the colonial government.

(*iii*) Irwin's unwillingness to negotiate forced Gandhiji to start his salt March which was joined by thousands. It developed the feeling of nationalism.

(*iv*) People in different parts of the country broke salt law and manufactured salt and demonstrated in front of government salt factories.

(*v*) People unitedly followed Gandhiji's words. They refused to pay taxes, revenues, picketed liquor shops, boycotted foreign clothes, resigned from government jobs and violated forest laws. *(Any **three** points to be considered)*

7A. 'In Britain the formation of the nation-state was not the result of a sudden upheaval or revolution but was the result of a long-drawn-out process.' Analyze this statement with suitable reasons. **5**

Ans. (*i*) In Britain the formation of the nation-state was not the result of a sudden upheaval or revolution. The primary identities of the people who inhabited the British Isles were ethnic ones - such as English, Welsh, Scot or Irish.

(*ii*) The Act of Union (1707) between England and Scotland resulted in the formation of the 'United Kingdom of Great Britain' meant that England was able to impose its influence on Scotland. Scotland's distinctive culture and political institutions were systematically suppressed.

(*iii*) The Scottish Highlanders were forbidden to speak their Gaelic language or wear their national dress and large numbers were forcibly driven out of their homeland.

(*iv*) The English helped the Protestants of Ireland to establish their dominance over a largely Catholic country. Catholic revolts against British dominance were suppressed. Ireland was forcibly incorporated into the United Kingdom in 1801.

(*v*) The symbols of the new Britain - the British flag, the national anthem, the English language were actively promoted and the older nations survived only as subordinate partners in this union.

OR

7B. 'The Treaty of Vienna was drawn up in 1815 with the object of undoing most of the changes that had come about in Europe during the Napoleonic wars.' Highlight the significant provisions of this treaty. **5**

Ans. (*i*) The Bourbon dynasty, which had been deposed during the French Revolution, was restored to power, and France lost the territories it had annexed under Napoleon.

(*ii*) A series of states were set up on the boundaries of France to prevent French expansion in future. Thus the kingdom of the Netherlands, which included Belgium, was set up in the north and Genoa was added to Piedmont in the south.

(*iii*) Prussia was given important new territories on its western frontiers, while Austria was given control of northern Italy.

(*iv*) The German confederation of 39 states that had been set up by Napoleon was left untouched. In the east, Russia was given part of Poland while Prussia was given a portion of Saxony.

(*v*) The main intention was to restore the monarchies that had been overthrown by Napoleon, and create a new conservative order in Europe.

8. Read the given text and answer the following questions: (1 + 1 + 2 = 4) **4**

Why Newspapers?

Krishnaji Trimbuck Ranade inhabitant of Poona intends to publish a Newspaper in the Marathi Language with a view of affording useful information on every topic of local interest. It will be open for free discussion on subjects of general utility, scientific investigation and the speculations connected with the antiquities, statistics, curiosities, history and geography of the country and of the Deccan especially... the patronage and support of all interested in the diffusion of knowledge and Welfare of the People is earnestly solicited. *Bombay Telegraph and Courier, 6 January 1849*

"The task of the native newspapers and political associations is identical to the role of the Opposition in the House of Commons in Parliament in England. That is to critically examine government policy to suggest improvements, by removing those parts that will not be to the benefit of the people, and also by ensuring speedy implementation.

These associations ought to carefully study the particular issues, gather diverse relevant information on the nation as well as on what are the possible and desirable improvements, and this will surely earn it considerable influence".

Source: Native Opinion, 3 April 1870

8.1 Explain the main reason for publishing newspapers by Krishna ji.

8.2 How was the task of native newspaper and political association seen identical to the role of the opposition?

8.3 Analyze the reasons for the popularity of newspapers during the 19th century.

Ans. 8.1 Krishnaji wanted to publish significant information about societal developments in the areas of politics, science, and other fields in order to inform the public.

8.2 The media used to criticise and analyse government policies were local newspapers and political organisations. As a result, both of these served as the government's opposition.

8.3 Reasons for popularity of newspapers during 19th century are:

(*i*) The political developments in the country began to interest a sizable portion of society, and this information was skillfully presented in the newspapers.

(*ii*) Newspapers started to serve as a source for societal advancements in social, cultural, and scientific

MAP SKILL-BASED QUESTION (2 Marks)

9. Two places A and B have been marked on the given outline map of India. Identify them and write their correct names on the lines marked on the map. **(1 + 1 = 2)**

(*a*) The place where the Civil Disobedience Movement was launched.

(*b*) The city where Indian National Congress session was held in September 1920.

Ans. Marked on the map.

SECTION - B

GEOGRAPHY (20 Marks)

10. What is essential for resource development to contribute to overall development? **1**

(*a*) The availability of resources alone is enough.

(*b*) The presence of foreign invaders and their governance.

(*c*) Technological development and institutional changes.

(*d*) Only human resources can contribute to development.

Ans. (*c*) Technological development and institutional changes.

11. Identify the appropriate option to fill in the empty boxes: **1**

Classification of Soils

Alluvial	?	?
Ideal for the growth of sugarcane, paddy, wheat and other cereal and pulse crops.	Ideal for growing cotton	suitable for crops like cashew nut.

(*a*) Black soil, Red and Yellow soils

(*b*) Laterite soil, Black soil.

(*c*) Red & Yellow soils & Black soil.

(*d*) Black soil & Laterite soil

Ans. (*d*) Black soil & Laterite soil.

12. A total of 628 tigers died in India during the past five years due to natural causes and other reasons, including poaching, according to government data. Meanwhile, 349 people were killed in tiger attacks during this period, with Maharashtra alone recording 200 deaths.

[source: https://www.ptinews.com/story/national/628-tigers-died-in-india-in-past-five-years-govt-data/1685133t/]

Which of the following is the most significant indirect consequence of poaching on the tiger population? **1**

(*a*) Reduction in the prey species, dwindling tiger's food supply.

(*b*) Increase in human-wildlife conflicts in protected areas

(*c*) Rise in the tiger population.

(*d*) Decrease in tourism revenue in national parks.

Ans. (*a*) Reduction in the prey species leading to the tiger's dwindling food supply

13. Based on the classification of forests, which of the following statements would most likely apply to states like Jammu and Kashmir, Andhra Pradesh, and Kerala? **1**

(*a*) These states mostly have forests managed as reserved or protected forests for conservation.

(*b*) They rely on unclassed forests and local community management for forest conservation

(*c*) They have forest resources and primarily focus on industrial development.

(*d*) There are no classified forests and forest management is entirely left to private ownership.

Ans. (*a*) These states have a significant portion of forests managed as reserved or protected forests for conservation.

14. Which one of the following states has made roof top water harvesting compulsory in India? **1**

(*a*) Haryana

(*b*) Punjab.

(*c*) Assam

(*d*) Tamil Nadu

Ans. (*d*) Tamil Nadu

15. Which of the following statements best evaluates the overall goal of the *Pradhan Mantri Krishi Sinchaee Yojana?*. **1**

(*a*) Addressing the negative ecological effects of large dams by reducing water usage.

(*b*) To provide better irrigation systems and sustainable water conservation practices for farmers.

(*c*) Shifting farmers from traditional crops to more commercial, water-intensive crops.

(*d*) Preserve the natural river flow and prevent the fragmentation of aquatic ecosystems.

Ans. (*b*) To provide better irrigation systems and sustainable water conservation practices for farmers.

16. Rice is grown as a commercial crop in Haryana and Punjab, but as a subsistence crop in Odisha. Using your understanding of geographical factors and economic practices, explain why rice cultivation differs in these regions. **2**

Ans. Climate and Irrigation:

- Haryana and Punjab have a well-developed irrigation system (e.g., canal irrigation from the Sutlej-Yamuna Link Canal), which allows for large-scale commercial cultivation of rice. The climate is suitable for high-yielding varieties, and irrigation ensures water availability.
- In contrast, Odisha has a more monsoonal climate, and while rice is grown, the farming is often rainfed and primarily for local consumption. The lack of large-scale irrigation systems limits its commercialization.

Economic Factors (Market Access):

- In Punjab and Haryana, rice is grown for commercial purposes to meet national and international demand. The proximity to markets, government procurement systems, and well-developed transport networks enable these states to export surplus rice.
- In Odisha, rice is mostly grown for personal or local use, with less access to large markets for profit-driven farming, making it a subsistence crop.

Farming Practices:

- In Punjab and Haryana, the use of modern farming techniques, machinery, and high-yielding varieties supports commercial rice cultivation.
- In Odisha, rice farming is more traditional and focused on family sustenance rather than large-scale production, which reflects the subsistence nature of cultivation.

Or any other relevant point(s) (**Any 2** point to be considered out of which at least one should be related to climate and one economic).

17A. Person P is willing to establish a mineral based industry. He has been advised to set up a bauxite industry in Odisha as a suitable way to make a profitable venture.Analyse the possible reasons behind the advice given to her. **5**

Ans. (*i*) Odisha was the largest bauxite producing state in India in 2016-17. Panchpatmali deposits in Koraput district are the most important bauxite deposits in the state.

(*ii*) Aluminium is an important metal because it combines the strength of metals such as iron,

(*iii*) It is a good alternative to other metals due to its extreme lightness and

(*iv*) also has good conductivity and

(*v*) great malleability *(any other relevant point - 5 points)*

OR

17B. 'Coal is the most important and abundant fossil fuel in India.' Justify the statement by evaluating the significant role it plays in the growth of the Indian economy in its different forms. **5**

Ans. Significance:

(*i*) It is used for power generation,

(*ii*) To supply energy to industry as well as for domestic needs.

(*iii*) India is highly dependent on coal for meeting its commercial energy requirements.e.g., in metallurgy

any other relevant point (at least 2)

Variety of coal types-

Coal, is found in a variety of forms depending on the degrees of compression and the depth and time of burial.

(*i*) **Peat** - Decaying plants in swamps produce peat. Which has a low carbon and high moisture contents and low heating capacity.

(*ii*) **Lignite** - is a low grade brown coal, which is soft with high moisture content. The principal lignite reserves are in Neyveli in Tamil Nadu and are used for generation of electricity.

(*iii*) **Bituminous coal**- Coal that has been buried deep and subjected to increased temperatures. It is the most popular coal in commercial use. Metallurgical coal is high grade bituminous coal which has a special value for smelting iron in blast furnaces.

(*iv*) **Anthracite** - is the highest quality hard coal.

18. Read the given text and answer the following questions: (1 + 2 + 1 = 4) **4**

Global pollution is rising due to rapid economic growth, population increases, and insufficient environmental management. This poses serious health risks for people and ecosystems, particularly in low- and middle-income countries. Contributing to these challenges, the global economy relies on deeply intertwined supply chains, sustained by more than 100 billion tons of raw materials entering the system each year. Intensive material consumption depletes natural resources and causes negative environmental impacts at every stage of the product lifecycle. Global waste is expected to increase to 3.4 billion tons by 2050. Pollution of all types hinders development outcomes. Exposure to air pollution, water pollution, and hazardous chemicals and wastes like mercury, lead and persistent organic pollutants (POPs) causes debilitating and fatal illnesses, creates harmful living conditions, and destroys ecosystems. Pollution undermines sustainable economic growth, exacerbates poverty and inequality in both urban and rural areas, and significantly contributes to climate change. Poor people, who cannot afford to protect themselves from the negative impacts of pollution, end up suffering the most.

Pollution is the largest environmental cause of disease and premature death. It is estimated to be several times more deaths than from AIDS, tuberculosis, and malaria combined. Global health crises, such as the COVID-19 pandemic, are reminders of the strong linkages between environment and health and of the need to address such linkages systematically.

Source: https://www.worldbank.org/en/topic/pollution]

18.1 Why do you think is global waste expected to increase by 2050?

18.2 How do manufacturing industries cause pollution of different types? Explain with examples.

18.3 Is it correct to consider pollution as a possible cause for worsening of the current global trends of poverty and inequality? Justify.

Ans. 18.1 Due to intensive material production and consumption.

18.2 Manufacturing industries are a major cause for-

(*i*) Air pollution – Smoke is emitted by chemical and paper factories, brick kilns, refineries and smelting plants, and burning of fossil fuels in big and small factories that ignore pollution norms. Toxic gas leaks can be very hazardous with long-term effects.

(*ii*) Water pollution is caused by organic and inorganic industrial wastes and affluents discharged into rivers. The main culprits in this regard are paper, pulp, chemical, textile and dyeing, petroleum refineries, tanneries and electroplating industries that let out dyes, detergents, acids, salts and heavy metals like lead and mercury pesticides, fertilisers, synthetic chemicals with carbon, plastics and rubber, etc. into the water bodies.

(*iii*) Thermal pollution of water occurs when hot water from factories and thermal plants is drained into rivers and ponds before cooling.

(*iv*) Dumping of wastes specially glass, harmful chemicals, industrial effluents, packaging, salts and garbage renders the soil useless.

(*v*) Rain water percolates to the soil carrying the pollutants to the ground and the ground water also gets contaminated.

(*vi*) Industrial and construction activities, machinery, factory equipment, generators, saws and pneumatic and electric drills also make a lot of noise. *(Or any other relevant point) – Any **two** points*

18.3 Poor people, cannot afford to protect themselves from the negative impacts of pollution, end up suffering the most. This also leads to social disparity/inequality due to the ill effects of poverty. (Can be explained with the help of an example)

MAP SKILL-BASED QUESTION (3 Marks)

19. On the same outline map of India locate and lable the following with suitable symbols: **1**

I. (*p*) The dam in the Sutlej-Beas river basin, which is being used both for hydel power production and irrigation

OR

(*q*) The dam in the Mahanadi basin that integrates conservation of water with flood control.

II. Any two of the following: **(1 × 2 = 2)**

(*i*) A major sea port in West Bengal

(*ii*) An international airport in Tamil Nadu

(*iii*) An international airport in Punjab

Ans. Marked on the map

SECTION - C

POLITICAL SCIENCE (20 Marks)

20. **Which of the following statement(s) are true with respect to the ethnic composition of Belgium?.** **1**

I. 59 percent of the total population of Belgium lives in the Wallonia region and speaks French.

II. 40 percent live in the Flemish region and speak Dutch.

III. One percent of the Belgians speak German.

IV. In the capital city Brussels, 80 percent people speak French while 20 per cent are Dutch speaking.

Choose the correct option:

(*a*) I and II (*b*) III and IV (*c*) I, II and III (*d*) I and IV

Ans. (*b*) III and IV

21. **The cartoon below depicts Germany's government that was formed after the 2005 elections. It included the two major parties of the country, namely the Christian Democratic Union and the Social Democratic Party. The two parties are historically rivals to each other. Which of the following options best explains the cartoon?** **1**

Source-Democratic Politics, NCERT

(*a*) Coalition Government. (*b*) Two Party System (*c*) Democratic government. (*d*) Bi-party system.

Ans. (*a*) Coalition Government.

22. **Consider the following case and choose the correct option-** **1**

Suppose the Government of India plans to issue new currency notes of different denominations in order to curb the influence of black money. The Government of one state is opposed to this policy of the Central Government. Can the state government stop the union government from implementing this policy?

(*a*) Yes, because Currency is the subject of State List

(*b*) No, because Currency is a subject of Union List

(*c*) Yes, because the approval of both the governments is necessary to implement this change.

(*d*) No, because any such change must be approved by the local government also.

Ans. (*b*) No, because Currency is a subject of Union List

23. **Two statements are given as Assertion (A) and Reason(R). Study the statements carefully and identify the correct alternative** **1**

ASSERTION (A): Exclusive attention to caste can produce negative results in democracy.

REASON (R): It can divert attention from other important issues thus leading to tensions, conflicts and even violence.

Choose the correct option:

(*a*) Both A and R are true, and R is the correct explanation of A.

(*b*) Both A and R are true, but R is not the correct explanation of A

(*c*) A is true but R is false.

(*d*) A is false but R is true

Ans. (*a*) Both A and R are true, and R is the correct explanation of A.

24. **Highlight any two key features of federalism.** **2**

Ans. **Features of federalism:**

(*i*) There are two or more levels (or tiers) of government.

(*ii*) Different tiers of government govern the same citizens, but each tier has its own jurisdiction in specific matters of legislation, taxation and administration.

(*iii*) The jurisdictions of the respective levels or tiers of government are specified in the constitution. So the existence and authority of each tier of government is constitutionally guaranteed.

(*iv*) The fundamental provisions of the constitution cannot be unilaterally changed by one level of government. Such changes require the consent of both the levels of government.

(*v*) Courts have the power to interpret the constitution and the powers of different levels of government. The highest court acts as an umpire if disputes arise between different levels of government in the exercise of their respective powers.

(*vi*) Sources of revenue for each level of government are clearly specified to ensure its financial autonomy.

(*vii*) The federal system thus has dual objectives: to safeguard and promote unity of the country, while at the same time accommodate regional diversity. Therefore, two aspects are crucial for the institutions and practice of federalism. Governments at different levels should agree to some rules of power sharing. They should also trust that each would abide by its part of the agreement. An ideal federal system has both aspects: mutual trust and agreement to live together.

*(Any **two** point to be considered)*

25. 'Women in India face discrimination, disadvantages and oppression in many ways.' Highlight any two aspects of life where you witness this inequality. **2**

Ans. (*i*) **Education** – Literacy rate among women is only 54% as compared with 76% among men. Parents prefer to spend their resources for their sons' education rather than daughters.

(*ii*) **Low Proportion of women in highly paid and valued jobs** – Women still have a small share in the highly paid jobs. Even if a woman works for more hours than a man, her work is not given importance. This results in low paid and low valued jobs for women.

(*iii*) **Women are paid less than men** – Despite the Equal Wages of Act women are paid less than men, even when both do exactly the same work.

(*iv*) **Preference for Son** – In many parts of India parents prefer to have sons and find ways to have the girl child aborted before she is born. This has led to decline in child sex – ratio (927)

(*v*) **Exploitation at workplace and domestic violence** – Women are exploited and harassed at the workplace. They have to face different forms of domestic violence at home. *(Any 2 point to be considered)*

26. 'Democracy leads to peaceful and harmonious life among citizens in every sphere.' Support this statement with suitable arguments. **3**

Ans. (*i*) Democracies accommodate various social divisions. For example, Belgium has peacefully solved her ethnic problems and solved the differences.

(*ii*) All democracies usually develop a procedure to conduct competition, i.e. conduct elections, power-sharing, etc. This reduces the possibility of tensions, due to social divisions, turning violent or explosive.

(*iii*) Democracy teaches people to respect the differences and resolve conflicts among different groups peacefully. In non-democratic countries, rulers either turn a blind eye to or suppress internal differences. For example, Sri Lanka. The plus point in democratic regime is the ability to handle social differences, divisions and conflicts.

(*iv*) A democracy is not just a rule by majority opinion. The majority always needs to work with the minority so that the government represents the general view.

(*v*) A democratic government ensures that the rule by the majority does not become autocratic in terms of religion, race or linguistic group etc. It tries to show that in every election, different persons and groups can form a majority. It tries to see that every citizen has a chance to be in majority at some point of time and is not barred on the basis of birth. All these things ensured by a democratic regime lead to a peaceful and harmonious life. *(Any **three** points to be considered)*

27A. 'Political parties play a significant role in the effective working of a democracy.' Explain.. **5**

OR

27B. 'The challenge of dynastic succession is undoubtedly a major challenge for political parties in India.' Analyse the statement'. **5**

Ans. (A) Political parties play a significant role in the effective working of a democracy. To fill political offices and exercise political power, political parties are needed to perform a series of functions, which are the following

(*i*) Parties contest elections. Elections are fought mainly among candidates put up by political parties.In India, top party leaders choose candidates for contesting elections.

(*ii*) Parties put forward different policies and programmes. Political parties in a democracy group together similar opinions, to provide a direction in which government policies can be formulated.

(*iii*) Parties make laws for a country. Laws are debated and passed in the legislature.

(*iv*) Parties that lose elections play the role of the opposition. Opposition parties voice their views by criticizing the government for its failure or wrong policies.

(*v*) Parties shape public opinion. They raise and highlight issues and resolve people's problems. Many pressure groups are the extensions of political parties.

(*vi*) Parties provide people access to government machinery and welfare schemes. For an ordinary citizen it is easier to approach a local party leader than a government officer. *(Any 5 points)*

OR

Ans. (*b*)

(*i*) Most political parties do not practice open and transparent procedures for their functioning. So there are very few ways for an ordinary worker to rise to the top in a party.

(*ii*) Those who happen to be the leaders are in a position of unfair advantage as they favour people close to them or even their family members.

(*iii*) In many parties in India, we see a trend of dynastic succession. The top positions are always controlled by members of a particular family, which is unfair to other members of the party, and bad for democracy.

(*iv*) This is so because people who do not have adequate experience or popular support come to occupy positions of power.

(*v*) More than loyalty to party principles and policies, personal loyalty to the leader becomes more important. This tendency is seen all over the world, even in older democracies.

28. Read the given text and answer the following questions: (1 + 1 + 2 = 4) **4**

Sri Lanka emerged as an independent country in 1948. The leaders of the Sinhala community sought to secure dominance over government by virtue of their majority.

As a result, the democratically elected government adopted a series of MAJORITARIAN measures to establish Sinhala supremacy. Over the years, it created feelings of alienation among the Sri Lankan Tamils. They felt that none of the major political parties led by the Buddhist Sinhala leaders was sensitive to their language and culture. As a result, the relations between the Sinhala and Tamil communities strained over time. On the other hand, the Belgian leaders took a different path. They recognised the existence of regional differences and cultural diversities. Between 1970 and 1993, they amended their constitution four times to work out an arrangement that would enable everyone to live together within the same country.

Source-Adapted from Power Sharing,NCERT

28.1 State any two demands of Tamils in Sri Lanka.

28.2 State the results of the Majoritarian Government in Sri Lanka.

28.3 Explain any two provisions of the Belgian model of power sharing.

Ans. 28.1(*a*) To recognise Tamil as official language

(*b*) Regional autonomy

(*c*) Equality of opportunities in securing education and jobs. *(Any **one** to be considered)*

28.2 The Majoritarian Government in Sri Lanka created a distrust between Tamils and Sinhala communities which resulted in civil war. As a result, thousands of people of both communities were killed and many families were forced to leave the country as refugees.

28.3

(*i*) The Constitution prescribed that the number of Dutch and French Any two speaking ministers shall be equal in the central government. Some special laws require the support of majority of members from each linguistic group. Thus, no single community can make decisions unilaterally.

(*ii*) Many powers of the central government have been given to state governments of the two regions of the country. The state governments are not subordinate to the Central Government.

(*iii*) Brussels has a separate government in which Dutch and French have equal representation.

(*iv*) Apart from the Central and the State Government, there is a third kind of Government. This 'community government' is elected by people belonging to one language community - Dutch, French and German - speaking - no matter where they live. This government has the power regarding cultural, educational and language - related issues.

*(Any **two** to be considered)*

SECTION - D

ECONOMICS (20 Marks)

29. Underemployment is caused when - **1**

(*a*) More workers are employed than actually required

(*b*) Fewer workers are employed than actually required

(*c*) Workers are paid more than their actual output

(*d*) Jobs are given only to highly educated workers

Ans. (*a*) More workers are employed than actually required

30. What can be inferred about the limitations of using per capita income (average income) to compare well-being across countries? Choose the correct option as the answer. **1**

(*a*) It shows how equally or unequally income is distributed among the people in a country

(*b*) The only measure needed to understand a country's development is Per capita income

(*c*) It gives a basic idea of economic well-being but hides the income inequality.

(*d*) It only reflects the industrial growth of a country and does not consider other important factors.

Ans. (*c*) It gives a basic idea of economic well-being but hides the income inequality, cost of living, or access to essential services.

31. Which of the following examples best demonstrates how the tertiary sector supports both the primary and secondary sectors?

(*a*) Farmers grow vegetables and sell them directly to consumers, with no transportation or storage involved.

(*b*) A factory makes shoes and uses raw materials like leather to create the product, relying on transport and retail stores to distribute the shoes.

(*c*) A bakery bakes bread and uses delivery services to send the bread to local shops for sale, without any direct involvement of raw materials.

(*d*) A company produces furniture from wood, but does not require any transport or retail services to sell the product.

Ans. (*b*) A factory makes shoes and uses raw materials like leather to create the product, relying on transport and retail stores to distribute the shoes.

32. Which one of the following issues currency notes in India? **1**

(*a*) Finance Ministry.

(*b*) Reserve Bank of India.

(*c*) State Bank of India.

(*d*) Central Bank of India.

Ans. (*b*) Reserve Bank of India

33. Person Z tries to explain how the requirement of a double coincidence of wants in a barter system limits trade and exchange. Which of the following justification do you think will be used by him/her? **1**

(*a*) It makes trade more complicated, as each person must have what the other person wants, limiting the pool of potential trade partners.

(*b*) The barter system allows trade to be conducted more efficiently since both parties already know what they need from the transaction.

(*c*) It increases the number of exchanges because each person can trade for exactly what they want..

(*d*) The system creates value for goods by ensuring that both parties have a direct need for each other's goods.

Ans. (*a*) It makes trade more complicated, as each person must have what the other person wants, limiting the pool of potential trade partners.

34. Recognize and choose the option that correctly matches the effects and consequent outcomes of globalization. **1**

	Column-A (Effects of globalisation)		Column-B (Outcomes)
1.	Increased foreign investment	i.	Expansion of global markets and access to technology
2.	Cultural exchange and awareness	ii.	Loss of traditional jobs due to automation and cheaper labor elsewhere
3.	Techonological exchange and awareness	iii.	Spread of cultural practices, ideas, and values across borders
4.	Growth of multinational corporations	iv.	Large companies becoming dominant players in global markets

Choose the correct option:

(*a*) 1-iii, 2-ii, 3-i, 4-iv (*b*) 1-iv, 2-ii, 3-i, 4-iii (*c*) 1-ii, 2-iv, 3-iii, 4-i. (*d*) 1-i, 2-iii, 3-ii, 4-iv

Ans. (*d*) 1-i, 2-iii, 3-ii, 4-iv

35. Evaluate the utility of public services in contributing to the overall well-being of individuals and society. **3**

Ans. **Healthcare and Public Health:**

- Accessible and quality public healthcare, is fundamental for maintaining, a productive and healthy population. It reduces mortality rates, ensures the well-being of the workforce, and allows individuals to contribute meaningfully to the economy. Inadequate healthcare can result in a higher burden of disease, lower life expectancy, and economic inefficiencies.

Education and Skill Development:

- Public education systems are essential for providing equal learning opportunities to all citizens, regardless of socioeconomic status. A well-educated population leads to increased literacy rates, skill development, and innovation, all of which are crucial for economic growth, reducing inequality, and fostering social cohesion.

Sanitation and Clean Water:

- Proper sanitation and access to clean water are vital for maintaining public health and preventing diseases such as cholera and dysentery. These services significantly improve life expectancy, reduce healthcare costs, and increase productivity, especially in rural or underserved areas.

Infrastructure Development:

- Public infrastructure, including roads, transportation, and energy, supports the functioning of markets, businesses, and industries. It enhances connectivity, stimulates economic activities, and improves the quality of life for individuals by providing easy access to essential goods and services. *Or any other relevant point(s) - Any* ***two***

36. 'Expanding access to loans in the formal sector is important, yet it is equally critical that these loans are accessible to all people for national development.' Justify the statement. **3**

Ans. (*i*) Higher cost of borrowing from informal sources means a larger part of the earnings of the borrowers is used to repay the loan. Hence, borrowers have less income left for themselves (as we saw for Shyamal in Sonpur).

(*ii*) In certain cases, the high interest rate for borrowing can mean that the amount to be repaid is greater than the income of the borrower.

(*iii*) This could lead to increasing debt (as we saw for Rama in Sonpur) and debt trap.

(*iv*) Also, people who might wish to start an enterprise by borrowing may not do so because of the high cost of borrowing.

(*v*) For these reasons, banks and cooperative societies need to lend more. This would lead to higher incomes and many people could then borrow cheaply for a variety of needs.

(*vi*) They could grow crops, do business, set up small-scale industries etc. They could set up new industries or trade in goods. Cheap and affordable credit is crucial for the country's development *-Or any other relevant point(s) - Any 3*

37. Highlight the significant three factors that have contributed to the growth of globalisation. **3**

Ans. (*i*) the movements of goods and services,

(*ii*) information and communication technology

(*iii*) Transportation technology

(*iv*) movement of people between countries

(*v*) Liberalisation of foreign trade and foreign investment policy *Any other relevant point (any 3 well explained)*

38A. A research student spoke with two people, M and N to learn about their work-related differences. On the basis of the interview conducted with both of them, the student concludes that while person M was working in an organized sector, person N was an employee of a workplace that was functioning in an unorganised way. Analyse the key differences between the two sectors that must have enabled the research student to come to this conclusion. **5**

OR

38B. Privatisation can have both positive and negative effects on the economy. Support the statement with argument. **5**

Ans. Working conditions of **person M** would have the following features:

(*i*) **Regular Employment:** Workers have assured, regular work with fixed terms of employment.

(*ii*) **Government Regulation:** Enterprises are registered with the government and follow legal rules and regulations (e.g., Factories Act, Minimum Wages Act).

(*iii*) **Security of Employment:** Workers enjoy job security with clear working hours and benefits.

(*iv*) **Overtime Compensation:** If workers work beyond regular hours, they are paid overtime.

(*v*) **Employee Benefits:** Workers receive benefits like paid leave, holidays, provident fund, gratuity, and medical benefits.

(*vi*) **Safe Working Conditions:** Employers are required to provide safe working environments (e.g., clean drinking water).

(*vii*) **Retirement Benefits:** Workers are entitled to pensions after retirement.

(*viii*) **Formal Processes:** The sector follows formal processes and procedures for employment.

Working conditions of **person N** would have the following features:

(*i*) **Irregular Employment:** Jobs are low-paid and often irregular, with no guarantee of continuous work.

(*ii*) **Lack of Government Regulation:** The sector operates largely outside government control, with few or no legal protections.

(*iii*) **No Employee Benefits:** Workers do not receive benefits like paid leave, overtime pay, or medical benefits.

(*iv*) **Job Insecurity:** Employment is not secure; workers can be dismissed without notice or reason.

(*v*) **Seasonal Work:** Employment is often dependent on seasons, and workers may be laid off during off-peak periods.

(*vi*) **Informal Jobs:** Many workers are self-employed, doing small jobs like street vending or repair work.

(*vii*) **Dependence on Employer:** Employment conditions are influenced by the employer's whims and needs.

(*viii*) **No Legal Protections:** There is little enforcement of rules or regulations related to working conditions or benefits.

OR

Ans. (B) Privatization: Positive Effects-

(*i*) Increased Efficiency and Productivity

(*ii*) Improved Quality of Services

(*iii*) Reduced Government Burden

(*iv*) Any other relevant point (s)

Privatization: Negative Effects-

(*i*) Exclusion of Public Welfare - Profit being the only motive

(*ii*) Loss of Employment Security

(*iii*) Wide gap between rich and poor - due to inaccessibility of basic facilities

(*iv*) Lower government accountability

(*v*) Any other relevant point (s)

(ANY 5 points to be accepted. However, at least 2 positive and 2 negative effects must be included in the response)

Map for Q. no. 9 (Section A) & Q. no. 19 (Section B)

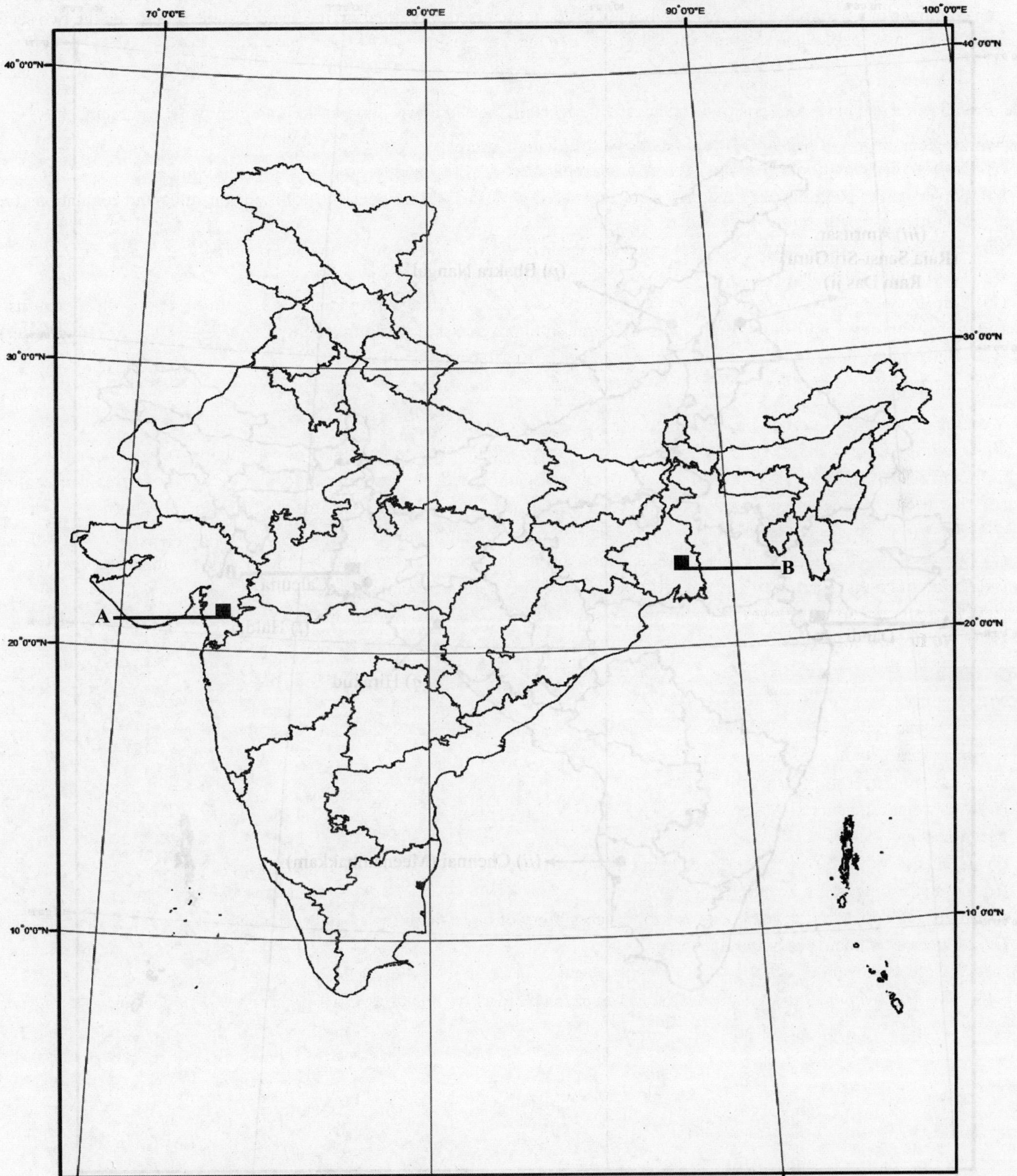

Published by Survey of India

Scale 1:16 M

Map for Q. no. 9 (Section A) & Q. no. 19 (Section B)

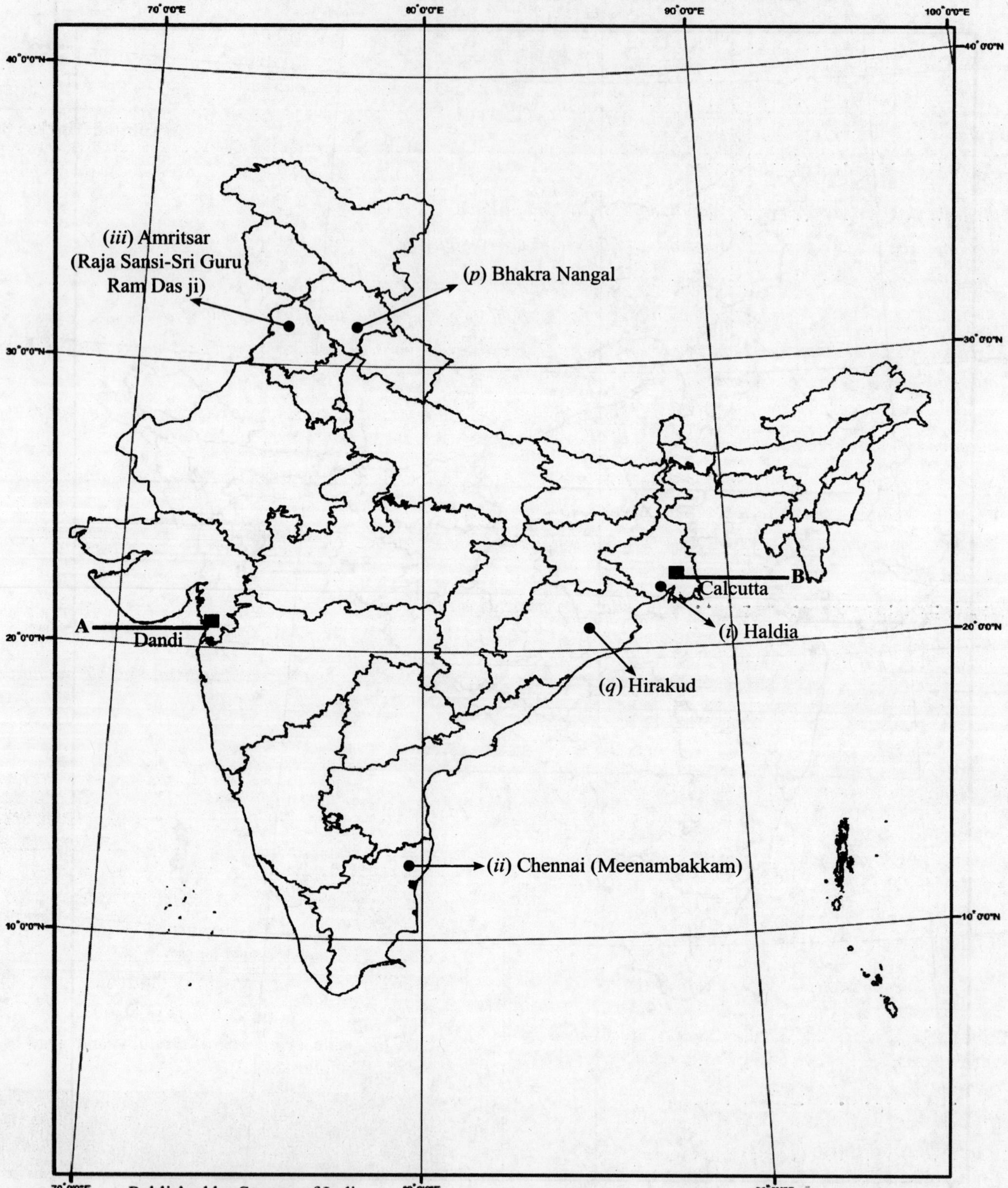

Published by Survey of India

Scale 1:16 M

CBSE Solved Paper 2024

Time allowed : 3 hours	Maximum Marks : 80

GENERAL INSTRUCTIONS:

Read the following instructions very carefully and strictly follow them:

*(i) This question paper contains 37 questions. **All** questions are **compulsory**.*

*(ii) Question paper is divided into **Six** Sections - Section **A, B, C, D, E** and **F**.*

*(iii) **Section A** – questions no. **1 to 20** are multiple choice type questions. Each question carries **1** mark.*

*(iv) **Section B** – question number **21 to 24** are Very Short Answer type questions. Each question carries **2** marks. Answer to these questions should not exceed **40** words.*

*(v) **Section C** – question number **25** to **29** are Short Answer type questions. Each question carries **3** marks. Answer to these questions should not exceed **60** words.*

*(vi) **Section D** – question number **30** to **33** are Long Answer (LA) type questions. Each question carries **5** marks. Answer to these questions should not exceed **120** words.*

*(vii) **Section E** – question number **34** to **36** are **Case-based/Source-based questions** with three sub-questions. Each question carries 4 marks.*

*(viii) In **Section F** – question number **37** is Map skill based question with two parts - **37(i)** History (2 marks) and **37(ii)** Geography (3 marks). This question carries total 5 marks.*

(ix) In addition to this, NOTE that a separate question has been provided for Visually Impaired candidates in lieu of questions having visual inputs, Map etc. Such questions are to be attempted by Visually Impaired candidates only.

SECTION-A

1. Which one of the following banks in India controls the issuance of currency and regulates the credit system in the country? **(*Re*) (1 M)**

(*a*) Punjab National Bank

(*b*) Indian Bank

(*c*) Reserve Bank of India

(*d*) State Bank of India

2. Primary, Secondary and Tertiary sectors are divided in which one of the following basis? **(*Re*) (1 M)**

(*a*) Nature of employment

(*b*) Nature of activities

(*c*) Nature of ownership

(*d*) Nature of income

3. Read the image of the cheque. Identify the cheque number from the given options: **(*Re*) (1 M)**

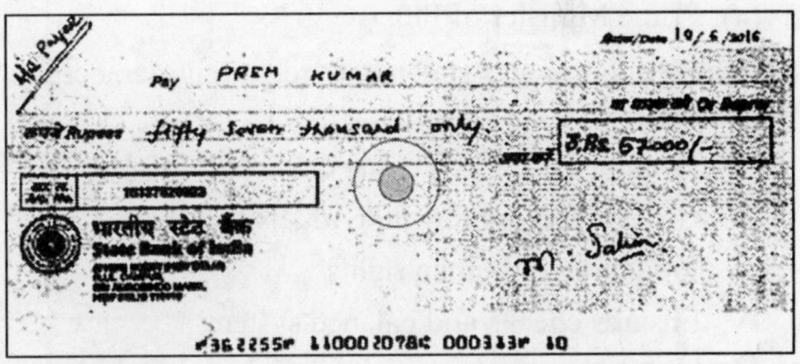

(*a*) 362255 (*b*) 110002078

(*c*) 000313 (*d*) 16137926023

4. Study the table given below carefully and answer the question that follows.

Country	Gross National Income (GNI) per capita (2011 PPP $)	HDI Rank in the world (2018)
A	12,707	73
B	6,681	130

C	4,961	148
D	5,005	154
E	3,457	143
F	4,976	134

Which of the following country has high Human Development Index Rank in the world? **(*An*) (1 M)**

(*a*) Country 'A' (*b*) Country 'C'

(*c*) Country 'D' (*d*) Country 'E'

5. Which one of the following definitions is most suitable for the 'Literacy Rate'? **(*Re*) (1 M)**

(*a*) The literate population at the global level

(*b*) The proportion of literate population in the seven years and above

(*c*) The total number of children attending school in a region

(*d*) The average number of schools in a region

6. Which one of the following is a significant aspect of globalisation? **(*Re*) (1 M)**

(*a*) Uniform Culture

(*b*) Environmental Support

(*c*) Support to Domestic Market

(*d*) Access to New Markets

7. Which of the following is responsible for resolving disputes between Centre and States? **(*Re*) (1 M)**

(*a*) Finance Commission of India

(*b*) Supreme Court of India

(*c*) President of India

(*d*) Prime Minister of India

8. Read the following statements regarding democracy and choose the correct option. **(*Un*) (1 M)**

I. Promotes equality among citizens

II. Government by few individuals

III. Protection of human rights

IV. Ensures checks and balance system

Options:

(*a*) I, II and III (*b*) II, III and IV

(*c*) I, III and IV (*d*) I, II and IV

9. How do Political Parties ensure accountability to the public? Choose the most suitable option from the following. **(*An*) (1 M)**

(*a*) Through Press Conferences

(*b*) Through Social Media Campaigns

(*c*) Through encouraging Partisanship

(*d*) Through Elections and Voter Support

10. Which one of the following statements, best describes women empowerment? **(*Un*) (1 M)**

(*a*) Encouraging men to take leadership roles.

(*b*) Promoting superiority of women over men.

(*c*) Ensuring equal opportunities and rights for women.

(*d*) Limiting the rights of men in all spheres.

11. Match Column-I with Column-II and choose the correct option from the following: **(*Ap*) (1 M)**

Column-I (Subject List in the Indian Constitution)		Column-II (Subject)	
I.	Union List	a.	Trade Union
II.	State List	b.	Banking
III.	Concurrent List	c.	Police
IV.	Residuary List	d.	Internet

Options:

	I	II	III	IV
(*a*)	d	a	c	b
(*b*)	b	c	a	d
(*c*)	a	b	d	c
(*d*)	c	d	b	a

12. Read the following informations and identify the crop.

- It is the staple food crop of majority of people in India.
- India is the second largest producer of this crop.
- It is a Kharif crop.
- It requires high humidity with of annual rainfall.

(*Un*) (1 M)

Crops:

(*a*) Ragi (*b*) Bajra

(*c*) Wheat (*d*) Rice

13. Which one of the following is the irrigation system in Meghalaya? **(*Re*) (1 M)**

(*a*) To irrigate land only during rainy season.

(*b*) To use large volumes of water for irrigation.

(*c*) To remove water from soil.

(*d*) To use bamboo drip irrigation system.

14. Arrange the following events of Indian National Movement in chronological order and choose the correct option. **(*An*) (1 M)**

I. Formation of Swaraj Party

II. Lahore Session of the Indian National Congress

III. Gandhi-Irwin Pact

IV. Formation of Depressed Class Association

(*a*) II, III, I and IV (*b*) I, II, IV and III

(*c*) I, III, II and IV (*d*) IV, III, II and I

15. 'Buddhism emerged from eastern India and spread in several directions.' Read the following reasons for its spread and choose the correct option. **(*Re*) (1 M)**

I. Due to Cultural exchange

II. Due to Silk route

III. Due to trade & travellers

IV. Due to European efforts

(*a*) Only I, II and IV are correct.

(*b*) Only II, III and IV are correct.

(*c*) Only I, II and III are correct.

(*d*) Only I, III and IV are correct.

16. Which of the following is a key indicator used to measure a country's development? **(*Re*) (1 M)**

(*a*) Primary Production

(*b*) Secondary Production

(*c*) Gross Domestic Product

(*d*) Net Domestic Product

17. Identify the primary objective of power sharing arrangements in Belgium from the following options. **(*Un*) (1 M)**

(*a*) Establishing a unitary form of government.

(*b*) Centralized political control of government.

(*c*) Establishing cultural and educational matters of Dutch.

(*d*) Accommodating linguistic and regional interest.

18. Two statements are given below. They are Assertion (A) and Reason (R). Read both statements and choose the correct option: **(*Ev*) (1 M)**

Assertion (A): On Prussian initiative 'Zolleverin' Custom Union was formed.

Reason (R): It was to create unified economic territory allowing the unhindered movement of goods, people and capital.

(*a*) Both (A) and (R) are correct and (R) is the correct explanation of (A).

(*b*) Both (A) and (R) are correct, but (R) is not the correct explanation of (A).

(*c*) (A) is true, but (R) is wrong.

(*d*) (A) is wrong, but (R) is true.

19. Match Column-I with Column-II and choose the correct option. **(*Un*) (1 M)**

	Column-I (Minerals)		Column-II (Examples)
I.	Ferrous	a.	Coal
II.	Non-Ferrous	b.	Granite
III.	Non-Metallic	c.	Bauxite
IV.	Energy	d.	Cobalt

Options:

	I	II	III	IV
(*a*)	b	d	c	a
(*b*)	d	c	b	a
(*c*)	a	b	d	c
(*d*)	c	d	b	a

20. Who among the following published 'Samvad Kaumudi'? **(*Re*) (1 M)**

(*a*) Rashsundari Debi (*b*) Tarabai Shinde

(*c*) Raja Rammohan Roy (*d*) Ram Chaddha

SECTION-B

21. "Trade and Cultural exchange always went hand in hand." Explain the statement in the context of pre-modern world. **(*Un*) (2 M)**

22. "Role of women is gradually enhancing in the politics of the country." Examine the statement. **(*An*) (2 M)**

23. (A) Suggest any two ways to solve the problem of land degradation. **(*Ap*) (2 M)**

OR

(B) Suggest any two ways for the conservation of resources. **(*Ap*) (2 M)**

24. How does the United Nations Development Program's (UNDP's) developmental criterion differ from the World Bank? Explain. **(*An*) (2 M)**

SECTION-C

25. "The development process of India has experienced transformation due to the significant influence of Information Technology (I.T.) and Electronic Industry." Explain the statement with examples. **(*Ev*) (3 M)**

26. (A) Analyse the process of German Unification. **(*An*) (3 M)**

OR

(B) Analyse the process of Italian Unification. **(*An*) (3 M)**

27. Describe any three challenges faced by the Political Parties. **(*Re*) (3 M)**

28. Why is cheap and affordable credit important for the country's development? Explain. **(*An*) (3 M)**

29. Examine the role of Tertiary sector in the development of the country. **(*An*) (3 M)**

SECTION-D

30. (A) "Democracy's ability to generate its own support is also its outcome and it cannot be ignored." Explain the statement. **(*Un*) (5 M)**

OR

(B) "Democratic systems are based on political equality." Explain the statement. **(*Un*) (5 M)**

31. (A) Explain the features of Commercial Farming. **(*An*) (5 M)**

OR

(B) Explain the features of Primitive Subsistence Farming. **(*An*) (5 M)**

32. (A) "There were variety of cultural processes through which Indian Nationalism captured people's imagination." Explain the statement with examples. **(*Un*) (5 M)**

OR

(B) How were the various social groups involved in the Civil Disobedience Movement? Explain with examples. **(*An*) (5 M)**

33. (A) Analyse the role of Liberalisation in the globalisation. **(*An*) (5 M)**

OR

(B) Examine five factors to promote the process of globalisation. **(*An*) (5 M)**

SECTION-E

34. Read the Following Source and answer the questions that follow:

Panchayati Raj

"We need to give more power to the panchayats to realise the dream of Mahatma Gandhi and the hopes of the makers of our Constitution, Panchayati Raj establishes true democracy. It restores power to the only place where power belongs in a democracy - in the hands of the people. Giving power to panchayats is also a way to reduce corruption and increase administrative efficiency. When people participate in the planning and implementation of developmental schemes, they would naturally exercise greater control over these schemes. This would eliminate the corrupt middlemen. Thus, Panchayati Raj will strengthen the foundations of our democracy."

34.1 How does giving power to Panchayats relate to the vision of Mahatma Gandhi? **(*An, Cr*) (1 M)**

34.2 Explain the primary objective of giving power to the Panchayats. **(*Re*) (1 M)**

34.3 How does the establishment of Panchayati Raj contribute to democracy? Explain. **(*An*) (2 M)**

35. Read the following source and answer the questions that follow:

Why Newspapers?

'Krishnaji Trimbuck Ranade inhabitant of Poona intends to publish a Newspaper in the Marathi Language with a view of affording useful information on every topic of local interest. It will be open for free discussion on subjects of general utility, scientific investigation and the speculations connected with the antiquities, statistics, curiosities, history and geography of the country and of the Deccan especially... the patronage and support of all interested in the diffusion of knowledge and welfare of the people is earnestly solicited.'

Bombay Telegraph and Courier, 6 January, 1849

The task of the native newspapers and political associations is identical to the role of the Opposition in the House of Commons in Parliament in England. That is of critically examining government policy to suggest improvements, by removing those parts that will not be to the benefit of the people, and also by ensuring speedy implementation. These associations ought to carefully study the particular issues, gather diverse relevant information on the nation as well as on 'what are the Possible and desirable improvements, and this will surely earn it considerable influence.'

Native Opinion, 3 April, 1870

35.1 Analyse the primary objective proposed by Ranade for publishing Marathi Language newspaper. **(*An*) (1 M)**

35.2 Why did the Bombay Telegraph emphasize the role of newspaper in promoting welfare of Deccan region? **(*Un*) (1 M)**

35.3 What were the key responsibilities attributed to native newspapers? Mention any two. **(*Re*) (2 M)**

36. Read the following source and answer the questions that follow:

Sacred Groves - A wealth of diverse and rare species

Nature worship is an age old tribal belief based on the premise that all creations of nature have to be protected. Such beliefs have preserved several virgin forests in pristine form called Sacred Groves (the forests of God and Goddesses), These patches of forest or parts of large forests have been left untouched by the local people and any interference with them is banned.

Certain societies revere a particular tree which they have preserved from time immemorial. The Mundas and the Santhal of Chota Nagpur region worship mahua (Bassia latifolia) and kadamba (Anthocaphalus cadamba) trees, and the tribals of Odisha and Bihar worship the tamarind (Tamarindus indica) and mango (mangifera indica) trees during weddings. To many of us, peepal and banyan trees are considered sacred.

Indian society comprises several cultures, each with its own set of traditional methods of conserving nature and its creations. Sacred qualities are often ascribed to springs, mountain peaks, plants and animals which are closely protected. You will find troops of macaques and langurs around many temples. They are fed daily and treated as a part of temple devotees. In and around Bishnoi villages in Rajasthan, herds of blackbuck, (chinkara), nilgai and peacocks can be seen as an integral part of the community and nobody harms them.

36.1 How does sacred groves relate to the belief in nature worship? ***(Un)* (1 M)**

36.2 How do communities incorporate trees into their cultural practices? Explain with example. ***(Un)* (1 M)**

36.3 Explain the cultural values that contribute to the coexistence of nature. ***(Ev)* (2 M)**

SECTION-F

37. *(a)* Two places **(A)** and **(B)** have been marked on the given political outline map of India. Identify them with the help of the following information and write their correct names on the lines drawn near them:

(i) The place where Jallianwala Bagh Massacre took place. ***(Re)* (1 M)**

(ii) The place where the session of Indian National Congress was held in 1927. ***(Re)* (1 M)**

(b) On the same political outline map of India, locate and label **any three** of the following with suitable symbols: ***(Un)* (3 M)**

(i) Bhakra Nangal - Dam

(ii) Noida - Software Technology Park

(iii) Tarapur - Nuclear Power Plant

(iv) Haldia - Sea Port

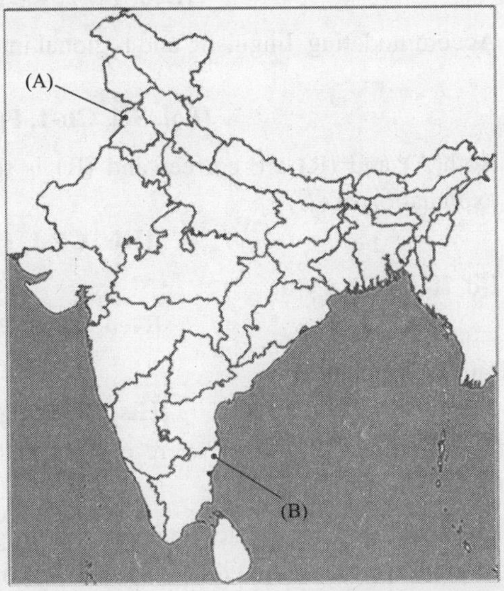

EXPLANATIONS

1. *(c)* Reserve Bank of India controls the issuance of currency and regulates the credit system in the country. ***(1 Mark)***

[Eco, Ch-3, Pg. no. 40]

2. *(b)* On the basis of the nature of activities sectors of the Indian economy are divided into Primary, Secondary, and Tertiary sectors. ***(1 Mark)***

[Eco, Ch-2, Pg. no. 19-20]

3. *(a)* Cheque number is 362255. ***(1 Mark)***

[Eco, Ch-3, Pg. no. 40-41]

4. *(a)* Country 'A' has the highest HDI rank among the countries given in the above table. Its ranking is 73. ***(1 Mark)***

[Eco, Ch-1, Pg. no. 13]

5. *(b)* Literacy Rate measures the proportion of the literate population in the 7 years-and-above age group. ***(1 Mark)***

[Eco, Ch-1, Pg. no. 10]

6. *(d)* "Access to New Markets" is a significant aspect of Globalisation. ***(1 Mark)***

[Eco, Ch-4, Pg. no. 62]

7. *(b)* Supreme Court of India ***(1 Mark)***

[Pol. Sci, Ch-2, Pg. no. 15, 17]

8. *(c)* I, III, and IV ***(1 Mark)***

[Pol. Sci, Ch-5, Pg. no. 64, 71-72]

9. *(d)* Through Elections and Voter Support. ***(1 Mark)***

[Pol. Sci, Ch-4, Pg. no. 49]

10. *(c)* Ensuring equal opportunities and rights for women ***(1 Mark)***

[Pol. Sci, Ch-3, Pg. no. 31]

11. *(b)* I-b, II-c, III-a, IV- d ***(1 Mark)***

[Pol. Sci, Ch-2, Pg. no. 16-17]

12. *(d)* Rice is India's staple food, a Kharif crop needing high humidity and rainfall. India is the second-largest producer globally. ***(1 Mark)***

[Geo, Ch-4, Pg. no. 32]

13. *(d)* In Meghalaya, bamboo pipes transport water from streams to agricultural fields, ensuring efficient water usage and conservation. ***(1 Mark)***

[Geo, Ch-3, Pg. no. 28]

14. (*b*) I, II, IV and III (*1 Mark*)
[His, Ch-2, Pg. no. 38-39]

15. (*c*) Only I, II and III are correct (*1 Mark*)
[His, Ch-3, Pg. no. 53-54]

16. (*c*) Gross Domestic Product (GDP) is a key indicator used to measure a country's development. (*1 Mark*)
[Eco, Ch-2, Pg. no. 24-26]

17. (*d*) Accommodating linguistic and regional interest. (*1 Mark*)
[Pol. Sci, Ch-1, Pg. no. 4-5]

18. (*a*) Both(A) and (R) are correct and (R) is the correct explanation of (A). (*1 Mark*)
[His, Ch-1, Pg. no. 10]

19. (*b*) I-d, II-c, III-b, IV-a (*1 Mark*)
[Geo, Ch-5, Pg. no. 43]

20. (*c*) Raja Rammohan Roy (*1 Mark*)
[His, Ch-5, Pg. no. 121]

21. Trade and cultural exchange were closely linked in the pre-modern world:

(*i*) **Silk Routes:** These routes enabled trade of goods like silk and spices, along with the spread of religions like Buddhism. (*1 Mark*)

(*ii*) **Missionaries:** Christian missionaries and Muslim preachers used these routes to share their beliefs. (*1 Mark*)
[His, Ch-3, Pg. no. 53-54]

22. (*i*) The above statement is true. Women's participation in Indian politics is rising. It is evident from the increasing number of women in government and local movements. (*1 Mark*)

(*ii*) Special efforts, like reserved seats in local governance, have helped them become more empowered. This also shows progress toward gender equality in politics. (*1 Mark*)
[Pol. Sci, Ch-3, Pg. no. 35]

23. (A) Two effective ways to address land degradation include:

(*i*) **Afforestation:** Planting trees can prevent soil erosion, enhance soil fertility, and restore land health. (*1 Mark*)

(*ii*) **Proper Management of Grazing:** Regulating grazing prevents the overuse of land, allowing vegetation to recover and soil to maintain its integrity. (*1 Mark*)
[Geo, Ch-1, Pg. no. 6]

OR

(B) Two ways for the conservation of resources are

(*i*) **Avoiding Irrational Consumption**: Minimize the overuse and wasteful consumption of resources to prevent socio-economic and environmental issues. (*1 Mark*)

(*ii*) **Proper Waste Management**: Involves reducing, reusing, and recycling waste to minimize environmental impact and conserve resources. (*1 Mark*)
[Geo, Ch-1, Pg. no. 3-4]

24. UNDP's development criterion differs from the World Bank in the following ways:

(*i*) UNDP measures the development of the countries based on the educational levels of the people, their health status, and per capita income whereas World Bank uses only per capita income to measure the same. (*1 Mark*)

(*ii*) UNDP has a broader framework while World Bank has a narrow framework to measure development. (*1 Mark*)
[Eco, Ch-1, Pg. no. 13-14]

25. The IT and electronics industry has transformed India's economy, fostering growth, innovation, and global connectivity.

(*i*) **Growth in IT Exports**: India's IT industry, including software services from hubs like Bengaluru and Noida, drives significant global exports. (*1 Mark*)

(*ii*) **Employment Generation**: IT and electronics industries have created millions of jobs, uplifting urban economies and empowering skilled youth. (*1 Mark*)

(*iii*) **Digital Revolution**: IT-enabled services, e-governance, and digital payments revolutionize India's economy, promoting efficiency, transparency, and inclusion. (*1 Mark*)
[Geo, Ch-6, Pg. no. 65]

26. (A) The process of German Unification:

(*i*) **Role of Otto von Bismarck:** Otto von Bismarck, the Prussian Chancellor, led the unification through his policy of "blood and iron" and diplomatic strategies. (*1 Mark*)

(*ii*) **Wars:** Prussia won wars against Denmark (1864), Austria (1866), and France (1870-71), consolidating German territories. (*1 Mark*)

(*iii*) **Proclamation of Empire:** In 1871, the German Empire was proclaimed in the Hall of Mirrors at Versailles, marking unification. (*1 Mark*)
[His, Ch-1, Pg. no. 19]

OR

(B) The process of Italian Unification:

(*i*) Italian unification was spearheaded by Giuseppe Mazzini, who inspired nationalism and unity through his secret societies like Young Italy. **(*1 Mark*)**

(*ii*) Count Camillo de Cavour, the Prime Minister of Sardinia-Piedmont, united Northern Italy through diplomacy, defeating Austria with French support. **(*1 Mark*)**

(*iii*) Giuseppe Garibaldi led armed volunteers in Southern Italy, uniting it with Northern Italy in 1861 under Victor Emmanuel II as king. **(*1 Mark*)**

[His, Ch-1, Pg. no. 20-21]

27. The challenges faced by political parties are as under: **(Any three)**

(*i*) **Lack of internal democracy:** In political parties, a small number of people hold the majority of the power. In such situations, a party's other members are given no consideration. Few members who have grown excessively powerful take charge of all decisions. **(*1 Mark*)**

(*ii*) **Dynastic succession:** Families of political party members typically receive very easy entry. In these situations, the unqualified family members attend the party while the deserving are excluded. **(*1 Mark*)**

(*iii*) **Factionalism:** Factionalism within the party, which can lead to a lack of unity and coordination. **(*1 Mark*)**

(*iv*) **Money and muscle power:** The influence of money and muscle power in elections, which can lead to corruption and unfair practices. **(*1 Mark*)**

(*v*) **Meaningful Choice:** Very often parties do not seem to offer a meaningful choice to the voters. **(*1 Mark*)**

[Pol. Sci, Ch-4, Pg. no. 57-58]

28. Cheap and affordable credit is important for the country's development because of the following reasons:

(*i*) **Encourages Entrepreneurship**: Affordable credit allows people to invest in businesses, leading to job creation and economic growth. **(*1 Mark*)**

(*ii*) **Enhances Living Standards**: People can borrow money for education, housing, and healthcare, improving their quality of life. **(*1 Mark*)**

(*iii*) **Agricultural Growth**: Farmers can buy seeds, equipment, and other inputs, increasing crop production and income. **(*1 Mark*)**

[Eco, Ch-3, Pg. no. 48-49]

29. The tertiary sector, or service sector, plays a crucial role. The role of the tertiary sector in the development of the country includes:

(*i*) **Economic Growth:** The sector contributes significantly to GDP through services like banking, IT, and tourism. **(*1 Mark*)**

(*ii*) **Employment Generation:** It creates vast job opportunities, especially in urban areas. **(*1 Mark*)**

(*iii*) **Improved Infrastructure:** Services like transport, healthcare, and education enhance quality of life and support other sectors. **(*1 Mark*)**

[Eco, Ch-2, Pg. no. 24-25]

30. (A) (*i*) Democracy's ability to generate its own support as an outcome signifies that people inherently value democratic principles and choose democracy over other forms of government. **(*1 Mark*)**

(*ii*) This preference is evident globally. People in various countries, regardless of whether they live in democratic or non-democratic regimes, tend to support the idea of democracy. **(*1 Mark*)**

(*iii*) People believe in having a government elected by them and feel that democracy suits their country. It reflects people's belief in democracy as a fair and just method of governance. **(*1 Mark*)**

(*iv*) Even when individuals criticize their democratic systems or express dissatisfaction with certain aspects, their engagement and demands for improvement further validate democracy's significance. **(*1 Mark*)**

(*v*) This continuous cycle of support, critique, and evolution underlines democracy's capacity to sustain and enhance itself. **(*1 Mark*)**

[Pol. Sci, Ch-5, Pg. no. 65-66]

OR

(B) (*i*) The statement "Democratic systems are based on political equality" highlights the fundamental principle of democracy, which says all individuals have equal rights and say in the democratic process and decision-making. **(*1 Mark*)**

(*ii*) In a democracy, every citizen gets one vote, and each vote has equal value, ensuring that no one has more influence over the government than anyone else. **(*1 Mark*)**

(*iii*) This core concept ensures that each person's voice holds equal weight, regardless of their social, economic, or cultural background. **(*1 Mark*)**

(*iv*) In democracies, political equality is fundamental, ensuring that elected representatives are chosen by the people, for the people, reflecting the collective will and preferences of the electorate. **(*1 Mark*)**

(*v*) This principle promotes inclusiveness and fairness, ensuring that all voices, regardless of socio-economic status or any other discriminatory factor, are heard and considered equally in the political process. **(*1 Mark*)**

[Pol. Sci, Ch-5, Pg. no. 69]

31. (A) Commercial farming is the large-scale production of crops for sale, using modern techniques. some features of commercial farming are:

(*i*) **High Input Usage:** Commercial farming extensively uses modern agricultural inputs such as high-yielding variety seeds and chemical fertilizers to enhance crop yields and productivity. (*1 Mark*)

(*ii*) **Single-Crop Focus:** This type of farming typically concentrates on one cash crop like cotton or wheat, allowing for specialized production techniques and greater efficiency. (*1 Mark*)

(*iii*) **Market-Oriented:** The primary aim is to sell the produce in the market, often targeting both domestic and international markets, aligning production with market demand. (*1 Mark*)

(*iv*) **Capital Intensive:** Significant investment is required in advanced technology, machinery, and infrastructure to facilitate large-scale production and increase profit margins. (*1 Mark*)

(*v*) **Labour Characteristics:** Commercial farming often depends on skilled and migrant labour for various farming activities, focusing on efficiency and expertise in agricultural practices. (*1 Mark*)

[Geo, Ch-4, Pg. no. 30]

OR

(B) Primitive subsistence farming is small-scale, traditional agriculture using basic tools and relying on natural environmental conditions. some features of primitive subsistence farming:

(*i*) **Small Scale and Labor-Intensive:** It is practised on small patches of land using family/community labour and primitive tools like hoes, daos, and digging sticks. (*1 Mark*)

(*ii*) **Dependence on Natural Resources:** This farming relies on monsoon rains, natural soil fertility, and environmental conditions suitable for the crops. (*1 Mark*)

(*iii*) **Slash and Burn Technique:** Known as 'slash and burn' agriculture, farmers clear a land patch, cultivate it until soil fertility decreases, and then move to a new patch, allowing nature to replenish the old land's fertility. (*1 Mark*)

(*iv*) **Low Productivity:** Due to the non-use of fertilizers or modern inputs, the productivity of this farming type is low. (*1 Mark*)

(*v*) **Known by Various Names:** It has different names across regions, like 'Jhumming' in Northeast India, like Assam, Meghalaya, Mizoram, Nagaland, etc. reflecting its widespread yet localized practice. (*1 Mark*)

[Geo, Ch-4, Pg. no. 33]

32. (A) Indian nationalism captured people's imagination through various cultural processes:

(*i*) **Symbolism of Bharat Mata:** The image of Bharat Mata, created by Bankim Chandra Chattopadhyay, and her hymn "Vande Mataram" united people emotionally. Abanindranath Tagore's depiction showed her as calm and spiritual, invoking pride in the nation. (*1 Mark*)

(*ii*) **Promotion of Folklore:** Nationalists like Rabindranath Tagore collected folk tales, ballads, and nursery rhymes to revive traditional Indian culture and instill pride in the nation's heritage. (*1 Mark*)

(*iii*) **Development of National Symbols:** The tricolour flag, with symbols like the spinning wheel and lotuses, was a powerful representation of unity and defiance against colonial rule. (*1 Mark*)

(*iv*) **Reinterpretation of History:** Indians glorified ancient achievements in art, science, and philosophy to counter British propaganda of Indian inferiority and inspire self-belief. (*1 Mark*)

(*v*) **Religious Inclusivity:** Figures like Bal Gangadhar Tilak emphasized unity through references to religious institutions like temples, mosques, and churches, fostering a collective national identity. (*1 Mark*)

[His, Ch-2, Pg. no. 47]

OR

(B) Various social groups participated in the Civil Disobedience Movement, each with distinct motivations and aspirations:

(*i*) **Rich Peasants:** Groups like the Patidars of Gujarat and Jats of Uttar Pradesh joined due to their inability to pay high land revenue during the economic depression. They viewed the movement as a fight against unjust taxes. (*1 Mark*)

(*ii*) **Poor Peasants:** Tenant farmers sought rent reductions as their incomes dwindled. The Congress, however, hesitated to support their demands to maintain alliances with landlords. (*1 Mark*)

(*iii*) **Business Classes:** Industrialists opposed colonial restrictions on trade and supported the movement to secure economic freedom. They helped finance the movement but withdrew when militant activities rose. (*1 Mark*)

(*iv*) **Women:** Women from urban and rural households participated by picketing shops and manufacturing salt. They viewed their involvement as a duty towards the nation. (*1 Mark*)

(v) **Tribal Groups and Plantation Workers:** Tribals protested restrictions on forest use, while plantation workers demanded freedom to return home. *(1 Mark)*

[His, Ch-2, Pg. no. 41-42]

33. (A) The role of liberalisation in globalisation:

(i) **Market Expansion:** Liberalisation reduces trade barriers, fostering an environment where goods and services move freely across borders, significantly expanding global markets. *(1 Mark)*

(ii) **Increased Competition:** By opening domestic markets to foreign competition, liberalisation forces local businesses to improve efficiency and innovation to stay competitive. *(1 Mark)*

(iii) **Attraction of Foreign Investment:** Liberalisation policies, including deregulation and reducing restrictions on foreign investments, attract multinational corporations seeking new opportunities, boosting local economies. *(1 Mark)*

(iv) **Technological Transfer:** The entry of foreign companies accelerates the transfer of technology and expertise to developing countries, enhancing their industries and infrastructure. *(1 Mark)*

(v) **Economic Growth:** By stimulating competition, attracting foreign direct investment, and enabling access to larger markets, liberalisation can boost economic growth and development. *(1 Mark)*

[Eco, Ch-4, Pg. no. 64]

OR

(B) To promote the process of globalisation, here are five key factors:

(i) **Reduce Trade Barriers:** By cutting down on taxes and quotas, countries can make it easier to buy and sell goods across borders. *(1 Mark)*

(ii) **Encourage Foreign Investment:** This means allowing foreign companies to start businesses or invest in local ones to bring more money into the country. *(1 Mark)*

(iii) **Improve Technology:** Having good technology, especially in communication and transport, makes it easier to do business all over the world. *(1 Mark)*

(iv) **Support from International Organizations:** Groups like the World Trade Organization (WTO) can help by making rules that are fair for all countries. *(1 Mark)*

(v) **Government Policies:** Governments can create rules that make it easier for goods, services, and money to move between countries. *(1 Mark)*

[Eco, Ch-4, Pg. no. 62-64]

34.1 Giving power to Panchayats connects with Mahatma Gandhi's vision because it fulfills his dream of decentralized governance. Gandhi believed in empowering villages, and the Panchayati Raj achieved this by placing power in the hands of the people. *(1 Mark)*

[Pol. Sci, Ch-2, Pg. no. 24-26]

34.2 The primary objective of giving power to Panchayats is to establish true democracy by returning power to where it belongs: the people. It aims to ensure that decisions affecting local communities are made by those who understand their needs and concerns. *(1 Mark)*

[Pol. Sci, Ch-2, Pg. no. 24-26]

34.3 The establishment of Panchayati Raj contributes to democracy by promoting grassroots-level participation in governance. It allows local issues to be addressed more efficiently and ensures that the development plan matches with the community's needs. By decentralizing power, it strengthens democracy, making it more inclusive and representative. *(2 Marks)*

[Pol. Sci, Ch-2, Pg. no. 24-26]

35.1 The primary objective of Ranade for publishing a Marathi language newspaper was to provide useful information on various local interest topics and promote the diffusion of knowledge and welfare among the people. *(1 Mark)*

[His, Ch-5, Pg. no. 122]

35.2 The Bombay Telegraph emphasized the role of the newspaper in promoting the welfare of the Deccan region by intending to create an informed public through discussions on a variety of topics such as general utility, scientific inquiries, and regional history and geography, thereby contributing to the region's overall progress and development. *(1 Mark)*

[His, Ch-5, Pg. no. 122]

35.3 The key responsibilities attributed to native newspapers were:

(i) Critically examining government policies to suggest necessary improvements and remove any detrimental aspects, ensuring that the changes benefit the public. *(1 Mark)*

(ii) Conducting thorough research on various issues to gather diverse and relevant information, which would help in influencing public opinion and possibly policy decisions through informed debates and discussions. *(1 Mark)*

[His, Ch-5, Pg. no. 122]

36.1 Sacred groves are areas of forest conserved by local communities due to religious beliefs and are seen as abodes of deities. This tradition reflects nature worship as these groves are protected and revered, highlighting the community's respect and devotion to nature as a sacred entity. *(1 Mark)*

[Geo, Ch-2, Pg. no. 17]

36.2 Communities incorporate trees into their cultural practices by associating them with religious ceremonies and rituals. For example, the Bishnoi community in Rajasthan reveres the Khejri tree, around which many of their practices are centred. *(1 Mark)*

[Geo, Ch-2, Pg. no. 17]

36.3 *(i)* **Respect for Nature:** Many cultures hold a deep respect for the environment, viewing it as a living entity. This respect leads to practices that protect and preserve natural resources, contributing to ecological balance. *(1 Mark)*

(ii) **Community and Sustainability:** Cultural values that emphasize community and sustainability lead to shared efforts in conserving natural habitats and species. Traditions such as community-led forest management and water conservation practices reflect this synergy between cultural values and nature's coexistence. *(1 Mark)*

[Geo, Ch-2, Pg. no. 17]

37. *(a)* *(i)* Amritsar *(1 Mark)*

[His, Ch-2, Pg. no. 31]

(ii) Madras *(1 Mark)*

[His, Ch-2, Pg. no. 42]

(b) **(Any three)** ***(3 Marks)***

(i) **[Geo, Ch-3, Pg. no. 24]**

(ii) **[Geo, Ch-5, Pg. no. 53]**

(iii) **[Geo, Ch-6, Pg. no. 67]**

(iv) **[Geo, Ch-7, Pg. no. 77-78]**

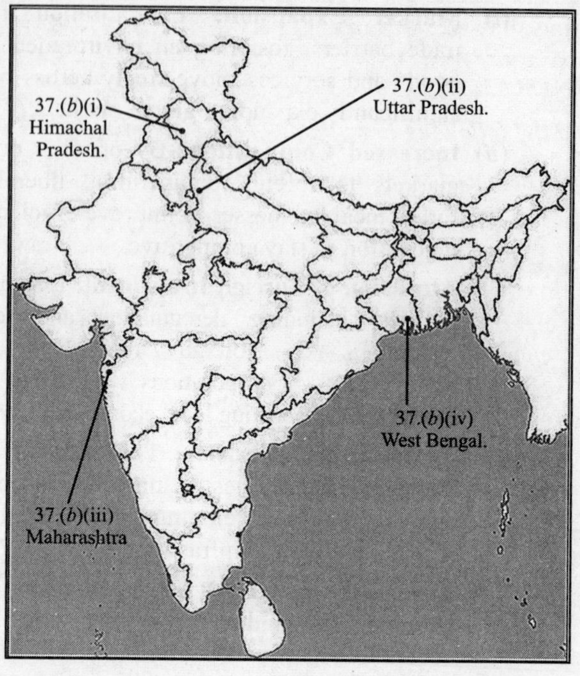

CBSE Solved Paper 2025

Time allowed : 3 hours **Maximum Marks : 80**

GENERAL INSTRUCTIONS:

Read the following instructions very carefully and strictly follow them:

*(i) This question paper contains 37 questions. **All** questions are **compulsory**.*

*(ii) Question paper is divided into **Six** Sections - Section **A, B, C, D, E** and **F**.*

*(iii) **Section A** – questions no. **1** to **20** are multiple choice type questions. Each question carries **1** mark.*

*(iv) **Section B** – question number **21** to **24** are Very Short Answer type questions. Each question carries **2** marks. Answer to these questions should not exceed **40** words.*

*(v) **Section C** – question number **25** to **29** are Short Answer type questions. Each question carries **3** marks. Answer to these questions should not exceed **60** words.*

*(vi) **Section D** – question number **30** to **33** are Long Answer (LA) type questions. Each question carries **5** marks. Answer to these questions should not exceed **120** words.*

*(vii) **Section E** – question number **34** to **36** are **Case-based/Source-based questions** with three sub-questions. Each question carries **4** marks.*

*(viii) In **Section F** – question number **37** is Map skill based question with two parts -*

*37**(i)** History (2 marks) and 37**(ii)** Geography (3 marks). This question carries total 5 marks.*

(ix) In addition to this, NOTE that a separate question has been provided for Visually Impaired candidates in lieu of questions having visual inputs, Map etc. Such questions are to be attempted by Visually Impaired candidates only.

SECTION-A

1. Arrange the following historical events in chronological order and choose the correct option: ***(An)* (1 M)**

I. Bardoli Satyagraha

II. Rowlatt Satyagraha

III. Champaran Satyagraha

IV. Kheda Satyagraha

Options:

(*a*) I, II, III, IV (*b*) III, II, I, IV

(*c*) II, I, IV, III (*d*) III, IV, II, I

2. Which among the following newspapers is related to Bal Gangadhar Tilak? ***(Re)* (1 M)**

(*a*) Hindustan (*b*) Bangla Patrika

(*c*) Veer Bhoomi (*d*) Kesari

3. In reference to the Germania allegory the "olive branch around the sword" symbolizes which one of the following? ***(Un)* (1 M)**

(*a*) Being freed

(*b*) Heroism and strength

(*c*) Willingness to make peace

(*d*) Beginning of a new era

4. The germs of which disease paved the way for Europe's conquest of America in the later half of the sixteenth century? ***(Re)* (1 M)**

(*a*) Cholera (*b*) Smallpox

(*c*) Jaundice (*d*) Malaria

5. Mrs. Monica, along with her family, clears a piece of land and grows grain and other food crops to feed her family. When the soil's fertility decreases, she prepares another piece of land for agriculture. Which of the following methods of agriculture does she use? ***(Un)* (1 M)**

(*a*) Plantation farming

(*b*) Slash and burn farming

(*c*) Intensive subsistence farming

(*d*) Commercial farming

6. Match Column-I with Column-II and choose the correct option: ***(Un)* (1 M)**

	Column-I (Minerals)		Column-II (Features)
A.	Sariska Wildlife Sanctuary	(*i*)	Uttarakhand
B.	Manas Tiger Reserve	(*ii*)	Rajasthan
C.	Periyar Tiger Reserve	(*iii*)	Assam
D.	Corbett National Park	(*iv*)	Kerala

(*a*) A-(*i*), B-(*ii*), C-(*iii*), D-(*iv*)
(*b*) A-(*ii*), B-(*iii*), C-(*iv*), D-(*i*)
(*c*) A-(*iv*), B-(*i*), C-(*iii*), D-(*ii*)
(*d*) A-(*ii*), B-(*i*), C-(*iv*), D-(*iiii*)

7. Two statements are given below. They are Assertion (A) and Reason (R). Read both the statements and choose the correct option: ***(Un)* (1 M)**

Assertion (A): Most of the jute industry in India is located in a narrow belt along the banks of Hugli river.

Reason (R): India is the second largest exporter of jute.

(*a*) Both (A) and (R) are true and (R) is the correct explanation of (A).
(*b*) Both (A) and (R) are true, but (R) is not the correct explanation of (A).
(*c*) (A) is true, but (R) is false.
(*d*) (A) is false, but (R) is true.

8. Choose the correct option to fill in the blank: ***(Re)* (1 M)**
The process of removing barriers on foreign trade and investment by the government is known as ________.
(*a*) Import Tax (*b*) Export Tax
(*c*) Liberalisation (*d*) Industrialisation

9. Identify the odd one out. ***(Re)* (1 M)**
(*a*) Hindustan Computers Limited
(*b*) Bharti Airtel Limited
(*c*) Hindustan Unilever Limited
(*d*) Bharat Heavy Electricals Limited

10. By which organization is the Human Development Report published? ***(Re)* (1 M)**
(*a*) World Trade Organisation
(*b*) Amnesty International
(*c*) United Nations Development Programme
(*d*) World Health Organisation

11. Why is it not easy to get loans from the formal sector? Read the following reasons and choose the most appropriate option: ***(Un)* (1 M)**
I. Availability of Banks
II. Availability of Collateral
III. Long and Complicated Loan Process
IV. Awareness of Borrower

(*a*) Only I, II and III are correct.
(*b*) Only II, III and IV are correct.
(*c*) Only I, II and IV are correct.
(*d*) Only I, III and IV are correct.

12. Identify the sector on basis of the following characteristics and choose the correct option: ***(Re)* (1 M)**
- The objective of this sector is to earn profit.
- This sector is owned by a person or company.
- Tata Iron and Steel is a example of this sector

(*a*) Cooperative Sector (*b*) Unorganised Sector
(*c*) Public Sector (*d*) Private Sector

13. Data related to an imaginary country is given below. Study these data and answer the question that follows: ***(Un)* (1 M)**

Age	Total Population	Net Attendance
7 and 8 years of age	1200	1000
14 and 15 years of age	1000	800
Total	2200	1800

The attendance percentage of this country of the age group of 14 and 15 years is ________.
(*a*) 90 percent (*b*) 80 percent
(*c*) 70 percent (*d*) 60 percent

14. Two statements are given below. They are Assertion (A) and Reason (R). Read both the statements and choose the correct option: ***(An)* (1 M)**

Assertion (A): Every party in India has to register with the Election Commission.

Reason (R): The Government provides election symbols to all political parties in India.

(*a*) Both (A) and (R) are true and (R) is the correct explanation of (A).
(*b*) Both (A) and (R) are true, but (R) is not the correct explanation of (A)
(*c*) (A) is true, but (R) is false
(*d*) (A) is false, but (R) is true.

15. Which of the following group is in majority in Sri Lanka? ***(Re)* (1 M)**
(*a*) Tamil-speakers (*b*) Sinhala-speakers
(*c*) Telugu-speakers (*d*) English-speakers

16. To reform the party system, which of the following tasks have been made compulsory for the political parties? Choose the most appropriate option. ***(Re)* (1 M)**
I. It is now compulsory for all the political parties to file income tax returns.
II. It is now compulsory for all parties to have one-third women candidates.

III. It is now compulsory for all the political parties to hold their organisational election.

IV. It is now compulsory for all candidates to disclose information about pending criminal cases against them through affidavit.

(*a*) Only I, II and III are correct.

(*b*) Only I, II and IV are correct.

(*c*) Only I, III and IV are correct.

(*d*) Only II, III and IV are correct.

17. Which of the following statements represent gender equality? ***(An)* (1 M)**

(*a*) The value of women's vote is more than that of men

(*b*) Restricting women to household chores

(*c*) Providing more rights to men.

(*d*) Providing voting rights equally to men and women.

18. Choose the correctly matched pair from the following: ***(Re)* (1 M)**

(*a*) Concurrent List - Education

(*b*) Concurrent List - Defence

(*c*) Concurrent List - Police

(*d*) Concurrent List - Trade

19. In which one of the following organs of India are women taking advantage of reservation? ***(Re)* (1 M)**

(*a*) Municipality (*b*) Legislative Council

(*c*) Rajya Sabha (*d*) Judiciary

20. Which one of the following languages is included in the Eighth Schedule of the Indian Constitution? ***(Re)* (1 M)**

(*a*) Bhojpuri (*b*) Magadhi

(*c*) Rajasthani (*d*) Tamil

SECTION-B

21. How is the distribution of power among different social groups beneficial for democracy? Explain. ***(An)* (2 M)**

22. Explain any two benefits of globalisation. ***(Un)* (2 M)**

23. Mention any two economic impacts of the First World War on India. ***(Un)* (2 M)**

24. (A) Describe any two features of 'arid soils' ***(Re)* (2 M)**

OR

(B) Describe any two features of 'forest soils'. ***(Re)* (2 M)**

SECTION-C

25. Explain any three aims of Jal Jeevan Mission (JJM). ***(Un)* (3 M)**

26. How does democracy establish an accountable, responsible and legitimate governance? Explain. ***(Ap)* (3 M)**

27. (A) Analyse the impacts of Gandhi-Irwin pact on the Indian freedom struggle. ***(An)* (3 M)**

OR

(B) Analyse the role of Alluri Sitaram Raju in the Indian National Movement. ***(An)* (3 M)**

28. Examine the importance of bank deposits. ***(An)* (3 M)**

29. Explain the main features of the Indian federal system. ***(Un)* (3 M)**

SECTION-D

30. (A) Analyse the contribution of Johann Gutenberg in the development of the printing press. ***(An)* (5 M)**

OR

(B) Analyse the development journey of print culture in India. ***(An)* (5 M)**

31. (A) "Secularism is the very idea of Indian Constitution." Justify the statement. ***(Ev)* (5 M)**

OR

(B) Suggest any five measures to establish the gender equality of labour. ***(Cr)* (5 M)**

32. (A) Distinguish between public and private sector of economy with examples. ***(Un)* (5 M)**

OR

(B) Suppose you are the Sarpanch of your village. What suggestions will you give for creating additional employment in the village, so that the problem of unemployment of the residents of rural areas can be reduced? ***(Ap)* (5 M)**

33. (A) Describe the features of cropping patterns in India. ***(Un)* (5 M)**

OR

(B) Describe the main characteristics of major millet crops grown in India. ***(Un)* (5 M)**

SECTION-E

34. Read the given source and answer the questions that follow:

IRON ORE

Iron ore is the basic mineral and the backbone of industrial development. India is endowed with fairly abundant resources of iron ore India is rich in good quality iron ores. Magnetite is the finest iron ore with a very high content of iron up to 70 per cent. It has excellent magnetic qualities, especially valuable in the electrical industry Hematite ore is the most important industrial iron ore in terms of the quantity used, but has a slightly lower iron content than magnetite (50-60 per cent). In 2018-19, almost the entire production of iron ore (97%) accrued from Odisha, Chhattisgarh, Karnataka and Jharkhand. The remaining production (3%) was from other states.

34.1 In which iron ore is the maximum iron content found? ***(Re)*** **(1 M)**

34.2 Which is the most important industrial iron ore? ***(Re)*** **(1 M)**

34.3 "Iron ore is a basic mineral." Support the statement. ***(Un)*** **(2 M)**

35. Read the given source and answer the questions that follow:

ORGANISED SECTOR

Kanta works in the organised sector. Organised sector covers those enterprises or places of work where the terms of employment are regular and therefore, people have assured work. They are registered by the government and have to follow its rules and regulations which are given in various laws such as the Factories Act, Minimum Wages Act, Payment of Gratuity Act, Shops and Establishments Act, etc. It is called Organised Sector because it has some formal processes and procedures. Some of these people may not be employed by anyone but may work on their own, but they too have to register themselves with the government and follow the rules and regulations.

35.1 Mention any one feature of the working conditions of organised sector. ***(Re)*** **(1 M)**

35.2 Explain any one benefit provided by the employers to the organised sector employees. ***(Un)*** **(1 M)**

35.3 Why is it necessary for all self-employed people to register with the government? ***(Un)*** **(2 M)**

36. Read the given source and answer the questions that follow:

THE REVOLUTIONARIES

During the years following 1815, the fear of repression drove many liberal-nationalists underground. Secret societies sprang up in many European states to train revolutionaries and spread their ideas. To be revolutionary at this time meant a commitment to oppose monarchical forms that had been established after the Vienna Congress, and to fight for liberty and freedom. Most of these revolutionaries also saw the creation of nation-states as a necessary part of this struggle for freedom.

36.1 Mention any one political demand of the liberals. ***(Re)*** **(1 M)**

36.2 Mention the main cause for the rise of secret societies in European States. ***(Re)*** **(1 M)**

36.3 Analyse the reasons for many liberal-nationalists going underground after 1815. ***(An)*** **(2 M)**

SECTION-F

37. (*i*) Two places **'A'** and **'B'** have been marked on the given political outline map of India (on page 23). Identify them with the help of the following information and write their correct names on the lines drawn near them: **(2 M)**

(*a*) The place where the session of Indian National Congress was held place in 1927. ***(Re)***

(*b*) The place where Mahatma Gandhi broke the Salt Law. ***(Re)***

(*ii*) On the same political outline map of India, locate and label any **three** of the following with suitable symbols: ***(Un)*** **(3 M)**

(*a*) An international airport of West Bengal

(*b*) A software technology park of Karnataka

(*c*) A nuclear power plant located in Maharashtra

(*d*) A major sea port of Odisha

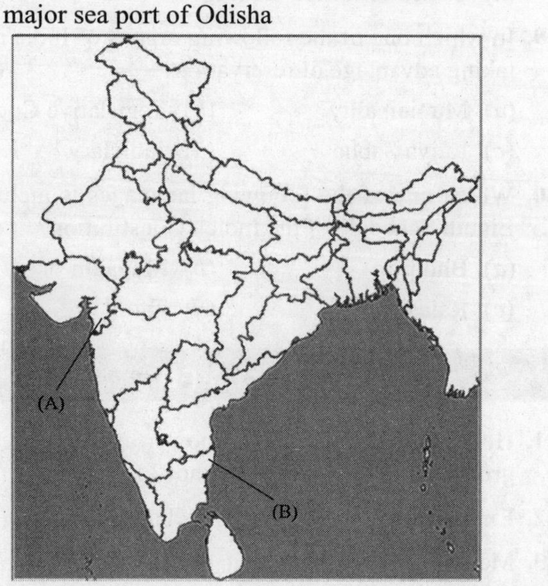

EXPLANATIONS

1. (*d*) The correct chronological order is:

III. Champaran Satyagraha- 1917

IV. Kheda Satyagraha - 1918

II. Rowlatt Satyagraha- 1919

I. Bardoli Satyagraha- 1928 ***(1 Mark)***

[His, Ch-2, Pg. no. 31,35]

2. (*d*) When Punjab revolutionaries were deported in 1907, Balgangadhar Tilak wrote with great sympathy about them in his Kesari. This led to his imprisonment in 1908, provoking in turn widespread protests all over India. ***(1 Mark)***

[His, Ch-5, Pg. no. 127]

3. (*c*) In the Germania allegory, the "olive branch around the sword" symbolizes the willingness to make peace. The olive branch traditionally represents peace, and when it surrounds a sword, it indicates a readiness to maintain peace without compromising strength. ***(1 Mark)***

[His, Ch-1, Pg. no. 24]

4. (*b*) Smallpox was the most devastating disease brought by Europeans to the Americas. The indigenous population, having no immunity to this new disease, suffered massive fatalities. ***(1 Mark)***

[His, Ch-3, Pg. no. 55]

5. (*b*) In **slash and burn farming**, farmers clear a piece of land, grow crops, and when the soil loses fertility, they move to another plot. This method is commonly practiced for subsistence farming. ***(1 Mark)***

[Geo, Ch-4, Pg. no. 30]

6. (*b*) A-(*ii*), B-(*iii*), C-(*iv*), D-(*i*) ***(1 Mark)***

[Geo, Ch-2, Pg. no. 15]

7. (*b*) Both statements are true. The jute industry in India is concentrated along the Hugli River due to the availability of raw materials, transport facilities, and labor. However, India's position as the second-largest exporter of jute is an independent fact and not the reason for the industry's location. ***(1 Mark)***

[Geo, Ch-5, Pg. no. 60, 62]

8. (*c*) Liberalisation refers to the removal of restrictions and trade barriers imposed by the government on foreign trade and investment. This policy aims to promote economic integration by allowing free movement of goods, services, and capital across borders ***(1 Mark)***

[Eco, Ch-4, Pg. no. 64]

9. (*d*) Bharat Heavy Electricals Limited (BHEL) is a public sector company owned by the Government of India, while the other three are private sector companies

(1 Mark)

[Eco, Ch-2, Pg. no. 33]

10. (*c*) The Human Development Report is published by the United Nations Development Programme (UNDP). It evaluates countries based on health, education, and per capita income indicators to measure overall human development. ***(1 Mark)***

[Eco, Ch-1, Pg. no. 13]

11. (*b*) The main difficulties in getting loans from the formal sector are the requirement of collateral, complex loan procedures, and lack of borrower awareness. Availability of banks is generally not an issue, but fulfilling the formal requirements is challenging.

(1 Mark)

[Eco, Ch-3, Pg. no. 49-50]

12. (*d*) The private sector is owned by individuals or companies with the primary objective of earning profit. Tata Iron and Steel is a prominent example of a private sector enterprise. ***(1 Mark)***

[Eco, Ch-2, Pg. no. 33]

13. (*b*) The attendance percentage for the age groups of 14 and 15 years is calculated as 80% using the given data.

Total Population (14 and 15 years): 1000

Net Attendance (14 and 15 years): 800

$$\text{Attendance Percentage} = \frac{\text{Net Attendance}}{\text{Total Population}} \times 100$$

$$= \frac{800}{1000} \times 100 = 80\%$$ ***(1 Mark)***

[Eco, Ch-1, Pg. no. 10]

14. (*c*) Every political party in India must register with the Election Commission. However, the government does not provide election symbols to all political parties.

(1 Mark)

[Pol. Sci, Ch-4, Pg. no. 53]

15. (*b*) Sinhala-speaking people form the majority in Sri Lanka, making up approximately 74% of the population.

(1 Mark)

[Pol. Sci, Ch-1, Pg. no. 2-3]

16. (*c*) It is compulsory for political parties to file income tax returns (I), holds organisational elections (III), and for candidates to disclose criminal cases through affidavits (IV). However, having one-third of women candidates (II) is only a suggestion, not a compulsory rule. ***(1 Mark)***

[Pol. Sci, Ch-4, Pg. no. 60]

17. (*d*) Gender equality means giving equal rights and opportunities to both men and women. Providing equal voting rights ensures that both genders have the same political power, which is a key aspect of gender equality. The other options either restrict women or favor either men or women, which do not represent equality. ***(1 Mark)***

[Pol. Sci, Ch-3, Pg. no. 31]

18. (*a*) Education is included in the Concurrent List in the Indian Constitution. Both the Union and State Governments can legislate on matters related to education. ***(1 Mark)***

[Pol. Sci, Ch-2, Pg. no. 16-17]

19. (*a*) Women taking advantage from reservation in local governance (municipalities and panchayats), where at least one-third of all seats are reserved for women.

(1 Mark)

[Pol. Sci, Ch-2, Pg. no. 24]

20. (*d*) Tamil is one of the 22 languages recognized in the Eighth Schedule of the Indian Constitution. ***(1 Mark)***

[Pol. Sci, Ch-2, Pg. no. 22]

21. Distribution of power among different social groups benefits democracy in the following ways: **(Any two)**

(*i*) **Reduces Social Conflict:** It reduces conflicts between social groups, ensuring peace and unity by preventing one group from dominating others. ***(1 Mark)***

(*ii*) **Enhances Inclusivity:** It ensures minorities and disadvantaged groups have a say in decision-making, promoting equality and fairness. ***(1 Mark)***

(*iii*) **Strengthens Democracy**: Power sharing is the core of a democratic setup. It involves people in the governance process, making them feel included and responsible, which increases the legitimacy and stability of the government. ***(1 Mark)***

[Pol. Sci, Ch-1, Pg. no. 9]

22. Two benefits of globalisation:

(*i*) **Increased Employment:** Globalisation has led to the growth of multinational companies, creating more job opportunities. ***(1 Mark)***

(*ii*) **Access to New Markets:** It allows producers to sell goods worldwide, expanding markets and boosting economic growth. ***(1 Mark)***

[Eco, Ch-4, Pg. no. 61-62]

23. Economic Impacts of the First World War on India were:

(*i*) **Increased Taxation:** The war led to higher defence expenditures, financed by war loans and increased taxes, including customs duties and newly introduced income tax. ***(1 Mark)***

(*ii*) **Price Inflation:** Prices doubled between 1913 and 1918, causing severe hardship for common people as the cost of living rose significantly. ***(1 Mark)***

[His, Ch-2, Pg. no. 29-30]

24. (A) Arid soils are characterized by unique properties due to climatic conditions and soil composition.

(*i*) **Low Fertility:** Arid soils are sandy, saline, and lack organic matter, making them less fertile for agriculture. ***(1 Mark)***

(*ii*) **High Evaporation:** Due to high temperatures, moisture quickly evaporates, leaving the soil dry and nutrient-deficient. ***(1 Mark)***

[Geo, Ch-1, Pg. no. 9]

OR

(B) Forest soils are found in regions with dense vegetation and exhibit unique characteristics.

(*i*) **Varied Texture:** These soils are loamy and silty in valleys, while coarse-grained in upper slopes. ***(1 Mark)***

(*ii*) **High Fertility:** Forest soils in lower valleys are rich in organic matter and highly fertile for plant growth. ***(1 Mark)***

[Geo, Ch-1, Pg. no. 9-10]

25. The Jal Jeevan Mission (JJM) aims to provide safe and adequate drinking water to every rural household.

(*i*) **Piped Water Supply:** It ensures potable piped water supply to rural households at 55 liters per capita per day. ***(1 Mark)***

(*ii*) **Water Quality:** It focuses on providing safe drinking water by addressing contamination issues and maintaining water quality. ***(1 Mark)***

(*iii*) **Sustainability:** JJM promotes water conservation through rainwater harvesting and groundwater recharge for long-term availability. ***(1 Mark)***

[Geo, Ch-3, Pg. no. 21]

26. Democracy establishes an accountable, responsive, and legitimate government in the following ways:

(*i*) **Accountable Government:** Through regular elections and other mechanisms like the right to information, citizens can question, scrutinize, and replace their representatives, ensuring accountability. ***(1 Mark)***

(*ii*) **Responsive Government:** Democracy encourages the participation of citizens in decision-making processes. Thus, the government must be responsive to their needs and aspirations to gain or maintain the support of the public. ***(1 Mark)***

(*iii*) **Legitimacy:** When people choose their leaders through voting, it makes the government more legitimate, strong, and respected. ***(1 Mark)***

[Pol. Sci, Ch-5, Pg. no. 65-66]

27. (A) Impacts of Gandhi-Irwin Pact on the Indian Freedom Struggle:

(*i*) **Civil Disobedience Halted:** Gandhi agreed to suspend the Civil Disobedience Movement. ***(1 Mark)***

(*ii*) **Political Prisoners Released:** The government agreed to release political prisoners except those involved in violence. ***(1 Mark)***

(*iii*) **Round Table Conference:** Gandhi participated in the Second Round Table Conference in London. ***(1 Mark)***

[His, Ch-2, Pg. no. 40-41]

OR

(B) Role of Alluri Sitaram Raju in the Indian National Movement:

(*i*) **Led Gudem Rebellion:** Raju led the tribal rebellion in Andhra Pradesh against colonial forest laws. ***(1 Mark)***

(*ii*) **Inspired by Gandhi:** He promoted Khadi and non-cooperation but believed in armed struggle. ***(1 Mark)***

(*iii*) **Folk Hero:** After his capture and execution in 1924, he became a symbol of resistance. ***(1 Mark)***

[His, Ch-2, Pg. no. 36]

28. The importance of bank deposits are:

(*i*) **Safety and Interest:** Bank deposits keep money safe while earning interest, ensuring the value of savings increases over time. ***(1 Mark)***

(*ii*) **Easy Access:** Depositors can withdraw money anytime through demand deposits, enabling smooth cashless transactions. ***(1 Mark)***

(*iii*) **Economic Growth:** Banks use deposits to provide loans, supporting businesses and promoting overall economic development. ***(1 Mark)***

[Eco, Ch-3, Pg. no. 40-41]

29. The following are some of the main features of the Indian federal system:

(*i*) **Division of powers:** The power is divided between the central government and the constituent units. ***(1 Mark)***

(*ii*) **Rigid Constitution:** The changes in the fundamental provisions of the Constitution require the consent of both levels of government to prevent abuse of power. ***(1 Mark)***

(*iii*) **Independent judiciary:** A federal government has an independent judiciary that serves as a check on the powers of both the central government and the constituent units. ***(1 Mark)***

[Pol. Sci, Ch-2, Pg. no. 15-17]

30. (A) Johann Gutenberg's contribution to the development of the printing press:

(*i*) **Invention of the Printing Press:** Johann Gutenberg, a German goldsmith, developed the first-known printing press in the 1430s. ***(1 Mark)***

(*ii*) **Inspiration from Olive Press:** He adapted the wine and olive press mechanism to create a printing press, enabling faster and more efficient printing. ***(1 Mark)***

(*iii*) **Movable Metal Type:** Gutenberg developed metal types for each letter of the alphabet, allowing reusable typefaces for different texts. ***(1 Mark)***

(*iv*) **Printing of the Gutenberg Bible:** The first major book printed was the Bible. Around 180 copies were printed, demonstrating the efficiency of the new technology. ***(1 Mark)***

(*v*) **Impact on Print Culture:** Gutenberg's invention made books cheaper, increased literacy, and spread knowledge across Europe, leading to the print revolution. ***(1 Mark)***

[His, Ch-1, Pg. no. 5-12]

OR

(B) The development journey of print culture in India:

(*i*) **Introduction of Printing Press:** The printing press first came to Goa with Portuguese missionaries in the mid-16th century. They printed religious texts in Konkani and Tamil, with the first Tamil book printed in 1579. ***(1 Mark)***

(ii) **Expansion by Missionaries:** Dutch Protestant missionaries printed 32 Tamil texts by 1710, including translations of older works. Catholic priests printed the first Malayalam book in 1713. ***(1 Mark)***

(iii) **Growth of English Printing:** James Augustus Hickey started the first printed English newspaper in India, the Bengal Gazette, in 1780, known for its independent stance. ***(1 Mark)***

(iv) **Emergence of Indian-Language Press:** Gangadhar Bhattacharya published the first Indian newspaper, the Bengal Gazette, in Bengali. Other regional newspapers, like the Bombay Samachar (Gujarati) and Jam-i-Jahan Nama (Persian), soon followed. ***(1 Mark)***

(v) **Role in Social and Political Movements:** Print culture helped spread reformist ideas, such as Rammohun Roy's campaign against social evils through his newspaper Sambad Kaumudi. ***(1 Mark)***

[His, Ch-5, Pg. no. 120]

31. (A) Secularism is the very idea of the Indian Constitution because:

(i) **No Official Religion:** The Indian Constitution does not recognize any particular religion as the state religion ensuring that all religions are treated equally. ***(1 Mark)***

(ii) **Freedom of Religion:** The Indian Constitution guarantees the freedom of religion to all citizens. Every citizen has the right to practice, profess, and propagate any religion or choose not to follow any. ***(1 Mark)***

(iii) **Prohibits discrimination:** It specifically prohibits discrimination on the basis of religion, ensuring that no individual or group is treated unfairly because of their religious beliefs. ***(1 Mark)***

(iv) **State Intervention:** The Constitution allows the state to intervene in religious matters to ensure equality. For example, it bans untouchability and prevents discriminatory practices based on religion. ***(1 Mark)***

(v) **Equality of all religions:** No religion is considered superior or inferior to any other religion. All religions are treated equally under the law. ***(1 Mark)***

[Pol. Sci, Ch-3, Pg. no. 37-38]

OR

(B) Five measures that may be taken to establish gender equality of labour are:

(i) **Equal Remuneration for Equal Work:** The Equal Remuneration Act, 1976 mandates equal pay for men and women for the same work. However, women still face pay disparities, so it's important to enforce this law more strictly in all sectors. ***(1 Mark)***

(ii) **Equal Education Opportunities:** Providing equal education for both boys and girls is crucial. When women get the same education, they can access better jobs and earn a fair income, just like men. ***(1 Mark)***

(iii) **Empowerment through Political Representation:** More women in politics help address their needs better. The Women's Reservation Bill, which sets aside seats for women in the Lok Sabha and State Assemblies, is important for their empowerment. ***(1 Mark)***

(iv) **Safe Working Conditions:** Implementing and enforcing laws to ensure safe working conditions for women in all sectors can help reduce harassment and make women feel more secure at work. ***(1 Mark)***

(v) **Recognizing Household Work:** Household work should be equally shared between men and women. Recognizing the value of domestic work and promoting shared responsibilities can help achieve this balance. ***(1 Mark)***

[Pol. Sci, Ch-3, Pg. no. 30-33]

32. (A) The distinction between the public and private sectors of the economy are: ***(5 Mark)***

Feature	Public Sector	Private Sector
Ownership	Owned and controlled by the government.	Owned and controlled by individuals or companies.
Objective	Provides services and welfare to the public.	Earns profit through business activities.
Examples	Indian Railways, Post Office	Tata Iron and Steel, Reliance Industries
Source of Funds	Funded by taxes and government revenue.	Funded by private investments and profits.
Service Priority	Focuses on public welfare and development.	Focuses on consumer satisfaction and profit.

[Eco, Ch-2, Pg. no. 33-34]

OR

(B) The suggestions to create additional employment and reduce unemployment in rural areas are: **(Any Five)**

(*i*) **Promote Irrigation Projects:** Developing irrigation facilities through wells, canals, or dams can enable farmers to grow multiple crops, creating more employment opportunities throughout the year. **(*1 Mark*)**

(*ii*) **Encourage Agro-Based Industries:** Setting up agro-processing units like dal mills, cold storage, and fruit processing industries can generate jobs for villagers beyond agriculture. **(*1 Mark*)**

(*iii*) **Skill Development and Education:** Providing vocational training in areas like carpentry, tailoring, and computer skills can equip villagers to find alternative employment. **(*1 Mark*)**

(*iv*) **Improve Rural Infrastructure:** Better roads, transportation, and storage facilities will help farmers transport and sell their produce efficiently, boosting the rural economy. **(*1 Mark*)**

(*v*) **Support Small-Scale Industries:** Promoting cottage industries like handicrafts, pottery, and handloom can create non-agricultural employment opportunities within villages. **(*1 Mark*)**

(*vi*) **Government Employment Schemes:** Implementing schemes like MGNREGA ensures 100 days of guaranteed employment, reducing seasonal unemployment. **(*1 Mark*)**

[Eco, Ch-2, Pg. no. 27-29]

33. (A) India's cropping patterns are shaped by geographical, climatic, and socio-economic factors, resulting in three major agricultural seasons.

(*i*) **Rabi Crops:** Sown in winter (October-December) and harvested in summer (April-June); examples include wheat, barley, gram, mustard, and peas. **(*1 Mark*)**

(*ii*) **Kharif Crops:** Grown during monsoon (June-September); key crops include rice, maize, bajra, cotton, soyabean, and pulses, requiring significant rainfall. **(*1 Mark*)**

(*iii*) **Zaid Crops:** Short-season summer crops grown between rabi and kharif; examples include watermelon, muskmelon, cucumber, and fodder crops. **(*1 Mark*)**

(*iv*) **Crop Rotation:** Farmers practice crop rotation to maintain soil fertility, reduce pests, and ensure balanced nutrient usage for sustainable farming. **(*1 Mark*)**

(*v*) **Regional Variations:** Different crops grow based on regions—rice dominates eastern India, while wheat thrives in northwestern and central plains. **(*1 Mark*)**

[Geo, Ch-4, Pg. no. 32]

OR

(B) Major millet crops in India, including jowar, bajra, and ragi, are known for their resilience and nutritional value. The main characteristics of these crops are as follows:

(*i*) **High Nutritional Value:** Millets are rich in iron, calcium, fiber, and micronutrients, making them an essential part of a healthy diet. **(*1 Mark*)**

(*ii*) **Drought Resistance:** These crops can withstand dry conditions and require minimal water, making them ideal for rain-fed areas. **(*1 Mark*)**

(*iii*) **Diverse Soil Adaptability:** Millets grow well in sandy, loamy, red, black, and shallow soils, suitable for dry and semi-arid regions. **(*1 Mark*)**

(*iv*) **Major Growing Regions:** Jowar is cultivated in Maharashtra and Karnataka, while Rajasthan and Uttar Pradesh lead in bajra production. **(*1 Mark*)**

(*v*) **Economic Importance:** Millets are not only consumed domestically but also exported, boosting farmers' income and agricultural sustainability. **(*1 Mark*)**

[Geo, Ch-4, Pg. no. 34]

34.1 Magnetite has the maximum iron content, with up to 70% iron, making it the finest quality iron ore. **(*1 Mark*)**

[Geo, Ch-5, Pg. no. 44]

34.2 The most important industrial iron ore is hematite due to the quantity used, although it has a slightly lower iron content (50–60 percent) compared to magnetite. **(*1 Mark*)**

[Geo, Ch-5, Pg. no. 44]

34.3 Iron ore is a fundamental mineral for industrial and economic development.

(*i*) **Industrial Backbone:** Iron ore is essential for steel production, which forms the foundation for industries like construction, transportation, and manufacturing. **(*1 Mark*)**

(*ii*) **Economic Growth:** It drives industrial growth, creating jobs and boosting economic development by supporting infrastructure and technological advancements. **(*1 Mark*)**

[Geo, Ch-5, Pg. no. 44]

35.1 One feature of the working conditions of the organised sector is job security, where employees have fixed working hours, regular wages, and benefits like paid leave and health insurance. **(*1 Mark*)**

[Eco, Ch-2, Pg. no. 30-31]

35.2 One benefit provided by employers in the organised sector is provident fund, which ensures financial security for employees after retirement, along with paid leave and medical benefits. ***(1 Mark)***

[Eco, Ch-2, Pg. no. 30-31]

35.3 The reasons for the necessity of self-employed people to register with the government are:

(*i*) **Access to Benefits:** Registration allows them to avail government schemes, loans, and subsidies that support business growth. ***(1 Mark)***

(*ii*) **Legal Protection:** It ensures their business operates under formal rules and regulations, protecting them from legal issues. ***(1 Mark)***

[Eco, Ch-2, Pg. no. 30-31]

36.1 One major political demand of the liberals was the establishment of a constitutional government with national sovereignty and protection of individual rights and freedoms. ***(1 Mark)***

[His, Ch-1, Pg. no. 12]

36.2 The main cause for the rise of secret societies in European states was the fear of repression by conservative forces after the Vienna Congress of 1815, which aimed to restore monarchical rule and suppress liberal and nationalist movements. ***(1 Mark)***

[His, Ch-1, Pg. no. 12]

36.3 Reasons for Many Liberal-Nationalists Going Underground After 1815:

(*i*) **Fear of Repression:** The Congress of Vienna (1815) aimed to restore conservative monarchies, leading to strict surveillance and suppression of liberal-nationalist movements. ***(1 Mark)***

(*ii*) **Opposition to Monarchical Rule:** Liberal-nationalists, who sought freedom and democratic reforms, were targeted by conservative regimes, forcing them to operate secretly to avoid persecution. ***(1 Mark)***

[His, Ch-1, Pg. no. 12]

37. (*i*) **A:** Madras ***(1 Mark)***

B: Dandi ***(1 Mark)***

[His, Ch-2, Pg. no. 40,44]

(*ii*) **(Any three)** ***(3 Mark)***

(*a*) **[Geo, Ch-7, Pg. no. 79]**

(*b*) **[Geo, Ch-6, Pg. no. 67]**

(*c*) **[Geo, Ch-5, Pg. no. 53]**

(*d*) **[Geo, Ch-7, Pg. no. 79]**

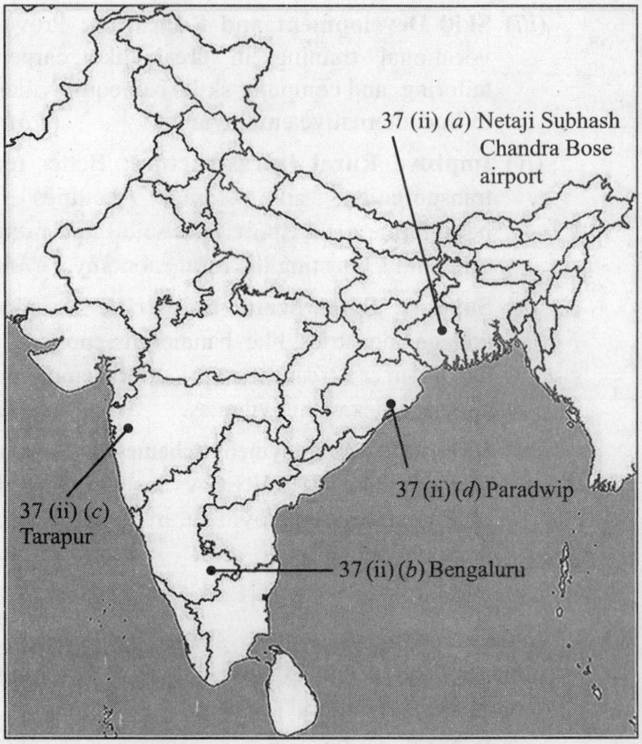